William Butterfield

1　William Butterfield, from a drawing by Lady Coleridge at Ottery St Mary

William Butterfield

Paul Thompson

Department of Sociology
University of Essex

Routledge & Kegan Paul London

First published 1971
by Routledge & Kegan Paul Ltd
Broadway House, 68–74 Carter Lane,
London EC4V 5EL
Photoset and printed in Great Britain by BAS Printers Ltd,
Wallop, Hampshire
and set in Monophoto Baskerville 169

© *Paul Thompson 1971*

ISBN 0 7100 6930 8

To Stephen and Sarah

Contents

Part Two

Colour Illustrations

Illustrations

Preface

Something should be said at the start of my purpose in shaping this book as I have. It is, in the first place, a monograph, and I have attempted to include in it all the essential ingredients of a complete architectural biography. I have, however, relegated the descriptive chronological surveys which normally form the core of such a book to the second part, for two reasons. The first is that Butterfield's purpose and style in design are fundamentally contentious, so that survey before analysis would be meaningless. The second is that I wish not merely to describe Butterfield's work, but to interpret it: to discover the forces which shaped it, and the meaning which he and his patrons and contemporaries found in it.

I have tried to do this on a series of levels—personality, patronage, technology, religious, social and aesthetic conventions and values—which are all *potentially* relevant to other situations; but I do not wish to suggest that explanations of Butterfield's work necessarily apply to other men or other periods. Factors such as religion or individual personality can be dominant in some situations and irrelevant in others. In particular, I do not believe that Worringer's polarities have any universal explanatory value, however much they may illuminate certain phases of architectural history; in other periods quite different ideal types of style are more helpful. Equally I do not accept the crude technological determinism so common in modern architectural history. Building is, of course, a material art, and some technological and economic influences upon its form are inevitable, in a certain sense primary; but they are by no means always dominant, and indeed have very often been merely passive limitations. In this book I have tried to indicate the contribution made by each level of interpretation, but not to impose any universal hierarchy of importance upon them; for ultimately this is an issue which depends not upon fact, but upon one's concept of man.

Nor does it seem necessary to me to establish a universal predictive power in my interpretations, such as some social scientists would demand. Events are the results of *conjunctions* of causes, each of which can be rationally explained if separated; but

xxiii

the particular conjunction may be the result of coincidence rather than logical connection. Thus it was not inevitable that a man of Butterfield's personality should have become the leading architect of the Ecclesiological movement; he might have died young, like his rival, Carpenter. Without Butterfield there would have been a High Victorian style, and High Victorian mannerism, but no church quite like Babbacombe. Nor, even if such an imaginative creation were the inevitable expression of a particular social situation, would it be possible to foresee it in advance from a different situation. The demand for prediction is, therefore, a search for the impossible.

This book is, nevertheless, intended as a contribution both to the history and sociology of architecture; and I have tried to write it as straightforwardly as possible, without mystifying either kind of reader with technical jargon.

Acknowledgments

In writing this book I have depended upon the help of a great many people for information and access to documents and I wish to thank them all. I should like to express my special gratitude to Captain and Mrs Stephen Starey, Mr John Starey, Mrs C. R. Riley and Mrs Betsy Lewis for allowing me to use their collection of letters, account books, drawings and other Butterfield relics (Starey Collection) and for their unfailing encouragement and hospitality, and to Mr A. D. R. Caroë for showing me the set of notebooks which Butterfield gave to his father. Mrs W. L. Hogg very kindly showed me her Butterfield furniture and album of Milton Ernest, and Dr Christopher Starey, Mr Jocelyn Drew, Mr Robert C. Butterfield, Mr John Joseph Butterfield and Mr Lawrence Butterfield helped me to construct the family tree.

Many descendants of Butterfield's patrons have helped me in a similar way. I owe a particular debt to Lady Elton, who provided me with the extracts relevant to Butterfield from a large section of the voluminous diaries of Sir Arthur Elton; to Lord Heytesbury for the use of his collection of papers on Heytesbury and Knook; to Mrs Tritton for the correspondence of Henry Tritton; to Lord and Lady Coleridge for their hospitality at Ottery St Mary.

A very large number of clergy have helped me with the records in their custody and in many cases provided me with much additional information. I am especially grateful to Rev. D. B. Haseler for his hospitality while I examined the Bursea box; and I should also like to record the particular assistance of Canon D. E. Evans of Aberystwyth, Rev. K. J. Benzies of Ambatoharanana, Rev. J. R. M. Johnstone of Ashton Keynes, Rev. A. B. de T. Andrews of Babbacombe, Rev. W. A. Colley of Bamford, Rev. E. G. Parke of Belfast, Rev. C. J. W. King of Belmont, Rev. R. Brownrigg of Bletchingley, Rev. F. W. Camp of Brigham, Rev. Hereward Hard of All Saints' Cambridge, Rev. D. A. Rogers of Cautley, Rev. G. L. Rowe of Charlton, Rev. H. N. L. Edwards of Colkirk, Rev. J. F. L. Eagle of Hargrave, Canon F. S. Fairclough of Hathersage, Canon C. J. Cobern of Hitchin, Rev. J. S. Habgood of Jedburgh, Rev. G. L. Treglown of Latton, Rev. E. Davies of Llanbadarn, Rev. K.

C. Herbert of Llangorwen, Rev. K. N. Ross of All Saints' Margaret Street, Rev. W. J. Kingston of Christ Church Albany Street, Rev. E. B. Wood of Mapledurham, Very Rev. T. W. Thomas of Melbourne, Rev. H. W. Dunn of Ogbourne St Andrew, Rev. C. J. Hubbold of Sedgeberrow, Rev. J. V. Philip of Sheen, Rev. E. Bannister of Sparsholt and to Rev. I. N. Miller of Thurlaston; and also to Canon C. K. Sansbury, Warden of St Augustine's College, Canterbury; Dr Austin Farrer, Warden of Keble College, Oxford; and Very Rev. George Douglas, Provost of Cumbrae.

I should also like to thank for similar help Mr J. C. Irwin of Adelaide, Mr. John Freeman of Ardleigh, Mr F. T. Smallwood of Battersea, Mr W. F. Ayres of Highbury Chapel, Bristol, Colonel Firth of Dinton, Mrs C. H. Webster of East Grinstead, Dr Roger Highfield of Merton College, Oxford, Miss M. Tamplin of St Dunstan's Abbey School, Plymouth, Mr M. C. Kittermaster of Rugby School, Mrs E. Carr of Trumpington and Mr John Harvey of Winchester College. Mr C. A. Hartridge very kindly provided me with information on Balsham, Mr F. J. Penn on Coalpit Heath and Horfield, Mr Anthony Symondson on Hursley and Pitt, Mr Denis Serjeant on Keble and Merton Colleges and Mr John Newman on Buckland. I owe my knowledge of Butterwick to Mr John Hutchinson, of Gillingham to Mr David Lloyd, of Ruston to Mr Raymond Fieldhouse and of Wick to Mr D. C. W. Verey, and of much of Butterfield's activity in South Africa to Mr R. R. Langham-Carter. In Australia I was particularly helped with information from Mr David Saunders and I also owe a great debt to the help and hospitality, among many others in Australia, of Mr and Mrs Randolph Creswell, Mr George Tibbitts and Professor Joseph Burke of Melbourne. This journey was itself only made possible by the generosity of my father-in-law, Mr J. C.-L. Vigne.

For more general information, I was greatly helped by many archivists, and especially by Mr Anthony Wood of Warwick, by Dr W. Urry of Canterbury, through whom I learnt of Mrs K. S. Urry's discovery of Broad Street School, and by Mr John Harvey (the Winchester College archives are cited by permission of the Warden and Fellows). Mr W. A. Carter generously allowed me to use the records of the Incorporated Church Building Society, and Mr Patrick Feeny those of John Hardman and Company. Mr Michael Waterhouse very kindly showed me the sketchbooks of Alfred Waterhouse, and Mr John Brandon-Jones his letters and sketchbooks of Philip Webb; Sir John Betjeman gave me a copy of Butterfield's drawings of Shottesbrooke church; and Mr M. G. Murray showed me his thesis on 'The Nineteenth-century External Polychromatic Revival'. Mrs Shirley Bury generously gave me information from her forthcoming study of nineteenth-century plate; Mr John House information on Ardleigh, St David's and other points from his article on Butterfield in _Transactions of the Ancient Monuments Society_, 1963; and Sir Nikolaus Pevsner answered many questions arising from _The Buildings of England_. I am also very grateful for many suggestions to

Dr Mark Girouard, Mr Peter Howell, Mr Charles Handley-Read and Mr Nicholas Taylor.

In the task of extracting information from periodicals I was initially greatly helped by my father and my wife. Miss Margaret Templeman completed this work for me, and Mrs Elspeth Burrows helped me with other documentary research. They were both research assistants provided by the University of Essex, who also generously gave me a grant towards my travelling expenses.

Lastly, I am deeply grateful for their criticism to Dr Royston Lambert, who commented on my earlier articles (in Peter Ferriday (ed.), *Victorian Architecture*, Jonathan Cape, London 1963, and in *Architectural History*, (8) 1965), to Dr Stefan Muthesius and to my wife, who read the present book.

Illustrations

I am particularly grateful to Mr John Lane, Mr Peter Burton, Mr Gordon Barnes, Sir Arthur Elton, Mr R. R. Langham-Carter, Bishop O'Ferrall and Dr Stefan Muthesius for giving me photographs, and to the other owners of copyright indicated in the list of illustrations, and also to the owners and incumbents of the buildings illustrated.

Abbreviations

A	*Architect*
AAS	*Associated Architectural Societies' Reports*
Accnts	Butterfield's accounts, Starey Collection
AR	*Architectural Review*
B	*Builder*
BA	*British Architect*
BE	Nikolaus Pevsner, *Buildings of England*, London, Penguin Books, 1951 onwards
BN	*Building News*
CB	*Church Builder*
CC	see Metalwork (page 503)
DNB	*Dictionary of National Biography*: Paul Waterhouse, Supplement 1, pp. 360–3
E	*Ecclesiologist*
G	*Guardian*
I.C.B.S.	Incorporated Church Building Society
ILN	*Illustrated London News*
Notebooks	Butterfield's notebooks, Caroë Collection; numbered, except the continental notebook
R.I.B.A.	Royal Institute of British Architects
TFB	see Stained Glass (page 469)

Note: bracketed references in the text are to illustrations

Part One

1   Old and New Interpretations

'To sum up. The first glory of Butterfield is, to me, his utter ruthlessness. How he hated "taste"!' wrote Sir John Summerson in 'William Butterfield, or the Glory of Ugliness'. 'The second glory is a wonderful, childish inventiveness. He was, I repeat, an innocent . . . Lastly, one word about Butterfield's "ugliness". It seems absolutely deliberate—even systematic: a calculated assault on the sensuous qualities latent in the simplest building-forms . . . Is it possible, I wonder, to parallel this purposeful sadism in the whole history of architecture?'[1]

Summerson's essay of 1945 opens this book because it was its starting point. It has undoubtedly influenced all subsequent criticism of Butterfield. It lies behind the comments of Henry-Russell Hitchcock and Sir Nikolaus Pevsner when they call Butterfield's architecture 'cranky', 'gawky', or 'original to the extreme of harshness and demonstrative ugliness'.[2] Summerson sent a whole generation of architectural enthusiasts—including myself—to Butterfield's buildings looking for harshness, oddity and discordance, anticipating strange sensual experiences of aesthetic brutalism. Helped by the simultaneous turn of contemporary architecture towards the ruthless functionalism of the New Brutalism and the primitive expressionism of Le Ronchamp, we quickly found the qualities we sought. The discovery made Butterfield a pioneer of the modern movement, a New Brutalist a hundred years ahead of his time.

Ugliness, still more than beauty, is subjective, in the beholder rather than the object. It is remarkable how easily what to one generation was rich, becomes florid to another; how boldness becomes coarse, or tenderness and restraint turn to sadism. In architectural style, as in all social manners, the meaning of a gesture can only be understood in its proper context. Out of context it can be interpreted completely differently—and often, just because the interpretation is untempered by reality, with astonishing conviction. For Ian Nairn, for example, All Saints' Margaret Street 'can only be understood in terms of compelling, overwhelming passion'. If Butterfield would certainly have thought it blasphemous 'to describe a church as an orgasm', this does not make Nairn's feelings any less vivid. His reaction is in fact so strong that he cannot accept the real Butterfield, and conceives him instead as the hero of *Wuthering Heights*.[3]

Becoming a Brutalist pioneer has in fact doubly hindered understanding of Butterfield. Not only is his architecture expected to supply contemporary justification, and therefore examined dogmatically. There is also the development of a Butterfield myth. Ian Nairn's 'unexpected Heathcliff' is but one example. One can find a still more striking fantasy in such an admirable architectural history as Peter Collins' *Changing Ideals in Modern Architecture*. In Butterfield's work, Collins asserts, 'ugliness was achieved . . . by simply ignoring the problem of "design" altogether . . . Butterfield himself possessed neither a drawing-board nor a T-square, and created most of his designs from small sketches, or by personal intervention on the site. He was thus a pioneer of what in recent years has been called "Action Architecture".'[4] Like all mythical figures in periods of change, Butterfield must suffer regular rehabilitation.

There are, however, other aspects of his legendary character which can only be explained as by-products of the interpretation of Victorian architecture as a whole. As the architect of All Saints' Margaret Street, the model church of the Ecclesiologists designed in 1849, Butterfield has from the first been recognized as a pioneer of the original High Victorian phase of the Gothic Revival. It was at All Saints' that constructional colour in brick and marble, the hallmark of High Victorian architecture, was first displayed (I, X). Inevitably Butterfield has always been a central figure in the interpretation of Victorian architectural style.

'Whence came this inclination for ugliness?' asked Summerson. 'It might plausibly be argued that it represents a surgence of that hard *bourgeois* puritanism half-hidden in the eighteenth century which had never expressed itself emotionally but at last seized the opportunity to do so.' It has indeed been widely accepted by architectural historians that the cause of the mid-nineteenth-century collapse in taste and architecture was the rise of the industrial middle class.

'The ironmaster and mill-owner, as a rule self-made men of no education, felt no longer bound by one particular accepted taste as the gentleman had been who was brought up to believe in the rule of taste,' declared Nikolaus Pevsner. 'The new manufacturer had no manners, and he was a convinced individualist. If, for whatever reasons, he liked a style in architecture, then there was nothing to prevent him from having his way.'[5] Worse still, because he lacked the time and the training essential to the development of sensibility, his eyes could only appreciate crude shapes and vivid colours. His armchairs and teapots reflected this deficiency. 'As against other styles favouring curves, the Victorian curve is generous, full, . . . bulgy. It represents, and appealed to, a prospering, well-fed, self-confident class.'[6]

The explanation of stylistic development through general social change can be used, as Arnold Hauser shows in his *Social History of Art*, for any period from ancient Egypt onwards, provided that the mediating mechanics of patronage are never examined in detail. It can also be applied in a bewildering variety of ways. Robert Furneaux Jordan in his *Victorian Architecture*, to take a recent example, focuses his argument on the High Victorian period of about 1860, which he regards as the moment of transition to the age of coal, steam, iron, cotton and *laissez faire*.

The High Victorian decades were thus dominated by Manchester, and Alfred Waterhouse, whose career was launched from Manchester, was its typical architect (315). His patrons were either confident, philistine, crude industrial magnates, or aristocrats who sensed that economic change had undermined their social position, and were thus forced into equally vulgar display in order to draw attention to themselves. The prosperous architect of this period was consequently a professional without a soul, often effective in his planning and organization of buildings, but always prepared to dress them in any style and with as much ornament as his patron could afford. The typical High Victorian building had no style of its own. Style in the nineteenth century developed outside the successful professional office: either with the engineers, whose structural achievements were the underlying architectural realities of the age; or with the romantic medievalist, the alienated Bohemian artist, who sought alternative values in craftsmanship or even pure imaginative fantasy transcending structure.

In this particular scheme Butterfield becomes an extreme case of romantic medievalism, a religious visionary who believed that Gothic must be made into a modern style, fit for its own time. His delight in ugliness followed from a search for the structural realities of the age; his buildings were useful rather than pretty, ruthlessly realistic like the early industrial buildings of the late eighteenth century. Consequently All Saints' represents 'a more curious kind of functionalism'. While this is a difficult interpretation to apply to Butterfield's architecture, it requires less biographical imagination than most. We are in fact given only one entirely new story: 'Butterfield's building operations were as highly disciplined as had been those of the Middle Ages – prayer and the rule of silence were the accompaniment of manual labour.'[7]

More commonly, however, Butterfield has been regarded as the classic expression of the new middle classes. To Summerson he was not so much an architect as a Victorian builder. This was why he delighted in common brick, pit-sawn rafters and ordinary Birmingham tiles. He was the pupil of an insignificant Pimlico builder, 'to all intents and purposes self-taught'. He remained essentially uncivilized, according to Hitchcock 'a man who never wrote a book or an article', and who did not care much for reading. Summerson was 'quite prepared to believe that he never bothered much' with *The Stones of Venice*, despite the evidently Ruskinian characteristics of All Saints' Margaret Street. Hitchcock asserted that Butterfield was probably little travelled, and 'knew continental work only through the drawings of less insular architects brought back from their sketching tours abroad'.[8] Insular, ill-trained, impervious to literary influence, he was able to remain a primitive, a child who could glory in ugliness, a barbaric genius who could speak for the *bourgeois* philistine.

This character is in fact a travesty, and there has never been any hard evidence to support it. It is, however, garnished with embellishments from the reminiscences of surviving contemporaries such as A. T. Bolton and Harry Redfern, which suggest a denial of the ordinary pleasures of life truly worthy of an aesthetic sadist. Butterfield would stubbornly refuse to provide heating in a north-country church because there was no medieval precedent for such comfort; he would allow his staff no time for lunch; he never permitted himself a holiday. These stories also turn out, on investigation, to be unfounded.[9]

The general argument equally crumbles at a touch. It was not the new middle class, the philistine industrialists, who were the influential patrons of mid-nineteenth-century architecture, but the old aristocracy. It is difficult to think of a single building commissioned by a manufacturer which was crucial to the development of the High Victorian style. Certainly Samuel Sanders Teulon, who was probably the most outrageously 'ugly' architect of the period (57), relied almost entirely on an aristocratic clientele.[10] Butterfield himself scarcely received a single commission from a manufacturer.

And even if the industrialists had ousted the aristocracy, what evidence is there that their architecture would have been crude and philistine? We have no analysis of the architectural taste of the different social classes in the early nineteenth century; but a reminder of the intellectual group around Matthew Boulton and James Watt in Birmingham, or a glance at J. M. Richards' *The Functional Tradition in Early Industrial Buildings*, suggest the rashness of any such generalizations.

In short, it is not merely necessary to reconstruct Butterfield's character and career, to show his relationships with the architectural profession and the building industry, to discover his theories of design, and to look at his buildings with fresh eyes. Equally, he must be placed within a new interpretation of High Victorian architecture.

Notes on chapter 1

1 *AR* (98) 1945, pp. 166–75, reprinted in John Summerson, *Heavenly Mansions*, London, Cresset Press, 1949.

2 Nikolaus Pevsner, *An Outline of European Architecture*, revised edition, London, Penguin Books, 1951, p. 253.

3 Ian Nairn, *Nairn's London*, London, Penguin Books, 1966, p. 95.

4 Peter Collins, *Changing Ideals in Modern Architecture*, London, Faber & Faber, 1965, p. 245.

5 Pevsner, *op. cit.*, pp. 245–6.

6 Nikolaus Pevsner, *High Victorian Design*, London, Architectural Press, 1951, p. 49.

7 Robert Furneaux Jordan, *Victorian Architecture*, London, Architectural Press, 1966, pp. 89–92.

8 Henry-Russell Hitchcock, *Early Victorian Architecture*, London, Architectural Press, 1954, pp. 572, 596.

9 A. T. Bolton, *R.I.B.A. Journal*, (xxxi) 1924, p. 344; Harry Redfern, 'Some Recollections of William Butterfield and Henry Woodyer', *Architect and Building News*, (clxxvii) 1944, pp. 21–2, 44–5.

10 Mark Girouard, 'The Victorian Country House: Clients and Architects' in *Victorian Rural England*, Victorian Society Third Conference Report, 1966.

2

Affection

William Butterfield's personal life remains mysterious, but, so far as it can be un-ravelled, remarkably empty. Perhaps it is worth noticing that Butterfield's personality shows the elements which psychologists have most commonly found in an original thinker.[1] We shall find in him the self-reliance, independence of criticism, and self-confidence of an eldest son; and exceptional persistence, driven perhaps by the need to release emotional tension; a certain willingness to take risks; and an undeniable streak of aggressiveness. But these attributes are certainly not unique to a creative genius. They cannot explain why Butterfield became a great architect. Nor, even if we knew much more about his childhood, could his personal background. It has proved impossible to discern any persistent pattern in the early lives of creative men. Why then trouble with Butterfield's personal life at all?

Even if we must assume his creative talent, it is probable that Butterfield's tempera-ment affected his architectural development in subtler ways. A need for emotional security could help to explain aesthetic obstinacies. Similarly, his choice of manner within the High Victorian style might be related to his personality. Wilhelm Wor-ringer believed that the contrast between the contorted, disembodied Gothic of northern Europe in the late Middle Ages, and the rounded calm of the Florentine Renaissance, reflected the religious fear of one civilization and the confident, nature-loving rationalism of the other. In a similar way one can associate the stylistic manner of the individual artist with his attitude to the world in which he works; an attitude which is constructed partly of religious beliefs, partly from social assumptions, and partly upon the quality of his personal life. For this reason it is worth discussing whether Butterfield's professional confidence concealed private insecurity, and to what extent his inner life was founded upon a circle of personal affection.

Butterfield's early life is extraordinarily obscure.[2] We know that he was born on 7 September 1814 and that his father, William Butterfield, was at that time a chemist and druggist with a shop opposite St Clement Danes at 173 in the Strand. His mother Anne was the daughter of Robert Steven, a city leather broker, who had come to

London very young from Scotland. He was, according to an obituary in the *Missionary Chronicle*, a very pious man, a director of the London Missionary Society, and attended the Kingsland Chapel. Although Butterfield's parents were married in their parish church on 21 February 1811, they were evidently Nonconformists, for none of their children was recorded in the baptismal register, and three were entered in the private register which was kept by dissenters at Dr William's Library in Cripplegate. Anne Steven's sister Mary was also to marry a strict Nonconformist, the Bristol tobacconist William Day Wills, in 1820.

At the time of their marriage William Butterfield senior was aged twenty-eight, but Anne was only sixteen. He had set up shop only a few months previously, very likely on the death of his father. This prudence, and the age at which he married, were characteristic of the middle classes at this date, but Anne was unusually young for a bride, so that the marriage looks to have been genuinely romantic. Certainly it lasted until William died in the winter of 1866 aged eighty-three, and his wife only survived him by eight months (2). They had nine children. William must have been the eldest son, since he took his father's name and was eventually his father's sole heir. There were six other sons, an elder sister who married Benjamin Starey, and a younger sister who married George Allnutt.

It seems that each of the five related families prospered during Butterfield's childhood and youth. The Wills of Bristol were the most successful and were to

2 William Butterfield senior and his wife Anne c. 1860 (Starey Collection)

Family Tree

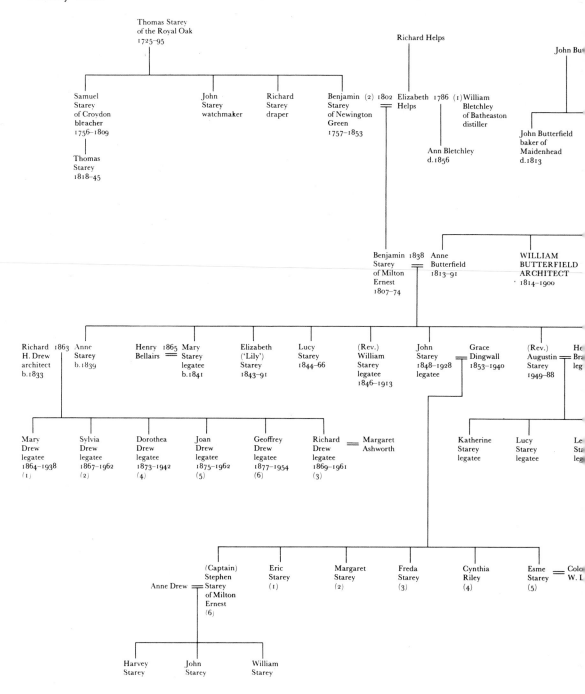

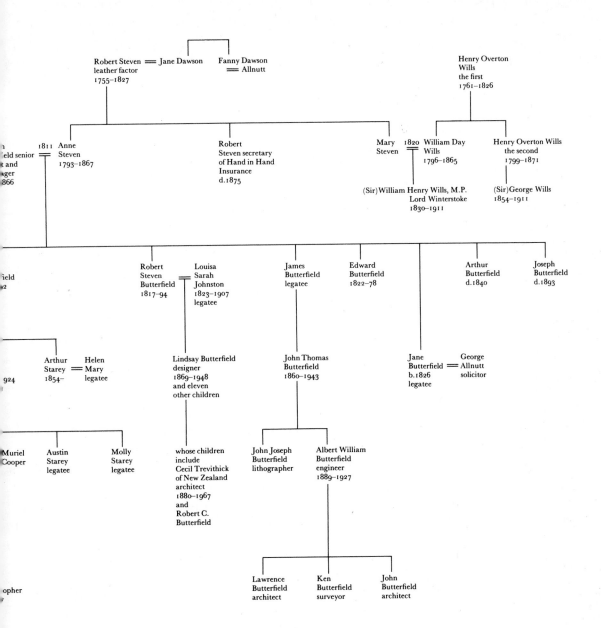

receive a baronetcy in 1897, right at the end of Butterfield's life. Their patronage was to be crucial at the start of his career. Of the Stevens and Allnutts we know less. Robert Steven junior succeeded to his father's business in 1815, and by 1836 had become secretary to the Hand in Hand Fire and Life Office, with a country home at Upper Tooting. He does not seem to have employed Butterfield, but at any rate gave him a Hand in Hand Insurance policy for £1000. As an old man he lived at Apsley Guise in Bedfordshire, writing to the Stareys in a pious Evangelical manner. George Allnutt set up as a Chancery Lane solicitor in the early 1840s, and by 1855 had moved to a new house in Ladbroke Villas; probably Charles Allnutt, one of Butterfield's executors, was his son. There was another family of Allnutts, related through Steven's sister-in-law, who were in touch with the Stareys in the 1870s, living in Portsea and supporters of High Churchmanship; possibly Butterfield's commissions in the town came through them.

It was with the Stareys, however, that he was to be most closely connected. The family had come to London from Tenbury in Worcestershire in the mid-eighteenth century, and there were various branches in different businesses. The most successful was probably the bleacher and coal merchant Samuel Starey, who bought the Old Palace of the bishops of London at Croydon in 1780. After the relatively early death of his son Thomas in 1845, this passed to his younger brother Benjamin, who was a wholesale linen draper and lived at Newington Green. Benjamin himself had married a wealthy widow, whose first husband had been a Bath distiller, although it was not until the death of his spinster stepdaughter Ann Bletchley in 1856 that this fortune was also to pass to his family. Ann's correspondence shows her to have been a strongly religious woman of great character, with a number of close friendships among High Churchmen, and it may be that it was through her influence that the family was drawn into this circle, although there is no sign that the Stareys ever passed through a phase of Nonconformity.

The younger Benjamin Starey is said to have invented a plaited wick that did not need stuffing, and certainly the family later had considerable shareholdings in Price's Patent Candle Company, of which he was a director. Where his main business interests lay is uncertain. Fortunately, however, we have an unusually full account of how he came to marry Butterfield's sister Anne, written for the benefit of her children fifty years afterwards. Some pains had been taken with Anne's education, as her exercise books in algebra and French poetry testify, and when she was twenty-two her mother saw an advertisement in *The Times* for a governess. She did not want to leave home, but believed it was the religious duty of a girl to submit to her parents' wishes, and so she entered service with Mr and Mrs Peek in north London. It happened that Benjamin Starey was friendly with the Peeks, and would frequently call on his way home to Newington Green. 'Sometimes he would join us in our evening walk down the green-lanes, or in Seven Sisters Road, at that time quite in the country, surrounded by pleasant fields, where the children gathered handfuls of wild flowers. . . . Our conversation was always natural and unconstrained, no thought ever crossed my mind that our acquaintance would lead to any further intimacy'. One day, however, instead of calling he left a message that he had gone on a business journey, and 'expressed a hope that he should not find I had gone away on his return'. She was left astonished and full of suspense, 'wondering what was going to happen to me, but I kept my own counsel, and shewed no sign of a ruffled spirit'. While Benjamin Starey was away the youngest of the Peek children died after a sudden illness, and he returned on the day of the funeral. Afterwards, in the evening, 'we walked up and down together in the garden talking quietly. He told me about his sister and his house and presently asked me if I would consent to be his wife and share it with him. More conversation followed, and then he took a small prayer book out of his pocket, and read to me those words from the marriage service: "Reverently, discreetly, advisedly, soberly, and in the fear of God".' Two years later, in April 1838, they were married.[3]

Their first home was in Millfield Lane, Highgate, but in 1853, the year of his father's death, Benjamin Starey, convinced that recent gold discoveries would cause inflation and make land the safest form of investment, decided to buy an estate of 590 acres at Milton Ernest in Bedfordshire. It cost him £22,000, and he was to spend another £14,000 on building work, including a country house, all to be designed by Butterfield (259). Earlier, it was no doubt partly due to family influence that Robert Brett, godparent and doctor to the Starey children, secured Butterfield as architect of St Matthias Stoke Newington; while later he was to work for the Stareys at Tottenham, and for an old friend of the family in designing St Mary Brookfield.

In a more modest way William Butterfield senior had meanwhile built up his own business, and in 1821 he had been able to purchase his freedom of the City of London. In 1831 he moved into one of the alleyways leading down to the river from the Strand, just behind his previous shop. He was now called variously a dairyman and a wharfinger, and was presumably taking milk from the wharfs. From 1835 he is simply a wharfinger; and then, as his scope widens, he becomes a coal merchant and a wharfinger. His increasing prosperity no doubt partly explains why his eldest son, apprenticed to a builder in 1831, decided two years later to become an architect. Socially this was a more ambitious career, and it was also initially more expensive; for it seems unlikely that Butterfield was self-supporting before 1842 or even 1844.

The second son Robert had purchased his freedom of the City in 1843, and with his brother James he took over the flourishing family business when their father retired in 1846. Three years later the directories show William Butterfield senior for the first time with a private address of his own, at 24 Doughty Street; and finally he moved to a superior house at 7 Gordon Street, Bloomsbury, in 1854, where he lived for the remaining dozen years of his life.

At this point the tantalizingly uninformative documents suggest a possible catastrophe. Butterfield's father's will was entered at Somerset House for under £200, a sum which would have scarcely exceeded a year's rent at Gordon Street. Possibly he had retired on a life annuity; but it may have been equally relevant that his sons had gone out of business in 1852. Was there a family crisis in the years when Butterfield was building All Saints' Margaret Street?

Certainly the Stareys received a serious set-back shortly afterwards. After a number of disasters on the Stock Exchange, in 1872 Benjamin Starey was forced to sell Milton Ernest for less than a third of the money which he had put into the estate, and his health appears to have been broken by the shock of the failure. It was only through his younger son John, who went to Ceylon for thirty years in 1871 as a tea planter and developed other business interests in rubber plantations in Malaya, that the family were able to repurchase the estate in 1919. Meanwhile they moved to a smaller house in Tottenham. This misfortune to his sister's family must have certainly shaken Butterfield, for even before his father died he had come to regard Milton Ernest as the family home. His parents were buried there in the parish churchyard. To some of the children he was godfather, and being childless he took this responsibility especially seriously. No doubt, now that he was eminent as a church architect, he was also attracted to the Stareys as country gentry and good churchmen. His brothers were less like the architectural patrons among whom he now moved; socially inferior, probably still dissenters. Moreover there are signs that the Starey family circle had become the centre of Butterfield's emotional life: that here, among his relations, this austere bachelor, already notorious for his remoteness, at times unfolded.

Butterfield's choice of homes suggests a family-centred man. Although he never married, he had lived until he was eighteen in a family household. Nothing is known of his early education, but it is inconceivable that a tradesman would have sent his child to any of the unreformed boarding schools of the 1820s. He must therefore have first left home in March 1831 when he was apprenticed, aged sixteen, to a Pimlico builder, Thomas Arber. Here he was to live with the family. Arber agreed to provide him with board and lodging, while his parents were to supply his clothes and pocket money, see to his washing and mending, and pay any doctor's or nurse's fees.

From the cancellation of this indenture two years later, when he became an architectural student, Butterfield apparently lived on his own. On the other hand, he remained almost all his life remarkably close to his parents' home. As a student he lodged in Norfolk Street, a few yards away;[4] in 1840 he set up office at 38 Lincoln's Inn Fields; and two years later he moved into the office at 4 Adam Street in the

Adelphi, which he kept for the rest of his professional life. By middle age he had taken over the adjoining house. Eventually in the 1880s he decided, again following his parents, to move into a house in Bloomsbury, 42 Bedford Square, where he died on 23 February 1900. Even his club, the Athenaeum, which he joined in 1858, was within the same square mile. It is true that Butterfield was constantly travelling to supervise building work, and regularly took holidays on the Continent; and also that for a short time before 1840 he was an architect's assistant in Worcester. Even so, one has the impression that he demanded a stability and security from his physical environment, and was happiest in the district he had known as a child.

Similarly, he allowed himself little change within his home.[5] He kept his own study in the Adelphi for forty years almost as he found it, with its Adam chimneypiece and grate, a richly plastered ceiling with a painted central medallion, furnished with an old Turkey carpet on the floor, and a few pieces of late-Georgian and early-Victorian furniture, including a plain square writing-table. Behind his chair for thirty years stood a large portfolio containing the working drawings of All Saints' Margaret Street; but apart from this, he made no attempt to assert his own Gothic tastes, preferring to accept the pleasant old-fashioned surroundings he had always known. Nor did he wish to move with fashion in his personal appearance. A tall, thin figure, grey-haired by the 1870s, with long side-whiskers and round steel spectacles (1), he invariably dressed in a black frock-coat, white linen shirt, high collar, loosely tied black bow, grey trousers and immaculately polished black capless shoes.

Above all, he insisted on a quiet and regular daily routine. He worked alone, answering all his correspondence in his own hand, and receiving clients and criticizing his assistants' drawings in his study. He never intruded on the drawing-office in the next room. His own living rooms were on another floor. Here he was looked after by his housekeeper and manservant, Mr and Mrs Loader, assisted by their daughter, who were apparently responsible for him for some thirty years.[6] Butterfield would start work early, and after a long morning he would lunch in his own rooms. Then in mid-afternoon, wearing a tall chimneypot hat, he would walk out 'for a visit to his club, the Athenaeum, to get his "dish of tea", and perhaps to hold conversation with those persons whose privilege it was to know him, or to write occasional letters on Church matters, in which his trenchant and caustic humour found a congenial outlet'.[7] This slight relaxation ended, he would return to his study, and as dusk fell Loader would bring in his shaded reading lamp.

Occasionally, if Butterfield felt that he had 'straightened things a little', he might call on a congenial fellow-architect like Philip Webb after dinner. He also saw something of Henry Woodyer, who had been his assistant for a few months in 1844, and had then set up his office in the same house in Adam Street. Butterfield undoubtedly enjoyed a circle of architectural acquaintances, including both colleagues and patrons. Nevertheless, apart from the afternoon interlude, he did not allow them much time. He was too often 'excessively pressed with arrears . . . Works in the country have kept me running about'.[8] In any case, there is no sign that these were close friendships. Webb's real circle, for example, was with William Morris and Burne-Jones; while Woodyer, flamboyantly dressed in a rough-blue serge suit, loose collar and crimson tie, wide hat and long green cloak, puffing a rare cigar, can scarcely have entirely pleased the abstemious and old-fashioned Butterfield. He may not have been very sorry when Woodyer moved his office to a Surrey farmhouse in 1857.[9]

Friendships with his architectural patrons appear at first sight to have been more important to Butterfield. He formed a close group with his Ecclesiological patrons of the 1840s: Benjamin Webb, Alexander Beresford-Hope, Sir William Heathcote, and the Coleridges of Ottery St Mary. Similarly, one can find later friends such as C. T. Arnold at Rugby, or Canon Hyde Beadon who secured many of Butterfield's Wiltshire commissions. It was to be among these patron-friends that he joined the Athenaeum, of which Lord Coleridge was also 'for many years an habitué'. Butterfield and Coleridge are said to have been 'close and intimate friends, constant companions and frequent correspondents'.[10] Their correspondence has not survived, but Butterfield's relics include a copy of *The Vicar of Wakefield* inscribed from the Coleridges: 'W. Butterfield from his friends . . . in memory of much kindness, February 1858'.

Yet what kind of relationships were these? No doubt they were both necessary and pleasant for Butterfield, but could they have been genuinely intimate? It is difficult to believe that he ever forgot either the superior social situation of these patrons, or the necessary distinctions between architect and client. Both were well – indeed acutely – understood in Victorian society, and Butterfield believed them important. Nor could these relationships have ever been relaxed if, as seems probable, Butterfield was from the first presenting only one side of himself.

In the 1840s he had pushed himself forward into the Ecclesiological circle with great assurance, giving the impression that he had, 'as an architect', a good deal of work to his credit.[11] Yet as far as we know, when he first wrote to the *Ecclesiologist* he had not designed a single building; and his first major commission, a Nonconformist chapel for his Bristol uncle, must itself have been an embarrassment. Criticism was consequently dangerous. He reacted in two ways: where possible, especially with clients, he was cool, and stood on his professional dignity; but occasionally he responded with explosive rage. For example, at his first church, Coalpit Heath (5), the eminent surveyor to the Incorporated Church Building Society, a pupil of Sir John Soane, suggested that 'better means should be provided to protect the walls of the aisle from the lateral pressure of the lean-to roofs'. Butterfield altered his plans, but with incredibly bad grace: 'I really do not understand Mr Good's objection. I can only suppose that he has never examined our old churches, from which source alone information and experience in such matters can be obtained.'[12]

Throughout his life Butterfield was liable to behave in this fashion. If his professional life had been an easy one it might not have mattered much. But in fact he was very much open to attack, in the first place as the architect of extreme High Churchmen, and in the second place as a stylistic innovator. Moreover some of the worst criticism came from former supporters. Beresford-Hope, with whom he had spent 'many a happy hour' in planning St Augustine's College, Canterbury,[13] and who had chosen him as the architect of All Saints', became neurotically hostile in the 1850s, and published a series of anonymous attacks in the *Ecclesiologist*. Butterfield decided not to answer. The fight would have been unequal. He tried instead to contain his fury. But inevitably it burst out sometimes, generally upon foolish builders, but also upon the occasional unsuspecting client or architect who crossed his path.

In middle and old age, as he stuck to his own style in spite of the change in architectural fashion, criticism was if anything less sympathetic. Butterfield replied in public only once, when Keble College was attacked by his favourite newspaper, the High Church weekly *Guardian*.[14] In private he tried to convince himself that true principles were never popular – a favourite conservative doctrine – and that a genius was rarely recognized in his own time. He copied into his book of 'Extracts' translations of Michelangelo's later sonnets, meditating upon the loneliness of the artist. From Renan's *Recollections of My Youth* he noted, a little ambiguously: 'I am well assured that no really great man has ever imagined himself to be one, and that those who during their life time browse upon their glory while it is green do not garner it ripe after their death.' In Emerson he found a defence for shyness: 'A constant effort is needed to keep genius unalloyed by the common places of a tyrannical world. Each must stand on his glass tripod if he would keep his electricity . . . There is an instinct in genius to possess its own soul apart, and to resist as an injury the attempts of society to break it in the yoke of its ordinary conventionalism.'

Increasingly thus Butterfield withdrew within himself, generally courteous but always remote, 'living as quiet and retired a life as is consistent with my public work'.[15] He was persistently reluctant to accept invitations to ceremonies when his buildings were opened, or to country-house parties. Lord Heytesbury, for example, found it difficult to persuade him to come even when his friend Hyde Beadon was there, although Butterfield confessed – 'I want to see him much.'[16] He could not even be induced to attend the meeting in 1884 at which he was awarded the R.I.B.A. Gold Medal. He began to resist any attempt, however sympathetic, to give publicity to his work. 'I have always had to regret when I have at all given way in the direction of publicity', he told the editor of the *Building News*. Altogether he cultivated an impression of morbid shyness, and would have been glad to see the obituary which asserted that 'he led the life of a recluse'.[17]

It was only to a few friends that he remained rather more open. 'Grave and unsympathetic as he was supposed to have been to many,' Swinfen Harris recalled after his death, 'he was by nature one of the kindliest and most hospitable of men to those few who had the good fortune to possess his friendship.' One undoubtedly close friend of the 1870s was C. T. Arnold, an assistant master at Rugby from 1841, who got to know Butterfield in the 1860s, and came to value him greatly. 'It was his habit of mind in any crisis of his life which moved him deeply to turn to you for sure sympathy,' wrote his widow in 1878. 'You knew him as few people knew him . . . Margaret begs me to send her love.' Butterfield noted on the back of this letter, 'some precious photographs'; and it leaves no doubt that he was capable of strong emotional friendships.[18]

Yet how much did such friends know of Butterfield's own problems? Did they realize that, for all his 'old-fashioned courtesy of manner',[19] he was smothering an emotional volcano? Certainly in 1880 Joseph Clarke, a fellow Ecclesiological architect, was astonished when he kept the plans of Ardleigh church for a few days without Butterfield's permission, in order to apply for a grant to the Essex Church Building Society; for his pains he 'received a very angry letter from the gentle Butterfield, and he could not understand it'.[20] But it seems unlikely that closer friends were generally unaware of the repeated quarrels with builders, or of the incidents, increasingly frequent as he grew older, which 'sometimes led his clients to consider him crotchety'.[21] And surely they knew of the extraordinary anonymous letters to the *Guardian* which he wrote from the 1870s onwards, meticulously pasting them into a cuttings book? He wrote them under their very noses, scribbling his wrath away after a courteous conversational exchange over his dish of tea at the Athenaeum. 'We have been suffering from unseasonable weather of late, year after year,' he writes, warming to a favourite theme. '"Rural Dean" is satisfied that our national iniquities have not deserved suffering or punishment. Many persons think otherwise. Godless education, a people largely estranged from religion, divorce established as an institution, the marriage law threatened, clergy suffering from their starvation incomes, ruinous trade strikes, and a multitude of other national evils, are too little taken into account . . .'[22]

It is difficult to be certain, but it seems likely that at the Athenaeum both sides were playing a conscious game. As early as 1875 Sir Arthur Elton was in London to persuade Butterfield to design him a church at Clevedon (281), and before seeing Butterfield he explained his anxieties to their mutual friend F. H. Dickinson, whom he saw at the Athenaeum.[23] On the next day, emerging with great relief from a successful interview with Butterfield, Sir Arthur met Dickinson in the street, 'who shrieked with laughter in the public ways when I said I had – "given myself up to Butterfield like a lamb"'.[24] There must have been more laughter of this kind in the privacy of the clubroom after Butterfield had walked back to his office. One is driven to conclude that even in the most intimate friendships with his patrons, as with the Coleridges, a considerable distance was maintained by both sides. At the end of his life Lord Coleridge wrote to a friend: 'Architects and contractors are an unstable lot of fellows in general, though I have been spoiled by old Butterfield, who kept his time to an hour, never exceeded his estimates by a shilling, and whose work, some of which I have known for forty years, seems as if it would last for ages.'[25] There is affection here, but it is a little patronizing; and certainly Coleridge could have scarcely implied that Butterfield was a stable personality, unless their relationship had remained, in its essentials, professional.

The truth therefore seems to be that only among his relations could Butterfield hope for friendship uninhibited by his professional situation, and all the elaborate barriers that this required. Certainly some of his letters to his uncle and his nephew have a warmth which can be found in no other surviving correspondence.

The earliest group of family letters are those to his Bristol uncle, for whom he was building Highbury Chapel in 1842–3 (76). In one of these, Butterfield had been seriously ill, and since he could scarcely write, his brother-in-law George Allnutt was acting as his amanuensis. Another mentions a Christmas visit to Bristol, and takes up an offer which his uncle then made of a loan of £20, 'procure a few things which would be extravagant in the present condition of my purse . . . I should not have thought of asking it of any one else but just recollected your kind offer'. Earlier, in 1836, when Butterfield was still an architectural student, his uncle had lent him £500. In all these letters he signs himself either 'your affectionate nephew' or 'yours very affectionately'.[26]

The letters to his nephew, William Starey, extend over a longer period. William, his godson, as his sister's eldest son probably named after him, became a clergyman, and remained a bachelor like himself; almost certainly he was Butterfield's favourite among the Starey children. Two letters were written to him at Cambridge in 1867 and 1868. In the first, Butterfield chats about 'what to read on the subject of the old Guilds', proposes a visit to Cambridge, and hopes to see him at Milton Ernest over Christmas; in the second he suggests another visit to Cambridge, and encloses some money towards 'such things as breakfasts'. He had also given him a writing table. He signs himself: 'with love to Augustin, I am, yours very affectionately'. The warm tone of these letters sets them apart from all his other correspondence. There were undoubtedly others: in letters to his mother in 1869 William refers to 'a very nice kind letter from Uncle William', who was helping to find him a curacy in a suitable parish. It was through Butterfield's efforts that Butler of Wantage, although 'rather overstocked with curates', was persuaded to take him on. On the whole, however, the later letters which have survived are those giving advice, generally about business matters such as house leases, but also on other questions, and their tone is unattractive. 'Certainly this lease is a very slovenly affair. I cannot make out from it who is to do the painting and repairs', he comments characteristically: 'You must have more definite terms.' And then as a postscript, he criticizes the way in which William had addressed a letter 'so as to give trouble to the Post Office. Why do you put "Islington"? It will not be delivered by an Islington postman, and it simply puts the Post Office on the wrong scent . . . There is a right and a wrong in all things'. It is as if Butterfield, unable to develop a more adult relationship with his godson who was now aged nearly thirty, was desperately attempting to perpetuate his earlier closeness to him through this hectoring advice on trivialities. When William was well into middle age, Butterfield was still addressing him in the same way. A letter of 1891 opens: 'You have often said that your memory is indifferent. Do you take pains to assist and supplement it?' He should start keeping a cuttings book of extracts from books and newspapers. And he should take more interest in church questions and church principles. 'Do not live as if the preaching of sermons was the great object of a clergyman's life. Anybody must get dull if that is the sole view. A clergyman has a relationship primarily to the Church, secondarily to his parish'.[27]

No doubt these letters give a one-sided picture. They were probably singled out to be kept just because of the pertinent advice which they contained. One would not imagine from them that Butterfield trusted William Starey sufficiently to choose him as his principal executor, or so enjoyed his company that he frequently visited him and on at least one occasion joined him on a continental holiday. Nevertheless, it is clear that Butterfield's concern for the Starey children was most easily expressed when he was instructing them. Of the other sons, he was closest to Augustin, whom he trained as an architect, and who later also became a clergyman. Augustin's praise for Butterfield when he was his pupil was unstinted: 'He is made of goodness and unselfishness'. John, as one might expect of a businessman, found Butterfield's attitude to life much less attractive. When, at the height of the family crisis which led to the sale of Milton Ernest, he had to decide whether or not to go to Ceylon, John seems to have felt Butterfield's opinion more important than his father's, and was glad of the 'very salient good advice' he received; but he complained that though Butterfield did not oppose him going, 'he holds such strong conservative and unenterprising ideas if I may say so that as was naturally to be expected, he does not anxiously encourage my going'. The pattern with the girls is similar. The saintly Lucy, whose pathetic death after a lingering illness aged only twenty-two was commemorated in a privately printed account of her last days, *In Memory of Lucy Starey*, regarded Butterfield as one of those rare inspiring examples of men 'who have spent their lives with no other thought but working for Christ, and look upon this life as only a preparation for the heavenly'. The equally devout Emily, on the other hand, was irritated to discover that when she sought a practical expression of her religious convictions in keeping house for her brother William in his Oxfordshire parish, 'His Uncleship' conveyed his disapproval by completely ignoring her in all his letters to William: 'I wonder what I *am* meant to do in the world according to his view?'[28]

This unequal success is hardly surprising when one read the letters which Butterfield wrote to his sister in about 1850, when the children were still young. His intense concern for the children is quite obvious; he regards the responsibilities of parents, and of godparents, as 'fearful to contemplate'. There is also much sensible advice in the letters, particularly his warnings against superficial tests of education such as French, music or Scripture reading rather than the development of character, and also in his awareness of the problems of a mother sharing her responsibility with a governess. A long letter on this second question is especially shrewd, showing how the governess's precarious authority must be supported by giving her a good room, allowing her to preside over the children at table, and in other ways giving her '*real substantial* respect . . . You must treat her generously and never by word or look thwart her plans in detail . . . You trust her thoroughly without suspicion. *She is yourself*. The children cannot serve two masters.' It was for this reason that he was never happy at the engagement of a governess in the first place; a mother's responsibilities were too serious to be handed over to another. But however sensitive to the essentially adult problems of a governess, his understanding of children was woefully inadequate. He had an idealized concept of the unspoilt little child, 'most beautiful to think of', pure and modest, reverent and obedient, simple and trustful. But although this character was a figment of extreme Victorian sentimentality, he wished to preserve it from corruption by a ruthlessly realistic discipline of Benthamite rigour. Punishment, by degrees adjusted to the fault, must be imposed for all disobedience, 'and there must be no escape from it. It must be as certain as the fault. If it comes one day and not the next, it has the appearance of temper in the inflictor'. The children must be taught by discipline to show reverence to their elders, to be punctual, to control their tongues. 'It is *quite* unsafe to allow children any greater licence *than speaking when they are spoken to*. Above all they ought not to ask questions'. In this method of upbringing it followed that the expression of affection must take a distinctly inferior place. Children were 'no toys to be fondled and caressed. They are intended for God's service in this world and the next'.[29]

If, in spite of these harsh views, Butterfield retained the affection of the Starey family, it was because his genuine concern for their well-being was never in doubt. Alone among his brothers, he was certain to attend every Starey family occasion. He was constantly in touch; his sister's diary for the last year of her life records a visit or a letter from him every ten days. A diary of Emily's for 1872 shows him joining the family for a seaside weekend at Whitsun, discussing the Sunday evening sermon as they walked down to enjoy the moonlight over the water. He helped the children in their careers, took them on holidays, encouraged them in suitable recreations such as embroidery and painting. In his last years he joined with them as a 'constant attendant' at Tottenham church.[30] There was never any doubt that he would choose his burial place next to his sister in Tottenham graveyard: 'no other has a claim on you'.[31] The low, weathered, cross-capped tomb chests which he designed for himself and the family form a distinctive group among the headstones of the cemetery. And when his will was read, his attachment to the Stareys was conclusively demonstrated: for although his sister Jane, his brother James and his brother Robert's widow were, with William Starey, the principal beneficiaries, more than a dozen other members of the Starey family were mentioned, and William was his principal executor.[32]

Thus Butterfield possessed the ultimate security of a family circle throughout his life. The presence of his family in the background gave a human meaning to the apparently empty regularity of his daily life, so that his own stable routine reminded him of the other households which he had known. In a published letter he wrote: 'Parents and home lie at the root of Church and State. There must be piety and prayer, discipline, good government, and affection in our households. Each family must be a small, well-administered kingdom in itself . . .'[33] It was this foundation which enabled Butterfield to build his career on firm religious beliefs and architectural principles, and to stick to them in spite of constant criticism and even at the cost of personal isolation. In an age when religious doctrine was shaken in its fundamentals, and when architectural fashion shifted from decade to decade, this was a remarkable achievement.

Yet in spite of the strength of his convictions, and for all the small ways in which he sought stability, in his regular timetable, his constant environment, and his professional and social punctiliousness, it was a course which subjected Butterfield to perpetual strain. He needed the warmth of human friendship, and however important his family, it was impossible that occasional and not always satisfactory contact should be sufficient. His outbursts of temper with relative strangers are indications that he needed more. In short, he was caught in a vicious circle; not a hard, cold man, but a man full of unexpressed emotion, needing more intense, more frequent human contact, and for lack of it driven more and more to an obstinacy and ill temper which left him still more isolated. No wonder, as he grew older, he became increasingly pessimistic, railing against the world, his voice hysterical. The loneliness of his last letters about All Saints' is especially pathetic. He found himself in continual conflict with the vicar over the details of the work, and his only consolation was a sympathetic churchwarden. 'As you to some extent know,' he wrote, 'I have been used singularly ill by the present incumbent. For love of the building, I have *given* my professional services ever since the Church was consecrated, but I was treated lately by him as if a child in his hands . . .' 'Certainly the architect of All Saints' does not lie upon a bed of roses . . .' 'It is hard work for an old man to have to carry on such an unworthy correspondence in the night hours . . .' And then, to his distress, the churchwarden wrote that he was obliged to resign, and Butterfield was obviously dismayed by the loss of his support: 'I should be very sorry to miss you – For I feel that our intercourse, so far as I am concerned, has been very helpful and pleasant. That it should come to an end so suddenly is a great loss to me . . . But perhaps I shall now be dismissed altogether'.[34]

It is scarcely surprising that occasionally he wondered whether the price had been worth paying. 'The world is not a Goddess in petticoats but the devil in a strait waistcoat,' he noted from Samuel Taylor Coleridge. 'It is the strait waistcoat which makes life endurable.' We do not know what temptations Butterfield faced. We have no indication why he never married. Much of the evidence is missing, and there may always be more which has been deliberately concealed. One thinks of William Morris, who also had a furious temper, but none of Butterfield's religious motives for secrets; yet much of his personal life has been only very recently discovered. We know very little of Butterfield's attitude to women in general, except that silence was 'modest and womanly', and that he accepted the conventional Victorian view that they should develop the heart rather than the mind: 'Are women estimable in society for what they *know* or what they *are*? Surely only for the latter . . .'[35] But for this very reason women could be a wholesome influence upon men, and he argued that young men benefited from mixed church congregations: 'the idea of separate services for the sexes is suggestive of evil thoughts and still more of evil language'.[36] There is also an ambiguous reference in a letter of 1881: 'Have you seen Dean Burjon's sermon last Trinity Sunday preached before the University of Oxford, on the subject of this craze about women?'[37]

Yet that Butterfield was struggling with himself is clearly revealed by some of the quotations in his book of 'Extracts'. 'All this is anything but human and natural, you may say,' he took from Ernest Renan. 'No doubt. But strength is only manifested by running to nature. The natural tree does not bear good fruit. The fruit is not good until the tree is trained, that is to say until it has ceased to be a tree.' And again from Renan, more explicitly: 'And more especially I noted that nature does not in the least encourage man to be chaste.' Butterfield did not seek justification in suppressing his passions, but in controlling his actions: 'Feelings or no feelings are quite independent of one's will, and God asks for one's will only.'

Notes on chapter 2

1 Liam Hudson, *Contrary Imaginations*, London, Methuen, 1966, pp. 100–52.

2 Apart from his date of birth and his father's trade, published information is unreliable: e.g. *R.I.B.A. Journal* (VII) 1900, p. 242, states that he was born in Gordon Square, then as yet unbuilt. The information in the following paragraphs is based upon contemporary street directories, the St Clement Danes parish registers, the wills of Butterfield and his father at Somerset House, and Butterfield's indenture of apprenticeship at the R.I.B.A.; Butterfield's correspondence, 'Extracts', an account book of 1863–4, newspaper cuttings and other personal relics, and also the journal of Benjamin Starey and other family papers in the Starey Collection; information from the Starey, Butterfield and Drew families, including family trees; and, for the Wills connection, an architectural thesis by F. J. Penn on 'The Early Life of William Butterfield', and also the Wills family ledger book (Messrs W. D. and H. O. Wills) and other documents kindly shown to me by Dr B. W. E. Alford.

3 Anne Starey to her children, 14 September 1886, Starey Collection.

4 Architectural Society, list of members 1835, R.I.B.A.

5 The next three paragraphs are based on Redfern, *op. cit.*, an unreliable source, but the only one available. The writing-table is at Milton Ernest. The account book of 1863–4, which runs from October to January only, shows Butterfield's expenses at that time: wages, ranging from £15 to £22 10*s* a quarter; £5 for the chief assistant's holiday; £36 5*s* a quarter's rent; offertory, averaging £1 weekly; a Gothic model book (£2); Christmas boxes (16*s*); subscription to the *Guardian* (30*s*); 'Chappels bill for boots' (£2 6*s*) and 'Hall for cravats' (£1 7*s*). Some other items are obscure: payments to Mrs L. F. Allnutt, to M. P., and to Mr Molyneux 'for schools' (£20).

6 Redfern, who was in Butterfield's office in 1877, called them 'a faithful couple', and they received £400 by Butterfield's will. They do not appear in the account book of 1863–4.

7 E. Swinfen Harris, 'The Life and Work of William Butterfield', *A*, (83) 1910, pp. 129–30, 145–7.

8 Butterfield to Webb, 28 October 1878, John Brandon-Jones, 'Letters of Philip Webb and his contemporaries', *Architectural History*, (8) 1965, pp. 52–66.

9 The description of Woodyer is also from Redfern. Street directories show that the younger Salvin, and later G. M. Hills, took over his rooms at 4 Adam Street.

10 E. H. Coleridge, *Life and Correspondence of Lord Coleridge*, London, Heinemann, 1904, 1, p. 217, and 2, p. 390.

11 *E*, (1) 1842, p. 55, signed W. B., but the phraseology unmistakable.

12 J. H. Good's report, 30 May 1844, and Butterfield to Good, 7 June, I.C.B.S. file 3434.

13 R. J. E. Boggis, *History of St Augustine's College, Canterbury*, Canterbury 1907, p. 65.

14 Copy in Starey Collection, February 1875.

15 Butterfield to M. B. Adams, editor of *BN*, 28 December 1878, explaining his 'desire that my works should be illustrated as little as possible', partly because of their dependence

on colour, but also because 'my natural disposition inclines me strongly to this'. This letter, which was partly quoted by the *BN* (see n. 17), was kindly shown me by Mr T. A. Greeves.

16 Butterfield to Lord Heytesbury, 7 September declining invitation to church reopening, and 26 June 1875 and 15 April 1879 to house parties; the visitors' book shows three visits with the Beadons in the 1880s: Heytesbury Collection.

17 *BN*, (78) 1900, p. 292.

18 Jenny Arnold to Butterfield, 22 May 1878, Starey Collection.

19 *The Times*, 26 February 1900.

20 Rev. R. B. Mayor to Canon F. W. Perry, 15 March 1880, Ardleigh chest.

21 *The Times*, 26 February 1900.

22 15 September 1897.

23 Dickinson was an active Ecclesiologist in the 1840s. The secretary of the Athenaeum Club kindly informs me that when Butterfield was elected a member in 1858 he was proposed by Dickinson and seconded by Coleridge. Butterfield was later a committee member.

24 Diaries of Sir Arthur Elton, 10–11 June 1875.

25 E. H. Coleridge, *op. cit.*, 2, 381. This slightly patronizing tone also occurs in his letter to Butterfield about the R.I.B.A. Gold Medal presentation: 'My dear B, Nothing can be better than Mr Christian's speech . . . He must be a very nice fellow whom to thank. I really think you must write your own thanks'; 13 June 1884, Starey Collection.

26 Butterfield to W. D. Wills, 16 December 1842 and 30 March 1843, Highbury Chapel chest. I am grateful to Messrs W. D. and H. O. Wills and to Dr B. W. E. Alford for informing me of this loan of £500. Butterfield, who paid interest at 5 per cent per annum, closed the account in 1860, when his uncle wrote off the £114 4s 7d still outstanding.

27 Butterfield to William Starey, 15 November 1867, February 1868, 22 February 1875 and 27 February 1891, Starey Collection.

28 Augustin Starey to Benjamin Starey, 24 October 1870, John Starey to Anne Starey, 19 April 1871, and Elizabeth (Lily) Starey to Anne Starey, 29 January and 17 February 1880, Starey Collection.

29 Butterfield to Anne Starey, 2 February 1848, 3 July c. 1850 and 3 March c. 1855, Starey Collection.

30 *DNB*. William Starey was curate at Tottenham from 1883. Other local connections were Canon and Mrs Twells at Enfield, and Prebendary Arthur Wilson, according to Swinfen Harris 'his attached friend'.

31 Anne Starey to Butterfield, 27 January 1891, Starey Collection.

32 Butterfield left £16,214; of which Mrs Jane Allnutt received £5232, James Butterfield £2616, Rev. William Starey £1000, Mrs Robert Steven Butterfield £800, and twelve other Stareys fractions of £2616. In addition, Rev. T. S. Barrett (for whom Butterfield had provided two minor restoration schemes without charge) received £500, Mr C. Allnutt (his second executor) £450, Rev. E. S. Medley £199, Mr and Mrs Loader £400, and six others, probably also employees, smaller sums. Mrs Jane Allnutt also received £43 for

board and lodging for Joseph Vincent for the next eighteen months. It is not clear who he was. A manuscript fragment of the late 1890s also refers to him: 'Whether Joseph or you added up the amounts of his list from October to February which I am keeping, I am *anxious* to know . . . He is so untidy' (Starey Collection).

33 'A Layman', *G*, 16 September 1885.

34 Butterfield to F. H. Rivington, 27 January 1894, 17 October, 2 and 4 November 1895, All Saints' chest.

35 Butterfield to Anne Starey, 2 February 1848 and 3 July c. 1850, Starey Collection.

36 'B.D.', *G*, 2 September 1885.

37 Butterfield to Canon Perry, 4 August 1881, Ardleigh chest.

3

Belief

There can scarcely have been a more propitious moment than 1840, during the last four hundred years of English history, for Butterfield to start a career as a church architect. An unprecedented number of churches, church schools, parsonages, convents and other religious buildings were to be constructed during the next fifty years. Churches were given more attention and were more frequently illustrated in the mid-nineteenth-century weekly magazines than any other type of building. In these decades churches could make an architect's reputation more quickly even than country houses; and in fact nearly all the future leaders of the architectural profession who started work in the early Victorian period made their names in church design. If one lists the best known English architects of the generation born between 1810 and 1830, two in three names are church architects: Pugin, Scott, Butterfield, Carpenter, Street, Pearson, Bodley and so on. Perhaps Teulon, although he designed more than sixty churches, started rather as an estate architect. There were also a few architects able to step into a family practice of a different character, such as P. C. Hardwick or E. M. Barry; but nearly every well known mid-nineteenth-century architect of another tradition – whether classical, official or even engineering – belonged to an older generation. There was only one outstanding new name made in secular architecture – Waterhouse. His career, so far from being typical of the High Victorian architect, is strikingly exceptional. And the secular nature even of his work was largely due to a fortuitous lack of opportunity, for Waterhouse in his early years also depended upon a religious connection, the Quakers: the only sect which escaped the chapel-building fever of the period.[1]

The penetrating influence of religion in Victorian life, which this professional pattern implies, came about through two successive religious revivals, each unusually persistent: the Evangelical and the Oxford Movement. Butterfield himself had strong views on both revivals.

The Evangelical Movement had begun in the eighteenth century as an attempt to raise practical moral standards in private and public life, using as its instruments private prayer, a regular daily life, and emotional preaching. No doubt Butterfield accepted, without realizing the source, its profound influence on the Victorian home: the regular ritual of morning prayers, grace at meals, and Sunday observance; and the mother's role as religious teacher and embodiment of virtue – and above all of the virtue of chastity. One can see its influence clearly in his own personal life; in his abstemious tastes (although he never showed any support for public temperance campaigns), and especially in the unanswerable reply which he often gave to hostile critics: 'Mr —, I have a conscience.'[2] Emotional preaching, on the other hand, he could not tolerate. To a devoted Anglican it might indeed be regarded as a disastrous instrument, for the Evangelical Movement had soon broken out from the respectable centres in which it had started – Oxford, Bath, Brighton and London – and spread down the social scale, bringing in its wake a series of secessions and new sects. Again and again local preachers would arise, generate a following, march out to some desolate and secluded moorland, and there hold great camp meetings attended by thousands of working people; there would be suspicion and criticism of the violent emotional scenes at these meetings, and the intoxicated preacher would decide to form his own church. The original Wesleyan Methodists were followed by Primitive and Free Methodists, Bible Christians, and by all the Baptist sects. Butterfield never concealed his dislike for 'the type of modern ranting Missioner, who has well-nigh made the word "Mission" a reproach';[3] or his fear of 'extempore prayer, and in the laity being absolutely abandoned, as the Dissenters are, to the mercies of the minister'. The 'expressions of a vague and Methodistical nature' which he detected in the Occasional Services suggested in 1889 revealed the decadence of the whole proposal. 'Methodism may need them. They are not the healthy outcome of the Church . . .'[4]

The Oxford Movement was not, as we shall see, without its own emotionalism, but this was the revival from which Butterfield drew his own religious inspiration. It began, at just the moment when he decided to become an architect rather than a builder, principally as a defensive response to the spate of reforms in the 1820s and 1830s which undermined the established position of the Church of England. The abolition of the Test Act in 1827 opened the civil service, local government and the House of Commons to Nonconformists. In the 1830s school education was for the first time taken partially under government control; the church monopoly of baptism, marriage and burial was broken by civil registration; and the ancient obligations of landowners to support the Church were ended by the commutation of tithes. The abolition of local church rates, which were used to raise money for church building, was only delayed by the House of Lords. Nor, even under a Conservative Prime Minister, was the government now willing, as on past occasions, to provide state money for parish church building. In short, England had effectively ceased to be an Anglican state; and if radical pressure groups were to have their way, disestablishment itself was in sight. In Ireland and in Wales the threat was in fact to be realized.

Equally serious was the possibility that the Church of England, before being cast out, would be disembowelled. The end of the Anglican monopoly of the state did not loosen government control of the Church: indeed, the vesting of bishop's revenues in a body of Ecclesiastical Commissioners appointed by the government, although a means towards the urgently needed redistribution of clerical incomes, revived the fear of secularization. Here again the danger was not to be entirely averted: in due course the Anglican universities of Oxford and Cambridge were to be secularized, and even Anglican parish graveyards were to be opened to other denominations. This last measure was particularly resented as an interference with church doctrine as well as property. 'In prospect of dissenters burying in our Churchyards,' wrote Butterfield to Lord Heytesbury in 1880, 'I hope that your Churchyard is closed for general interments.'[5] The ultimate secular control of Anglican doctrine had earlier been shown by the notorious Gorham Judgment of 1850, by which the Privy Council reversed a church court decision on baptismal regeneration; and it was also indirectly asserted by the secular appointment of bishops.

Although the Oxford Movement was launched to defend church property (John Keble's sermon of 1833 was in defence of the absurdly unequal Irish dioceses), it soon became more concerned with doctrine. It reasserted the catholic inheritance of the Church of England, the apostolic succession, the sacraments and the Prayer Book, the priesthood rather than the pastorate. Its rapid success came from the need in the Church for a new spiritual authority to replace its lost institutional state privilege; and it was because this need was especially felt by the parish clergy, who had to face dissenters without their old legal weapons, that Keble was always regarded as its leader. As vicar of Hursley he shared their experience while, as an Oxford don, at a date when all dons were in Anglican orders, and generally moved after a few years to a parish living in college patronage, his influence could spread easily from the common-rooms to the vicarages. On the other hand, it was not until the end of the nineteenth century that the bishops were sympathetic. Their problems were different – and in any case they were appointed by the government, and the Queen never liked High Churchmen. It is characteristic that Gilbert Scott, rather than Butterfield, was the architect employed in the cathedrals: as Scott recalled, 'Carpenter and Butterfield were the apostles of the high-church school – I, of the multitude.'[6]

Thus to the Oxford Movement in its early decades both state and church authority were in practice enemies. Butterfield, canvassing in 1872 against a Lessons Book of biblical extracts ('We shall thus have a National Bible instead of the Catholic one, and all for the mere sake of saving trouble which it will do men good to take'), calls Archbishop Tait 'this new sectionary'.[7] In other letters to the *Guardian* he attacked the archbishop for his irregular conduct of confirmation services. 'He *says* a great deal more, and *does* a great deal less, than is directed'; and instead of a cope, he wears 'a dress in which with sleeves a little less developed an ante-Reformation Bishop would have walked about his house and garden.' In general the bishops 'take more liberties with the Prayer-book, and are rather more lawless than people in general . . . I love authority and simple loyalty, and I do not despair if the Bishops will work in the spirit of the Prayer-book and obey its orders.' It would also be better if they did not desert their dioceses for the London season.[8] 'We laymen are in a sore plight . . . as sheep scattered by the shepherds.'[9] The Queen however meets with little more approval: he is angered by her failure to provide sufficient church accommodation in the New Forest, so that a retired admiral 'is doing that which the Crown should do for its own tenants and refuses to do – and he is the only person in the district who is not poor.'[10] Butterfield's hostility is also betrayed in an attack on the Accession Day service, 'not prayers of the old description, but conversation of a very prosy kind, ponderous talking . . . verbose in an excited way.'[11]

In this case Butterfield's attitude was reinforced by his dislike of any alteration in the old forms of prayer, which he regarded with as much reverence as medieval precedents in Gothic architecture: 'The Prayer-book is our *terra firma*.'[12] Moreover, he found that the essential hostility of the state brought its compensations, in providing justification for 'refusing to agitate his heart and soul in the party questions which agitate the community.'[13] Nor was this attitude surprising in an age in which religious questions provoked serious public uproar. Butterfield knew men who had suffered public violence: Charles Lowder, for example, whose services were invaded by organized gangs of London roughs; or the rector of St Columb in Cornwall, who lived for a time in a state of siege, his windows barred, with alarm bells fixed to the shutters, because he had put on a surplice to preach. Public controversy, such as the outcry which followed the re-establishment by the Pope of bishops and cathedrals in England, could only cause damage. If Cardinal Wiseman's effigy was burnt on Guy Fawkes' day 1850, a High Churchman might be the next victim.[14] Butterfield wrote to a Roman Catholic friend early in 1851: 'I suppose we must not expect much more row until Parliament meets and then it is just possible there may be some new event to divert people and so we may be let alone. But as I always felt we and not you will suffer. It has already dealt us several heavy blows but we needed some cudgelling. Some men's common sense had deserted them.'[15]

The year 1850 was indeed a second moment of crisis for the Church of England. Once the question of spiritual authority had been raised, the certainty of Rome beckoned. The re-establishment of the Roman hierarchy immediately following the Gorham Judgment was an invitation to the High Church clergy to secede, to follow the path which Newman, their finest theologian, had taken as early as 1845. We have no evidence of wavering in Butterfield himself, but he had worked with at least a dozen clergy who were converted. They included four from All Saints' Margaret Street and two from Stoke Newington; Henry Wilberforce of East Farleigh and his curate; Coleridge's brother Henry who was curate at Alfington; J. H. Hungerford Pollen with whom he was restoring Merton College chapel (348); and Archdeacon Manning of Chichester and his curate Laprimaudaye, who thus never used the church and vicarage (266) which Butterfield was building for him at West Lavington.[16] For many of Butterfield's friends these secessions were devastating blows. Henry Coleridge's father, John Taylor Coleridge, eminent as a lawyer and judge, seriously considered abandoning his career for ordination 'by way of confession of his own unswerving loyalty to the Church of his Fathers'.[17]

It is inconceivable that Butterfield was not himself shaken by these desertions. He sensed, quite correctly, that authority was but one of the attractions of Rome. Butterfield himself to a large extent sympathized with the attitudes of the old High Church school which had preceded the Oxford Movement, with its emphasis on authority and the Prayer Book, its suspicion of emotion, its sobriety, earnestness and austerity. To the new generation, deeply influenced by the revolt of romanticism against cold reason, the old High Churchmen were 'high and dry'. Keble's poetry of religion corresponded to the young Ruskin's *Poetry of Architecture*. Enthusiasm was characteristic of the Oxford Movement. Coupled with the medievalism equally typical of the romantics, enthusiasm made possible a new devotional type of piety very close to Roman Catholic methods. Devotional books for private prayer were translated, and confessions and retreats became a regular practice. Above all, monastic life was revived with the formation of sisterhoods at Regent's Park, Oxford, Wantage and Devonport in the late 1840s. The leading part in many of these developments was played by Canon Pusey, who was especially the protector and benefactor of the monastic revival.[18]

Butterfield certainly sympathized with the new sisterhoods, for he designed the first convents at Plymouth (213) and Osnaburgh Street without a professional fee.[19] Earlier, he had entered with enthusiasm into the rebuilding of St Augustine's, Canterbury, which was conceived as 'some sort of restoration of the old Monastery of St Augustine, and not a mere college'.[20] He also assisted the revival of two quasi-monastic almshouses: St Nicholas' Hospital at Salisbury,[21] and the Hospital of St Cross and Almshouse of Noble Poverty at Winchester. St Cross seems to have been especially close to his heart, perhaps because Pugin had chosen it as the symbol of medieval charity, opposed to a prison-like workhouse, in his *Contrasts*. Its condition had become notorious after 1845, for the master, whose duties were nominal, was the Earl of Guildford, a pluralist who also held the wealthy livings of Alresford and Southampton St Mary. After a series of Chancery suits he was persuaded to resign in 1853, and the new master called in Butterfield to restore the buildings. He remained architect to the hospital until the end of his career, advising the trustees on policy as well as buildings, 'for your dealing with the fabric seems to have imbued you with the spirit of those who originally designed it'.[22]

On the other hand, to the revival of catholic practices in private prayer Butterfield was distinctly hostile. He believed the first task to be to revive the regular observance of formal services, to open 'the churches closed from Sunday to Sunday'.[23] Special 'days of prayer' were unnecessary: 'the Church has a day of humiliation and fasting in every week.'[24] The effectiveness of private prayer, with its meditation upon sacred pictures, 'is much exaggerated, because, perhaps, not one Englishman in a thousand possesses any such amount of imagination as can invest a picture with such power.'[25] More seriously, private prayer gave excessive importance to feeling rather than belief, and to isolated parts of the Gospel, particularly to the Crucifixion. He insisted that the most prominent positions in Keble College chapel should be given to the Last Judgment and Revelation, rather than to the Crucifixion.

> Did not the later part of the Middle Ages put forward the passion of our Lord with undue prominence, out of all proportion with other things? It was death much more than life that men were compelled to meditate on, the past much more than the future, instead of the two in their proper relationship. This gave a strong Puritan and melancholy tinge to the Christianity of Europe . . .
> Early Christian art told a different story, because a more complete one.[26]

If the mosaics at Keble were to end with the Crucifixion, or even with the Ascension,

> I should very naturally be asked ' 'Is this all? What do you believe of these 1800 years past and of we know not how many more years to come?' My answer is in this mosaic: 'I believe that our Lord is in the midst of His Church as He Promised.' . . . Our Lord's relationship to His Church must be all important. It crowns His whole work. He came to purchase to himself a glorious Church. And the more we see that Church divided and at variance in Christendom, so much the more is it necessary to go back to St John's vision of her at Unity, with Our Lord in the midst.[27]

This insistence on the complete story was linked to Butterfield's belief in the Bible. Here he shared the attitude of a wholehearted Protestant. 'Those who have tried it know that the Bible, taken as a whole, is the only true way of teaching God's will and ways, and their duties. To those who know it as a whole it is a wonderful book.'[28] So that for him, the attempt to revise the majestic language of the Authorized Version was 'very like an attack upon religion itself.'[29]

Early Christian art had not only told a more complete story, but told it in a dignified manner. 'A Crucifixion for instance with our Lord's arms stretched out straight upon the Cross expressed no agony. The figure was calm and impassive. It was only at a later date that such figures became anatomical and aimed at affecting the feelings, and that was as we know the period of its decay.' Thus for Butterfield the Victorian revival of catholic devotional piety was a sign of decadence. 'We are living in an age most terribly subjective and sensational . . . Creeds and definite principles are out of fashion. Our feelings take their place. Religion is losing strength and dignity, and I fear that the sceptic has too much cause for scorning it when presented to him in such a human and piecemeal fashion.'[30]

Butterfield believed that the proper character of religion, and consequently of architecture, was objective rather than subjective, a creed rather than a sermon. 'Not our feelings but our faith must sustain us. In the thoughtful repetition of the Creed there is the most real, the only real strength.'[31] 'The highest function of art is I think an objective one. It succeeds in a Creed, perhaps because it is in its nature a fixed and unchanging thing, better than it can do in a sermon.'[32] Whatever the modern eye may detect, 'purposeful sadism' was the very reverse of Butterfield's intention in Keble College chapel. 'Distortion and disorder for supposed good ends must have no permanent part in a building erected for [public worship] and which is to last for generations. We must of course endeavour to stamp upon it what is divine, rather than what is human. To give the restfulness and strength, and sense of communion that come of quiet order, completeness and proportion, must be our aim.'[33] Keble College chapel was conceived as a statement of faith; as a Te Deum, strictly ordered but manifestly triumphant.

Ritualism, which was a natural counterpart of the revival of catholic methods of devotion, as well as of the medievalism of the Oxford Movement, was equally repugnant to Butterfield. 'I have no sort of sympathy with lawlessness of any kind, whether Episcopal, Evangelical or Ritualistic.'[34] Thus while he supported the re-assertion of Holy Communion as the principal Sunday service, 'not to be largely put out of sight in the early hours',[35] because this was sanctioned by the Prayer Book, he disapproved of Benediction, and of the reservation of the sacrament in hospitals.[36] 'Is it *certain* that Reservation was only authorized for the short period between 1552 and 1549?' he was asked by Canon Perry of Ardleigh.[37] On such a question the law – even if state-imposed – would be decisive. He did not attend either All Saints' Margaret Street or St Alban's Holborn probably partly because of the ritual innovations – incense, lights, vestments and the elevation of the sacrament – with which they were associated. According to one recollection, although he took 'the minutest interest in the details of traditional worship, he held in horror anything like fancy ritual'.[38]

Certainly – in contrast to his attitude to the Gorham Judgment[39] – he accepted the Privy Council's 1857 decision that crosses were allowed *behind* the altar, or on a chancel screen, but not on the table itself: until the 1880s (by which date opinion had changed) his designs for plate include candlesticks, chalices, patens and flagons, all of which were legal, but not altar crosses. Similarly, he showed his conservatism in generally providing designs for altar cloths, which had been common before the Oxford Movement, but only occasionally for a frontal, and it seems never for vestments.

Perhaps one example of his meticulous attitude on such points should be given. When copies of the lost medieval brasses at Winchester College were to be relaid in the chapel, Butterfield wished them to face east: west-facing monuments were a Roman Catholic innovation of the seventeenth century, intended to distinguish lay-men from ecclesiastics. Knowing that Baigent, the maker of the copies, was a Roman Catholic, he expected a struggle, and 'warned the masons that he would endeavour so to lay them, and that they were not to yield'. When Baigent appeared in the chapel and attempted to instruct the masons, they reported his intervention to Butterfield. 'The news reached me on a Sunday morning in the country and I at once sent over a messenger five miles, and telegraphed to the Warden.' Butterfield of course carried his point. 'It seems strange to me, that Mr Baigent should feel such a protest to be worthwhile. But he has a strong will.'[40] However, he had met his match.

Such incidents were only possible in a society to which religion, and so religious controversy, was intensely important. Even the anti-ritualist riots were in one sense a demonstration of public religious feeling. But the obsessive concern of Butterfield and his contemporaries with the outward forms of religion was also partly due to a fear of examining the fundamental situation of religion in the nineteenth century. For in two ways the foundations of the Church were slipping.

Firstly, the intellectual justifications of faith had been shattered. It was not merely that the Oxford Movement had raised questions of spiritual authority which for the moment could only be settled by 'a desperate leap into blind fanaticism', the final authority of Rome.[41] At least the movement for the revival of Convocation, which could then take responsibility for church doctrine, offered some answer to this problem. Much more serious was the undermining of the authority of the Bible. German biblical scholars had shown the divine book to be a historical patchwork, some of it fraudulent, much of it mythical, and in his *Leben Jesu*, translated into English in 1846, D. F. Strauss presented a human Christ stripped of the historical Christ myth. If Butterfield did not know this book, he had probably read Ernest Renan's *Life of Jesus*, translated in 1865, a compelling humanist biography, in which Christ's miracles and resurrection are assumed to be false, and explained. Certainly his book of 'Extracts' shows that he read Renan's autobiography, and was familiar with the agnostic writing of the American poet Emerson. He was also in touch with liberal English theology, for Temple of Rugby was one of the authors of *Essays and Reviews*, published in 1860; although no doubt he had little more sympathy for this book than for the High Church liberalism of *Lux Mundi* which was published in 1889 and which he advised William Starey not to read.[42]

Equally, he must have been aware of the threat to Christian doctrine in the advance of the natural sciences. Sir Charles Lyell's *Principles of Geology* of 1830–3 had refuted the literal meaning of the book of Genesis. With Darwin's *Origin of Species* of 1859 the biblical story of the Creation took a still more serious blow. The possibility was emerging that life might not be a divine creation at all; that man might be a mere chemical automation. 'The consciousness of this great truth weighs like a nightmare, I believe, upon many of the best minds of these days,' wrote Huxley, the champion of scientific agnosticism,[43] and there can be no doubt that to Butterfield scientific advance was menacing. It was not so difficult to deal with biblical criticism. The minor inconsistencies in the Bible were 'there by God's providence, . . . warnings against the old error of seeking to find a mathematical certainty for our faith'.[44] He could effectively ridicule the liberal Sunday School teacher who tried 'to reduce a Divine operation to common sense' by saying, when the children asked 'Did the ass of Balaam really speak?' that he thought 'the ass looked at its master, with speaking eyes, so that he understood its thoughts'; as Butterfield remarked, 'We need, of course, to be told how the ass could possibly so turn its head as to bring its eyes to bear upon a rider seated upon its back.'[45] Again, some accommodation to the geological discoveries of Lyell proved possible. One could hardly forget them in the heyday of railway travel, when each new line revealed a fresh geological slice of the countryside; but familiarity itself could ease anxiety. Probably this was one reason for the geological activity of a man like Ruskin, even when the geologists' hammers left his faith fluttering in weak rags: 'I hear the clink of them at the end of every cadence of the Bible verses.'[46] Permanent polychromy, Butterfield's own doctrine from 1849 onwards, was in one sense a reassertion of the divine element in English clays and rock. But to the man of science of the 1860s and later, and the 'modern form of infidelity'[47] which he represented, Butterfield's generation produced no such reply.

There were some, such as Matthew Arnold, who preferred to accept agnosticism, seeking emotional support in the family and in personal love. Few Victorian agnostics found much pleasure in this new intellectual insecurity. Hurrell Froude, for example, wrote in later life that he would 'gladly give away all I am, and all I ever may become, all the years, every one of them, which may be given to me to live, but for one week of my old child's faith, to go back to calm and peace again, and then to die in hope. Oh, for one look of the blue sky, as it looked when we called it Heaven.'[48] Perhaps there were times when Butterfield felt this himself; for there can be no doubt of his genuine sorrow at the situation of such agnostics, 'following that Will o' the Wisp, their own poor feelings and fancies as to what is true and right, studying themselves instead of looking to God.'[49]

More commonly, however, Victorians cured themselves by feverish work, by church-building, parish organization, tract-writing and constant campaigns for reform and improvement, 'persuading themselves and others with spasmodic agony that the thing they love is not dead, but sleeping'. As early as 1835 Keble had advised Arnold to put down his doubts by 'main force'; take 'a curacy somewhere or other, and cure himself not by physic, i.e. reading and controversy, but by diet and regiment, i.e. holy living.' The same attitude lay behind the central emphasis of Carlyle, Ruskin and Morris on work – as suppressing 'self-listenings, self-questionings . . . diseased self-introspection . . . Properly speaking all true Work is Religion'.[50] Here is one reason for the shift of the Oxford Movement in the 1840s from its early concern with doctrine and authority, to the church-building activity of the Ecclesiologists. Equally, it helps one to understand the relentless pace of Butterfield's own professional life.

We have still to record the second fundamental weakness of the Victorian church: its social bias. The religious census of 1851 showed that church attendance among the upper and middle classes was probably more general than ever before. Nor is this surprising. With few exceptions they regarded the church as an essential instrument of social order in a revolutionary age. Even the cynical Disraeli saw Christianity as 'the only security for civilization and the only guarantee of real progress'.[51] Through his travels on the Continent Butterfield may well have seen something of political upheaval, and certainly Alfred Gerente, who designed much of the glass for All Saints' Margaret Street, had fought on the Paris barricades in 1848.[52] Right to the end of his life Butterfield could write: 'Our generation is living in a new and revolutionary period' – and his pen trembled at the rising tide of secularism and 'worldli-mindedness'.[53]

The working classes not only felt little attraction to the Church as an instrument of social order, but in some of the larger cities, and especially in London, they had been so neglected by the Church for generations that they regarded religion with positive hostility. In 1839 the inhabitants of Bethnal Green broke up the foundation-laying ceremony of the first of Bishop Blomfield's new churches by driving an infuriated cow at the bishop, lord mayor and choir. A canvasser for sixpences was told that they would give a shilling to hang the bishop, but nothing for church-building; the people needed food, not churches.[54] Later, when the clergy had widely taken up residence in their slum parishes and when many new churches had been built, attitudes softened. But the problem of low church attendance remained. The surveys of London by Charles Booth and Richard Mudie-Smith at the end of the century showed that in working-class districts four-fifths of the population never went to church; and 'the poorer the district, the less inclination is there to attend a place of worship'.[55]

One of the most heroic aspects of the Oxford Movement was its attempt to re-convert the urban working classes, and in this effort Butterfield played his part. His

church at Manchester (58), and several in London, are examples. All Saints' itself
was built in an area of 'dirty shops and dingy private dwellings, where the streets
seem never swept, the shops never clean, the houses never painted, and the amphibious
children, equally happy in the court or the gutter, never washed'.[56] The approach
to St Alban's Holborn was still worse.

> There is no blacker spot upon the map than that on the east of Gray's Inn
> Lane. It is the haunt of the lowest prostitutes and the worst thieves. Filth,
> squalor, ignorance, and sin are here huddled together without distinction of
> age and sex . . . Let any man button up his coat, empty his pockets, and walk
> through the several alleys or 'gardens' which form dirty channels between
> Gray's Inn and Leather Lane, and he will see work enough for the church
> which a noble-minded man has founded there.[57]

Exactly the same purpose inspired the campaign, in which Butterfield played a
leading part, against rented pews. One essential change he imposed on every church
which he touched was to cut down the old high family pews. But experience showed
that this was insufficiently drastic. In one country parish, for example, a member of
the congregation promptly converted his two new seats into one square pew: 'not
high, but yet a pew: his plea for doing this is that at times he suffers very much from
the gout, and at such times he is unable to sit without resting his leg at full length.'[58]
Thomas Hubbard, the vicar of Butterfield's church at Newbury, believed that any
discretion left to the churchwardens was likely to be disastrous. He had secured
crowded Sunday congregations of six hundred or more, four-fifths of whom were
poor, and 'many have come who would not have come but for the entire freedom of
the church.' 'We know what has been the fate of the poor under such management in
times past . . . Not many years will pass before we see the poor again put into back
seats and unpleasant corners, and virtually excluded from Church.'[59] Indeed there
was a later incident at St Mary Brookfield when some poor children sat in the front
pews, and after complaints that 'the children looked disagreeably, smelt disagreeably,
and brought *fleas* into Church . . . *they actually were turned out*'.[60] It was to prevent
such regressions that for a time during the 1850s Butterfield tried, where possible, to
introduce movable seats on the continental model. He succeeded in imposing this
against his patron's wishes at All Saints'[61]; but probably the best-known instance
was the restoration of St Peter's Sudbury (372), which was specially mentioned in the
Report of the House of Lords Committee on Spiritual Destitution. 'At service times
accommodation is given by means of chairs, of the same simple and inexpensive kind
with which most of us are familiar in the churches of France and Belgium,' reported
the *Building News* in 1858. 'During the weekday services, when there is only a small
congregation, only so many of the chairs are brought into use as the congregation

requires; the worshippers form a compact little flock around their pastor, and the rest of the building is left to produce all the effect of its spaciousness and dignity.'[62] The point continually aimed at in the Sudbury restoration was 'the making this house of God equally free to the poor and rich throughout, and the abolishing every-thing which might lead to a restoration of the slightest distinction'.[63]

There is no doubt of Butterfield's strong feelings against any social distinctions in church. Even hassocks were intolerable on such grounds.[64] He never believed that sufficient efforts had been made to overcome traditional attitudes to the poor. 'The working men have never been heartily welcomed in our towns.'[65] He entirely rejected the need for special services in slum parishes.

> I have seen the poorest and most ill-clad congregation saying the Church's evening services throughout (not 'portions of it'), kneeling on the floor of some gutted dwellings arranged reverently in church order. I have knelt with them. I have heard them chant the musical parts of that service, and generally respond with a vigour and thoroughness which I do not find in the congrega-tions which the Bishop of Bedford would consider as used to and able 'to take part in our beautiful Church service', and to whom he is satisfied to permit the use of the entire Prayer-book. Such poor folk as I allude to certainly appeared to need no extraordinary condescension to their supposed mean capabilities. If we give the poor man an equal Church chance in every way, he will soon, as many have proved, shame the rich man in the matter of hearty worship.[66]

Butterfield knew that the Church had failed to win back the urban working classes; and he was well aware of the disastrous implications of this failure. During his lifetime England changed from a predominantly rural to an urban society. In 1851 half the population still lived in rural districts; by 1901, through the continuous growth of towns and the collapse of agricultural prosperity in the 1870s, only one quarter. The ebbing rural population would leave almost empty churches which he had once built or enlarged. By the late 1870s it seemed necessary for a vicar to apologize for money spent on a country church: 'it is too often forgotten that the village is the nursery of the town, and that the country youths may leave the town, to which they are drawn, with the influences brought with them from their native homes.' For this reason 'our country parishes have a special claim on the capitalists of England'.[67] But such appeals only emphasized the fact that the real challenge was now in the towns.

Thus as he grew older Butterfield had good reason for pessimism. The youthful optimism which had inspired the Oxford Movement in the 1840s was long forgotten. Butterfield held on to his creed, to Prayer Book and Authorized Version, to strict observation of the law; to objective rather than subjective religion. 'Not our feelings but our faith must sustain us.' It was an austere faith.

Perhaps it is most attractively put in a story of his own, about a working man.

A poor journeyman, working for the great houses for the manufacture of shoes in Northampton in his own cottage in a village a few miles from Northampton, as used to be the custom twenty years since, and may be so now, was lying on his deathbed. A valued friend of mine, at that time vicar of the parish, was my informant. He was calling on his sick parishioner one day and found him singularly depressed. He asked the reason; the sick man said, 'I have had a visit from a fellow-workman in Northampton, who heard that I was ill. But he was no comfort to me. He has no religion, and he talked against it in many ways. He said to me, "You don't believe that the whale swallowed Jonah?" ' To the vicar's question, 'And what did you say?' he replied, 'I told him, sir, that if God wished the whale to swallow Jonah the whale could do it.' The man's faith in God made him see at once that it was not the whale that was being attacked, but God himself. He knew that all things are possible to Him. It was a noble reply . . . The faith of this poor dying man was enviable.[68]

But faith without feeling cannot have satisfied Butterfield. His pleasure in the almost Franciscan naivety of the story betrays his longing for a less artificial religion.[69] And was it indeed only for its architecture that he modelled his two most famous buildings upon the upper church at Assisi? Surely in the spontaneity and joy of the Franciscan legend Butterfield, whose own religion was so utterly different, felt that he could sense the spirit of early Christianity, the spirit which the Oxford Movement had hoped to recapture?

Notes on chapter 3

1 *R.I.B.A. Journal*, (XII) 1905, p. 608.
2 Swinfen Harris, *op. cit.*
3 'A Layman', *G*, 17 November 1880.
4 'A Churchman', *G*, 17 July 1889; Butterfield secured offprints of this letter.
5 Heytesbury Collection.
6 G. C. Scott, *Personal and Professional Recollections*, London, Low, 1879, p. 112.
7 Butterfield to Rev. G. S. Holmes, 26 January 1872, Holme upon Spalding Moor chest.
8 'A Layman', *G*, 20 May 1874; unlike the other anonymous *G* letters here quoted, this is not from Butterfield's cuttings book which starts only in 1880, but is identified by its style and content.
9 'A Layman', *G*, 20 August 1884.

10   Butterfield to secretary, 9 June 1863, I.C.B.S. file, 6095 (Emery Down).

11   'A Layman', *G*, 26 May 1897.

12   *Ibid.*, 20 May 1874.

13   Edward Irving, *Collected Writings*, London 1864–5, I, p. 243, noted in 'Extracts'.

14   Owen Chadwick, *The Victorian Church*, A. & C. Black, 1966, pp. 220, 292–6, 496–7. Indeed, during the disturbances at Stoke Newington in 1867, John Starey did see an effigy of Robert Brett prepared for the fire: John to Anne Starey, Starey Collection.

15   Hardman Collection.

16   E. G. K. Browne, *Annals of the Tractarian Movement*, London 1861, pp. 539–48.

17   E. H. Coleridge, *op. cit.*, 1, p. 196.

18   Owen Chadwick, *The Mind of the Oxford Movement*, London, A. & C. Black, 1960.

19   T. J. Williams, *Priscilla Lydia Sellon*, London, S.P.C.K., 1950, pp. 96–9.

20   Boggis, *op. cit.*, p. 55.

21   C. Wordsworth, *St Nicholas' Hospital*, Salisbury, 1902.

22   *Victorian Church*, *op. cit.*, p. 513; Clement Esdaile to Butterfield, 20 August 1881, Starey Collection.

23   'A Churchman', *G*, 30 August 1899.

24   'A Layman', *G*, 18 March 1885.

25   Butterfield to the Warden of Keble College, 22 January 1873, copy in Starey Collection.

26   Butterfield to Dr Liddon, 7 January 1873, copy at Keble College.

27   Butterfield to H. H. Gibbs, 11 October 1874, Gibbs Collection, Guildhall.

28   'Another Layman', *G*, 20 October 1897.

29   'B. D.', *G*, 9 December 1896.

30   Butterfield to the Warden of Keble College, 20 January 1873, copy in Starey Collection.

31   Manuscript fragment, Starey Collection.

32   Butterfield to Warden, *op. cit.*

33   *Ibid.*, 22 January.

34   'A Layman', *G*, 20 May 1874.

35   *Ibid.*, 6 August 1884.

36   'A Churchman', *G*, 28 December 1898. The Axbridge Sisters noted his attitude to Benediction in their Journals, 28 September 1882.

37   Perry to Butterfield, 24 June 1887, Starey Collection.

38   *DNB*. William Starey supplied some of the information for this article.

39   Signatures collected at the great protest meeting held at St Martin's Hall, Long Acre on 23 July 1850 were built into the wall behind the font. Some years later they were removed to Lambeth Palace Library (Michael Reynolds, *Martyr of Ritualism*, London, Faber & Faber, 1965).

40   Butterfield to J. D. Davenport 25 January 1882, Winchester College archives.

41   Thomas Arnold: quoted in W. F. Houghton, *The Victorian Frame of Mind*, Yale, 1957, pp. 100–1.

42   'Leave modern books alone, and keep to the writing of proved men', 11 March 1890, Starey Collection.

43 Houghton, *op. cit.*, p. 71.

44 'B.D.', *G*, 9 December 1896.

45 'Another Layman', *G*, 1 December 1897.

46 J. D. Rosenberg, *The Darkening Glass*, London, Routledge & Kegan Paul, 1963, p. 30.

47 Cutting of 1896, in 'Extracts'.

48 Houghton, *op. cit.*, pp. 86–7.

49 Manuscript fragment, Starey Collection.

50 Houghton, *op. cit.*, pp. 133, 254–5, 262.

51 J. A. Froude, *Lord Beaconsfield*, London 1898, p. 177.

52 *E*, (10) 1849, p. 97.

53 'A Churchman', *G*, 21 September 1898.

54 *Victorian Church*, *op. cit.*, p. 331.

55 R. Mudie-Smith (ed.), *The Religious Life of London*, London 1904, p. 26.

56 *BN*, (5) 1859, p. 486.

57 *Ibid.*, (7) 1861, p. 46.

58 Rev. C. S. Holthouse to secretary, 3 March 1847, I.C.B.S. file 3759 (Hellidon).

59 Rev. Thomas Hubbard to secretary, 23 August 1860 and 2 June 1861, I.C.B.S. file 5456.

60 1875, I.C.B.S. file 7137.

61 H. W. and I. Law, *The Book of the Beresford-Hopes*, London, Heath, Cranton, 1925, p. 176. He later thought the experiment a failure: 'No, chairs are a weakness and favour crowding which does not promote devotion' (Butterfield to F. H. Rivington, 5 September 1893, All Saints' chest).

62 (4) p. 1083.

63 *ILN*, (31) 1857, p. 261.

64 To the I.C.B.S. question, 'Will hassocks or kneeling boards be provided? Hassocks are to be preferred', Butterfield always scribbled: 'Kneeling boards as being most cleanly and durable . . . and as making no distinction between rich and poor': e.g. file 7513 (Poulton, 1873).

65 'A Churchman', *G*, 13 September 1899.

66 'B. D.', *G*, 9 November 1881.

67 Vicar's appeal, c. 1877, Winterborne Monkton chest.

68 'Another Layman', *G*, 1 December 1897.

69 One of his last letters describes C. P. M. Sabatier's *Life of St Francis of Assisi* (translated 1894) as 'most interesting and full of wholesome religious thoughts'; a book he can 'strongly recommend . . . as holiday reading . . . I see it at the Athenaeum—but shall most likely buy it'; Butterfield to F. H. Rivington, 29 July 1895, All Saints' chest.

4   Patronage

The sympathy for the poor which brought an egalitarian strain to Butterfield's religion was a distant reflection of the democratic forces in mid-nineteenth-century England. It is hard to find such influences in the patronage which supported him. His career depended almost entirely upon the old upper classes.

The beginning, it is true, was different. Butterfield's first known work was Highbury Congregational Chapel (76), built for his uncle W. D. Wills, the Bristol tobacco manufacturer. Moreover, when the chapel was completed in the spring of 1843 and Butterfield was short of work, he not merely lent him money, but tried to introduce him to the patronage of the new railway magnates. Wills was a substantial shareholder in the Great Western Railway, which had opened from Paddington to Bristol in 1841. When the company promoted the building of a church for its new works town at Swindon, he encouraged Butterfield to enter the competition for its design.[1] But Gilbert Scott's designs were preferred; and Butterfield had in any case already found a more profitable opening for himself.

The emphasis of the Oxford Movement, shaken by doctrinal controversy, was at this moment shifting to the less dangerous medievalism of church architecture. The foundation of the Oxford Architectural and Historical Society in 1839 was an indication. The principal instrument of the change, however, was the Cambridge Camden Society, formally established in the same year by two undergraduates, Benjamin Webb and John Mason Neale. The last of the Oxford series of *Tracts for the Times* was published in 1841: *Tract 90*, in which Newman shattered his own faith in the Church of England, and shook that of many of his friends, by attempting to show that the thirty-nine Articles were compatible with catholic doctrine at the time of the breach with Rome. In the same year the Cambridge Camden Society issued the first number of a periodical devoted to church design, the *Ecclesiologist*. Lacking rivals – it was the first practical English architectural journal in which buildings were systematically criticized, preceding even the *Builder* by a few months – the *Ecclesiologist* was quickly established as the High Church authority on matters of design. The Cambridge

Camden Society's numbers swelled to nearly a thousand by 1845, while the first part of its *Few Words to Churchwardens*, issued in 1841, sold the astonishing number of thirteen thousand copies in two years.[2] By 1843 Alexander Beresford-Hope, a friend of Webb's at Cambridge, later Member of Parliament for Maidstone and son-in-law of the Marquis of Salisbury, had become the society's chairman. Inevitably its growing prominence at last drew an attack on the Romish tendencies of its medievalism; but the *Ecclesiologist* had wisely avoided theological controversy, and after the crisis of 1844–5 the society was able to sever its Cambridge connection and reform itself as the Ecclesiological Society.

The *Ecclesiologist* remained important until it ceased publication in 1868, but there is no doubt that its first ten years were the most influential, when its supporters were a close-knit group and its standpoint was relatively clear. Moreover, in propagating their architectural views Webb, Neale and Hope had the special advantage, through Cambridge friends who had become parish clergy, of offering patronage to sympathetic architects; while Hope's personal wealth allowed him also to promote his own building schemes. Thus from the beginning the *Ecclesiologist* recorded the election of a steady stream of architects. Gilbert Scott, always quick to sense an opportunity, was announced a member in February 1842; and the same issue contained a letter, signed 'W. B.', which can be identified as Butterfield's first attempt to introduce himself to the society. He argued two points, briefly and cogently: first, that choir stalls should never be placed at the east end of the nave – 'It seems to me a very unmeaning and awkward arrangement; and I have as an architect had occasion to protest against it'; and, second, that altar rails were an innovation which should be superseded by chancel screens – 'If we restore this beautiful feature, what need is there of any second fence of rails to the Altar, and why should the congregation go within the screen to receive the Holy Eucharist?'

Butterfield wrote this letter 'although not at present a member of the Camden Society, yet, as hoping when an opportunity offers to become one of them'. Does the second point betray the inquiring mind of a medievalist recently converted to the Church of England? The *Ecclesiologist* replied instinctively: 'We could not but feel some prejudice in favour of an arrangement so warmly advocated by Laud, Montague, Wren, Bridges and other holy Bishops, who suffered for the Church.' Nevertheless, Butterfield persisted in the idea for some years, and suggested it at All Saints' Margaret Street, thereby provoking Hope to discern 'the stuff of a heresiarch in him, he is of the stamp of Tertullian, Eutyches, etc., stiff, dogmatic, and puritanical, and pushing one side of Catholicism into heresy . . . He puts himself above the Western Church.'[3] This, however, was in 1849, when Hope and Butterfield were already drifting apart after a period of close co-operation.

Later in 1842 Butterfield had again written to the *Ecclesiologist*, this time suggesting that the society should 'engage some goldsmith in the manufacture of chalices of the ancient form . . . Goldsmiths must be checked, for they are running perfectly wild in their designs for what they call "Gothic church plate".' The society took up the suggestion, and in March 1843 announced that its committee had 'entered into arrangements with a gentleman of much taste and skill, W. Butterfield Esq', who had kindly agreed 'to undertake the practical superintendence of the execution of sacred vessels or other ecclesiastical furniture from designs which shall have been approved of by our Society. It will be his object to select artists who in their respective branches of art will execute the work entrusted to them in a right spirit.'[4]

Butterfield had secured an office which, although honorary, brought him both reputation and influence. He became, in effect, the arbiter of ecclesiological taste in all church fittings from office books and plate to stoves, pulpits and lychgates. The publication of his designs as *Instrumenta Ecclesiastica* began in May 1844 and the twelfth and final part was published by 1847. Butterfield was elected a member of the society in May 1844.[5] The Oxford Architectural Society – whom he had approached as early as 1843, sending drawings of Shottesbrooke church, which they published in 1844 – elected him an honorary member in 1848.[6]

Such a growing reputation brought with it work. Butterfield received his first major commission from Hope himself in June 1844: the rebuilding of St Augustine's Canterbury as a missionary college (168). The work took four years. In 1844 Butterfield was also asked to design his first church and parsonage, at Coalpit Heath, a mining district near Bristol 'proverbial for vice and irreligion'. James Woodford, the vicar, was a Cambridge man, and secretary of the Bristol and West Architectural Society.[7] In the following year he began his second church at Cautley in Yorkshire,[8] and his first two schools: at Jedburgh, for the Cambridge Camden Society's co-foundress, the Marchioness of Lothian, and at Wilmcote for the energetic and wealthy curate, Edward Knottesford Fortescue, who 'lived in good style', and went on to employ Butterfield on his parsonage.[9] He no doubt introduced him to his cousin Henry Wilberforce, for whom Butterfield built a third school at East Farleigh in 1846.[10] By this date he had been given six restoration schemes, including one at Horfield through the Bristol society, and the important work at Dorchester Abbey (8) for the Oxford society; and he was invited to join the limited competition for the restoration of Eton College chapel in 1845.[11]

The decisive years, however, were from 1847 to 1849. The number of commissions was in itself now impressive: eleven restorations, four new churches, three churches by other architects to complete, three houses, two schools, a college, a workhouse chapel, a cemetery chapel and two cathedrals. Still more important, however, were a number of connections established by these commissions. Two major schemes were for the future Earl of Glasgow, George Frederick Boyle, who had returned to Scotland from Oxford – where he had been secretary of the Architectural Society – to build a Tractarian college on the Isle of Cumbrae (270) and provide most of the funds for a new Anglican cathedral and choristers' college at Perth. This missionary enterprise, in a town where the congregation had been extinct since the eighteenth century, corresponded to colonial cathedral-building; and at this time Butterfield supplied his first designs for Adelaide, Fredericton and Cape Town.[12] Nearer home, a series of Cardiganshire commissions began with some alterations to Llangorwen church[13] for its vicar, Lewis Gilbertson, who had become a follower of Newman while at Jesus College, Oxford; three small chapels – two designed without a fee[14] – secured the influential support of the vicar of Wantage, W. J. Butler; and the restoration of Merton College chapel established a foothold in Oxford itself. Butterfield's long association with the Coleridge family began with the restoration (IX) of Ottery St Mary church;[15] and he very likely owed his Winchester connection from the late 1850s to the recommendation of the Coleridges, who were close friends of Keble and his squire, Sir William Heathcote. The accession of the seventh Viscount Downe in May 1846, began eleven years of vigorous building activity on the extensive Dawnay estates in Rutland and Yorkshire (264). Downe was another Oxford graduate, whose father-in-law was a bishop and father had been a parson, and Butterfield was to describe him at his death as 'a most really good man and a great loss in many ways though he lived in so retiring a manner. It has been one of the pleasures of my life to have been connected so much with his good works and to see how he did them'.[16] And finally – although in this case Butterfield's relationship with his patron was to deteriorate rapidly – he was chosen by Hope as architect of the most influential of all his buildings, the model church of the Ecclesiologists, All Saints' Margaret Street.

Beyond this point the story becomes too complex to recount in detail. However, the pattern both of patrons and commissions remained little changed. His principal commissions are shown in Table 1 overleaf.

A few comments should be added to these figures. Judged in terms of new commissions, Butterfield's popularity would seem to have reached its climax in the 1850s and 1860s, although his personal income did not reach its peak until the later 1870s, when he was earning roughly £2200 as against £1900 a year. This was, however, chiefly due to a few very large buildings, such as Keble College and Melbourne Cathedral (XIX); and as these tailed away in the early 1880s his income dropped sharply to less than £1000 a year.[17] On the other hand, in terms of the variety rather than the total of new commissions, the 1850s were clearly more notable than the 1860s. The death of Downe was a factor in this, but it was largely balanced by work for Heathcote in the 1860s and in later years for the Gibbs family, who were principal benefactors of Keble College (XX), and subsequently employed Butterfield

Table 1

Principal Commissions (excluding those abandoned)

	Churches	Parsonages	Schools	Restorations	Other Buildings		Total
1840–9	▪	▪	▪	▪	▪	Two cathedrals, two colleges, one workhouse chapel, one cemetery chapel and one school-chapel.	46
1850–9	▪	▪	▪	▪	▪	Three estate villages, two farms, one cemetery, two convents, one country house, one watermill and one school-chapel.	98
1860–9	▪	▪	▪	▪	▪	Two cottage groups, one college, one alms house, one hospital, and one new town plan.	95
1870–9	▪	—	▪	▪	▪	One cathedral, one college, one office, two farms with cottages, one village inn.	57
1880–92	▪	—	▪	▪	—	One country house and one convent.	46
Total	69	29	44	167	33		342

in other work. A more important reason for the change was the steady increase in requests from parish clergy for restoration schemes, especially in areas such as Wiltshire, where an old supporter like Hyde Beadon was now Rural Dean, so that his recommendation carried added weight.[18]

This change meant that in later years Butterfield was sometimes exposed to a test of wider popularity in the form of fund-raising. At Aldbourne, for example, the parishioners were circularized by a committee no doubt anxious to deny any Romish intentions: 'The earnestness of my desire that this interesting fabric may in all its pure protestant beauty shadow forth the Presence Chamber of the Great Jehovah – may be my excuse for the liberty I now take in asking you to inclose if it be only a few stamps in aid of so good a work.' Or, more bluntly, the people were asked to 'aid a Moonraker, who, having turned his attention to his Church, is endeavouring to rake up a fund for its restoration'.[19]

At Aldbourne, as in a number of other cases, the need for money led to the appointment of a Restoration Committee, who took charge of the building work as well as the fund-raising. Butterfield thus found himself responsible to a collective patron, rather than to an individual clergyman or eminent parishioner. The rise of the Building Committee was an important development in nineteenth-century patronage, which could considerably complicate an architect's task. At its best, as in the design of the county hospital at Winchester (25), it could produce a more sophisticated building; but more often collective patronage simply involved the architect in time-consuming disputes. Butterfield's worst experiences were with Oxford colleges, particularly at Merton, where two parties among the fellows struggled over the proposal to shift the old library to a different position, in order to allow the college to expand; and Butterfield became the victim of exaggerated rumours, petitions of protest, and letters to *The Times*. Colleges, however, were exceptional in being corporate bodies of equals; and Butterfield was more fortunate in school and church-building because the initiative of a headmaster or vicar was less frequently questioned. Very often the building committee was only set up when, as at Aldbourne, the 'vicar and his friends' had already decided the plans, and had even started work, only to find their resources insufficient; and Butterfield himself clearly regarded the change as nominal, corresponding with the vicar as before, and entering his name only in his account book. The case of Great Berkhamsted, where five or six names appear in the accounts, and Butterfield consulted different members of the building committee on different parts of the restoration scheme, was very unusual if not unique in his experience.

The crucial question was not, in fact, whether or not the client was a building committee rather than an individual, but whether the original initiative had come from an individual with a position of clear authority. Butterfield's plans were nearly always submitted to a full parish meeting, since this was necessary to obtain a faculty, but questions on these occasions were unusual. Nor is there any case in which Butterfield can be shown to have changed his plans as a result of such a meeting. At Dinton, for example, where he had been chosen on the suggestion of the curate rather than the vicar, and the principal landowners the Wyndhams had been less enthusiastic for the restoration than some other leading inhabitants, there seems to have been a tense moment at the meeting when 'Mr Wyndham asked some questions and made some objections to some details'; but in fact he agreed to the plans, and there were no subsequent hesitations.[20] Christleton, another divided parish, caused rather more difficulty. Butterfield had advised the incorporation of the old tower, rather than a complete rebuilding: 'Half the buildings in Europe owe their character and interest to their system of preserving what is sound in the older parts . . . Unless you want a much larger Church than you have led me to expect, you had *better keep the old Tower* and so look a little different to the modern new Churches which are generally so noisy and pretentious.' The parish meeting accepted this advice, but, perhaps because the Duke of Westminster had been among the minority, more ambitious proposals were revived nearly a year later – although once again Butterfield eventually had his way.[21]

If such vexations were relatively rare in Butterfield's experience, the principal reason clearly lay in the social class of the majority of his patrons. Even in his later years, a high proportion of his clerical support came from men of independent means. Something like a fifth of the clergy who appear in Butterfield's account books are immediately recognizable by their names as members of landed families: Berkeley, Heathcote, Houblon, Nelson, Sykes and so on. Some of these names speak of the old unreformed church of the eighteenth century, whose parish stipends had provided relief for impoverished gentry. The two Beadons came from a West country family once famous for its pluralists, while Edward Cheese had gained the rich living of Haughton-le-Skerne through the benevolent simony of his father-in-law, Bishop Villiers, as late as 1861. Equally old-fashioned, although scandalous for different reasons, was the appointment of the Honourable Augustus Duncombe as Dean of York in 1858, on the ground that only a wealthy Yorkshire aristocrat could afford to hold that office for the meagre salary of £1000 a year. In response to protests that dean's salaries should be adequate for any clergyman suitable for appointment, Duncombe's stipend was doubled, thereby provoking more uproar: the whole episode was described as 'the great job of the session'.[22]

It would be wrong to suggest that, because Butterfield's patrons tended to be wealthy younger sons of gentry, they were not active pastors in their parishes. On the contrary, many were impressively vigorous. J. B. Sweet of Colkirk, for example, besides restoring the church, reforming its services, and asserting his rights over the parish glebe, interested himself in housing, sanitation, footpaths and Poor Law administration, personally led the fire brigade, and was author of a biography of Henry Hoare and of a booklet on *How to Train Your Infants*.[23] John Sandford recorded his vigorous parish organization at Dunchurch in *Parochialia*, which he published in 1845. Benjamin Webb himself took Hope's living at Sheen in Derbyshire in the 1850s, hoping to form a choir school, reformatory and other institutions in that 'ecclesiastical Australia.'[24] At Rownhams, Keble's former curate R. F. Wilson introduced – apart from the usual church improvements and school – a convalescent home in some converted cottages. He had noticed that while the sick could not recover quickly in their own overcrowded homes, if the father or mother of a poor family was removed to the county hospital the whole family was liable to disintegrate.[25]

Butler of Wantage got to know his people equally well: his parish journals record years of systematic visiting. When the town was threatened by the cholera epidemic of 1849, it was Butler who went down to the cottagers in Queen's Row, who had piled dung heaps for their allotments on the Potato Land in front of their doors, and persuaded them to move the manure to a safe distance. Butler's diaries in fact show that the re-assertion of spiritual authority by the clergy frequently demanded very considerable social confidence. The nearby hamlet of Charlton, for example, was 'a peculiar place . . . ruled by farmers clever at hoarding but not making money – without any family or clergyman to raise the tone. Two families Stone and Barnard have from time immemorial held the sway.' Perhaps because they did not realize its implications, when Butler provided the hamlet with a cheap brick chapel designed by Butterfield (56), 'the farmers helped a little, at least not opposing it'. But it was a different matter when he criticized them for personal immorality. 'Spoke to Stone of Charlton on his evil life, having Miss Castle in his house. He very angry with me. People of that kind have been so little found fault with for doing wrong by a Minister that it seems quite presumptuous to them one does one's duty.' Butler's persistence was undoubtedly helped by the social assurance which permeates the diaries. For example, he comments on the dinner to celebrate the opening of Butterfield's cemetery chapel: 'It was a most pleasing sight to see tradesmen, farmers, squires, clergy, ladies, tradesmen's wives, &c, all dining together in perfect equality – without restraint, but in perfect subordination, and the whole character of the meeting distinctly after the Church, the weight of the Church in fact keeping all perfectly balanced.'[26]

One would expect to find the notion of equality still further qualified when one turns to Butterfield's secular patrons. Not all were as arrogant as Colonel Sibthorp, who thought it impertinent for the government to introduce important measures in the summer, with 'grouse shooting approaching, and Goodwood races on, and other amusements';[27] nor were many as tactless as Hope, who threatened to question the legality of his tenants' marriages if they resisted the reconsecration of Sheen church.[28] A more sympathetic landowner, for example, was Charles Duncombe of Waresley Park, who refused to call for a church rate in 1856 because the majority of the rate-payers were dissenters: 'I thought it desirable to avoid asking them to contribute to rebuild a place of worship not their own if it could be avoided, although probably they would not have refused it being my own Tenants.'[29] Nevertheless, many of Butterfield's patrons were grand figures, and they demanded respect. When in 1851 Sir John Ramsden paid his first visit to Huddersfield – most of which belonged to his estate – in order to lay the foundation stone of Butterfield's church built there to his father's memory, the homage was social rather than religious. Church bells ringing, the young landlord rode through the gaily decorated streets to be received by the magistrates and clergy, the Improvement Commissioners and the local gentry; and the principal speech was not a sermon, but a eulogy by Earl Fitzwilliam – 'He declared to you the satisfaction with which he heard of the growing prosperity of this great population (Hear, hear) . . . He addressed you in a manner and with a modesty which must have won your hearts (Cheers).'[30]

No doubt one reason for the decision of Earl Nelson to send out his house chaplain to live in the estate village across the river from Trafalgar was the desire for respect from his tenants. Not only were the villagers frequenting a dissenting meeting room in a cottage, but 'it was scarcely possible for a respectable person to walk down the village street without being in some way molested or insulted.'[31] Not that such factors made their religious concern any less genuine: the Earl of Glasgow, for example, died a bankrupt from his generosity to the church, and Hope seriously impoverished his heirs in the same cause. One can find lesser sacrifices in more cautious men: Lord Heytesbury's son, for example, agreed that 'the church had better be done thoroughly at once . . . I think myself giving up the new wing would be the best way of doing it, for though the billiard room &c would be very nice and convenient ·I think that it could be well done without.'[32]

Nevertheless, if one were to look for a single patron who sums up the qualities of Butterfield's lay support, the choice would probably be Sir William Heathcote, the squire of Hursley. He was, like almost all of them, well educated: from Winchester he had gone on to Oxford, where he had been a pupil of Keble and a fellow of All Souls, and thence to London to read for the Bar, although he was not called because he succeeded his uncle in 1825. Equally characteristically, he was a man of culture, a friend of Southey, the Coleridges and Gladstone.

The estate to which he succeeded at the age of twenty-four was no easy respons-ibility, for his uncle had sold or left to others all the family property except what was legally entailed. As Heathcote later recorded, 'In my accession to a station of some importance in the county . . . I had succeeded to a house with bare walls.' He was forced to borrow, not merely to buy back land, but to secure the furniture, and even the stocks of wine in the house. The wine alone cost him over £2000. The estate, he wrote, 'cannot enable its owner to fulfil the duties of his station satisfactorily without economy, and rigid regularity in accounts.' Nor was Heathcote helped by his sons, whose debts in one year rose as high as £13,500.[33] But if these difficulties made Heathcote a serious man, they in no sense reduced his impressiveness as a public figure. In Hampshire he was chairman of the Quarter Sessions, chairman of the hospital governors, and Warden of Winchester College: acknowledged leader of the county. The Hursley estates were run with strict paternalism. Tenants were expected to be loyal churchmen, and although, especially in the depressed 1870s, Heathcote often had several large downland farms empty, he never relaxed this rule. The men were paid on saints' days, and encouraged to attend church in the morning and play cricket in the afternoon. The repair of their cottages, and the attendance of their children at school, were carefully watched. Keble was persuaded to Hursley as their vicar, and new churches were provided for the outlying hamlets. In the church, Sir William would sit on the same benches as the peasantry in their white smock coats; but without, he was their acknowledged master. The American author, Richard Henry Dana, was a guest at Hursley in 1856, and remarked how 'almost every man, woman and child either in Winchester or on his estates' touched the hat to Sir William. Dana was driven to Hursley, down the long avenues of the park, after evensong in Winchester: in the cathedral close 'Sir William's full style equipage was waiting for us, an open barouche with arms and baronet's helmet emblazoned; four prancing horses, with two postillions in full livery and a livery servant also on the seat behind the carriage. It made a grand show as it drove through the narrow streets of Winchester.'[34]

Heathcote regarded the country gentry as the real 'aristocratic class' of England, and he would have been glad that on his death in 1881 he was described in *The Times* as 'the very representative and pattern of the class . . . the highest product of a class and school of thought which is fast disappearing . . . the old University culture, the fastidious taste, the independence of thought, the union of political life with country associations.' Certainly Heathcote stuck to his old-fashioned political views as firmly as Butterfield to his religious principles. He was a leader of the country Conservatives in the House of Commons, refusing to follow the efforts of Peel and Disraeli to adapt party policy to an increasingly urban and industrial England. Heathcote seconded the wrecking amendment against Peel's Corn Bill in 1846; and he regarded the later Disraeli – even at the height of his career – as an incubus: 'Cold and warm in all that might serve the Church or Religious Education and thus (to place it on its lowest level) real conservatism, he is earnest only in sensational claptrap . . .' To follow the popular will rather than the right principle he regarded as 'the most irreligious

F

principle which can be laid down in politics', while the middle classes with their demands for political reform were dismissed as 'the worst and most unprincipled stratum of English society'.[35]

Several more of Butterfield's patrons were Conservative Members of Parliament of similar views: for example, Hope, Hubbard, Melville Portal and Sotheron Estcourt. Lord Coleridge, a radical who regarded the aristocracy as indolent, corrupt and utterly detestable, was the one notable exception.[36]

Table 2

Principal Patrons 1858–92[37]

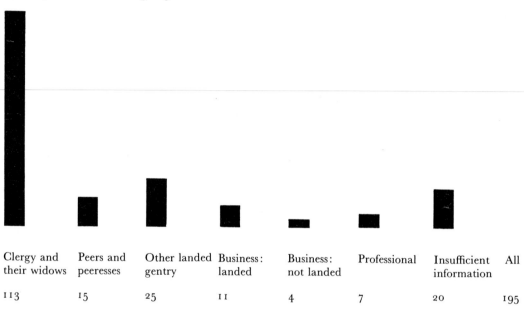

Clergy and their widows	Peers and peeresses	Other landed gentry	Business: landed	Business: not landed	Professional	Insufficient information	All
113	15	25	11	4	7	20	195

Butterfield, in short, depended upon a clientele in which the rising middle classes, whether professional or manufacturing, had scarcely a place. Of just over sixty substantial clients recorded in his accounts, a quarter were peers and peeresses, and altogether over half were landowners without major business affiliations. By contrast the professions were barely represented: three lawyers (two from old county families), four army and naval officers; and a Stoke Newington doctor.[38] There are a larger number of patrons with substantial business interests, but on examination nearly all are found to come from old dynasties, already well established as country landowners: the brewers, Bass and Charrington; the bankers, Hoare and Tritton; the South American merchants and bankers, Gibbs; the Ulster linen magnate, Ewart; and the banker and Russian merchant, Hubbard.[39] They brought fresh elements into the English upper classes – just as inheritance through a nephew or cousin introduced a lawyer like Heathcote, a parson's son like Downe, or a connoisseur's son like Hope; but this was the process by which the English upper class had renewed itself for centuries. Two names only represent the new manufacturers: Butterfield's uncle Wills; and a Derbyshire millowner, W. C. Moore of Bamford.

Moore was a tyrant in his own domain. His great grey mill buildings still dominate the Bamford valley, the mill chimney taller than the church spire; and the village remembers the extortions of his truck shop, and the justice of his eventual financial crash. One might think that this domineering man found Butterfield's blunt style to his taste. But the truth is that Butterfield was chosen to design Bamford church (223) by the vicar, who had previously employed him at Hathersage. New money provided the funds, but old patronage chose the style.

Here is the crucial objection to any interpretation of High Victorian architecture as a reflection of new manufacturing taste. Industrial wealth was essential to much of Butterfield's work. Baroness Windsor's church at Penarth depended upon the docks, Ramsden's at Huddersfield upon the mills. The bankers and brewers flourished upon it. But leadership in taste remained with the old families, because they were better educated, moved in a wider world, and had the confidence to choose between architects of national standing. When the manufacturers wished to exercise taste, they had little choice but to defer to their social superiors; for the local architects they knew were likely to be conservative, lagging behind metropolitan fashion – and metropolitan fashions were created by the old upper classes.

A crucial change was to come with the assimilation of the new middle classes, through the growth of the public school, into a national upper and middle class culture. Some of Butterfield's building contributed to this change: notably the reconstruction and enlargement of Rugby School (67) and Winchester College, and the rebuilding of Exeter Grammar School (288) on a new site, where 'what was essentially a school for the children of tradesmen and the better class of working men' could be converted into a 'high-class school' of the new type.[40] Equally important was the fact that, with the growth of a weekly building press from the 1840s, an architect could win his clients through good publicity as well as through good personal recommendations. Middle-class architectural taste could therefore be a creative influence, instead of a faint shadow; and Norman Shaw might well be claimed as the first major architect to bear its mark.[41]

Butterfield, as we have seen, worked under the more personal patronage of the past. This was, of course, another reason for his lack of interest in publicity: it was only a handicap. He liked to work with patrons whose confidence in him was unquestioned – and some of them, showed remarkable loyalty in the face of criticism.

At Rugby, for example, Temple refused to submit to the distaste for Butterfield's brick patterns expressed by the school governors and by the boys, and later, as bishop at Exeter and London he continued to employ him.[42] Similarly, William Gibbs supported Butterfield's much criticized plans for Keble Chapel without the slightest hesitation. When Butterfield felt that he could not rely upon such support, at least in later years, he would at once resign.[43]

Confidence, however, by no means implied unquestioning subservience. Butterfield expected criticism from his patrons and he expected them to listen to his own arguments. Lord Downe, for example, was eventually persuaded that representations of Christ were legal in a Transfiguration scene, and 'had he lived I believe that he would have yielded altogether'.[44] Again, criticism from the Master of Balliol was received and countered in good spirit: 'You must not judge of that red doorway as it *now* stands. There is a great plain wall of white coming above it which would have looked badly unless there had been some strong colour below to give a strong and not toy-like look to that arch. I have little doubt about it when finished. I like however to hear your remarks from time to time.'[45] Butterfield never claimed the unquestioning deference on which, by the end of the century, an architect like Charles Voysey could insist: 'All artistic questions you must leave to me to decide. No two minds ever produced an artistic result.'[46] Voysey's patron, himself a professional man, was prepared to allow a sphere of absolute professional discretion – and indeed the growth of such trust was an essential precondition of the acceptance of a modern style of architecture which, to the layman, is essentially 'abstract'. For Butterfield's patrons, by contrast, architecture remained a well understood social language, and the exercise of architectural taste an accepted social skill.

Probably the best summary of Butterfield's relationship with his patrons, and certainly the best documented, is in Sir Arthur Elton's diaries. These were two strong-minded men; and Sir Arthur had been warned that Butterfield was 'disposed to decline being architect as he did not like not having *entirely* his own way'. At their first interview in Butterfield's office, however, after some initial skirmishing about art criticism, it emerged that he 'thought I meant to insist on a Perpendicular Style! Finally we found we were really much of one mind on all points.' When Butterfield came to see the site for the church at Clevedon (281) in the autumn of 1875, he lunched at the Court, and they 'talked much on Church matters – on poor, etc. A very interesting, religious minded, and I would think truly honest man.'

This happy start was followed by a set-back. Sir Arthur's first proposal, was for a relatively inexpensive church built in brick and iron, and to his distress he found that the Ecclesiastical Commissioners considered Butterfield's construction inadequate. Butterfield wished to fight it out, and offered to resign. Certainly he was determined to convince Sir Arthur, and the question was only settled after a battle in a neighbouring country house. 'Butterfield and myself debated the difficulty with the E. Commissioners about the thickness of brick arcade. He invoked Sir W. Heathcote who joined us in the library and without (seemingly) mastering the facts flourished about and backed Butterfield . . . Finally at B's wish I wrote to E. C. practically waiving the whole question by intimating my wish to build in stone.'

In August 1876 the plans were ready, and the crucial moment took place at which Butterfield discussed them with his client.

> Waited on Butterfield punctually at 11 and stayed near two hours. He was pleasant, kind, and in making casual conversation interesting. I liked the plans of the Church on the whole much. He at once altered the vestry and also modified a rose window in North Transept to please me, and on the few other points stated was ready to agree if pressed – i.e. modification of chimney stack at West Gable and substitution of stone for brick in walls of Nave.

Butterfield seems, in fact, to have been very accommodating, particularly in accepting this fundamental change in materials. They went on to talk a good deal of the strange career of Waldo Sibthorp ('twice went to Rome, stayed there the second time'). On the next visit he was again 'kind and courteous', and in February 1877 Sir Arthur invited him to a second lunch at Clevedon Court, when there was again talk 'of the Church and other matters. I do like him'.

Later in the year there were other difficulties about the organ builder and the stained-glass windows. The latter caused Sir Arthur great anxiety, for he disliked the designs submitted by Gibbs, whom Butterfield had recommended. 'I wrote a careful letter yesterday to Butterfield explaining our preference for Heaton as artist for the windows in St John's. What will he reply?' In fact he received only another 'kind letter'. And by the autumn, for the first time at Clevedon, 'Butterfield dines and sleeps. We talked of lawyers, of Congress at Croydon, of Penge Starvation Case, Burglars, etc. Rather late to bed.'[47] In short, the forbidding architect had become an intellectual companion; and for Butterfield, such intellectual exchange, combined with personal trust, was the heart of a professional relationship.

Notes on chapter 4

1   Butterfield to W. D. Wills, 30 March and 11 April 1843, Highbury Chapel chest.
2   J. F. White, *The Cambridge Movement*, Cambridge 1962, pp. 42, 114–15.
3   Law, *op. cit.*, p. 175. It was at this time that Butterfield made 'an impossible request' that Neale 'would write a short popular History of the Greek Church': E. A. Towle, *John Mason Neale*, London, Longmans, 1906, p. 284.
4   *E*, (2) 1842, p. 25, and 1843, p. 126.

5   *Ibid.*, (3) 1844, p. 132.

6   *Ibid.*, (9) 1848, p. 49; Oxford Architectural and Historical Society Minutes, 10 May 1843. The minutes of 6 June 1842 show that the tile tracings at the Victoria & Albert Museum, said to have been given by Butterfield, were in fact the gift of Joseph Clarke.

7   Penn, *op. cit.*

8   I.C.B.S. file 3652, plans approved July 1845.

9   *Church Times*, 21 and 28 September 1906. Following this article, the V.C.H. (3, p. 42) attributes the church, consecrated on 11 November 1842 (*British Magazine*, March 1842), to Butterfield. There are, however, none of Butterfield's personal touches in the building; and if he was its architect, one wonders why he did not contradict the assumption that Highbury Chapel was his first building. Moreover, a Wilmcote scrapbook (Shakespeare's Birthplace Library) reveals that the church was started at least in early 1840, if not earlier, and designed for a tower and steeple, which were subsequently abandoned for the present bell turret. But the bell turret and west front could not conceivably be the design of a follower of Pugin (C. H. Corbett to Fortescue, 19 September 1840). Finally, to start building early in 1840 would imply a commission in 1839, which is probably before Butterfield had set up his practice. The school, on the other hand, looks clearly Butterfieldian (contract in scrapbook, 1 September 1845), while for the parsonage his responsibility is documented (contract in scrapbook, 3 September 1846); the same builder, Joseph Mills of Stratford, was employed for both.

10 *E*, (5) 1846, p. 159. The present master's house is by Joseph Clarke, and the school has been entirely rebuilt (school plans, Kent Record Office).

11 *B*, (3) 1845, p. 275.

12 Several of the new colonial sees were given High Church bishops, because funds for their endowment came from supporters of the Oxford Movement. Edward Coleridge in particular—a master at Eton later vicar of Mapledurham—helped to found the Cape Town and Adelaide sees, as also St Augustine's College Canterbury: Boggis, *op. cit.*, p. 31.

13 *E*. (9) 1849, p. 382 and (11) 1850, p. 210; the original church was not by Butterfield, but by H. J. Underwood of Oxford (accounts, 1841, chest).

14 A. J. Butler, *Life and Letters of W. J. Butler*, London 1897, pp. 57–8; Wantage parish diaries, 22 September 1849, p. 156 (Berkshire Record Office).

15 Westhill church was designed by Wollaston: *B*, (4) 1846, p. 487.

16 Butterfield to the Master of Balliol, 27 January 1857, Balliol College archives.

17 Accnts.

18 E.g. cutting of 4 November 1872, Purton chest.

19 Leaflets, c 1867, Aldbourne chest.

20 Cutting and accounts, Dinton chest.

21 Rev. L. Garnett to Dixon, 17 March 1875, Christleton chest.

22 Geoffrey Best, *Temporal Pillars*, Cambridge 1964, pp. 406, 438–40.

23 *History of Colkirk Church*, Cambridge 1960.

24 Law, *op. cit.*, pp. 185–7.

25 R. F. Wilson, *Short Notes of Seven Years' Work in a Country Parish*, Oxford 1872.

26 Wantage parish diaries, 17 June and 4 July 1848; 21–22 August 1849; 29 July 1850.

27 Best, *op. cit.*, p. 379.

28 Rev. Henry Pritchard, *A Letter addressed to the Parishioners of Sheen*, 1850 (copy in parish chest). A parish poll had voted against the rebuilding of the church.

29 Duncombe to secretary, 7 February 1856, I.C.B.S. file 4958.

30 *Huddersfield Examiner*, 18 October 1851.

31 Nelson to Warden of Winchester College, 1 November 1848, and parish logbook, Charlton chest.

32 Hon. Holmes à Court to Heytesbury, 19 March 1865, Heytesbury Collection.

33 Increase and Diminution Book, Southampton University Library.

34 F. Awdry, *Memoir of Sir William Heathcote*, London 1906, pp. 84–5, 96, 112.

35 *Ibid.*, pp. 121, 188, 191, 207–9; Robert Blake, *Disraeli*, London, Eyre & Spottiswoode, 1966, p. 564.

36 E. H. Coleridge, *op. cit.*, 1, p. 237.

37 Accnts: all patrons who paid a total of £50 are included. Of those for whom information is insufficient, at least seven were probably landed gentry.

38 Coleridge, Erle and Ford (Brookfield); Admiral Boultbee (Emery Down), General Smith (Caterham and barracks' fountains), Colonel West and Colonel Chambers; Robert Brett (Stoke Newington).

39 M. T. Bass paid for Rangemore, C. E. N. Charrington for Baverstock, Ewart for Dundela and Hubbard for Holborn.

40 *B*, (39) 1880, p. 435.

41 E.g. Mark Girouard, *op. cit.*

42 J. B. Hope Simpson, *Rugby Since Arnold*, London, Macmillan, 1967, pp. 46–8; *Meteor*, 15 December 1867, etc.

43 E.g. Stratford-on-Avon, *A*, (25) 1881, p. 298, where he resigned on realizing 'the temper of the parish'; or Report of Sub-Committee on Drainage, Winchester Hospital, 1879–80, Hampshire Record Office.

44 Butterfield to H. H. Gibbs, 11 October 1874, Gibbs Collection, Guildhall.

45 Butterfield to the Master, 27 August 1856, Balliol College archives.

46 Jenkins, *op. cit.*, p. 196.

47 Diaries of Sir Arthur Elton, 10 and 11 June and 23 September 1875; 20 June, 21 July, 10 August and 27 November 1876; 2 February, 12 and 17 April, and 11 October 1877. Only once, for a brief moment, do the diaries record bad temper on Butterfield's part—25 May 1878: 'Letter from Butterfield as if he had got out of bed the wrong side. Excited about Thompson's hassocks in Church not unnaturally'.

The modern architectural profession was a nineteenth-century creation. During Butterfield's lifetime its essential characteristics began to crystallize: professional ethics, standard charges, accepted conditions of employment and definitions of responsibility, effective training, a range of professional journals, and a national professional association. The foundation of the (Royal) Institute of British Architects in 1834, a year after Butterfield became an architectural student, was the first essential condition of the consolidation of the profession which followed. We shall find Butterfield opposed to many of these changes. Does this mean that he was opposed to the whole concept of professional architecture, and can be better understood as 'a Victorian builder'?[1] Was this Halsey Ricardo's meaning when he said that Butterfield was, 'if not actually on the scaffolding, at least on its verge'?[2]

It is true that Butterfield began his architectural training in 1831 as the pupil of Thomas Arber, a Pimlico builder. But it is important to remember that until the late nineteenth century the distinctions between architects and builders were not easy to maintain, because it was possible for any builder who wished to call himself an architect to do so. One consequence of the growth of the educated middle classes in the nineteenth century was a greatly expanded demand for creative architecture, so that many builders who had once prospered on straightforward pattern-book designs were obliged to become, or at least give the impression that they had become, artists with some pretence to originality. Such a change was generally signified by a change of title to 'architect', with the result that the number of architects recorded by the census more than quadrupled between 1841 and 1881; but this did not necessarily imply any abandonment of practical building activity, and indeed the title of 'architect and builder' was quite common. This relatively fluid situation meant that Butterfield's first three years of training were not professionally ignored, and he was able to enrol as a student member of the Architectural Society, which laid down five years' training as a condition of membership.[3]

In any case the three years which Butterfield spent from 1833 until 1836 as an architectural pupil would have been generally accepted as a sufficient apprenticeship in itself.[4] He was articled to E. L. Blackburne of Clement's Inn, a young antiquarian architect of some repute in the 1830s, who was a committee member of the Architectural Society. Blackburne had published an *Architectural and Historical Account of Crosby Place*, which according to the *Architectural Magazine* of 1834 displayed 'an intimate historical knowledge of ancient English domestic architecture',[5] and which secured his appointment as architect of the restoration of Crosby Hall in 1836, in succession to the much better-known Edward Blore. At the same time he was announced to be preparing a second book *On the Pointed Architecture of England During the Middle Ages*, and in later years he published a finely illustrated *History of the Decorative Painting applied to English Architecture during the Middle Ages*. He was a Fellow of the Society of Antiquaries.[6]

No doubt Butterfield joined Blackburne chiefly because of his competence as a scholar. Certainly Blackburne's later work does not give the impression of an able designer: his church at Ospringe (1857) is florid, while his designs for *Suburban and Rural Architecture* are an indiscriminate mixture of striped Italianate, Swiss weatherboarding, spiky half-timbering and coarse late French gothic. Nor does his office appear to have been effectively organized, for he was continually overdue with his drawings for the work at Crosby Hall, failing to produce his 'long promised north elevation', or even the 'pen or pencil directions' for a doorway: 'all the workmen profess themselves at a loss how to proceed with it.'[7]

It was fortunate that Butterfield had received a more practical grounding from a builder, for Blackburne's practice must have discouraged him. It was probably at this point that he spent a short time in the distinguished family firm of William and Henry Inwood, despite the fact that most of their work was classical.[8] Perhaps he was still with them when he entered drawings, which have unfortunately not been rediscovered, for the rebuilding of Gillingham parish church in Dorset.[9] Butterfield must have these uncertain years in mind when as an old man he wrote a note on his career: 'His choice of a vocation in life was made before any accurate and detailed study of church architecture had been made. There were then, in fact, no practising church architects of any repute, except Pugin, who was beginning work – Rickman's catalogued examination of English churches was a useful pioneer but no more.'[10] One can almost sense the combination of shock, disheartenment and excitement with which he opened *Contrasts*, Pugin's first great manifesto, published in 1836, to find a devastating comparison of the Inwoods' thin Somers Town church with the robust gothic of a medieval Yorkshire chapel.

The notes give the impression that Butterfield regarded his years after leaving Blackburne as the most useful part of his education. 'At the close of his articles, he spent a considerable time in laboriously visiting old buildings, and specially churches, throughout many parts of England – In their then neglected condition they were in many ways far more interesting and instructive for purposes of examinations, than they can ever be again . . .' There is, however, a characteristic element of exaggeration in the statement which suggests something of a grand tour. It is clear from the drawings which he published in *Instrumenta Ecclesiastica* that Butterfield's first knowledge of English medieval architecture was based upon Kent, Cambridgeshire and other areas explored from London. The only other examples came from the district around Worcester, where he took work for a while, and, in the company of a 'sympathetic head clerk of archaeological tastes, . . . measured and drew the cathedral' and examined the buildings in the county.[11] Since some of the Kent and Cambridge examples can be shown by his earliest surviving notebook[12] to have been collected in his spare time after he set up on his own, it seems likely that he spent most of 1838 and 1839, and possible longer, working in the architectural office in Worcester.

The name of his Worcester principal is unknown, but there was only one church architect of any reputation working in the town at the time – Harvey Eginton. During the late 1830s and 1840s Eginton built more than a dozen churches in Worcestershire, and although little of his work from before 1840 survives, there can be no doubt that he was an unusually serious and competent gothic designer. His details were remarkably careful, and it was characteristic that he employed Thomas Willement, the best artist of the day, for the stained glass at St Michael's Worcester.[13] Butterfield followed him in using Willement in his own first work, and one may imagine that he gained a great deal of other useful experience while with Eginton. At any rate, by 1840 he had sufficient confidence in his own ability to return to London and set up independently at 38 Lincoln's Inn Fields; and even if he scarcely received a significant commission during his first four years, his work with Eginton was probably in his mind when he spoke of his experience 'as an architect.'[14]

We have some indication of Butterfield's later opinions on the best methods of training architects from the fact that although he trained two pupils in his own office, he supported the development of architectural schools. His second pupil, Galsworthy Davie, won a Royal Academy scholarship in 1872,[15] and perhaps attended the school there, which was effectively organized after the move to Burlington House in 1870. Butterfield himself supported the Architectural Association school, launched in 1847, which, together with the new courses at King's College (from 1840) and University College (from 1841), provided the best architectural teaching available in the mid-nineteenth century.[16] Although far too shy to think of lecturing, he 'took a keen interest' in what was being taught, and even sent one instructor 'a long letter carefully pointing out the best method of laying tiles upon a roof and desiring him to impress upon the students the results of his experience.'[17] He indicated his support by becoming a member of the Architectural Association in 1875.[18]

Support for such voluntary self-improvement was, however, as far as he would go in improving the qualifications of architects. Like the majority of the best-known architects of his generation, he strongly opposed the limitation of entry to the profession by examination and legal registration. He argued not only that 'architecture as an art' would suffer from efforts to impose examinable standards, but also that scientific knowledge was insufficiently stable for such a step. 'I fancy that the favour of the public is being gained for this Registration Bill on the score of architects being deficient in sanitary science, as it is called.' But as far as London was concerned, the performance of the experts had been pathetic: when the new sewage pumping systems had been built, 'so firm was the belief that success had been attained that the Prince of Wales opened the new works'. Yet within months the Thames was again full of floating sewage, and dumping barges had to be introduced, a return to 'the days when sewage was carried away by the nightman . . . The truth is that sanitary principles are in a very elementary state . . . How blunderingly it goes along!'[19]

It was perhaps because he could see that the R.I.B.A., in spite of its disclaimers, already hoped to achieve architect's registration, that Butterfield never became a member. Like quite a few gothic revivalists, he felt more at home as a Fellow of the Society of Antiquaries, to which he was elected in 1881.[20] In any case, less than one tenth of the architectural profession belonged to the R.I.B.A. in the 1870s, and such distinguished architects as Bodley, Webb, Nesfield and Norman Shaw were non-members.[21] Shaw had left the R.I.B.A. after finding its meetings 'intolerably dull, and its members interested in architecture not as an art but as a more or less lucrative profession', and its policy in the hands of 'business men'.[22] The same attitude lay behind Butterfield's scorn for 'firms' of architects, 'being quite unable to understand how each, having a mind of his own, could manage to work comfortably with that of any other.'[23] Shaw, on the other hand, was a good deal fiercer in his opposition than Butterfield, for he twice turned down the offer of the R.I.B.A. Gold Medal, treating it on the second occasion as an insult.[24] Butterfield, after the humiliation of being twice proposed for the medal by the Council in 1865–6 and defeated by classicist opposition at a general meeting, accepted the award in 1884, only insisting that he should not be obliged to receive it in public.[25] His non-membership of the Institute was thus much less significant than it might at first appear, and indeed the offer of the Gold Medal, and even the counter-lobbyings and heated speeches which it provoked, indicate his wide reputation as a leading member of the architectural profession.

Certainly Butterfield insisted on the highest professional standards in his own practice. The proper regulation of competitions, for example, was a recurrent concern of the R.I.B.A. and in one of his earliest letters we find Butterfield asking whether a definite figure is mentioned for the church at Swindon: 'If this is not made clear and competitors are not tied to a sum there can be no competition, as some of the designs may double or treble that sum.'[26] In later years he became so hostile to competitions and the scandals which they provoked that he cancelled an arrangement to take W. R. Lethaby as a pupil, after hearing that he had entered a students' competition – 'for competitions were very upsetting to quiet and steady work'.[27] Another contemporary issue upon which he took a strong professional line was the ownership of drawings by an architect: this was one reason for the surprising anger expressed towards Joseph Clarke, which has been mentioned earlier. Equally characteristic was his attitude to the rising profession of quantity surveyors, who were regarded in architectural circles as interlopers. Butterfield suspected them of being in league with the builders – certainly in London – 'because their plan of having the "quantities" taken out for all of them by one Surveyor who may be right or wrong brings their amounts generally very near to each other . . . There is frequently an agreement come to between them.'[28]

The architect's role in protecting the client from the builder, implied here by Butterfield, was a crucial concept of the new profession. This is again shown by the consistent accuracy of Butterfield's estimates, which is revealed by comparing newspaper reports with his final accounts. Coleridge exaggerated when he claimed that Butterfield 'never exceeded his estimates by a shilling',[29] for fluctuating prices alone made such a performance impossible, but realistic predictions were an essential element in the confidence of his patrons. Bishop Temple, for example, according to his somewhat apologetic biographer, 'cared but little for the colours which were dear to the architect, but he greatly admired the boldness and dignity of his designs, and he recognised with kindred spirit the reverence which pervaded the whole conception, and the truthfulness which always ensured correspondence between estimated and actual cost.'[30] As one would expect, Butterfield's own fees never varied from the traditional five per cent of building cost, plus travelling expenses, unless he decided to waive the fee altogether in a good cause. The only variation was for unexecuted designs, where there was no standard custom, and Butterfield's account depended on the circumstances; more often than not, however, he made no charge unless he had gone to considerable pains, or felt himself unjustly treated. Sir Arthur Elton was impressed by Butterfield's scrupulous treatment of discretionary fees. 'I think he is very liberal not to charge commission on divers things on which other architects make money such as Stained Glass and Bells. He only charges "superintendance" at a very moderate sum. On the Church itself he charges usual commission, but his travelling expenses are very moderate.'[31]

The client was also protected by the rigid control which Butterfield exercised over the execution of his work. Like many Victorian architects, he seems to have found it necessary to produce an ever-increasing number of drawings in order to leave no loopholes for the negligent contractor. Thus his first church at Coalpit Heath required only nine drawings altogether – plan (323), elevations and general sections of the building;[32] while for the chancel of St Mark's Dundela, completed in 1891, the contract was accompanied by about forty drawings, including many working details and fittings down to the bootscrapers.[33] His specifications, on the other hand, changed little over the years. They were divided, as was the convention, into sections for the excavator, mason, bricklayer, carpenter, plumber, smith, glazier and tiler or slater; generally running to more than five thousand words of detailed instructions altogether. Invariably they concluded with a clear assertion of authority:

> It shall be in the power of the Architect to reject any part of the materials
> which he may think unfit for the work, or cause any part of the work to be
> altered which is in his opinion unsound . . . It shall be in the power of the
> Architect to direct such alterations to be made in the work during its progress,
> as may be found expedient, which alterations shall not vitiate or make void
> the contract, but shall be performed by the contractor according to the
> directions he may receive, and the value of the same whether an addition or
> deduction shall be added or deducted from the amount of Contract according
> to the price at which the work was undertaken, the award of the Architect
> in every case to be final. No allowance will be made to the Contractor for
> extra or additional works unless the same shall have been ordered in writing
> by the Architect.[34]

We can well believe that Butterfield rejected the doctrine of Ruskin and William Morris that free craftsmanship was essential to the spirit of gothic architecture: 'He was opposed to the new cult of letting the workman think and act for himself.'[35] Nor do the specifications mean that he was likely to intervene impetuously on the site, ordering last minute alterations of plan. It might be necessary in restoring an old building to take decisions by stages, depending upon the state of the fabric, but in general he resisted change: 'Of course there can be a vestry. But I wish it had been thought of in time. I do dislike extras and additions. How am I to act?'[36] In any case the purpose of his occasional visits during the building process was not to reassess his designs, but to watch some of the crucial stages, such as setting out the foundations, completing the roof, securing the right tone of stain in the wood or colour in the plastering, and clearing up on completion.[37] In a church restoration the specification might state that the opening of a blocked arch should wait until 'Mr Butterfield is on the spot'.[38] But for most of the time the responsibility would be left with his own clerk of works on the site.

It was only because he worked through reliable and loyal assistants, whom he did not irritate with frequent changes of plan, that Butterfield was able to maintain such accurate control over the production of his buildings. He normally had six or more clerks on the various sites, each provided with accommodation by the builder, and paid directly by the client. Although their names are rarely documented, nearly half of them can be shown to have worked for Butterfield for several years, including Wheeler, whom he first employed in the 1860s and left a small legacy in 1900, and Breathwaite, who was killed by a fall from a scaffolding at Keble.[39] He would deploy these men in a strategy concealed from the builders: 'I want to remove Boulden for about ten days, to see to some finishing of a work he has formerly been engaged on in Cornwall. It is best that the workmen at Balliol Chapel should not know for what time he is going'.[40] Meanwhile Butterfield himself was constantly on the move. His accounts for the early 1860s record his travels in some detail, and show that at least a third of his days were spent away from London. Sometimes he was out of town for as long as a fortnight. On 27 September 1863, for example, he set out for Winchester, went on to Wales for four days, returned by way of Reading to Cornwall, turned back and crossed to Lincolnshire, and finally returned to London through Northamptonshire and Oxford, making eleven separate visits in all. In mid-Victorian England such travelling demanded long hours and considerable energy. On his visits to Bursea chapel he normally left the Dean of York's household in time to catch the 7 a.m. train, and went on to another client in the evening.[41] When supervising Balliol Chapel we find him arriving by the 6 a.m. train, and still forced 'to run for my train' to get on to the next job; two weeks later he was 'again obliged to run'; and on another occasion he even travelled up to Oxford in the morning for five hours, and returned in the afternoon in time to catch the Great Northern Mail train to York the same evening.[42]

It was an implication of such constant and feverish travelling that Butterfield could depend upon his Adam Street office to work smoothly and independently in his absence. Certainly some of his assistants and office clerks were trusted employees who stayed with him for many years. His quarterly account for 1863–4 records payments to four assistants. The senior, Daniel, received £90 a year; Alders, £80; Keates, £60; and Middleton £50. We know that Middleton was still employed by Butterfield as late as 1895, while Keates, who had just joined the office, only left to set up his own architectural practice in 1882, by when Butterfield's work was noticeably contracting.[43] It is hard to believe that such long service had anything to do with the wages offered, which were no more than the earnings of some artisans, and less than his site clerks, who were paid up to £150 a year. The attraction must have been in the conditions: paid holidays,[44] alternate Saturdays off, and the security which Butterfield returned to a reliable employee. It was characteristic that Butterfield always respected the privacy of the drawing office in which most of his assistants worked.[45] Such details must be seen in their contemporary context, and not, as in the rather exaggerated reminiscences of Harry Redfern of his youthful experiences as Butterfield's assistant, in contrast to modern office practice. Certainly Augustin Starey, who was articled to Butterfield in 1870, wrote in unqualified terms of Butterfield's kindness: 'He is made of goodness and unselfishness'. As a nephew he received special attention, accompanying Butterfield to dinner with Trollope or on a visit to Germany with Boxall, curator of the National Gallery, who was apparently 'a great friend of his'. But it was above all the work itself – chiefly drawing, although measuring a church for restoration is mentioned – which he found so enjoyable: 'I can hardly bring myself to give up sometimes in the evenings, even though I stay after hours, and I take the greatest delight in my work all day long, and find the time pass much too quickly. In fact I am never tired of it'.[46]

Butterfield was prepared to employ men with very different backgrounds. Keates had been fully trained at the Architectural Association; but an earlier assistant (who died of a fever) was John Dawes, a Norfolk village boy who was used as a carpenter and then taught to draw by the artist-squire of Hunstanton, Henry le Strange.[47] On the other hand he had little sympathy for anybody who lacked the confidence to speak out plainly. In the winter of 1871, for example, an impecunious architect friend of Philip Webb, named Robert Chamberlain, was desperately hunting for congenial work. He wanted a salary of £130, although he would have been prepared to take less than a £100 from Butterfield. Foolishly, instead of waiting for an intro-duction, he decided to call on Butterfield, and began rather evasively.

> I said I'd called to ask if he would be so good as to remember me when he
> should be in want of a clerk – If I was likely to suit him. He turned sharp
> round on me with 'So good as to *remember* you Sir! Why should I do that?
> When I know nothing of you.' I put in that I'd said 'if I was likely to suit him',
> to which he said, 'Take a seat, Sir, you begin at the wrong end, at present I
> know nothing of you.' Whereupon he put a few short questions to which I
> gave equally short answers (being riled); and it ended by his saying he had
> others in view when he wanted assistance.[48]

Butterfield's travelling, and also his method of producing a design, required that his assistants should have self-confidence and independence. Although he handled the clients, inspected the site or made notes of the building to be restored, pro-grammed the work and defined the working areas,[49] and prepared the first drawings himself, in his later years all the working drawings and details were left to his staff, and brought to their final state by a process of tireless criticism and correction.[50] Thus in spite of his relatively large practice, every building from his office clearly was his own. It is this method which explains the many small changes between the outline elevations and sections produced by the office and the details as finally executed.

Halsey Ricardo, when a boy at Rugby, was shown by Butterfield's clerk the alterations which he had made in the outlines of the cusping to the tracery cinquefoils in
the chapel windows.[51]

At Rugby Butterfield had purposely left the decision on this crucial detail to the
last possible moment. But Ricardo was clear that there were no sudden changes of
plan inspired by site visits – nothing which could be said to anticipate 'action architecture': 'In his buildings there are no accidents of construction, no growth that
came during erection, there is nothing permitted but what had been foreseen.'[52]

Control, in short, was essential from start to finish. In the case of his colonial designs,
Butterfield was obliged to leave the execution to local architects. Such distant supervision could prove disastrously ineffective, and in the case of Melbourne Cathedral
it was to lead to his resignation before the completion of the building. Not surprisingly,
when Baroness Windsor suggested a similar procedure at St Augustine's Penarth, he
at once rejected the offer. 'There could not be two persons acting upon the same building in the capacity of architect . . . The superintendence and inspection of a building
by the architect who designs it is essential to its being what he means it to be . . .'
At best the local man could be his clerk of works – but his proposition the Penarth
architect in turn found unacceptable:

> I could agree with any professional man if I were associated with him on a footing
> of equality. But at my age and with my professional knowledge to accept such a
> subordinate position would be to confess an inferiority I cannot admit without
> doing myself a grievous injustice. I have been regularly educated as an Architect –
> served my time to one of the most eminent men in London . . . and though
> circumstances have compelled me to reside in a country town, I believe I am as
> well qualified in my profession as most London architects.[53]

Butterfield, despite his natural conservatism and his profound feeling for construction as the basis of design, had no doubt upon which side of the fence he stood. He
belonged to the élite of the Victorian architectural profession, and his practice was
governed by the strictest professional standards.

Notes on chapter 5

1 Summerson, *op. cit.*, p. 169.
2 Halsey Ricardo, *AR*, (7) 1900, p. 259.
3 Barrington Kaye, *The Development of the Architectural Profession in Britain*, London, Allen & Unwin, 1960, p. 63.
4 Jenkins, *op. cit.*, pp. 160–1.
5 p. 130.
6 T. F. Bumpus, *London Churches Ancient and Modern*, London, Laurie, 1908, 2, p. 268; Basil Clarke, *Church Builders of the Nineteenth Century*, London, S.P.C.K., 1938, p. 251.
7 *BN*, (3) 1857, p. 151; Maria Hackett to Blackburn, 15 May 1838, etc., Maria Hackett Collection, Guildhall.
8 Lethaby, *op. cit.*, p. 68: 'He told my friend Halsey Ricardo'.
9 *Somerset and Dorset Notes and Queries*, XV, 1917; the competition was won by William Walker, but the building was eventually erected to the design of Henry Malpas.
10 Memorandum ('He left behind the following notes . . .'), Starey Collection, used in several obituary notices.
11 *DNB*.
12 Notebook 12 includes the Northfleet floor cross (*Instrumenta Ecclesiastica*, plate xvi, published 1844), Teversham church Cambridge (*E*, (3) 1844, p. 134) and the pulpit at Westerleigh, near Coalpit Heath—the only example not from the Home Counties.
13 Willement Collection, British Museum Add. MSS. 34871 and 52143. In addition to the churches listed in Goodhart-Rendel's card index (R.I.B.A.), he designed Fernall Heath (demolished) and Headless Cross (rebuilt 1867 by Preedy) (both 1842, I.C.B.S. files 3033 and 3064). His Broseley church (1842–5) is described by Nikolaus Pevsner as 'remarkably serious' and his Holy Trinity Dawley (1843–5) as 'very competent' (*BE, Shropshire*, pp. 86, 119) both in the Perpendicular style; while Trimpley (1844) is an unusually scholarly essay in the neo-Norman style. Catshill (1838) and Broadway (1838) are, however, much less impressive essays in Early English.
14 *E*, (1) 1842, p. 55. In spite of searches of faculty papers, parsonage mortgage deeds, and the I.C.B.S. files for 1842–5, not a single previously unmentioned work by Butterfield has been found earlier than 1847—while some previous attributions have been disproved. Even for the period 1847–52, for which Butterfield's notebooks are available, five sixths of his buildings have been previously documented; and the same is true when we come to the 1860s, which are covered by his office accounts. It is improbable that any substantial works of the early 1840s remain to be discovered.
15 *A*, (7) 1872, p. 270.
16 Jenkins, *op. cit.*, pp. 166–73.
17 Swinfen Harris, *op. cit.*
18 *B*, (33) 1875, p. 226.

G

19 *The Times*, 12 April 1888, 3 March 1891; Jenkins, *op. cit.*, pp. 223–6.

20 3 March, 'honoris causa', I am kindly informed by Mr A. R. Pike.

21 Barrington Kaye, *op. cit.*, pp. 174–5.

22 Reginald Blomfield, *Richard Norman Shaw*, London, Batsford, 1940, p. 21.

23 Swinfen Harris, *op. cit.*

24 Blomfield, *op. cit.*, p. 79.

25 B, (23) 1865, p. 230 and (24) 1866, p. 165; *BN*, (12) 1865, p. 193 and (46) 1884, pp. 735 and 905. On the first occasion there was a 'private whip' for Pennethorne, and Sidney Smirke made a 'heated speech' against Butterfield; in 1866 Butterfield withdrew just before the general meeting, which had drawn a huge crowd 'on the chance of a fight'.

26 Butterfield to W. D. Wills, 11 April 1843, Highbury Chapel chest.

27 Lethaby, *op. cit.*, p. 69.

28 Butterfield to the Master, 1 March 1856, Balliol College archives.

29 E. H. Coleridge, *op. cit.*, 2, p. 381.

30 E. G. Sandford (ed.), *Memoirs* of Archbishop Temple, London, Macmillan, 1906, I, p. 512.

31 Elton Diaries, 12 August 1878.

32 R.I.B.A.

33 Dundela chest.

34 Church restoration, June 1849, Trumpington chest; c.f. Canterbury Broad Street School, October 1847 (Cathedral Library) and Great Woolstone rectory, March 1851 (Bodleian Library).

35 Swinfen Harris, *op. cit.*

36 Butterfield to Rev. G. S. Holmes, 27 January 1870, Holme upon Spalding Moor chest.

37 Butterfield's accounts give details of his site visits. For most buildings three or four visits sufficed.

38 1872, Purton chest.

39 B (32) 1874, p. 977; he is first mentioned at Hitchin. Wheeler first appears at Babbacombe. Boulden, Benham, Burdett and Nash were other trusted clerks of works.

40 Butterfield to the Master, 13 January 1857, Balliol College archives.

41 Butterfield to Holmes, 31 October 1869, 17 August 1871, Holme upon Spalding Moor chest.

42 Butterfield to the Master, 12–20 February and June 1857, Balliol College archives.

43 Middleton—Butterfield to R. H. Styles, on his income tax, 2 May 1895, Starey Collection; Keates—*Who's Who in Architecture*, London 1914.

44 The quarterly account (Starey Collection) includes £5 for Daniel's holiday.

45 Redfern, *op. cit.*

46 Augustin Starey to Benjamin Starey, 24 October 1870, and John Starey, 17 September 1871, Starey Collection.

47 Jamesina Walker, 'Recollections of Hunstanton Hall', Norfolk Record Office.

48 Chamberlain to Webb, 11 February 1871, *Architectural History* (8) 1965, pp. 52–66. Redfern also mentions that Butterfield would tell off his clerks for speaking indistinctly.

49 E.g. Butterfield to the Master, 23 October 1855, describing his proposals for hoardings

completely enclosing Balliol Chapel. The workshops and stone were to be on the north side of the garden. 'I think that the entrance for the builder's men and carts should be entirely by the new gateway and he should be bound by his contract if you like it, to keep a gatekeeper there during the hours his men are working, to open and shut the gate. I think that if this arrangement were followed out the buildings would not be any great annoyance to the College.' On 12 March 1856 he advises: 'No time should if possible be lost and if the Chapel could be taken down during the vacation a good many persons would be saved from the annoyance of dust'. Balliol College archives.

50 Harris, *op. cit.*,; Waterhouse, *op. cit.*

51 Lethaby, *op. cit.*, p. 68.

52 *AR*, (7) 1900, p. 259.

53 Butterfield to Baroness Windsor, 1 March and C. G. Bernard to James Tomson, 14 March 1864, Plymouth Estate Collection, Glamorgan Record Office.

6   The Builders

We have already introduced Butterfield's builders to some extent, but we need to look at them more closely. Who were the men who constructed Butterfield's architecture? How did they influence the quality of his work? And what was it like to work for him as a builder?

One of the first important effects of the industrial revolution upon architecture was the rise of the block contractor, who undertook a complete building at a firm price, in the place of the old master craftsman, who was paid on a basis of time and materials, and worked on until the job was finished. This change resulted in the lowering of standards of execution, for while the old craftsman made his name for quality, the new contractor's success depended upon speed and cheapness. Even if he exaggerated the point by making it into a general principle, there can be no doubt that Ruskin was right when he declared in 'The Nature of Gothic'[1] that the vitality of medieval architecture depended upon the superior work situation of the medieval craftsman. It would therefore be very much in accordance with his medievalism if Butterfield had disapproved of block contracting.

His practice was, however, quite the reverse. There are only three clear exceptions when he used the old system, and the last occasion, Melbourne Cathedral, was a choice made in desperation. The first occasion was at St Augustine's Canterbury, where in 1846 it was reported there was 'no master builder engaged: the committee employ their own men, and have at this time eighty-two engaged there'.[2] This was perhaps an experiment suggested by Hope, but the fact that it was given no publicity in the *Ecclesiologist* suggests that it was not especially encouraging. The other case was in the restoration of Brigham church, Cumberland, in the 1860s, where there was a master builder, but no contract, and 'the work was executed, by day-labour, by the parishioners'.[3] The Robinson family were responsible for the delightful painting of the roof (119). At Bacton in Suffolk a village artist also painted a church roof under Butterfield's direction; but the remainder of the work there, as for all other buildings for which we have information, was put out to contract.

In some buildings the contracts for the carcase and the furniture were separated, but even this was unusual. The only fittings which were normally given to specialists were the font, stained glass and metalwork. It was in fact a cause of Butterfield's dispute with the builder of Christleton church, James Holland, that his father (who died before the work was finished) 'did not distinctly know that the Bills of Quantities had the choir seats separate from the nave and aisle seats . . . It was a great pity Mr Butterfield thought it necessary to take the seats out of our hands . . . knowing as I do the serious amount which my Father lost under the contract, and which each member of his family knows only too well helped to hasten his end.'[4]

While almost invariably insisting upon a block contract, Butterfield was less happy with the system of tendering. We have seen that when a surveyor was used, especially in London, he knew that the builders often operated a ring, deciding among themselves who should take the job and ensuring that the other tenders were higher. This he could counter – at least until the advent of the telegraph,[5] by bringing in country builders. But a more serious problem was that of builders who were short of money and tendered below the real cost, and then attempted to skimp the execution. 'One wonders how men can live on such contracts', he commented on Kassell's estimate for Bursea chapel;[6] and trouble was certainly in store there. Consequently he would sometimes advise a client to invite a trusted builder 'to come over and look at the drawings and specification on the spot. You would then if you liked ask him for a tender but would tell him that he must understand, you did not bind yourself to accept it'.[7]

Whether or not tenders were invited, Butterfield preferred to use a builder he knew wherever he could. Two thirds of the hundred and fifty buildings for which the names of the builders can be found were executed by a group of about twenty firms, and well over a third by seven firms only.[8] From the 1850s the most frequent name was that of Joseph Norris of Sunningdale, who was given more than twenty buildings. It is also noticeable that Butterfield was more prepared to experiment in the country than in London, where three quarters of his work was given to Norris or George Myers. This does not mean, however, that he preferred small country firms, with an easy-going tradition of good craftsmanship. He was infuriated by Holland, 'an unpleasant person in every way', whom he could not get to send an accurate statement: 'He sends me bills with the most absurd mistakes. He evidently does not keep any proper accounts.'[9] Similarly he lost patience with Ruddle and Thompson of Peterborough, whose reputation was undoubtedly high, because they had to be paid large advances in order to bring sufficient masons to work on Balliol chapel, and even then could not finish before the frosts set in: 'I cannot put energy into him about those gables. I imagine the reason is a too small capital for the works he has in hand'. 'I do not understand *Mr Ruddle's* insensibility.'[10]

Butterfield's favourite builders were therefore substantial and well-organized firms, who could be expected to finish on time whether or not a penalty clause was incorporated in the contract,[11] and who would not place unexpected extras on their bill. Such firms invested in advanced machinery: at Keble, for example, Parnell used a steam winch to hoist materials up to the top of the scaffolding; while at Clevedon, Sir Arthur Elton noted with excitement that Restall was 'sawing planks with steam'.[12] An inventory of the equipment used in constructing Melbourne Cathedral includes a gas engine, mortar mill, grindstone, horizontal and vertical saws, tramway and trucks, hoisting and travelling gear and derrick crane;[13] some of these can be seen in photographs of the building in progress. (3) Large firms also had the necessary experience in ordering timber, slates, glass, facing stone and other materials from

3 Scaffolding at Melbourne Cathedral (Melbourne Cathedral)

suppliers of national reputation, for only tiles and brick or stone for general walling were still normally taken from local sources. The local expertise of the village crafts-men thus lost much of its relevance; they became dependent upon larger firms who acted as wholesale suppliers, and reduced often to minor repair work, whitewashing, or merely catching rats.[14] Butterfield showed no wish to reverse this trend, and even regarded a small job like a lych gate as 'beyond the power of an ordinary village carpenter'.[15] The only occasion when he can be found preferring the services of 'a smart carpenter' to those of a larger contractor was when the latter had presumed to give advice on the cracks which appeared in his church at Dundela – but the 'dis-approval of reports from builders' expressed on that occasion was merely an assertion of their subordinate role to the architect, however 'reputable and experienced' they might be in Belfast.[16]

4   Bursea chapel, interior

The use of large contractors was thus a natural consequence of Butterfield's insistence upon full professional control, and he was clearly influenced by this fact in his designs. His buildings are nearly always as sound as he meant them to be, 'playing confidently into the hands of time'.[17] The brickwork is laid with admirable precision, the flintwork glistens, or the stone rubble walls show the exact texture he wanted; the roof is raked precisely as the specification indicated. But in the features where some gothic revivalists encouraged the craftsman to show his hand, Butterfield rarely allowed any licence. Sculpture, for example, is almost eliminated, or confined to strictly repetitive models, while encaustic tiles are stamped, rather than painted. His interest in mechanized decoration provided by incised mastic patterns was character-istic. The only exceptions, and even these were limited, were in stained glass, and the occasional tile mosaic or decorative painting. Nowhere in his buildings are there features which he was not sure that 'the workman of his day could intelligently carry out'. This method was in many ways limiting, but there is no doubt that Butterfield's desire to accommodate to his builders' abilities was equally a stimulus to originality. His roofs, for example, were constructed of joists and rafters cut to 'reasonable modern sizes instead of the necessarily extravagant scantlings of medieval carpentry.'[18] In Oxford, although he already knew how unwilling dons were to accept anything without a local precedent, Butterfield wrote that he had 'taken the freedom to dis-regard this fact, and to use in the buildings of Keble College materials such as the nineteenth century and modern Oxford provides.'[19] Lethaby was surely right to call Butterfield's London works 'the most possible *buildings* erected in the name of revived Gothic'.[20]

What was it like to work for such an architect? For the men, we have a few indica-tions. When he visited the site he had a sharp eye for the quality of their workmanship and would not hesitate to correct them: on one occasion he is even said to have 'shown a workman how to drive in a nail'.[21] But it is clear that he was respected for his fairness, and had some sympathy for trades unionism, even though he thought the regulation of trades by the medieval guilds had been happier: 'a sort of pleasant brotherhood, with its Guildhall, on good terms with itself and society'.[22] At the time of the great London building strike of 1859, Butterfield was one of the architects nominated by the men to act as an arbitrator.[23] As a London architect some ex-perience of trades unions would have been difficult to avoid, but the discussion of the masons' by-laws which the men proposed implied considerable skill in the arbitrator, and it is interesting that Butterfield was thought suitable for this role. It suggests views considerably more democratic than those of most of his patrons and many of his builders. William Restall of Bisley, for example, complained to Sir Arthur Elton 'of Trades Union men annoying his men and injuring work' at Clevedon, and Elton asked the Chief Constable for protection 'which was very promptly granted'.[24]

For the workmen, as today, building was a dangerous occupation. It was a matter of comment if a major work was completed without an accident.[25] But there was one compensation which survived from an earlier period – the feasts provided for the workmen by patrons. Foundation-laying, roofing-in or completion normally provided a pretext. Sometimes even on these occasions the Victorian sense of hierarchy must have impaired the gesture, as at Aldbourne, where two hundred subscribers were invited to 'a plain and substantial luncheon' in a hired tent, costing 3*s*. 6*d*. a head, with wine and sherry (selected by the vicar) provided; while the workmen were given supper in the school-room, costing 2*s*., with only a quart of strong ale to drink.[26] But at Purton at any rate, after the ringers had celebrated on a traditional lunch of bread, cheese and beer, thirty-five men sat down to a dinner costing 2*s*. 6*d*. a head, with not only a quart of ale each, but whiskey, tobacco and cigars.[27]

When we turn to the master builders, it is more difficult to gain an overall impression. There is no indication that Butterfield ever made a friend of a master builder as he did of the stained glass and metal maker, John Hardman. On the other hand, we have seen the evidence which justifies his reputation for 'loyalty towards good builders'.[28] The difficulty is that surviving correspondence only breaks from mere formalities on occasions when the builders were troublesome. In addition, letters were more often preserved when there had been disputes, and litigation was a possibility. If we conclude by recounting Butterfield's quarrel with the builder of Bursea chapel (4), it is not because the relationship was typical, but rather for its indication of Butterfield's expectations.

Bursea was an isolated hamlet at the end of a long lane across the low-lying Spalding Moor, east of York, and the principal landowner, Sotheron Estcourt (whom Sir William Heathcote described as 'my *alter ego*'[29]), decided in the 1860s to provide the cottagers with a cheap chapel-of-ease. The architect first consulted was Hugall of Liverpool, and the site was determined before Butterfield was appointed. In June 1869 Butterfield sent a drawing for a chapel 'which is I think as simple as it can be made'. He accepted a tender which he thought 'very reasonable', and contracts were about to be exchanged, when Estcourt's local agent, Meek, intervened with a still lower tender from Kassell of Goole.[30]

Although hesitant, Butterfield advised: 'You had better accept Mr Kassell's estimate. It is *very* low, but if Mr Meek has so good an opinion of him, you must take the risk.' In order to save expense, Holmes the vicar agreed 'to act as Clerk of Works and report to me progress from time to time while the building goes on. I enclose to you the working drawings for the tender that you may look them over and hand them to [Kassell]. He must mount *the tracings* on stout paper *at once*, or they will soon be hopelessly torn.'[31]

Some discussion followed on the materials to be used. Butterfield had first hoped to use local stone – 'Surely you would not go to Bath for stone in a county so full of stone as Yorkshire?' – but changed his mind on finding that the sandstone had been 'too long out of the quarry. . . I don't wish any stone work to be prepared till they are nearly high enough with the building to set it in its place.' He was also anxious about the quality of the bricks: 'I wish Kassell would explain what he means by "black" bricks. Does he mean the Staffordshire blue brick which is coloured all through, or some nasty thing with a smear on the surface? . . . He may use white bricks instead of grey ones on the inside but I should prefer not using white ones on the outside.'[32]

Discussion led to suspicion: 'I do not like what you describe of the difference in size between the black and red bricks. It must look very odd. Can he get local white ones which agree in size and use them in place of black for *the inside*? Is the mortar good and white? Was a damp course of asphalt inserted just above the ground? . . . Has he inserted air bricks beneath the floor level?'[33]

On sending over George Burdett, his clerk then at York, suspicions were confirmed; and to aggravate matters, Kassell did not prepare for the inspection.

> He should have had a bricklayer on the spot to amend things. The masonry is not generally on its proper bed. A builder should attend to such things. One piece of cill on the south side is to be taken out. The common rafters are not framed as shown on the drawings, and must be *taken off* to be set right . . . They are too few in number . . . I am anxious about the tiling. *No mortar* is to be used in laying them, and 2″ stout cast iron pins are to be used. Will you report to me about all this?

A month later Butterfield enclosed 'a letter from Mr Kassell which may mean anything or nothing. I fear that he is slippery';[34] and when he came down to see the chapel himself early in October 1870, he found that the roof had indeed not been properly corrected. Moreover the ridge tiles and other details were incorrect, and the chapel had been floored without removing sufficient soil underneath. Worst of all, Kassell himself had not even appeared.

Butterfield sent him a furious letter:

> If your brother had not the power to authorise the men to make the necessary alterations, at any rate he led me to believe that he had, and in such case was guilty of deceiving me. If he had not full powers how is it that *you* did not come to meet me? It appears to me that there has been something extremely discreditable in the way you have acted about my visit . . . You laid the joists in defiance of me after you had been referred to the specification and reminded that the soil must be removed . . . You have been exceedingly careless and have altogether neglected to read the specification or at least to act upon it . . .

You have set the building at too high a level . . . The entrance porch is thrown
up to a very undesirable height and makes an additional step necessary . . .
The footings of the west wall and a certain length of the side walls are thus
also placed at too high a level and consequently on a less good foundation
than I provided for them.

He must either rebuild, or underpin these parts. 'The tiler (though, as I believe, a
good workman) was doing his work altogether wrong, as he had not seen the specification. He had succeeded to a man who had begun it and run away. He was not tilting
the tiles to the gables, he was not bedding the gable tiles in cement'. The ridge tiles
did not fit because Kassell had failed to tell the tilemakers the roof pitch. 'I am not
in the habit of ordering builders' materials. I give the builders sufficient instructions
and then leave them to do the rest.'[35]

Not surprisingly, Butterfield now regarded Kassell as 'thoroughly bad', and when
he started making excuses through Meek, he concluded that

his word is worthless . . . He does not answer my letters. I was never so treated
by a builder before. He *cannot* answer them and so prefers to write to others
who do not know the circumstances. Please keep all the letters carefully, and
be on your guard, for you are dealing with a very unscrupulous person. Mr
Meek ought to have found him out before this. He has deluded Mr Meek who
is no judge of builders' work or drawings any more than agents generally are,
though they think themselves very clever in building matters. They get work
done cheaply because the builders do as they like with them. Mr Meek did
very wrongly in cheapening this building below what it could be honestly
built for.[36]

Eventually Kassell wrote 'what was, I suppose, meant for a penitent letter', and by
March 1871 began correcting his mistakes. 'Please report to me *once a week* for I must
keep a tight hold on these men. Observe that no floor must be laid until I have
inspected the underparts', 'Should not Mr Meek be informed by you of the state of
things as we owe to his recommendation this admirable specimen of a builder?', 'Is
the building taking ill from exposure to the weather? I imagine it must have been
very much injured.' Butterfield had even received a 'straightforward letter' from
Kassell. 'Mr Meek must not hurry Mr Kassell unduly. I want the work carefully
done.' Had the floor boards been prepared and seasoned? 'The *edges* must be free of
sap, and must not have a new surface given them at this moment or they will shrink
even if the boards themselves are well seasoned.'[37]

More trouble, however, began in the summer. A large crack opened up as the
chimney settled, and Kassell tried various tactics to get Butterfield's next inspection
before the roof was finished. 'Mr Kassell has trebled my trouble in regard to Bursea

chapel. The correspondence alone in consequence of this extraordinary conduct runs to a most ridiculous length . . . He now expects me to come down the moment he summons me', 'The man is *deliberately* rude . . .'[38]

When Butterfield came in September, the visit was a fiasco. He had asked Kassell to bring with him a painter, joiner and bricklayer with their tools.

> He met us as you know with a labourer and a painter who brought neither tools, paints, nor stains, but only some stained boards of a wrong tint . . . (The staining should always be settled by experiments on the spot as I wished to do in this case) . . . His excuse for having no men on the ground is always the distance of Bursea from Goole. This makes me the more regret that the builder on the spot at Holme was not allowed to do the work . . . The ironwork is rusting in the windows, the entrance doors are hung as he was perfectly well aware on the wrong side, and without the proper hinges, the floor battens were lying rotting in the mud and grass outside, their edges which should have been shot months since, all rough . . . His plausibility is overwhelming. If you find fault with one thing he puts himself right by assuming that you are finding fault with another and so wearies you with talk . . . He hopes I suppose that I shall in time be worn out.[39]

Not much was achieved during the winter. Kassell continued to shuffle, and Butterfield was afraid to come down again: 'He may play some trick now and make my visit useless.' The only method was to drop all friendly coaxing: 'We shall do no good with such a man, I now see plainly, unless we are very stiff with him. He is losing time most needlessly . . . Pray be stiff and formal with him.' The trick seemed to work. Butterfield arranged a visit in April 1872:

> I expect him to have the Chapel in a thoroughly clean state, fit for the painter, who is to meet me there both with paints and stains as I will specify. The man ought to be there *at least the day before* preparing. And there ought to be men getting the chapel into a clean state, and touching up paint, cleaning glass and examining everything for several days this week. The plasterer ought to be there this week colouring the ceiling and walls if Kassell has not forgotten the colours I pointed out for them to follow.

Some of this was in fact done, and Butterfield was able to spend several hours setting the men to work. On his return, he was astonished to receive 'a *succession* of letters from Mr Kassell . . . It is perfectly marvellous.'[40]

Kassell's tactic seems to have been to delude Butterfield into certifying the completion of the chapel; but the architect was, not surprisingly, 'not at all disposed to be in such furious haste to certify'. Kassell did not in fact reappear at the chapel for weeks; and although glazing bars were put in the windows, the stone sills were not repaired, the bell-chain was not replaced by a rope, and the walls were left covered in stains and spots. Butterfield began to fear the worst: 'delay always tends to involve a case'; 'How many years has Bursea chapel been in building?'[41]

Escourt himself had been asking the same question, and despite his vicar's assurance that without Butterfield's vigilance 'we should have had a building not only imperfect, but insecure and not even weatherproof', he decided that Kassell had been 'driven mad by the requisitions of Mr Butterfield – The one a man quite unaccustomed to do work under a superior chief: the other a first rate architect who will not tolerate the least infringement of his directions. It is time to close our business with both.' The bills must be paid, and the odd jobs tidied up by the local builder.[42]

Butterfield, although glad to be finished with Kassell, was naturally insulted by Escourt's attitude: 'It is as if he had said that he believed that rogues in general were produced by the surveillance of the police.' He was still more astonished when he heard that he had been passed over for a new church because 'I gave so much trouble in the matter at Bursea!! Is this not adding insult to injury? . . . It is clear that in future I need not take so much trouble to keep a rogue in order.' But he may have had the last word. Three years later Escourt was foolish enough to think of paying Butterfield a friendly visit. The infuriated architect replied to his former clerk:'I had hoped never to hear of Mr Meek or Bursea again . . . I am sorry to hear that Mr Sothern Escourt is going to call on me. Can you prevent it? I shall tell him a bit of my mind if he calls . . .'[43]

Notes on chapter 6

1   *The Stones of Venice*, London 1851–3, 2, VI.

2   B, (4), 1846, p. 521.

3   *Ibid.*, (23) 1865, p. 753. This is confirmed by the restoration account, where the payments are for work and materials: Brigham chest.

4   James Holland to Rev. L. Garnett, 4 April 1878, Christleton chest.

5   Thus Henry Everett of Colchester, later Butterfield's builder at Ardleigh, wrote to four other firms, including Parnell, on 12 May 1874: 'We are invited to tender for brigade depot at Normanton. Happy to take a price from you by 18th inst.' They replied by telegram, Parnell's reading: 'Send in at £48,500.' Letter books, Henry Everett and Son, Colchester.

6   Butterfield to Rev. G. S. Holmes, 24 November 1869, Home upon Spalding Moor chest.

7   Butterfield to Rev. E. Coleridge, 3 February 1863, Mapledurham chest; the builder was John Wheeler of Reading.

8   Crook of East Dean, Hampshire (from 1850s); Gaskin and Godden of Canterbury (1860s—70s); Joseph Mills of Stratford-on-Avon (1840s—60s); George Myers of Lambeth

(from 1850s); Joseph Norris; Parnell of Rugby (from 1860s); and William Restall of Bisley, Gloucestershire (from 1860s).

9 Butterfield to Garnett, 16 April and 30 October 1877, Christleton chest.

10 Butterfield to the Master, 18 August, 23 September and 13 December 1856 and 3 January 1857, Balliol College archives; c.f. his initial anxiety in spite of a recommendation from G. E. Street, in giving a contract to Strong of Warminster, after one of their patrons had been bankrupted—'I fear that the church at Warminster has crippled them': Butterfield to Lord Heytesbury, 8 July 1865 and 17 March 1866, Heytesbury Collection.

11 E.g. Penarth, £5 a week: Plymouth Estate Collection, Glamorgan Record Office.

12 B, (32) 1874, p. 977; diaries, 21 April 1877, Clevedon Court.

13 1882, Melbourne Cathedral archives. The capital cost of this equipment was more than £1600, including £413 for the gas engine, £214 for the mortar mill, £180 and £130 for the saws, £173 for the travelling gear, £160 for the hoisting gear and £97 for the crane.

14 C.f. letter books and accounts of Henry Everett and Son and accounts of another local builder, Hardy of Great Yeldham, Essex Record Office.

15 Butterfield to Rev. E. S. Dodd, 2 October 1882, Starey Collection.

16 Vestry minutes, 31 August 1887, Dundela chest.

17 Halsey Ricardo, *R.I.B.A. Journal* (III) 1896, p. 369.

18 (Ricardo) Lethaby, *op. cit.*, p. 68.

19 G, February 1875.

20 Lethaby, *op. cit.*, p. 68.

21 B, (52) 1887, p. 684; the story came from Sedding.

22 Butterfield to William Starey, 15 November 1867, Starey Collection.

23 B, (17) 1859, p. 783; BN, (6) 1860, p. 126.

24 Diaries, 27 November 1877.

25 E.g. Exeter Grammar School, B (39) 1880, p. 340.

26 Restoration Committee minutes, August 1867, Aldbourne chest.

27 Accounts, October 1872, Purton chest.

28 Harris, *op. cit.*

29 Awdry, *op. cit.*, p. 142; he was co-Member for Oxford.

30 J. Hugall to Rev. E. W. Sharpe, 31 December 1864 and 18 February 1865, and Butterfield to Rev. G. S. Holmes, 9 June and 12 November 1869, Holme upon Spalding Moor chest. Hugall added: 'I had two hours at Selby on my way to Liverpool. What a glorious Church or rather Cathedral! How I should revel in the restoration of that Building with £30,000 paid in to the local Bank!'

31 Butterfield to Holmes, 24 November 1869 and 3 January 1870, *ibid*.

32 *Ibid.*, 14 December 1869, 3 January and 24 June 1870.

33 *Ibid.*, 2 July 1870.

34 *Ibid.*, 6 August and 4 September 1870.

35 Butterfield to Kassell, 12 October 1870, *ibid*.

36 Butterfield to Holmes, 12 October and 3 November 1870, *ibid*.

37 *Ibid.*, 4 February, 13 March, 11, 20 and 25 April, 1 May and 10 June 1871.

38   *Ibid.*, 13 June and 5, 14 and 17 August 1871.

39   *Ibid.*, 8 September 1871.

40   *Ibid.*, 10, 13 and 16 April and 8 May 1872.

41   *Ibid.*, 21 May, 24 June and 2 July 1872.

42   Holmes to Estcourt, 26 April 1872; and Estcourt to Holmes, 10 July 1872, *ibid.*

43   Butterfield to Estcourt, 24 July 1872, 19 March 1873 and 12 February 1875, *ibid.*

When we turn from Butterfield's treatment of his builders to his method of design, we are at once confronted with a fundamental paradox. How could an architect who so deliberately adapted to the new building methods of his own age regard himself, and be regarded by his contemporaries, as a strict historicist? To modern eyes, Keble College (71) appears a defiantly Victorian building, its gothic features merely minor trimmings. But when its first range of buildings was completed in 1870, the *Architect* described their style as Early Decorated, 'for the purity of which the name of Mr Butterfield is ample security'.[1] And when his own weekly paper, the *Guardian*, described the college chapel (70) as 'fantastically picked out with zigzag or chessboard ornamentation, in which Mr Butterfield delights', Butterfield's defence was to cite the precedents – the diapers which were 'a common decoration upon old red brick walls', and the chequer patterns which could be seen throughout East Anglia, as near to Oxford as Burnham or Reading, and indeed in 'hundreds of churches in the flint and stone districts of England'. Like the men who built those churches,

> I have sense to see that in mixing materials I may as well observe some order
> in the parts of the wall surface, and not always use them at random . . .
> My "delight" in these things is not greater than that of my predecessors
> centuries since, and I know that I am in very good company when I am thus
> acting "fantastically" . . . Taking my place in a long line of very worthy
> predecessors I am content . . .'[2]

There is no reason for treating this self-defence as insincere. For Butterfield, the examination of old buildings was by far the most valuable part of an architect's education, and he had begun his own career with an intensive study of this kind. His first major work, St Augustine's Canterbury, was designed on the basis of an intensive study of the ruins of the old abbey, including excavations, and where no authority could be found for essential missing details they were copied from elsewhere: the library windows (47) from the ruined archbishop's palace at Mayfield in Sussex, the library staircase from Howden in Yorkshire, the chapel footpace from Fountains Abbey, and so on.[3] Similarly, his first church and parsonage at Coalpit Heath are obviously derivative. The church (5) is intended to evoke, and in detail closely based upon, medieval examples of the Early Decorated style of about 1300. This was the style which the *Ecclesiologist*, following the taste of Pugin, at first favoured, so that in its commendations of Butterfield's work in the 1840s it was a well-understood mark of approval to say: 'The style is, of course, Middle Pointed.'[4] For the parsonage (6) medieval precedents were scarcely known at that date, but the design is clearly modelled upon the local Cotswold vernacular tradition.

A closer look, however, reveals some slight but very significant variations from the common small Cotswold house. Thus several of the windows are rather more elaborate than one would expect, especially the drawing room window, and there are chimney-breasts against the outer walls.[5] Cotswold chimneys were almost always on the ridge, except in substantial manor houses. External chimneybreasts are however common in timber-built cottages such as those of East Anglia, and the exaggerated tapering of the Coalpit Heath chimney seems also more East Anglian than Cotswold in character. Furthermore the great width of the base of this chimneybreast has made it necessary to cut one of the drawing room windows into its side. Although doors and windows can be found in medieval work, so that in principle this device was sanctioned by precedent, this particular detail is rare, if not unique. Finally, although the walling is in local limestone rubble with Bath stone dressings, there was no medieval precedent for the use of Welsh slates for the roof, rather than Cotswold stone tiles, or the clay pantiles characteristic of nearby Bristol.

These variations demonstrate important principles, each of which qualified Butterfield's historicism, and eventually, in combination, altered it beyond recognition. Firstly, from the start a design was modelled not upon a single precedent, but upon a combination of sources: at Coalpit Heath, East Anglian as well as Cotswold. Secondly, the style was adapted to the social customs of the time. The house was not only planned for the convenience of a Victorian parson, but also given sufficient stylistic elaboration to make the social standing of its occupant apparent; moreover the elaboration concentrated upon the fanciful chimneystack and traceried gothic window of the drawing room, where guests were to be received. Thirdly, in the organization of details, and also in the choice of materials, the principles of medieval design were given more weight than the precise precedents. Butterfield's position on this controversial issue was clear. When, on a later occasion, the fellows of Balliol criticized the reduced north-west bay of the college chapel (50), a detail comparable to the Coalpit Heath chimney window, Butterfield replied: 'There is such a good *reason* for the cramped look of the window next the stairs turret that I do not feel the least objection to it. A much less good reason in old work has often caused a similar

5 Coalpit Heath church, exterior

6 Coalpit Heath vicarage

treatment.'[6] Similarly, when attacked for using materials without local precedent in Keble College chapel, he declared his intention, 'as long as I continue to work, to take the responsibility of thinking for myself, and to use the materials, whatever they may be, which the locality and this age supply'. And lastly, when the application of these principles – 'of thinking for myself' – resulted in combinations of detail, plan and material for which no precedent existed, the overall design inevitably depended not upon medieval example, but upon Victorian concepts of proportion and harmony.

Although we shall consider these principles separately, they were of course inter-dependent. In particular, historicism cannot be isolated from the general develop-ment of ideology and social behaviour. Too often historicism has been treated as an aesthetic disease, a malevolent external which crippled nineteenth-century archi-tecture by burdening its creative imagination. But whether or not architects believe themselves to be following a style of the past – as all the major architects from the Renaissance to the twentieth century believed – originality will always derive from the transfer of remembered forms to new contexts, rather than from pure imagination. Historicism makes no difference to this process in principle, although it can – contrary to the usual impression – stimulate invention by providing a choice of forms far beyond the capacity of the unaided imagination. The essential point is that whatever the sources of the forms borrowed, their selection will depend upon the aesthetic, political and social taste of the age, rather than upon their original meaning.

The Victorian 'Battle of Styles', for example, was as much an expression of English political history as a conflict between rival antiquarian groups. Through the neglect of church building after the Reformation, gothic had acquired a special association with churches. The English country landowners, however, had resisted the classical style of Palladio when it was first adopted by the Stuart court. They eventually espoused Palladianism, when the court had gone on to baroque, because its Venetian origins provided convenient republican and oligarchical associations. Thus while in the sixteenth century the court favoured Italian and the country gothic, by the early nineteenth century the position was reversed. It was because he was a Whig that Palmerston refused to accept the High Tory symbolism of a gothic Foreign Office. Similar political associations can also be seen in the favourite Florentine style of the Victorian bank, or in the Queen Anne Board school, consciously contrasted to the gothic church school and parsonage. Equally, the astonishing rise of England to become the dominant shipping and trading nation of the nineteenth-century world had its direct impact on English historicism through opening up new sources for selection. Chinese motifs date from the middle and Indian from the end of the eighteenth century, but the Japanese fashion waited until trade was opened up in the 1860s. Similarly, in Europe it was the weakening of the Ottoman empire which allowed the thorough exploration of Dalmatia and Greece in the eighteenth century,

7 St Matthias Stoke Newington, exterior from the west (Stefan Muthesius)

8 Dorchester Abbey, exterior from the east

thus revealing the sources for the Adam style and the Greek Revival. Resistance to French influence, and consequently the special position of Italy, was reduced when France ceased to be a military rival after 1815. By the mid-century the classic internationalism of the *pax britannica* had been established. It is striking how quickly free trade in goods was followed by free trade in taste: within three years of the repeal of the Corn Laws, the insular nationalism of the *Ecclesiologist* had also collapsed.

The operation of such influences alone would modify historicism to give each age a style of its own. But there is the still more important consideration that architectural history is itself reshaped by each period in turn. The past is always seen in terms of the present. Thus the gothic ruin, once a barbarous relic, and then a picturesque feature, was first treated as serious architecture, and analysed, in the early nineteenth century. In the classification of English gothic into three major styles, the distinction between construction and ornament, according to the rationalistic architectural theory of the period, was a crucial influence. Equally, it was the growing ease of travel, and the consequent accumulation of descriptions of continental gothic, which

9 Cowick church, exterior from the west   **10** Lindisfarne parish church, exterior (*Country Life*)

allowed the systematic comparison of English gothic with other national styles. Thus the problem of purity of style, both of period and of nationality, was a direct consequence of the advance of stylistic analysis – a problem which the nineteenth century created for itself. This alone gives a unique flavour to the historicism of the 1830s and 1840s. But in addition, because the past can only be seen through the eyes of the present, the nineteenth century created a past which suited its own visual taste. Italian gothic, for example, to the German architect L. Runge in the late 1840s was interesting for its sharpness of form and line, and its colouring was a defect. His tastes were those of an earlier classicism. English travellers, by contrast, were already sensitive to contrasts of material and colour, and fascinated by the decorative qualities of brick and marble. Consequently English and German drawings of the same buildings indicate markedly different qualities.[7]

Butterfield's use of precedents shows how they could contribute to an architect's inventiveness. From his early days as an assistant at Worcester he was observing old buildings, jotting down sketches in a series of notebooks which become the dictionary of forms from which he worked. Sometimes it is possible to trace the origins of particular motifs. Thus the high conical-capped turret at St Dunstan's Abbey, Plymouth of 1850 (179), shows the impact of his visits to Scotland in the late 1840s. At St Matthias Stoke Newington (1850) the remarkable exterior (7) was based upon the buttressed east window of Dorchester Abbey (8) in Oxfordshire, which he had reconstructed in 1847, and also on the small saddleback tower at Thorpe Mandeville, north of Oxford, which he very likely saw at the same time on a visit to Hellidon. For Merton Chapel the roof form (348) was supplied by the chancel at Trumpington, where Butterfield was also at work in 1849 – and it was characteristic of his Victorian professionalism that he believed the two buildings to be designed by the same architect.[8] The west front of his Yorkshire church at Cowick of 1853 (9) is a remarkably faithful translation into brick of the lonely medieval parish church on Holy Island, off the Northumbrian coast (10). And another remote church, Lamphlugh in Cumberland, which he restored in 1870, seems to have inspired the series of upper traceried openings above the chancel arch, providing spatial interpenetration between nave and chancel, in Butterfield's last major churches.

Similar documentation could be provided for many of the more curious details in Butterfield's work. The odd hook corbels which terminated the wall shafts at St Alban's Holborn, for example, were adapted from Broadwater church in Sussex; while the tense, sharp lines of the east window tracery at Balliol was based upon the miniature churchyard chapel at Bodmin in Cornwall.[9] Perhaps it is significant that when Butterfield was revising the Balliol design (after criticism from the college) he had just received his first Cornish commission, the restoration of St Mawgan church.[10]

On the other hand, such coincidences can easily be overemphasized. The Balliol tracery, for example, is much closer in character to Butterfield's own windows at St Matthias Stoke Newington or to the choir arches of All Saints' than to the rustic toy shrine seen on a chance break in the railway journey. Nor would Lamphlugh have stirred his imagination if he had not already become interested in the linking of nave and chancel through floor-to-ceiling wooden screens. The pattern of precedents expressed Butterfield's changing taste, and still more the tastes of his contemporaries.

Like the other Ecclesiological architects, in the 1840s Butterfield cited only English Middle Pointed as precedent, but in later years became more openly eclectic. While it is clear from the highly sympathetic and full-bodied early gothic tower, which he added to Charles Dyer's Early English church at Wick (209), that Butterfield was always strongly attracted by the robust quality of early work, it was not before the late 1850s that one of his churches was openly described as Early English in style.[11] In the 1840s he used stumpy clasping buttresses of an early gothic type, but one could not imagine him writing, as he did in 1854, of the 'better and earlier form' of upright pilaster buttresses, which had 'greater dignity' than the typical projecting Middle Pointed form.[12] As general esteem for Early English increased, so did his willingness to cite its precedents; so that eventually, in the 1880s, he could design Ascot convent chapel (291) in the very earliest phase of northern English gothic – scarcely even 'pointed' – and he could speak of an Early English composition with unequivocal admiration: 'graceful and refined . . . This whole design is very dignified, and careful and perfect.'[13]

Exactly the same development can be seen in his use of late gothic precedents. In this case he was interested by the linear fantasies of curvilinear and flamboyant tracery, vaulting and screenwork. But although we know that his early sketchbooks were filled with studies of late gothic woodwork, and their influence can be discerned in details such as pulpit tracery in the 1840s, it was not until 1849 that the *Ecclesiologist* spotted his growing use of Third Pointed forms in disguise: 'We view this symptom, we confess, with especial apprehension'.[14] In time, however, this source also came to be accepted. In St Mary Brookfield of 1870, for example, Butterfield used square-headed windows and level parapets with waterspouts, while his last church, St Augustine's Bournemouth, even has some forms of the Tudor period.

In secular work, partly because of the rarity of suitable medieval precedents, Tudor forms were accepted much earlier by the Ecclesiologists. Thus clusters of moulded brick chimneys occur in Butterfield's Hursley lodges of the 1860s (139). His interest in building with brick also led him to look at seventeenth-century houses well before the Queen Anne revival of the 1860s had brought them common admiration. Their influence can be seen not only in the general form of some of his secular brick building in the 1850s (140), but even in the use of details such as cornices of angled bricks in a church of 1857.[15] Occasionally he made use of still later motifs, for

Butterfield was certainly not blind to the merits of classical architecture. He never tried to gothicize the Adam decorations of his own Adelphi offices, and in his restorations of Wren churches he was far more cautious and sensitive than most of his contemporaries. Even in the undistinguished late classical interior of Christ Church Albany Street he did not impose gothic furniture: the screen of 1883, for example, is neo-Jacobean. He was also interested rather earlier than most architects in the English baroque of James Gibbs. In 1887 he could be found arguing in the columns of *The Times*, on the basis of a wooden model which he had discovered, that if St Martin's in the Fields had to be shorn for street widening, it would suffer less from the loss of the inner columns of its portico, than from the steps on which the portico stood; and, a month later, he was leading a campaign for the sympathetic restoration of St Mary le Strand – 'in the main a sound, as well as an interesting patient, but it has been subjected during the last two months to the killing, rather than the curing process. The whole upper part which forms its outline has been wrecked . . .'[16] Just as earlier undercurrents of taste, which were to emerge as the Queen Anne revival, led him to look at seventeenth-century houses, here Butterfield seems to anticipate the baroque revival of the 1890s.

His attitude to continental gothic also followed the changing doctrines of the Ecclesiologists: national in the 1840s, international in the 1850s, and returning to Englishness in the later 1860s. Although the earliest of Butterfield's journeys for which certain evidence exists are those entered in his passport from 1851 onwards,[17] some of the comments on his plates in *Instrumenta Ecclesiastica* suggest that he already knew the continent. It is suggested, for example, that a type of chalice 'must be familiar to those moderately acquainted with medieval pictures in the continental galleries'; and the designs he used a Fra Angelico painting of the Nativity and a Taddeo Gaddi of the Ascension, which had almost certainly been seen abroad, for the Italian primitives were scarcely known in England in 1846–7. Another design, for a candlestick, acknowledges the influence of Early Christian mosaics in Rome, and refers to the common use of the crucifix in Lutheran churches in Germany; while a baptismal bucket was described as 'an adaptation from the design of an ancient metal pail not uncommon in parts of Germany'.[18]

It is possible that these comments resulted from recent travels in Italy and Germany. At any rate, there is no doubt that he explored both countries in later years. Apart from his passport, one of his continental sketchbooks survives, with notes of two German journeys, one up the Rhine and the other across the north of the country. It also contains drawings from northern France, Provence, and Turin. Another manuscript fragment with notes on Burgundy has survived. A chance reference in a letter shows that his visit to Italy in 1868 lasted five weeks, and there is a note in his 'Extracts' which indicates his admiration for the great polychromatic cathedral of Orvieto and its Signorelli frescoes.[19] But the most revealing information is fortunately for an earlier journey to Italy, made in 1854 with Benjamin Starey and another friend. Due to the unsettled condition of the Austrian Italian provinces the passport was stamped in almost every town, and Butterfield's route can be traced from France over the Alps to Milan, Verona, Venice, Ferrara, Ravenna, Bologna, Modena, Mantua, Bergamo, and then over the Alps again by the Splugen pass. Altogether he was a month in Italy. For three weeks the letters of Benjamin Starey to his family prove a rare and illuminating commentary on Butterfield's attitudes and behaviour.

Their first stay was in Basle, where they hoped to be joined by Butterfield's friend Hullah. Starey was afraid that Hullah, who was a musician, would prove too formidable: 'What I am personally afraid of in Hullah is his learning. William says that bad French, German, or Italian makes him positively unhappy. He has written, that we are to spend a day in learning irregular Italian verbs (assuming that we are perfect in the regular) but I don't intend to begin. My memory is not good enough to learn a new language now.' But although Hullah did not join them for two days, the next day he was 'dragged away nolens volens to take a lesson in Italian, and after a dose of grammar have read through the first chapter of St John, for pronunciation only. William has had a master, and this part of the language cannot be had otherwise than orally.' Meanwhile they had visited the cathedral, and Butterfield was going to draw there, attracted by the coloured stonework.

After Hullah's arrival they went on to Lucerne, visiting a Franciscan convent at Sursee on the way. 'It is all the better that Murray does not say a word about it. The monks would not be benefitted by English visitors. Your brother had formed a bad opinion of the Swiss from representations of their houses in pictures and models, which he now finds are libels, inasmuch as all the *old* houses we have seen, have high pitched roofs, and only the new ones the flattish kind'. He was also impressed by the ironwork. But their pleasure on the journey was marred by the sight of 'a horrid railroad making from Basle to Lucerne, that is cutting up hills and crossing valleys . . . Town and country alike given over to the spoiler and science brought to a perfection that leaves no room for further progress in its annihilating time and space; multiplying material and sensual pleasures at the expense of the beautiful and the true'. For Butterfield there was the added unpleasantness on arrival of meeting at Lucerne 'Mr Rhodes, a pervert to Rome, for whom he built a church in Yorkshire . . . He is shy of his acquaintance, but does not like to appear rude, in cutting him'.

The next day they left Lucerne by lake steamer, and crossed the Alps by the St Gothard pass, taking two days. Their difficulties included storms, an avalanche, and being held up for want of documents at the Austrian frontier. Starey was now missing his family, although he found Hullah 'a most accomplished and amusing person' – sketching, copying illuminations from church books, and at Como treating them to 'a grand performance at the organ of San Fidele, which took five bellows to keep him supplied'. Butterfield himself had been excited to discover at Monte Cenere 'a very large and beautiful fresco' by Luini, which he hoped to have copied, as he thought its colour better than those which Dyce was using at All Saints'; while in Como he was 'much interested by the Broletto, and made some discoveries there, that seem to have escaped Ruskin, and there and elsewhere many things that Murray would have told, if he had known them.' At St Mark's in Milan, for example, Butterfield took a drawing and measurements of the west front, 'which is not a *popular* sight', and was in fact to be replaced in 1871. In general, however, although heartened by the 'good honest brickwork' of Italy after the distressing 'universal whitewash in Switzerland', Starey was beginning to be bored by visiting buildings he had seen; while many of the new discoveries, like a cloister used as army stabling in Brescia, were so neglected that the party shared Ruskin's pessimism 'as to the rapid decay and destruction of monuments of art'. At Verona, as he feared, Butterfield was too absorbed by Santa Anastasia to stay less than three days; for this great medieval church, which was also to be singled out by George Edmund Street when he published *Brick and Marble* in the following year, came as a triumphant confirmation of the architectural position which he had already reached: 'Your brother has more than once referred to his satisfaction at having Margaret Street off his hands before he came here and has found that what he did in simplicity as his own development of gothic principles had been done before him.'

They next moved on to Padua, which Starey did not know, where all were impressed by the Giotto and Altichiero frescoes; and from there to Venice, with a visit to Torcello, and also the discovery of the paintings of Carpaccio and Basaiti, neither then known in England, in the Accademia. There are other pleasures mentioned: coffee and ices in the piazza, and open air theatricals in the evenings. But Starey had by now definitely decided to leave the party and return home by himself.

> My fellow travellers will only look at Lombard gothic churches and tombs and frescoes. Canvas paintings and classical buildings they avoid . . . I could not get William to go into one of the show churches, such as the Salute, Gesuiti or Scalzi. He said it would be like the men who go into vicious resorts that they may know the world. I believe he is right, in condemning them utterly, though unknown – no terms that Ruskin uses are too strong for Venetian renaissance.

But even if Butterfield was right, his approach to travel did not suit Starey: he saw the rest of the tour as a professional ordeal rather than as a delight.

> The places that have been but little altered, he likes best, and he hopes to find that the old cities he is now going to, have stood still for centuries . . . To me a

non-professional your brother's exclusive pursuit of architecture, and of one kind only, has become rather wearisome, and in the towns he is going to there is not the pretence of a single natural beauty. Ferrara is only six feet above the sea, a dead swamp, with flies as big as hornets and every other annoyance on a magnified scale.

It was to this uninviting prospect – not to mention the cholera epidemic which had already taken hold of western Lombardy – that Butterfield and Hullah departed on the night train for Ferrara.[20]

The architectural consequences of Butterfield's knowledge of continental gothic, whether acquired through such journeys or second hand, became suddenly obvious at the end of the 1840s. The design for St Matthias' school, Stoke Newington, showed 'an excellent idea, borrowed from German domestic Pointed, a high Pointed window-arch, with the tympanum not pieced'.[21] Thurlaston chapel school, also of 1849, has a pyramidal tower roof (24) like the city gate towers common in south Germany, while the half-timbering at Alfington (138) is central German rather than English in character.[22] Above all, in the design for the model church of the Ecclesiologists, All Saints', the form of the spire (I) was based upon St Mary Lubeck, the exterior of the choir upon Freiburg im Breisgau, and the vaulted interior (X) upon the upper church of S. Francesco at Assisi (11). These sources were openly acknowledged at the time.[23]

There can be no doubt, as with his use of English precedent, that Butterfield's use of continental sources reflected his own needs, rather than accidental observations while travelling. He went to north Germany because of the relative scarcity of English medieval brick architecture; and in the same way he went to Italy to study medieval colour. But it is noticeable how the willing acknowledgement of these sources is confined to the 1850s, when internationalism was accepted by the Ecclesiologists. The same sources clearly underlie some of his major later works: Keble College chapel, for example, is again inspired by the upper church at Assisi (81), while the west front of St Augustine's Queen's Gate (12) strongly resembles the towering German westwork at Chorin (13). By 1870, however, such influences were not noticed by critics, for Butterfield had come to be regarded as the leader of 'the English clique' of Gothic revivalists, 'the most conservative in their opinions, the most exclusive in their taste, and the stanchest admirers of traditional English Gothic among contemporary architects.'[24]

Butterfield was strongly sympathetic towards the turn of taste back to English gothic in the 1860s, and said that G. F. Bodley's All Saints' Cambridge – the first major manifestation of this change – was 'one of the few churches in which he could worship'.[25] It fitted in well with the Prayer Book fundamentalism of his religion to

11 *above left* S. Francesco, Assisi, interior of upper church (Italian State Tourist Office)

12 *above* St Augustine, Queen's Gate, exterior

13 Chorin, Kloster Kirke, westwork (*Deutsche Dome*)

be regarded as the most strictly Anglican of architects. He told the architectural historian T. F. Bumpus that this was why he used square rather than apsidal east ends to his churches: 'You do me justice in saying that I have remained firmly "English". I have great belief in tradition and in the good that comes of following it, and keeping private judgement under control'.[26] But, as the more observant critic Charles Eastlake noticed, the fact remained that, of all the 'English clique', Butterfield the most consistently flouted tradition: 'there is no one who in some respects has more deliberately discarded tradition than their leader.'[27] Why was this strange contradiction so little remarked at the time?

The answer lies in the profound difference between the historicism of the 1840s and that of the 1860s. Early nineteenth-century critics had analysed gothic as a style, and even in this they had shown the existence of gothic principles which could override medieval practice. The mid-Victorians, inspired by Carlyle's *Past and Present* and Ruskin's 'Nature of Gothic', analysed the social system of the middle ages, found its principles the reverse of those of nineteenth-century England, and showed that gothic architecture was the product of medieval society. 'Go forth again to gaze upon the old cathedral front, where you have smiled so often at the fantastic ignorance of the old sculptors', Ruskin wrote in 1853: 'examine once more those ugly goblins, and formless monsters, . . . but do not mock at them, for they are signs of the life and liberty of every workman who struck the stone; a freedom of thought, and rank in scale of being, such as no laws, no charters, no charities can secure; but which it must be the first aim of all Europe at this day to regain for her children . . .'

Ruskin's doctrine destroyed the whole basis upon which accurate revivalism had been founded. If medieval gothic had been the product of medieval society, it followed that the Victorian social system would not allow its precise imitation. It became logical for even a gothic revivalist to demand an original Victorian style, so that by 1860 a third-rate house architect such as Thomas Harris could issue a pamphlet entitled *Victorian Architecture*, which claimed that a terrace broken up with turrets and discharging arches, so as to 'make the front of each individual dwelling violently unlike any of its neighbours', was an 'honest, independent, simple expression of the true, God-fearing English character'.[28]

To Butterfield such licence must have seemed close to blasphemy. He was not a man to trim his sails in such a situation, like Gilbert Scott, and declare that 'if we had a distinctive architecture of our own day, I would be content to follow it.'[29] One would expect to find him whole-heartedly on the side of precedent and principle. But, as Pugin himself had written, the need was not for servile imitators, but for 'men imbued with the consistent spirit of the ancient architects, who would work on their principles, and carry them out as the old men would have done, had they been placed in similar circumstances, and with similar wants to ourselves . . . It is the devotion,

14   St Alban's Holborn, interior (*Builder*, 1862)

majesty and repose of Christian art, for which we are contending; it is not a *style*, but a *principle*.'[30]

This was the course which Butterfield followed throughout his architectural career. But Ruskin gave a deeper meaning to those words of Pugin. One can perhaps best see the change by comparing All Saints' Margaret Street, designed in 1849–50, with St Alban's Holborn, begun ten years later. At All Saints', in spite of the eclectic variety of precedents used and the strange originality of many of the details, the essential structure of the church was still Middle Pointed, and the most important decoration was sculpture and fresco. It was new wine in an old bottle. St Alban's was equally dependent upon precedents: the saddleback over the western narthex (225), for example, was based upon St Cunibert, Cologne. Painting was also still used. But sculpture had been completely eliminated, and instead the vast interior (14, 324) was dominated by mechanized abstract patterning, coloured brick, incised mastic and terracotta pipes. The spatial effect was equally Victorian, a great congregational space, from which mere passage aisles and a short chancel opened like vestigial tributes to medieval ancestry.

Through his logical pursuit of gothic principles, Butterfield had reached a wholly original style. It was in exactly these terms that his supporters welcomed St Alban's Holborn as a triumph of strictly traditional historicism. 'It is an English church, for the worship of the Church of England, and built in a thoroughly English style', declared the *Guardian*. 'It is such as an English medieval architect might have built, if he had to consider the needs of our own times and the ritual of our own church. Men cry out for a new style, and perpetrate eccentricities in a desire for orginality . . . A man of genius can speak to the heart in the old native style of architecture.'[31]

It is hard to imagine a contrast more surprising than these words, and the style of Butterfield's church. But the surprise is largely due to the reduced meaning which historicism now has, of stylistic copy rather than architectural principles. For the High Victorians, a building could be simultaneously gothic and modern. Sir Arthur Elton, for example, described Butterfield's church at Clevedon (281) as 'Early Decorated', but he was equally prepared to say that 'the style of Butterfield was the nineteenth-century style'. Butterfield's supporters were not aesthetically blind, as one might be tempted to suggest. Few eyes, indeed, were sharper, less conventional, that those of the young Gerard Manley Hopkins; and in June 1866 Hopkins, standing in drenching rain in the ruins of Tintern Abbey, concluded that its architecture was 'the typical English work and reminding one, as Street led one to expect, of Butterfield'. Equally there were others who strongly dissented, like E. A. Freeman of Oxford, a bitter critic of Butterfield from as early as 1850, whom Butterfield later justifiably described as 'savage and violent'. In such cases the difference was one of principle. Another incident, mentioned by Hopkins in his diary a month before his visit to

Tintern, makes one realize how much both supporters and critics of Butterfield had in common in their understanding of historicism. Benjamin Jowett had decided to reject Butterfield as the architect for the new Broad Street buildings at Balliol: 'In choosing Mr Waterhouse we hope to avoid eccentricity and Unenglish styles and fancies. Simplicity and proportion such (not colour) always seem to me the great merits of Architecture'.[32] No modern critic would think Waterhouse any more strictly historicist than Butterfield, but for Jowett the question of colour was decisive. For his generation historicism was not a style, but a system. It was this understanding which allowed Butterfield to achieve the fusion in his architecture of historicism and modernity.

Notes on chapter 7

1   (3) p. 322.
2   *G*, February 1875.
3   *Archaeologia Cantiana*, IV (1861), pp. 57–66; Boggis, *op. cit.*, pp. 133–45.
4   (Horfield) January 1847.
5   The peculiar position of the north-east buttress dates from the northward extension of the drawing room in 1863 (by W. Robinson: mortgage, Gloucester Record Office). External chimneybreasts had been recommended by Pugin: *True Principles*, London 1841, p. 52.
6   Butterfield to the Master, 7 November 1854, Balliol College archives.
7   I owe this point to Stefan Muthesius.
8   *R.I.B.A. Transactions*, 1869–70, p. 32.
9   T. F. Bumpus, *A*, (63) 1900, p. 195; *BN*, (3) 1857, p. 6.
10 Butterfield to the Master, 7 November 1854 and 27 June 1855, Balliol College archives; *E*, (17) 1856, p. 233.
11 *Short Account of the New District Church at Hammersmith*, 1858, Hammersmith Public Library.
12 Butterfield to the Master, 7 November 1854, Balliol College archives.
13 Notes supplied by Butterfield for a visit of the Royal Archaeological Institute, August 1887, Heytesbury Collection.
14 *R.I.B.A. Journal*, (VII) 1900, p. 241; (West Lavington), *E* (10), 1849, pp. 67–8.
15 (Hammersmith) *E*, (19) 1858, pp. 341–2.
16 13 and 21 July, 8 and 20 August and 14 September 1887.
17 Starey Collection: the journeys entered are listed in the chronology. There were certainly others where no entry was made: e.g. a 'short holiday abroad' in 1867 (Butterfield to Lord Heytesbury, 7 September 1867, Heytesbury Collection), and a visit to Germany with William Starey in 1872 (diary of Emily Starey, Starey Collection). Passports were not essential for foreign travel at this time.
18 *Instrumenta Ecclesiastica*, plates 51, 58, 59, 67, 68
19 Continental notebook; manuscript fragment, Starey Collection; Butterfield to Rev. G. S. Holmes, 21 October 1868, Holme upon Spalding Moor chest.

20 Benjamin Starey to Anne Starey, 10, 13, 18, 21, 24 and 28 August and 1 September 1854, Starey Collection.

21 *E*, (11) 1850, p. 145. The plans had been approved a year earlier: Metropolitan Buildings Office, Third Class approvals, 24, pp. 13–25, County Hall.

22 The latter was pointed out to me by Stefan Muthesius.

23 *ILN*, (26) 1855, pp. 267–8; *BN*, (5) 1859, p. 488.

24 'Art Cliques', *BN*, (12) 1865, p. 673; Charles Eastlake, *History of the Gothic Revival*, London 1872, p. 262.

25 Bumpus, *op. cit.*, 2, p. 271.

26 *A*, (63) 1900, p. 226.

27 *Op. cit.*, p. 262.

28 *BN*, (6) 1860, pp. 775, 827.

29 Gilbert Scott, *Remarks*, London 1857, p. 12.

30 *Apology*, London 1843, pp. 22, 44.

31 25 February 1863.

32 R.S.S., *Complete Guide to Clevedon* (the entry on St John's was by Sir Arthur Elton, diaries, 30 May 1878); diaries of Sir Arthur Elton, 11 June 1875 and 26 June 1878; H. House (ed.), *Notebooks and Papers of Gerard Manley Hopkins*, Oxford University Press, 1959, pp. 136, 140, 350.

'I am under the impression that architecture was made for man, and not man for architecture,' Butterfield wrote to *The Times* in 1884. He had proposed that the great fourteenth-century hammerbeam roof of Westminster Hall should be bodily lifted to provide more light for the interior – 'by the use of very simple machinery, an easy matter'. In reply to protests that the character of the hall depended on the low gloom from its broad, massive roof, he asked 'at what period it ceases to be lawful in respectful terms to criticise an architect's work? . . . A style is self-condemned, in my opinion, which does not require and welcome a good light.'[1] Precedent, in short, was no bar to convenience.

This was a principle which Butterfield observed from the beginning of his career. One might think that the long range of students' rooms at St Augustine's College (168), with its gothic cloister provided for wet weather exercise, would have incorporated the full rigour of medieval discomfort, if only as a preparation for missionary work overseas. In fact the rooms were as well equipped as some student accommodation which is being built today, for not only were they centrally heated, but each was provided with a built-in table, bookshelves, washstand and cupboard.[2] The building is in fact one of the first examples of the modern approach to residential student accommodation, and it was characteristic that Butterfield here – as later at Keble College (328) – arranged the rooms along corridors, instead of up the traditional Oxford or Cambridge staircase.

There are, of course, some cases of contemporary complaint of discomforts in Butterfield's buildings. At Sheen the well he provided for Benjamin Webb's parsonage (211) dried up in drought, and Beresford-Hope sarcastically commented that he ought 'to have an office with a man in it great in tanks, revelling in cesspools, a perfect Pan to play upon the pipes. Until he swallow the severe Christian artist sufficiently to do this messes will always occur.'[3] Rather fairer complaints were made by the curate of Wilmcote, who moved his family into the house built by Butterfield for his bachelor predecessor. 'You speak of the house as "desirable"', he wrote in fury to his bishop: 'allow me to say, if desirable, why so long unoccupied? For all ordinary purposes of existence it is most miserable.' The cellar was damp; of the two ground floor rooms, one was miniscule, and the other draughty; upstairs, there was not one room 'in which you could ask a married couple to sleep'; 'not one papered, not a shutter – not a window that is air-tight, nor water-tight'. Outside, there was scarcely a fence, no gate, no coal shed. 'No outhouse of any kind – the dusthole too near the house: worst of all, the impropriety of the place – turn which way you will, the eye falls upon a necessary – two belonging to the school, and two belonging to the house. Nor is there a cottage in Wilmcote, where the decency of keeping such things out of sight is not more consulted . . . So much for Mr Butterfield's domestic architecture.'[4]

One can sympathize with the curate, who was forced to convert the miniature oratory into a nursery, and write his sermons in the dining room. But of course the basic fault here was not Butterfield's; the house had not been planned for a family, and had not even been finished with the outbuildings which Butterfield proposed.[5] And there can be no doubt that in general, he built to the standards of comfort of his time. It was certainly not his habit to build draughty shutterless houses. Even Butterfield's churches were so thoroughly insulated, that he frequently installed Moore's patent ventilators in an attempt to reduce stuffiness.[6] His buildings were also heated, and well lit.

For village schools and houses he normally provided open fires. By the mid-nineteenth century hot water central heating had become common in large country houses, and Butterfield installed such systems at Highclere and at Ottery St Mary, although not at Milton Ernest Hall. In churches, on the other hand, he nearly always used either Porritt's traditional stoves, or the newer hot air heating of Haden's apparatus. The latter method unfortunately circulates dust and in time completely altered the effect of some of his interiors. It was used as early as 1851, at Perth Cathedral.[7] He was, however, fairly cautious in using new heating techniques: he advised against Perkins' method – 'He heats water to 700 degrees and there have been many instances of it bursting' – and did not think the Alpha Gas machine suitable for churches. 'I certainly think it is too delicate an affair for ordinary sextons and that it is much more suitable for a house', he told the rector of Christleton in 1877. 'I did not much like the agent who called on me. I never like to use these things till others, more adventurous, have well tested them.'[8]

Nevertheless, even if cautious, Butterfield clearly regarded the provision of heat in his buildings as essential, and there is no evidence that he himself ever made use of the antiquated circular coke brazier illustrated in *Instrumenta Ecclesiastica* (15). This charming wrought iron design is more indicative of his concern for the visual expression of heating methods. Butterfield's chimneys are always prominent, and

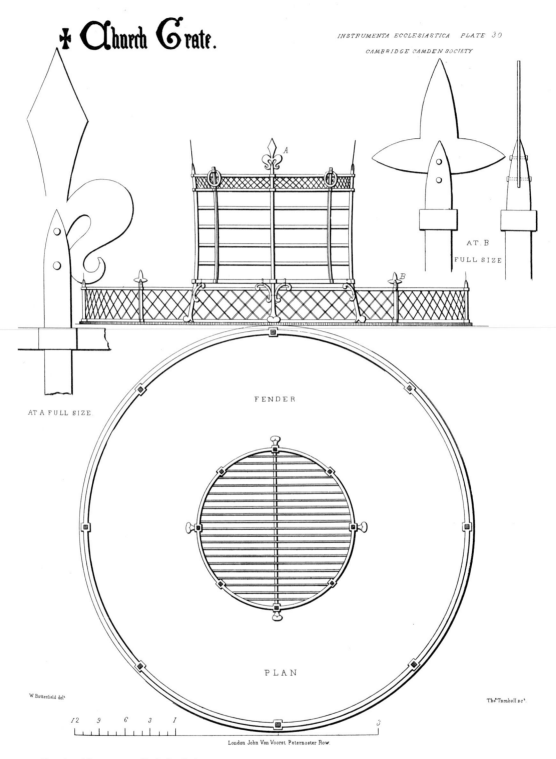

A

AT.B
FULL SIZE

B

AT A FULL SIZE.

FENDER

PLAN

12   9   6   3   I   3

W. Butterfield delt

Tho' Turnbull sct

London John Van Voorst, Paternoster Row.

15 Brazier (*Instrumenta Ecclesiastica*)

16 Wykeham church, chimneystack (John Lane)

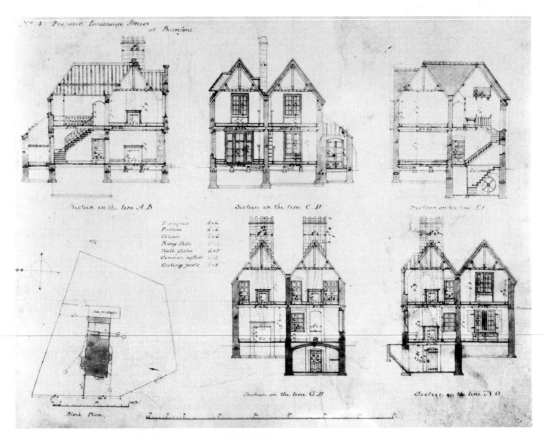

17 Bamford parsonage, section (Bamford chest)

18 Sudbury St Gregory, light brackets

19 Hensall vicarage

often splendid (16). Nearly every new or restored church was given a furnace chamber with a grand flue shaft on the north side of the chancel, although curiously one of the most dramatic examples of this aesthetic functionalism is at Pollington, rammed up against the south aisle. Internally, the chimneys were also designed with unusual care. Not only were the flue twists shown in the contract drawings (17) and emphasized in the specifications, but sometimes the builder was made to set them out for his approval on boards on the scaffolding. Halsey Ricardo claimed that in consequence 'of all the flues in Keble College not one requires a cowl or help to the draught' and for Lethaby, this was the true sign of Butterfield's greatness – 'Notwithstanding all the names, there are only two modern styles of architecture: one in which the chimneys smoke, and the other in which they do not.'[9]

Ricardo also regarded Butterfield's practice of indicating the positions for lighting as unusual. Certainly he led the way in designing gas fittings for town churches, where gas supply was available (18). *Instrumenta Ecclesiastica* had asserted as late as 1847 'that every one will grant that gas is not to be introduced for lighting Churches', yet by the early 1850s Butterfield's gas standards were described by the *Ecclesiologist*

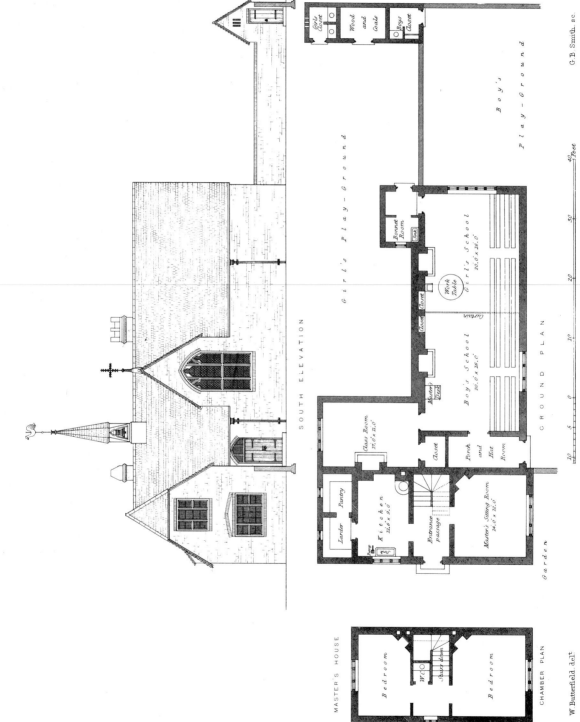

20 School and schoolhouse (*Instrumenta Ecclesiastica*)

as 'elegantly designed and wrought, and forming beautiful pyramids of flame when lighted'.[10] The turning-point seems to have been Perth cathedral, where in 1850 he used a combination of standards, hanging coronae, and concealed lighting behind the screen, creating 'an effect almost magical'.[11] Yet before the end of his life gas itself was to be superseded by electricity, and here again Butterfield led the way in adapting it to church use. He designed special electric light fittings when he restored All Saints' Margaret Street in 1895, and took tremendous pains to position them correctly.[12]

Natural lighting was disposed with equal ingenuity. Even in a large house such as Milton Ernest Hall (260) it is remarkable how well every room is lit, even including the servants' bedrooms. It was an advantage of gothic romanticism, fully exploited by Butterfield, that windows could be placed exactly where needed for internal light, rather than adjusted to external symmetry. Sash and latticed casement windows could be combined as desired, producing surprising variations to the fronts of many country vicarages; staircase windows were allowed to break the divisions between the stories (19); while on a tight London site such as Margaret Street the brilliantly ingenious planning was absolutely dependent upon the random fenestration of the exterior (26).

For churches a certain degree of darkness was generally thought appropriate by the Ecclesiologists. William White (who claimed Butterfield as 'one of his oldest friends') probably expressed the common view when he wrote that 'freshness of thought' was best secured by moderate light, while 'twilight is the most favourable to deep and close intellectual contemplation.'[13] Religious gloom had been one of the rediscoveries of the romantic movement, and it had the backing of precedent in 'the sombre and subdued light which was eminently characteristick of all Early-English churches'.[14] Butterfield to some extent shared this view; in his churches the nave is always rather lighter than the chancel. Nevertheless, he became a leader of the reaction to a more practical taste. Perhaps his Puritanism made him suspicious of excessively dark chancels; or it may be that he realized in Italy that constructional colour was particularly impressive where there was less distraction from stained glass. At any rate, as early as 1852 he was frightened that All Saints' would be too sombre; he experimented with light grisaille, pressed the stained glass artists to let in as much light as possible, and urged glazing 'at least just the chancel clerestorey with un-painted glass for fear the light should fail'.[15] On the last point his advice was rejected, and at All Saints', as in a number of Butterfield churches, the effect is damaged by the window glazing. An especially striking case is Holy Saviour Hitchin (159), where the lucid simplicity of the original interior as revealed by early photographs has com-pletely vanished in obscure confusion. 'It is an unfortunate circumstance that the need for light is so little considered by those who make gifts of stained glass', Butterfield

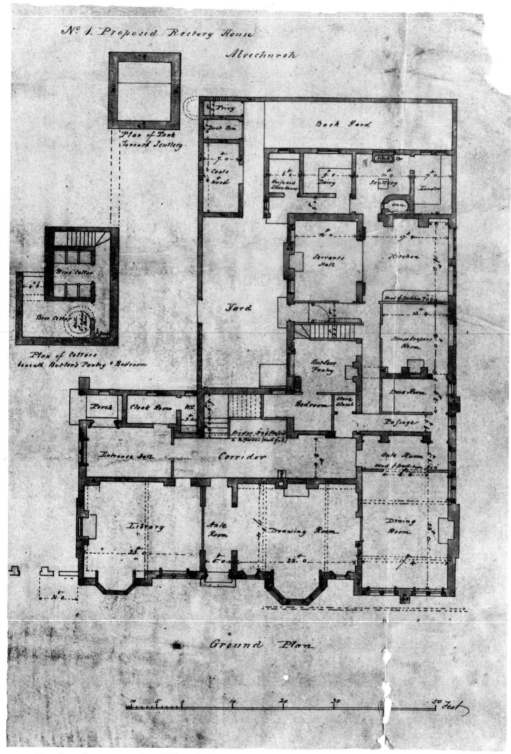

21 Alvechurch rectory, plan (Church Commissioners)

wrote with such experiences in his mind. 'Light is so great a blessing that all architecture is bound thankfully to accept it.'[16]

It would have been quite possible, given this high degree of control which he imposed on the internal environment, for Butterfield to have planned free interiors, open plans with one space flowing into another. He would have been attracted to such arrangements, for he provided just such effects in the half-enclosed spaces of building groups such as St Augustine's Canterbury or Keble College (XX). The reason why Butterfield did not use open plans was neither visual nor technical: it was social. In the planning of interiors, propriety is as important as convenience; and propriety in the Victorians was a highly developed social sense.

The separation of functions in Victorian buildings was an expression of the same instinct which made social reformers pin their hopes upon the classification, segregation and even solitary isolation of the wicked. Butterfield's village school in *Instrumenta Ecclesiastica* (20), for example, deliberately unfolds in two directions, so that the boys and girls would not meet at the entrance: 'All persons connected with Schools should be emphatically reminded, that very great moral evils may arise from the neglect of these precautions. No school can be considered properly arranged where there is not a separate door for exit into a separate yard for each sex.'[17] In a similar spirit, in the schoolmaster's house the ground floor, only 35 feet by 12, is divided into five spaces: hall, sitting room, kitchen, pantry and larder. The master was no doubt unnecessarily cramped in consequence, but he could at any rate observe some elementary gentility when the functions of reception, eating, and food disposal were distinguished. For a substantial servant-owning family segregation was naturally much more elaborate. In Alvechurch rectory (21) Archdeacon Sandford had his own library and prayer room; guests could be received in the drawing room and the dining room, each entered through an ante-room; dressing rooms allowed appearances to be maintained in the bedrooms; and the servants were provided with a completely separate territory in the north wing, with their own staircase, servant's hall, and special domains allocated to the butler and the housekeeper. The points of contact with the master of the house were, very appropriately, the dining room on the ground floor and the prayer room upstairs.

Such arrangements were not of course new to the Victorian era, even if the huge wings so frequently appended to country houses were often intended to supply territories, particularly for servants, which had not previously been sufficiently distinct. There were, however, several building types for which the nineteenth century, in response to the social challenge of urbanization and industrialization, produced wholly new planning forms. Perhaps the most famous is the radiating plan of the prisons and workhouses built all over the country in the 1830s and 1840s. A similar wave of cemetery building followed the public health campaigns against town churchyards and the Interment Act of 1852. This was a new building type which directly affected the Ecclesiologists. At Wantage (131), for example, Butler successfully campaigned for a cemetery to replace the old churchyard, which was 'entirely packed with graves, and rather covered with, than covering, quantities of human bones, for they appear all over the surface.'[18] In 1852 a whole section of *Instrumenta Ecclesiastica* was devoted to designs by Butterfield for the purposes of 'Extramural Interment, which the epidemic of 1849 has made a matter of pressing and present interest.' The designs are certainly astonishing: a circular chapel (22), based on an example at Nuremberg and the Holy Sepulchre at Jerusalem; and a saddleback gate tower astride a 'lich-house' for the reception of bodies (23), which it was suggested might reduce 'the exorbitance of the usual charges of Undertakers'. But, probably because the High Church party was too narrow-minded to gain control of many Burial Boards, which had to provide for dissenters as well as church-men, Butterfield's cemetery designs seem to have had little influence, and he was never given the opportunity to execute the model design himself.

Butterfield's most important contributions to the development of building types, however, lay rather in the refinement of old forms than in the creation of new ones. He was exceptional among his contemporaries both in the range of planning types which he devised, and in his ability in providing both a symbolical and a practical form for them. The full range is revealed by the survey of his work in the second part of his book. Here it will suffice to emphasize that the variety of convents, colleges, schools, houses and churches there discussed is exceptional for the mid-nineteenth century, and some sub-types, such as the Holborn clergy house with its bachelor flats and communal dining room, must be among the earliest of their kind.

This is undoubtedly true of Butterfield's chapel-schools, which represent a fusion as much as a subdivision of types. There are two, Thurlaston of 1849 (24) and Pitt of 1858, both designed for use as schools during the week and as churches on Sundays. In 1849 this was 'new in idea and practice'[19] and Butterfield produced a surprising symbolic combination of the two functions: a church-like brick building with the schoolmaster's cottage at the west end designed to look like a church tower. It is a three-storied cottage, with a square projection like a staircase, wide-eaved roofs, and a pyramid cap and bellcote. The effect is delightful, rather like a medieval German town gatehouse. Inside the chapel is a neatly concealed anteroom for hats and coats. The main room is wide, with low plastered walls, while the sanctuary walls are higher, of exposed brick (86). There are also distinctions in the window types. Pitt is less interesting, since it has no house attached, but it is also an attractive little building, of weathered brick and flint, with a little stone added to distinguish the sanctuary. It was also suggested that Bursea chapel should be designed partly for use as a school-room, but by this date Butterfield had turned against the idea. 'School chapels are a

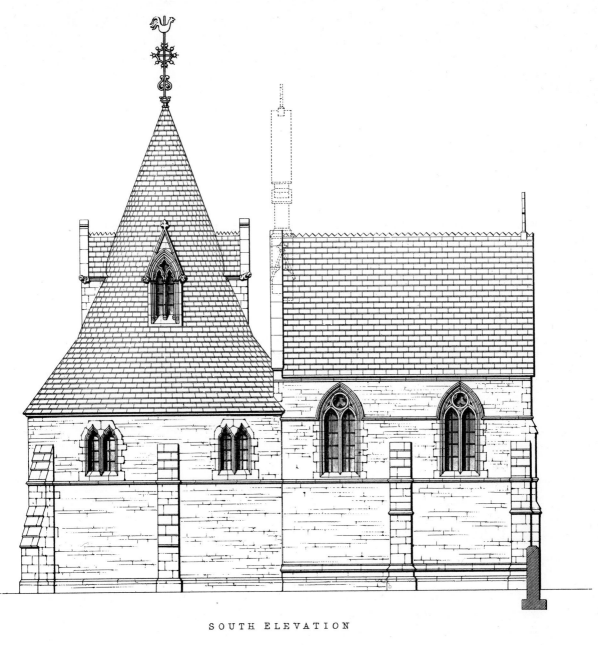

SOUTH ELEVATION

10 5   10   20   30   40   50
                                                    Feet

22 Cemetery chapel (*Instrumenta Ecclesiastica*)

failure. They obtain no reverence and can never inspire people with any notion of worship. They neither make School, nor Chapel.'[20]

If Butterfield's symbolical ingenuity is well illustrated by the chapel-schools, his practical skill is perhaps most impressively revealed by his one design for a public hospital – the Royal Hampshire County Hospital at Winchester (25).

The Winchester building committee wanted 'to invite an architect of first-rate eminence to undertake the work, who, upon all those disputed points of hospital construction which, if the plans were to be really well digested, ought to be settled by conference during their progress, should be in close and constant communication with themselves' and other advisers. They asked that 'no unnecessary expense should be incurred for doubtful experiments, still less for mere ornament'; and that there should be 'not one external feature which was not justified, and even required, by the internal arrangement.'[21] It might seem surprising that a Gothic Revivalist should be selected for such a commission, but it happened that the most recently built hospital in the county was that notorious classical folly, the Royal Victoria Military Hospital at Netley (27). The *Builder* had declared the sanitary planning at Netley would ensure that 'more disease will be generated there than is cured', and Palmerston that 'the comfort and recovery of the patients has been sacrificed to the vanity of the architect, whose sole object has been to make a building which would cut a dash when looked at from the Southampton River.'[22] The Winchester committee were more interested in moral qualities than in style, and Butterfield was familiar enough in the town, and especially with their chairman Sir William Heathcote, for his practical rationalism to be well known. In addition, there was to be a hospital chapel built by special private subscription in memory of the former hospital chairman, Warden Barter of Winchester College. Very probably Heathcote had already mentioned the hospital scheme to Butterfield and knew of his enthusiasm for it – an enthusiasm which was to be shown in a very substantial gift to the chapel fund.

Certainly Butterfield threw himself into the work 'with a zeal and interest far beyond the mere performance of a professional engagement', even sacrificing his annual holiday. With Heathcote he visited several new military and civilian hospitals, including the Herbert Military Hospital at Woolwich, which was the newly completed first example of the pavilion plan, providing maximum protection from cross-infection by spreading wards across the site, building latrines as separate structures, and linking the parts by open corridors. He also held frequent consultations with experts at the War Office, including Captain Galton who had designed the Woolwich Hospital, and on several occasions discussed his plans with the Winchester doctors. He listened patiently to the long letters which Florence Nightingale sent from her sickbed commenting on his proposals, and no doubt read both her *Notes on Hospitals*, of which she gave him an autographed copy ('from a fellow worker'), and also

SOUTH ELEVATION.

Scale of 10   5   0   10   20   30   40   50 feet

23   Lich house (*Instrumenta Ecclesiastica*)

24 Thurlaston school chapel, exterior

25 Royal Hampshire County Hospital, Winchester, exterior

26 All Saints' Margaret Street, exterior from street (A. F. Kersting)

numerous articles on hospital design published by the *Builder* at this date.

Florence Nightingale was on the whole 'quite delighted' with the final scheme: 'I think you may justly congratulate yourselves on having planned a model hospital'. Most of her criticisms were accepted by the committee and met by alterations. Her comments, and the Winchester plan, are thus as interesting as a test of her medical opinions as of Butterfield's architectural skill.[23]

In many ways the hospital certainly came up to the level of contemporary science and public health knowledge. The open site, sloping south from the Romsey road, was a great improvement on the cramped position of the former hospital within the walls of the insanitary old town. Butterfield's drainage system – a crucial feature of any nineteenth-century hospital – was a threefold separation of sewage, rainwater and bathwater, according to a report of 1879 'far in advance of the general practice of the time.'[24] The planning of the hospital was also ingenious. In contrast to the pavilion principle which Florence Nightingale herself supported, Butterfield designed a long slab running from east to west, with the wards opening at each end onto a balcony, bathrooms and lavatories in projecting semi-separate corner towers, and a central core of rooms for night nurses and a large, easily sloping, wide staircase. This core ensured the horizontal separation of the main wards, and they were cross-ventilated by immense, practically floor-to-ceiling plate glass windows, and heated by open fires rather than radiators in order to encourage air change. Externally the great utilitarian windows were relieved only by occasional stone bands in the brickwork, and by the more elaborate patterning and gothic windows of the chapel on the top floor. In contrast to the extravagantly spread pavilions of most later nineteenth-

27 Royal Victoria Military Hospital, Netley, by Mennie (Radio Times Hulton Picture Library)

century hospitals, Butterfield had evolved an economic and striking alternative especially suitable for confined urban sites. A similar approach, for example, was used by Alfred Waterhouse in University College Hospital, London, thirty years later.

In the arrangement of rooms within this plan, however, the Winchester hospital was much less satisfactory. It was already believed by some of the leading medical men of the period, and in particular by Sir John Simon, the brilliant Medical Officer to the Privy Council, that infection was spread by germs, rather than by noxious vapours sweated out by the sick into the atmosphere, as was then generally thought. The new theory meant that the isolation of infectious patients, and especially the separation of surgical and general wards, was much more important than the provision of constant ventilation. At Winchester no such precautions were taken. The venereal ward was isolated, but not the surgical ward. Some of the doctors wanted more small wards, but Florence Nightingale resisted. Accidents and operations were 'under much better care and supervision' in a large ward. Patients 'actually prefer a full large ward and think it "so cheerful" '. The one essential point was fresh air – and at Winchester 1500 cubic feet[25] of constantly changing air was assured to each patient.

There were two reasons for Florence Nightingale's advice. Firstly, she regarded germ theory and contagion as irrelevancies, not even worth consideration in hospital planning. Contagion was 'on the same footing as witchcraft and superstitions.' Her hostility to scientific advance was indicated by her lack of support for the Winchester doctor who wanted a special 'room for microscopic investigations'. Secondly, she was dominated by the need for moral order in the hospital. The matron and nurses, specially trained in her St Thomas's establishment, could supervise the large wards from their strategic rooms in the core. Small rooms, or separate day rooms, would need more staff, or they would 'look much like the parlour of a discreditable public house . . . the patients gossipping and lolling out of a window'. She thus underestimated the danger of cross-infection in surgical cases, but insisted on the isolation of the morally contaminating venereal patients, who required 'a head nurse of the utmost strength of character . . . . to prevent assignations for further vice by these wicked women under her very nose.'[26]

The 'model hospital' was thus in some respects less of a model than it might have been. Although Butterfield himself cannot be criticized for the expert advice upon which he acted, it is symbolic of the prime importance of propriety in Victorian planning that even in a public hospital it was allowed to prevail over advanced scientific opinion. It was above all propriety which prevented the Victorians from developing an architectural style which was, in the modern sense, strictly functional.

It was not merely that propriety affected the planning of buildings. It also helped to determine their style. It was a traditional assumption of European architecture that religious and social hierarchies in the functions of buildings should be expressed by corresponding hierarchies of material and ornament. Thus in many regions, where the common building materials were wood and mud, churches and the great houses would be built of stone. Within them, colour, sculpture and intricacy were concentrated upon the jewelled sanctuary, or the frescoed drawing room with its marbled fireplace. The Victorians did not question this assumption, until Ruskin showed them the effect of their social system, the extremes of limitless elaboration for the rich and mass-produced utter shoddiness for the poor which, in a society of great wealth and mass poverty, the division of labour produced. This was the under-standing which led William Morris from the 1870s to call for a return to egalitarian simplicity in art, and through this doctrine to provide one of the fundamental influences in the modern movement. It was too late to influence Butterfield, who thought an egalitarian society 'without shade or relief will be seriously untrue and uninteresting', and in any case had little interest in the reorganization of society to allow self-expression to workmen, when the whole basis of his professional practice had been the assertion of absolute control by the architect.[27]

Butterfield therefore organized his designs on the basis of a hierarchy. In his churches, for example, decoration is concentrated upon the sanctuary. Very often all the walls are bare, except for a rich display of alabaster or tile patterns behind the altar. Invariably the tile floors become progressively richer towards the east; very often the nave will be purely red and black, while in the chancel stone will be added, and patterned yellow tiles, with perhaps sea-blue also in the santuary. The point is emphasized by the arrangement of the sanctuary steps, which encircle the altar on three sides. When the Archbishop of York indicated that he preferred the steps to run right across the chancel, Butterfield indignantly replied: 'The Archbishop means that he likes to sit in a chair against the East Wall staring at, and stared at by, the people, as the principal object. He therefore dislikes a footpace.'[28] In a Butterfield church the principal object was the altar, and even the roof was normally designed to emphasize this fact, the open rafters of the nave giving way to lower panelling in the chancel, and the sanctuary roof picked out in coloured decoration. At Balliol (28), although externally the chapel had a single roof, Butterfield explained that internally 'the three varieties of roof are to answer to the three varieties on the floor, of Antechapel, Choir and Sanctuary. They are boarding and ribs of wood over the Sanctuary, plaster and ribs of wood over the choir, and common rafters over the Antechapel.'[29]

Exactly the same principle can be seen in secular work, in the concentration of ornament upon the drawing room in a house, and the distinction between various types of building. Thus at St Augustine's College (29) all the residential buildings were plainer than the chapel and the library, but the *Ecclesiologist* praised the 'some-what greater height, bulk and pretension of the warden's, as compared with the

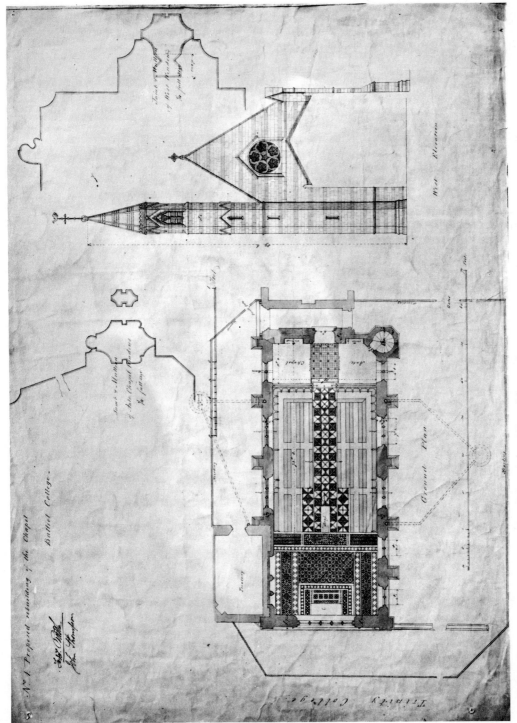

28 Balliol College chapel, tile floor plan (Victoria & Albert Museum)

29 St Augustine's College Canterbury, chapel, warden's and fellows' residences (St Augustine's College)

30 Baldersby, banded cottages

31 Baldersby, plain cottages

32 Baldersby almshouse

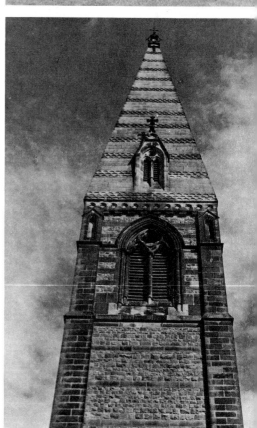

33 *above* Baldersby school

34 *above right* Baldersby vicarage

35 Baldersby church, exterior (John Lane)

fellows' residence; and the two-light windows of the latter bear a similar proportion to the plain lancets of the student's building.'[30] Similarly, in a group of buildings such as Baldersby village, each represents a step in aesthetic and social status. The humblest cottages (31) are of brilliant simplicity, of brick and tile, entirely depending upon the subtlety of their roof shapes for their effect. A second group (30) a little closer to the church has stone banding added, and simple mullioned windows instead of casements; while in the almshouses (32), halftimbering is also introduced. The schoolmaster, by contrast, has a stone cottage, attached to a richly gothic school (33) with halftimbering decorating the porch. Finally, in the vicarage (34) the same materials are contorted into shapes of bewildering confusion; and in the church a severe stone exterior conceals the ultimate climax of polychromatic splendour within (35, 36).

Building types, in short, represented a progression from utilitarian simplicity to architectural splendour. In accepting such a hierarchy Butterfield shared the common view of the mid-nineteenth century. The design reformer Owen Jones opened his famous *Grammar of Ornament* with the categoric statement that ornament 'must necessarily increase with all peoples in the ratio of the progress of civilisation'.

36 Baldersby church, interior (Gordon Barnes)

37 Edensor village, cottages
by Sir Joseph Paxton
(Architectural Press)

38 Ardingly College, Home Farm

39 Milton Mill

Ruskin's attitude was similar; for him, architecture only began when a building was taken beyond mere practicalities, so much so that 'ornamentation is the principal part of architecture' and unadorned buildings have little to do with art.[31] Even the great pioneers of structural functionalism such as Paxton and Brunel accepted this standpoint, attempted to make their designs more architectural in the conventional sense – Paxton's modifications of the Crystal Palace are an instructive example – and when they turned to cottages (37) and country houses, produced designs far more naively historicist than those of Butterfield. In fact Butterfield was probably unusual in the care which he was prepared to give to a simple building. When it was once suggested that a racquet court might be too insignificant a building for him to design, he replied with some vigour, 'I will build a pig-sty if it has got to be built.'[32] And certainly in the few cases where he designed buildings at the bottom of the hierarchy, he entered unhesitatingly into their utilitarian spirit, eliminating the unnecessary trimmings of architectural style and ornament with the thoroughness of any engineer. Perhaps the big-boned Sussex barns at Ardingly (38) are a trifle self-conscious, even if as structural as the wagons they once housed; but who would suspect the author of the noble vernacular watermill at Milton (39) in Bedfordshire? Confronted by the elementary grandeur of this mill, one realizes that Butterfield understood as well as any modern architect the merits of *The Functional Tradition in Early Industrial Buildings*. Milton Mill would have made a perfect example for J. M. Richards' book. It was not aesthetic blindness but social convention which made him think Milton Ernest Hall a finer achievement, and prefer the vicarage to the cottages at Baldersby.

Notes on chapter 8

1   2, 4 and 6 December.
2   Boggis, *op. cit.*, p. 162; *ILN*, (13) 1848, p. 5.
3   Law, *op. cit.*, p. 188. At Milton Ernest the water supply, with a basement main tank and pumps on the ground floor, was certainly eccentric, although it is uncertain when the attic tank was installed. In Victorian houses the water closets, here and elsewhere provided by Butterfield on the upper floors, were often filled by servants, just like the washstands. Baths were usually filled with hot water in the same way, and most of Butterfield's clients were apparently content to take them in the old fashioned manner in their bedrooms. (See L. Wright, *Clean and Decent*, London, Routledge & Kegan Paul, 1966).
4   20 April 1852, Wilmcote scrapbook, Shakespeare's Birthplace Library.
5   Butterfield to Rev. Knottesford Fortescue, 13 March 1847, *ibid*.
6   E.g. specification, 1865, Heytesbury Collection. Although the best that Victorian technology offered, they were not very effective: see Reyner Banham, *The Well Tempered Environment*, London, Architectural Press, 1969, p. 32.

7 *E*, (12) 1851, p. 26.

8 Butterfield to the Master, 19 September 1856, Balliol College archives; and to Rev. L. Garnett, 16 April 1877, Christleton chest.

9 Lethaby, *op. cit.*, p. 68.

10 (Stoke Newington) *E*, (14) 1853, p. 269. There are several designs for gas fittings in the Starey Collection, but all late in date.

11 *Ibid.*, (12) 1851, p. 26.

12 *Church Times*, 27 September 1895; correspondence, All Saints' chest.

13 *BN*, (47) 1884, p. 705; 'On Windows', *E*, (17) 1856, pp. 319–22.

14 *Ibid.*, (2) 1843, p. 120.

15 A. J. B. Hope to William Dyce, 10 April 1852, 'Life, Correspondence and Writings of William Dyce', Aberdeen Art Gallery.

16 *The Times*, 6 December 1884.

17 Vol. 2, plate 49.

18 Rev. W. J. Butler to Chapter Clerk, 18 June 1849, St George's Chapel, Windsor, archives.

19 *E*, (9) 1849, p. 321.

20 Butterfield to Rev. G. S. Holmes, 28 May 1869, Holme upon Spalding Moor chest.

21 Final report of the Building Committee, 1869, Hampshire Record Office.

22 *AR*, (139) 1966, p. 249.

23 Building Committee Minutes, 14 October 1863 and 12 April 1867 (Butterfield's gift of £500, one quarter of his total income in 1866), Hampshire Record Office; accounts, and *Notes on Hospitals*, Starey Collection; Anthony King, 'Hospital Planning', *Medical History*, October 1966.

24 Report of Sub-Committee on Drainage.

25 Some nineteenth-century hospitals provided still more air; half as much is now acceptable.

26 Royston Lambert, *Sir John Simon*, London, MacGibbon & Kee, 1963, pp. 267–8, etc.; Annual Report of Committee of Governors, 1868; Building Committee Minutes, 14 October 1863; Florence Nightingale to Sir William Heathcote, 11 September and 19 October 1863, Nightingale Collection, British Museum.

27 He was in fact complaining of children 'affecting to be *ladies* and *gentlemen*': Butterfield to William Starey, 17 January 1891, Starey Collection.

28 Butterfield to Rev. G. S. Holmes, 27 January 1870, Holme upon Spalding Moor chest.

29 Butterfield to the Master, 21 October 1854, Balliol College archives.

30 (9) 1848, p. 3.

31 (Lectures on Architecture) *Works*, xii, p. 83.

32. E. G. Sandford (ed.), *Memoirs* of Archbishop Temple, London, 1906, I, p. 512.

When Butterfield was restoring the little Wiltshire church of Knook, his patron, Lord Heytesbury, was distressed to find that the designs showed a chancel arch in wood instead of stone. Butterfield's answer sums up his attitude to the expression of structure: 'As you are aware the gable at the East end of the nave at Knook is only timber. There has never been a stone arch there. It is timber at present and *disguised*. I make it of timber and *avow* it. That is the difference.'[1]

In the notes Butterfield made for the restoration of old buildings, one finds again and again slight changes to bring out the structural function of architectural members. At St Cross, for example, he decided to 'uncoat the filling between the vaulting ribs, [and] point same neatly so as to shew the separate stones'; at Hathersage to provide 'angle buttresses of bolder character than at present.'[2] The changes indicate the intense concern which Butterfield shared with his contemporaries for 'truthfulness' and 'reality' in architecture – that structure should be seen and understood. 'Real' was one of the highest words of praise to the *Ecclesiologist*. Pugin himself had written, in the first page of *True Principles*, that all architectural ornament should be limited to

> enrichment of the essential construction of the building . . and even the construction itself *should vary with the material employed* . . . Strange as it may appear at first sight, it is in *pointed architecture alone that these great principles have been carried out*; and I shall be able to illustrate them from the vast cathedral to the simplest erection. Moreover, the architects of the middle ages were the first who *turned the natural properties of the various materials to their full account*, and made *their mechanism a vehicle for their art*.

What then were the materials which Butterfield used, and what did he make of them in his designs? It will be simplest to begin at the base of his buildings, and consider foundations, walls and roofs in turn.

The base of Butterfield's buildings, as one would expect, was the best which nineteenth-century techniques could have provided. The lighter buildings were

128

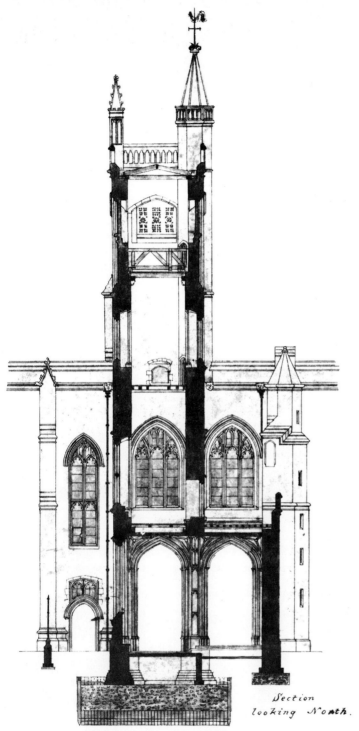

Section looking North.

40 Winchester College, section of tower (The Warden and Fellows of Winchester College)

constructed on foundations of rammed rubble, the heavier upon concrete. Churches, from Coalpit Heath onwards were generally given a complete concrete floor. In the specification for Broad Street School Canterbury, in 1847, the material is described as a mixture of 'ground stone, lime, gravel and stones, poured from a height into the trenches', to form a layer two and a half feet thick beneath the main walls.[3] In restorations of old buildings foundations of this type were also sometimes introduced: the medieval tower at Winchester College, for example, whose original baulks of beech and oak had rotted away into the boggy soil, was rebuilt on a concrete raft in

41   Broad Street School, Canterbury

1862 (40). In addition, for all new and most old buildings, the base of the wall was provided with a damp course. This was at first normally of slate, but from about 1860 Butterfield often used an asphalt mixture 'of coal tar, lime and sand', which was poured in hot. It was particularly suited to old buildings where the coursing was uneven, and since it was regarded by contemporaries as a 'clever expedient', Butterfield seems to have been adventurous in employing this method, even though it was a traditional vernacular expedient.[4] These foundations have, at any rate, almost everywhere stood the test of time. I know of only two buildings – Dundela and

42   Castle Hill school

Clevedon – where there was any complaint of settlement, and I have seen only one – Dalton – which obviously suffers from damp walls.

There was no expression of the strength of these foundations in Butterfield's walls, which normally rose clean and sheer from the ground. Even when there was a change of material in the upper wall, this usually took place at the level of the window sills rather than the base. Ruskin had argued in *The Stones of Venice* that the foundation was 'to the wall what the paw is to an animal. It is a long foot, wider than the wall, on which the wall is to stand, and which keeps it from settling into the ground. It is

43 St Mawgan vicarage

most necessary that this great element of masonry should be visible to the eye.'[5] His advice could be effectively followed, as in the subtle cambers which G. E. Street would give to a wall base. Butterfield on this point chose to ignore Ruskin.

For the upper walls of all his earliest buildings, and throughout his life for major buildings in the countryside, Butterfield preferred a facing of stone. For parts such as corners, copings and window tracery, where first class dressed masonry was essential, he most frequently used Bath stone, mined by Randall and Saunders at Corsham Down. In Kent, however, he used the traditionally popular Caen stone dressings (in Broad Street School from Luard Reedham's quarry), and in the north he would choose a Millstone Grit, sometimes the well-known Bramley Fall stone from Leeds, used at Baldersby, but also local freestones, such as Cowcliffe at Huddersfield and a Garsdale stone at Cautley.

For the main walling on the other hand a local stone was invariably chosen, often a quarry in the same parish, especially when it was for the restoration of an old building. At Chaddesley Corbett the pink and cream sandstone of the medieval work was matched from 'an adjoining quarry', and at Dodford the new work was of 'the same local stone as the whole church is built of'.[6] The rubble walling at Milton Ernest Hall was dug from the Ouse river bank four hundred yards away from the park, and brought down the river by barge.

The result was a wonderful variety of building stones, which beautifully match the surrounding landscape. One thinks of the rocky Kentish Rag of the Broad Street School (41), or the spongy brown Essex conglomerate at Ardleigh; of the classic white Wiltshire limestones from Tisbury at Netherhampton and from Chilmark at Amesbury, and a whole range of lesser grey limestone rubbles stretching up through Berkshire (Marcham stone at Wantage) and Bedfordshire into Lincolnshire. Beyond these are the glowing ironstones, the oolitic limestone at Gaer Hill perched on the brim of Dorset, the golden Cotswold stone at Milton (277), brown Rutland marlstone at Ashwell, and a last yellow Derbyshire limestone as far north as Sheen (211) astride the Pennine foothills; and then the range of sandstones, from deep Devonshire browns and blues at Castle Hill (42), to Cheshire pink and white at Christleton (51) and ginger Norfolk carstone at Hunstanton (271). Still further north and west one finds the blackening grits of the Yorkshire churches, and the clean grey island stone of Cumbrae, facing the peaks of Arran across the Firth of Clyde; the rough mountain rubble from the gnarled old Cardigan range at Elerch (274), and red-streaked grey Delabole slate in a wooded Cornish combe at St Mawgan (43). In short, all over the country, perfect responses to the subtle variety of landscape. If Butterfield's attitude to the builders was that of a Victorian realist, to the quarries at least his approach was consistently romantic. There must be a score of overgrown village pits where the last carts were brought out at his command.

Each type of stone demanded a facing appropriate to its quality. Some of them, particularly the ironstones and sandstones, were dressed to a relatively clean surface because they were easy to cut and weathered well. Most were less tractable. This did not worry Butterfield, who shared the characteristic romantic delight in rough texture. Pugin, too, had found that ancient rubble walls 'yet impress the mind with feelings of reverent awe', and showed in *True Principles* how their irregular patterns were preferable to those of regular dressed ashlar, where the jointing will 'by its *lines interfere* with those of the building.'[7] He illustrated a gothic window with an arch of narrow rubble stones, and surrounding masonry in 'jumper work', where thin horizontal courses are varied by large broader stones rising into the courses above. From the first this was Butterfield's favourite type of masonry. Even at Highbury Chapel, designed a few months after *True Principles* was published, there are rubble window arches, irregular quoins to the buttresses, and walls of rubble coursed in random jumper work (44). Where more sharply dressed stones were used, the masonry would be more regular, but the impact of the joints was reduced by laying the stones as closely as possible, keeping the mortar well back from the surface, and varying the thickness of the courses. Butterfield's aim was to produce a *continuous* masonry texture, varying in density according to the quality of the stone: dense when the stone was fine, but much looser when it was rough; using much more mortar to produce a surface when the rough stones were small, but allowing deeper crevices with large rough stones. Above all, the stone must show its natural quality. If weathered old stone is to be reused, he instructs that 'it is not to be redressed on the face, but only in the joint'.[8] New stone must be given the surface to bring out its character, and with the harder rocks, like Cornish slate-stone, this meant that the builder should 'take off quarry face from all building stone'.[9] Sometimes, as at Sessay, one can still see the rough marks of the chisel quite clearly (45).

Within these persistent characteristics, one can detect some gradual changes in Butterfield's treatment of masonry. In the 1840s and early 1850s he seems to be seeking as neutral a texture as possible, an undifferentiated, continuous, flat surface. As early as St Augustine's College (29) one finds the window tracery level with the wall, and running straight into it without the interruption of a hoodstone or drip moulding. The same is true of the windows of the Coalpit Heath vicarage (6), and soon church windows were treated in the same fashion. Internally the windows are punched through the thick walls to the outer surface with abrupt force, the edges scarcely splayed, almost rectangular (46).

The same desire to maintain the integrity of the wall surface can be seen in his treatment of hard rock masonry. At Canterbury (47) he used Kentish Rag, a popular stone with the early Ecclesiologists. But while at St Augustine's the stones are of extraordinarily varied size, and the effect a very rough irregular homespun texture, at Broad Street School (41) the masonry, although still random, is composed of stones of relatively even size. Butterfield had no doubt reacted, like the *Ecclesiologist*, against the 'prodigalities of irregularity' produced by builders when random work was specified. It was better if the spectator was 'neither induced to examine and commend the ingenuity with which the difficulties of a bad building stone are overcome, nor are you called on to join the vulgar admiration of "such big blocks." '[10] Even so at the Canterbury Broad Street School the blocks were still large and very rough. At Cumbrae, therefore, even though the island stone is a tough crystalline

44 Highbury Chapel, exterior

45 Sessay church, doorway (Peter Burton)

volcanic rock, it was cut to medium-sized rectangular blocks, and laid in courses of jumper work, with the smoothest face to the surface (270).

At the end of the 1850s one senses a reaction (48). The surface of the masonry becomes a little rougher, and is more often varied by smooth bands, projecting string courses and mouldings, and very slight projections or recessions in the plan. Internally the window splays become wider. Where limestone rubble is used, the mortar is no longer brought close to the surface, in spite of the wide joints. Sometimes, as at Highway church, a stone which would have previously received a fairly even surface is hammered. The tendency becomes especially obvious once more in the treatment of the hardest stones. At Clevedon, Wraxall and Axbridge (49) the stone was quarried from the Mendips, and its rough uneven texture clearly appreciated. The chaplain's house of about 1880 at Axbridge has craggy, utterly irregular walls, quarried at Draycott, and its rockiness is emphasized by two broad bands of smooth ashlar running below the windows.

The bands recall Ruskin's demand for 'smooth sheets of rock, glistening like sea waves, that ring under the hammer like a brazen bell, – that is her preparation for first stories.' Although at Coalpit Heath church Butterfield enlivened the rubble surface with a few pieces of dressed masonry, he had not repeated this experiment, and dressed bands only occur in his stone buildings from the late 1850s, beginning with Baldersby (35) and Ashford in 1857–8. *The Stones of Venice* had been published by Ruskin six years earlier, and Butterfield was well aware of his support for banded walls. But he did not follow Ruskin's suggestion that they should 'correspond to the divisions of its stories within, express its internal structure, and mark off some portion of the ends of its existence already attained.'[11] Nor did he always smooth the harder rock, according to the natural precedent cited by Ruskin. His bands are mostly of limestone of medium density, and they emphasize external rather than internal features: sometimes the springing of corbels or arches, but generally window sills.

A second, but much briefer experiment, can be directly attributed to the influence of Ruskin. Butterfield was always attracted to the varied natural colouring of stone, but he normally treated it in a subtle random manner appropriate to his method of coursing. It is quite wrong to think of his stone buildings as characteristically striped with strongly contrasted colours. Most of them give the impression of one colour only, at least until one looks more closely and sees the interwoven variations of which it is composed (II). In the few cases where the colour contrast is more obvious, it generally derives from the same stone, and the colours are naturally harmonious: Delabole slatestone, for instance. There are in fact only two out of more than seventy stone-faced new buildings in which Butterfield deliberately banded the colours. In addition there is Ashwell church, but this was a rebuilding, and the brown and grey bands probably follow the pattern of the original medieval stonework. There remain only

46 St Augustine's College Canterbury, windows

Balliol College chapel (50), designed in 1854, and Etal church, of 1856–8.

At Balliol for once the stone was not local, because Oxford had no longer any suitable building stone. This may have persuaded Butterfield that it was a case for experiment. For the main walling he used a white stone from Somerset and a reddish sandstone from Worcestershire, mixed in what the *Builder* saw as 'irregular and eccentric courses'.[12] There is, however, a system in their arrangement. At the base of the building there are broad red bands, occasionally interrupted by a narrower seam of white, and as the walls rise, the white becomes more frequent, and eventually dominant. In the east gable it is like a wave breaking into a spray of chequers at the crest of the gable. The turret has the same rhythm, but, to emphasize its verticality, the broader bands are white. The scheme clearly follows Ruskin: 'as, in all well-conducted lives, the hard work, and roughing, and gaining of strength comes first, the honour or decoration in certain intervals during their course, but most of all in their close, so, in general, the base of a wall, which is the beginning of its labour, will bear least decoration, its body more, especially those epochs of rest called string courses; but its crown or cornice most of all.'[13]

Butterfield himself clearly regarded the chapel as an experiment: 'It requires rather frequent visits, as I have never tried anything of the kind before.'[14] He repeated it only once, in a simplified form with local stone at Etal, and then abandoned Ruskin's method. The chapel was disliked at Oxford, and local critics at once proclaimed 'that the walls look like slices of streaky bacon',[15] but Butterfield took little notice of their feelings, as Keble College was to show. Probably he was dissatisfied with Balliol because the colour gives it an undeniably exotic flavour. In spite of all the English precedents – even the turret is based on that of the old chapel – the

47 St Augustine's College, library exterior

48 Little Faringdon parsonage

49 St Michael's Home Axbridge, chaplain's house

general form looks French, the materials Italian. Hence he turned to another method of enriching his wall surface, the heightening of texture which we have already noticed.

Internally Balliol was also richly polychromatic, and although most of the walls were covered by alabaster, the banded stonework was shown in the window splays (158). Again the chapel is exceptional. Apart from Penarth (XIV), where the banded stone arches and columns contribute to an essentially brick interior, there are only nine interiors which use systematically contrasted coloured stonework. The earliest, Yealmpton (IV), probably designed in 1849, has nave columns of banded light and grey marble, and thin grey strips diapering its white walls, intended as frames for frescoes which were never executed.[16] Balliol followed; and then in 1865 Babbacombe was begun (III). Here Butterfield's growing concern for varied texture was dramatically manifested. The rough red and grey sandstone walls are raised on smooth polished drums of Devon marble, in two shades of brown; and the walls themselves are not merely banded, but set with an irregular chequer of mastic patterns, and criss-crossed by a strange raised pattern like a diagonal trellis of sticks. The complexity

50 Balliol College chapel, exterior

51 Christleton church, interior (Simon Clements)

52 Rugby St Andrew, interior (Long)

of Babbacombe is unique. The remaining six coloured interiors were all designed after 1875, and are far quieter. Except for Christleton (51), where the upper chancel walls are prettily chequered, the banding is everywhere broad and the effect generally majestic: the white, pale pink and biscuit brown sandstone at Dundela (165); buff and pink in Rugby parish church (52); and cream with dark blue-grey in Melbourne Cathedral (XIX).

Earlier interiors were structurally plain. Usually the stonework was revealed only at arches and other openings, and the walls were covered by plain plastering, coloured a warm white. But there was a considerable use of stone for non-structural decoration (V): in fonts, sanctuary floors, reredoses and occasionally in pulpits. For these Butterfield chose alabasters and marbles which he very rarely used for structure. Some of them were foreign marbles – Sicilian white, Sienna, Belgian black, and Galway green and yellow; but most were English – Devon reds, browns, and yellows, Cornish serpentine, and most beautiful of all, grey Derbyshire fossil marble. Where local marbles existed they would be exploited, as in the earliest examples of 1850–1, the sparkling font at Ottery St Mary (VI) and the deep pink and grey at Yealmpton

53 Great Bookham school

54 Godmersham church, flint walling

55 Avington parsonage

(IV), both in Devon. Their exquisite colours roused strong feelings in the Victorians, to whom geology was a question of faith, but there is no doubt that the immediate inspiration came from Ruskin's famous call in *The Seven Lamps*: 'The true colours of architecture are those of natural stone, and I would fain see these taken advantage of to the full. Every variety of hue, from pale yellow to purple, passing through orange, red and brown, is entirely at our command; nearly every kind of green and grey is also attainable . . .'[17] If Butterfield's masonry owed little to Ruskin, he gave ample tribute in his marblework.

One type of stone has been left unmentioned, because its character is entirely different: flint. Traditionally flint was widely used in parts of the south and east where good stone was unobtainable, and often mixed with brick. Butterfield used it very early, in St Augustine's, and he always continued flintwork where appropriate in extending or restoring medieval buildings. From the late 1850s he also used flint mixed with brick in several buildings (53, 54), all in or close to Surrey and Wiltshire, where cottages are commonly a patchwork of this sort. It was given a suitably economical texture, roughly knapped, with 'the quiet look of an old building'.[18] Butterfield never attempted the close-fitted, dense blackness of medieval East Anglian work. Nor did he ever have occasion to use the rounded kidney flint technique of Norfolk cottage walling.

It might seem surprising, when as early as 1847 in Avington parsonage (55) Butterfield showed how flint could provide a charming and inexpensive vernacular material, that he did not use it more frequently in later years. The reason lay in the peculiar, almost passionate, liking which he developed for brickwork in all buildings where stone was not appropriate. The suddenness with which this feeling developed can be seen from the figures overleaf, which show the materials which he chose for new buildings. From an overwhelming preference for stone in the 1840s, the position is dramatically reversed in the 1850s, even though an estate village of cottages is counted as a single building. If cottages are counted separately, almost three quarters of Butterfield's work in the 1850s was in brick. His conversion to brick can, moreover, be dated precisely, to the year 1847.

Although Pugin had designed a number of brick buildings, including his own house at Ramsgate, the *Ecclesiologist* in the early 1840s had regarded brick as a very inferior material: 'we do abhor it, whether black, red or white, *most* cordially.' Gradually, as High Church enthusiasm for the reintroduction of colour in church architecture grew, and the medieval brick churches of Italy and north Germany were rediscovered, hostility to its use lessened, and by 1847 it declared that 'brick is by no means a proscribed material for church building.' It was more important that it should be candidly expressed: 'a material so mean' demanded a design 'of the severest and plainest kind', relying for effect upon the sheer scale of 'bold and broad masses', as

Table 3

Wall Materials (restorations excluded)

	Stone	Stone with brick interior	Brick and flint	Brick	Brick and timber	Total	% brick
1840–9						29	35
1850–9						63	59
1860–9						36	70
1870–9						31	61
1880–92						16	50
Total	76	3	7	74	15	175	57

for example in the great French cathedral at Albi, which had been described in a previous issue.[19]

These comments were inspired by the publication in the autumn of 1847 of two designs for colonial cathedrals in brick, Colombo by R. C. Carpenter and Adelaide by Butterfield. Moreover, at precisely the same time Butterfield presented the vicar of Wantage with a design (56) of extreme simplicity for a cheap chapel in the hamlet of Charlton, 'with room for about 90 people, which can be built for £120, . . . contrived so as to receive nave wall, a chancel, tower and good windows whenever money comes to pay for them.'[20] Although the Adelaide design was never used and Charlton chapel has been rebuilt, the remarkable design for the chapel fortunately survives to show Butterfield's first treatment of brick.

Clearly brick churches were a matter of general interest at the end of 1847. Perhaps this simply came from a gradual change in attitude; or it may have been stimulated by the publication of Thomas James's account of Italian brickwork – 'common brick, yet beautiful in form and colour' – in his book *On the Use of Brick in Ecclesiastical Architecture*.[21] At any rate, Butterfield took up the idea with such enthusiasm that by 1849 All Saints' itself was conceived as a brick church. Undoubtedly in London, and great industrial cities like Leeds and Manchester, brick had tremendous advantages: it lasted indefinitely, while even the best stones would finally succumb to the sulphurous air; it was a better protection against fire; and it was, in most such cities, by now the traditional material. 'London', the *Ecclesiologist* eventually recognized, 'is naturally a brick town'.[22] Principle, and in the south-east even precedent, was satisfied. Nevertheless, the use of brick for major buildings at a time when every Londoner who could disguise his house in stucco preferred to do so, was a bold break with conventional taste, and it brought Butterfield his first experience of hostile critism. All Saints', Charles Eastlake recalled,

> puzzled the antiquaries, scandalised the architects, and sent unprofessional
> critics to their wit's end with amazement. Passers-by gazed at the ironwork
> of the entrance gateway, at the gables and dormers of the parsonage, at the
> black brick voussoirs and stringcourses, and asked what manner of
> architecture this might be, which was neither Early English, Decorated nor
> Tudor, and which could be properly referred to no century except the
> nineteenth.[23]

Such reactions could only harden the conviction of a man like Butterfield, who eventually came to feel that he had a 'mission to give dignity to brick'.[24] At Keble College, although tightness of the budget gave him little choice except in the chapel, he was furious when its use was attacked: 'What has brick done that it is never to be used except under protest? After every great fire we always hear that it is the only

M

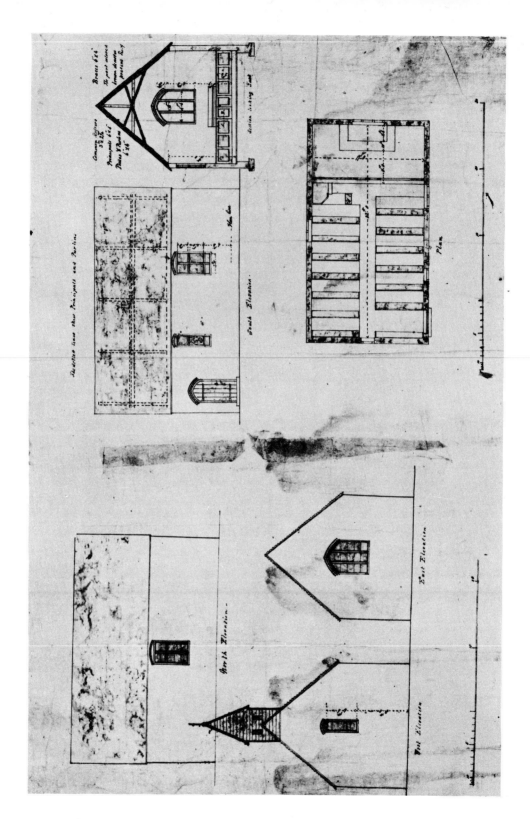

56 Charlton, Wantage, church plan (Berkshire Record Office)

material which has not failed. And we are always hearing of the decay of stone. And yet stone is to be considered the one sacred material.'[25]

Although brick was cheaper than stone in the great cities, this by no means implied that Butterfield's choice was wholly economic. Some brick was much more expensive than other varieties, and Butterfield worked with the best when he could. In London, for example, while a cheaper church like St Matthias Stoke Newington (7) was built entirely of light brown London stocks, for the more expensive St Augustine's Queen's Gate (12) blue Staffordshire and red Suffolk bricks from Ballingdon were added; while All Saints' (I) was almost entirely faced in a superb soft pink brick – so costly, in fact, that G. E. Street, an equally eager propagandist for the material, felt the church was hardly a fair demonstration of its use: 'I rather regret the unnecessary goodness (as it seems to me) of the bricks in this noble work'.[26]

The more expensive bricks at St Augustine's were not only made outside London, but in the case of the blue bricks they were made from the tough clay of the Midland coal measures which had only very recently been brought into use for brickmaking, as a result of the invention of the 'stiff plastic' (dry machine-moulded) brick in the late 1850s. Unlike the blue bricks of the softer southern clays, which were merely blackened on the surface by being closest to the flame in the kiln, this clay produced wholly blue bricks. One would expect Butterfield to prefer 'the Staffordshire blue brick which is coloured all through, [to] some nasty thing with a smear on the surface'[27], for this was a case in which Victorian mechanization had improved the quality of the material.

Similarly, the interior at St Augustine's (279) was boldly patterned with Pether's patent bricks, pale buff, moulded with fleur-de-lys; and Butterfield had also used a similar type of brick, moulded to form flower patterns, in the New Schools of 1868 at Rugby (282). Perhaps these two experiments in moulded brickwork were inspired by the first successful large-scale use of architectural terracotta in the Victoria & Albert Museum quadrangle of 1865. There are at any rate no other significant instances of Butterfield's use of this type of material, which he abandoned as it became fashionable in the 1870s. But a rather earlier use of terracotta should also be mentioned – the warm brown wall arcade shafts at St Alban's Holborn and in Balliol Chapel (158). Contemporaries regarded them as an 'extremity of oddity': who would imagine 'for one moment that the red shafts of Balliol College are hollow, were made by Mr Minton, and are nothing more or less than field drain pipes? So accurately, however, had they to be made, that the cost was considerably more than the expense of marble would have been'.[28]

All these experiments with new Victorian materials were, however, confined to ornament. One never finds drainage bricks used for the main walls of a church, as in Teulon's strangely defiant dockland church of 1861 at Silvertown (57); nor did

57 Silvertown church, by S. S. Teulon, exterior

Butterfield vary the thickness of courses, as here and also in work by William White in the 1850s (XXII); nor was he tempted by the weather-proof qualities of fully glazed bricks. For general walling his choice of brick was in fact distinctly conservative. He never favoured the cheap mass-produced brick which, following the introduction of wire-cutting, machine-grinding, the 'stiff plastic' method and the continuously worked Hoffman Kiln, began to oust local hand-made bricks in many parts of the country from the late 1850s. Outside London he always preferred the best local brick: Culm Davy for Exeter School, Forest bricks for Emery Down, 'good hard blunt local bricks' for Letcombe Bassett, Rugby's own bricks for the elaborately patterned New Schools and chapel.[29]

Thus there is a range of local colour in Butterfield's brickwork just as in his masonry. At the Trumpington schoolhouse he uses a soft Cambridgeshire honey grey; at Baldersby and Snaith the rough dull pinks of the Yorkshire plain (62); and at Ashwell in Rutland, a richly glowing iron red (152). Similarly in the towns, although contemporaries thought that the local red and grey-blue bricks used at St Thomas's Leeds (73) had brought 'an Italian hue and refinement to the coarse and disheartening vicinity of coal-smoke and mill chimneys',[30] today one is more struck by the intensely local quality of the material: St Cross in Manchester (58), its majestic walls, soot-stained with mill-smoke, rising sheer from a melancholy sea of brick

58 Manchester St Cross, exterior

terraces; or the vivid Welsh red interior at Penarth (**XIV**), daringly contained by the bluntness of the arcades.

All these bricks are richly textured and of attractively uneven colour, as was almost always the case with good hand-made bricks. They are exact only in size, which allowed Butterfield to keep the mortar joints relatively fine – less than a quarter inch. He chose the thinnest bricks normally available, two and five eighths thick, and laid them generally in English bond, rows of headers alternating with rows of stretchers. In a few early buildings he tried Flemish bond, in which headers and stretchers alternate in the same course, but it is very rare in buildings after 1855. Since his walls were solid, he had no need to use the modern method of facing almost entirely with stretchers. The result is a fine, dense texture, to which the varied colouring of the brick gives life. One has to read the early specifications, which instruct the builder to select 'the most even coloured' bricks for facing, with the very varied

59 Brick bonding: Flemish (left) and English (right)

60 Great Woolstone parsonage, exterior

hand-moulded bricks in mind. At Great Woolstone (60) in 1851 the result was not the dead-even colour of machine-made material, but a subtly speckled pattern of individually perfect bricks.[31]

Even in the south-east however, where mechanization was slow, a higher standard of uniformity gradually followed from competition with the new methods. In some brickworks machine-grinding or the new kiln slightly modified the old methods, but sufficiently to produce a much more uniform and slightly cheaper brick; and although the traditional hand-moulded brick was not significantly challenged before the 1880s, there are a few later buildings for which Butterfield seems to have been forced to a rather lifeless material.[32] There can be little doubt that he regretted this loss of texture. It is significant that he always wanted the rougher brick, even for blue or grey headers, which were semi-vitrified rather than glazed. Certainly in later years when he was able to find a good local brick of naturally varied colour, he exploited its wayward quality with evident delight. Horton church (VIII) of 1867–8 was close to the south Oxfordshire grey brickfields. The 'grey' bricks in its walls run from a rich yellow ochre, through buff and cream to almost white; and some are flushed with pink. The blues are equally changeable: some steely and silvery, others a richer purple; while the 'reds' vary from mauve to orange. Within the basic patterns, all these colours are laid random, so that they merge into each other; the pattern here

61 Pollington church, window and pier

62 Cowick school

distinct, there blurred, flickering on the brick surface like the mottled light and shade from a tree.

Very likely the growing use of colour patterns in Butterfield's brickwork was itself partly in response to the growing uniformity in the material itself. Until the late 1850s, with the notable exceptions of All Saints' (I) and St Thomas Leeds (73), only the slightest variations are introduced to relieve the plain brickwork: a lightly sketched diaper running under the eaves, or perhaps a white half-timbered gable or porch. Sometimes only a short cornice of angled bricks over the principal window,

63   Kirby Maxloe cottages

or voussoirs of smoothed rubbed bricks – both post-medieval devices – are used (140). Similarly, in the interior areas of plain brick are contrasted with stone and white-washed plaster in the simplest possible manner. It is also noticeable that the elementary qualities of the wall are emphasized by windows punched through at right angles (61), and flush to the external surface, even in his very earliest design for Charlton in 1847; and that very often in the 1850s the whole front of a row of cottages, or a school and schoolhouse, will be on the same plane, perhaps distinguished by a varied roofline, but with the wall surface continuous and flat (62, 63).

64 Baldock rectory

From the 1860s, as with stone walls, the trend is reversed (64, 65, 66). Such
continuous flat surfaces disappear, the windows are set distinctly further back from
the wall face and more often given added depth by drip mouldings, and the roof,
previously often finely clipped to within an inch of the gable edge, is now invariably
projected with a brick cornice or bargeboarding. In a few especially elaborate
buildings, such as Keble College and the New Schools at Rugby, Butterfield even
breaks his straight gable and eaves lines by introducing horizontal parapets, with
crowstepping at the gable feet. In most buildings the diaper spreads over more of the

65 Burleigh Street
parsonage

surface, especially the gable, where it often cuts across the rake of the roof; and whereas the earlier diaper was blue, it is now more often picked out in white, giving an added piquancy. At the same time a series of interiors almost completely covered by diaper patterns begins with St Alban's Holborn in 1859–62 (14). Other interruptions to the wall surface come from projecting wall shafts, boldly sunk foliate circles and other shapes in the arcade spandrels (XIV). Externally, besides the bands of indented flowers, and the lozenges and diapering of the brickwork, the Rugby New Schools (67) have windows set back in square or arcaded recesses, oriel windows

66 St Alban's Holborn, clergy house

corbelled out on long wall shafts, a chamfered corner squinched out on the second floor, and a chimney-breast projected on sharp tall vertical ribbing. The continuous brown, white and grey patterning leaves not a square foot of surface untouched.

Outside the library at Keble College the blank wall arcading is combined with buttresses, again in order to enliven the wall surface. Comparisons in Butterfield's handling of buttresses are difficult, because their use in his work is more often hierarchical than purely structural: for, as Ruskin complained in *The Stones of Venice*, buttresses were supposed 'to have something of the odour of sanctity about them;

67 Rugby School, New Schools

otherwise one hardly sees why a warehouse seventy feet high should have nothing of the kind, and a chapel, which one can just get into with one's hat off, a bunch of them at every corner.'[33] Butterfield's churches are indeed always better buttressed than his secular work. In either case the placing of buttresses is normally symbolical, to indicate the entrance doorway, or the orientation of a church, or the division of its nave and chancel, rather than in a position dictated by structural needs. Because of this approach there is more variation in the treatment of buttressing in a single group like Keble College, from the unsupported Warden's House to the tremendous but-

68 Sir Walter St John's School, Battersea, exterior (Sir Walter St John's School)

tresses of the chapel, than there is between one phase of Butterfield's work and the next. Even so, differences are observable. In the plain brick churches of the mid-1850s the buttresses are broad, and entirely of brick, simply shaped with a single massive batter into the wall (9). By the 1860s stone copings become common even in the cheaper churches, and the buttresses become thinner, often with a double batter. Instead of standing at the angles in the direct line of the wall they are moved a few feet to one side, as if to emphasize their structural irrelevance (72). An extreme example is the Margaret Street parish school of 1870, where the spindly porch

69   Newbury St John, parsonage

buttresses clearly support nothing more than the unusually ornate arched stone hoodmoulding applied to the gable.

It is also noticeable that in the more elaborate buildings of the 1860s and 1870s, and especially in the most famous of them all, Keble College, far more stonework is used in the walls. Butterfield's brick churches, it is true, always made some use of stone, and stone bands, and not brick diapers, were the principal decoration of the splendid interiors at Leeds, Baldersby and Alvechurch (III, XII). He also very early realized in London the dramatic effects which could be obtained by contrasting stock brick, which would blacken in time, with the rain-washed white of broad stone window sills, copings and bands. Sir Walter St John's School in Battersea was an especially striking example of the late 1850s (68). From that time, however, ashlar bands also appear in simpler country churches, such as Landford. They are introduced in the later cottages and the agent's house at Baldersby (31), and in the gaunt parsonage at Newbury (69), while in earlier work, such as All Saints', stone had been reserved for the church alone. Besides banding, stone chequers sometimes occur, especially where brick is combined with flint. As the density of these bands and chequers increases, the building gradually loses its essentially brick character, and becomes an indeterminate mixture – the logical consequence of the search for a continuously varied texture (70). Keble College Chapel, as Butterfield himself remarked, 'might nearly as well be called a stone building as a brick one. It is, in fact, neither the one nor the other, but a mixture of both, to the great advantage of each material.'[34]

We shall need to return to the aesthetic meaning of these continuous patterns. But it is essential, however restless and even neurotic they seem, to understand them as a *reaction* to the severe plain flat surfaces of the 1850s. The new elaboration is conceived to provide *relief*: at Keble College (71), for example, where Butterfield could not afford the roofing materials which he preferred, he told Philip Webb that he hoped 'the gay walls would carry the eye somewhat away from the slating'.[35] A century of Oxford smoke sadly obscures their colour now, but in the sunlight one can sense their original gaiety. One can also see, underlying the new texture, reminders of the unrelieved surfaces to which it is deliberately contrasted. Stone tracery is sometimes brought flush to the wall surface, and most windows are still without dripmoulds; string courses and the upright stone verticals of the bay window are so sharp that they break the brick surface without confusing it. In the little church at Dropmore (72) the east window shows the same contrast on a simpler level: the hoodmoulding is raised from the rough brick and flint wall like a clean knife-edge, while the tracery itself is a pattern of thin linear cusping attached to a plate-flat frame. Similarly, in the stone interior at Babbacombe (III) the stone trellis pattern is like a spider's web stretched between the hoodmoulding and the wallplate. Behind it, the continuous surface remains, modulated but intact.

70 Keble College, chapel
from west

71 Keble College, south
quadrangle

The texture of Butterfield's earlier brick buildings was a direct and natural consequence of their method of construction. With his later brickwork this was clearly no longer the case. The structural colour does not penetrate the walls, even though from Baldersby (36) onwards it is carried round window jambs as if it did; the external stone bands in fact rarely correspond to those within. The external banding is used, as in stone buildings, to link external sills and cornices rather than to indicate 'epochs in the wall's existence' such as internal floor levels. The diapers lengthen the shadows under the eaves, or draw together a set of windows into a continuous band, or provide a horizontal link between traceried window-heads (334). Only in the largest buildings, such as Keble College chapel, is there a marked distinction between the strongly banded load-bearing base walls and the lightly chequered upper 'wall veil'; and even here the distinction is not consistent, so that the buttresses are treated almost as if they were extensions of the lower load-bearing walls, but with slight and apparently arbitrary distinctions (70). The system is in fact no more consistent than at All Saints' (I), where the exterior was built before Ruskin had published his theory of structural aesthetics in *The Stones of Venice*: here decoration is progressively reduced as the wall's load increases, and the giant buttresses are left absolutely plain, soft pink, taut at each angle of the building.

The internal structural decoration of All Saints' (X), it is true, owes much more to Ruskin. The basic plans for the church, which had been ready by the summer of 1849, were radically revised after the publication of Ruskin's *The Seven Lamps*. As Beresford-Hope wrote, explaining the rapidly rising estimates for the building, the original costing had been 'on the supposition of its being merely built of common materials. Since then the aesthetic possibilities of different materials have become more and more clear, and the present scheme is that of a church whose character and beauty and effect of colour shall arise from *construction* and not from *superaddition*, namely that, the pillars shall be *made of granite*, and . . . the diaper be an encrustation of tiles, and not the track of a paintbrush.'[36] Butterfield's debt to Ruskin is emphasized by the fact that All Saints' was his only experiment in 'encrustation', that is a mere skin of brick and tile mosaic rather than structural colour.

There were, however, clear limits to Ruskin's influence even here. In *The Seven Lamps* he had supported the use of chequers, stripes and zigzags, and urged that 'geometrical colour-mosaic' should be strenuously taken up.[37] The use of circular patterns in the spandrels is reminiscent of the Doge's Palace at Venice, and the first volume of *The Stones of Venice* had in fact been published before this part of the interior had been completed. On the other hand, Ruskin had unequivocally declared stone to be a superior building material to brick, and he had definitely not advocated the use of tiles rather than natural marbles for mosaic work. Moreover, in the detailing there are as many conflicts as parallels, and many of the parallels which have been suggested by Professor Hitchcock are hardly convincing: for example, Butterfield's colour schemes are far from the blotched and irregular sea shells and bird feathers described by Ruskin. In particular, it is not true that the patterns are disposed, as Hitchcock suggests, 'almost regardless of the architectural forms that cut across them'.[38] If this were so, Butterfield would have been following Ruskin's argument for colouring that, as in nature, 'never follows form, but is arranged on an entirely separate system'.[39] The colour patterns at All Saints' are in fact clearly defined by the architectural surfaces, as may be seen from the placing of circular motifs. The

72 Dropmore church, east end

most obvious case of apparently arbitrary irregularity is the junction between the cross-wall above the chancel arch and the side walls of the nave; but this is deliberate, indicating that the cross-wall is a subordinate division, allowing the main lines of the design to carry through into the chancel. Butterfield's constructional colour was undoubtedly inspired by Ruskin's *The Seven Lamps*, but his system was his own.

This is equally clear in his second experiment in constructional polychromy, St Thomas Leeds (73), which must have been well advanced before the first volume of *The Stones of Venice* was published, for it was consecrated in February 1852. Internally

73   St Thomas Leeds, exterior elevation (R.I.B.A.)

Butterfield here abandoned encrustation for banding in brick and stone, with the voussoirs of the arches also picked out in colour. Externally the system is still as at All Saints', with patterning confined to structurally less significant parts of the wall. The buttresses are again absolutely plain, and at corners, as in the porch, even the stone bands stop short immediately above the buttresses, leaving an absolutely bare wall surface.

There was of course no structural need for the banding to break off thus abruptly. Butterfield's system was not so much the rational expression of structure, as the

74 Pinchbeck Bars parsonage

utmost manipulation of structure for aesthetic ends which was consistent with contemporary demands for reality and truthfulness. He was undoubtedly a daring – if wholly successful – constructor by contemporary standards. From the first his buildings surprised the surveyors to whom they were submitted: even at Coalpit Heath he was obliged to strengthen the aisle walls.[40] At All Saints' the surveyor to the Metropolitan Buildings Office insisted that over a foot should be added to the north wall. Nor was it only the regular surveyor who was sometimes surprised by Butterfield's nerve. Even his colleague G. E. Street, who was the Oxford diocesan surveyor, thought the tower piers which he proposed for Milton church were 'likely to be very weak . . . unless the construction of the work is most carefully attended to.'[41] It is noticeable that as he grew older, Butterfield became more inclined to resist criticism however authoritative its source. Already in the small parish school for St Matthias Stoke Newington, although agreeing to buttress the outer walls, he refused to spoil the roof with tie beams: 'the roof timbers are strongly bolted. The room is but 18 feet wide and the walls two bricks thick upon a sound foundation. The whole building appeared to Mr Butterfield as substantial as any amount of extra buttress could have made it.'[42] At Emery Down, while thickening a south wall to 22 inches and adding a buttress to please the Incorporated Church Building Society, he requested them to allow the internal north wall to remain, 'as the 4″ is a great object in the vestry which is a small one, and a good 18″ wall will bear far more than this one has to carry. The wall above the Chancel arch is hollow for the sake of avoiding unnecessary weight. But if the Society insist upon its being solid I will make it so . . . But they will add needless expense if they do insist.'[43] And at Clevedon, in 1875, he was so angered by Ewan Christian's insistence, on behalf of the Church Commissioners, on thickening the brick walls, that he would have given up the church altogether rather than concede the point.

Structure was thus often bold, sometimes in the cause of economy, but equally often simply to gain effect. Certainly the expression of structure was carefully controlled. Sometimes it was deliberately exaggerated, as in the Balliol west doorway with 'relieving arches of different shapes piled up above it in wonderful confusion.'[44] In other cases it was consciously deceptive, as in the stone-faced churches which conceal brick interiors. Butterfield was even prepared, unlike almost all the other Ecclesiological architects, to conceal a brick wall with roughcast. At Harrow Weald, for example, the nave which he added to a stone chancel was in rendered brick,[45] and a parsonage at Pinchbeck (74) survives with a roughcast upper storey above a limestone rubble ground floor – a charming house, which anticipates Voysey's roughcast style of the 1890s. At Milton, but for the criticisms of Street, cement would have replaced dressed masonry even in the arches: 'a little economy in some other respect might allow perhaps at any rate of the construction of the Tower arches in stone'.

Roughcast was a deception peculiar to the 1850s, when Butterfield was attracted to its grey uniform surface. As his taste developed, and he became more concerned with linear patterns contrasted to the wall plane, another deceit became more appropriate: half-timbering. Butterfield's half-timbered features are always purely superficial, tacked onto the outer surface of a brick wall and filled in with cement. They illustrate the limits of the concept of structural 'reality'; for if contemporaries objected to Butterfield's roughcast, they never complained of the picturesque un-reality of his half-timbered walls. Structural reality – like twentieth-century structural functionalism – was in truth an aesthetic rather than a constructional concept; it operated as part of, rather than in conflict with, the prevailing aesthetic attitudes of the period. The doctrine in no sense implied that Butterfield's walls were the most economic, or the most structurally rational, that he could have built. And when we turn to his roofs, we shall immediately be confronted by the same paradox.

Notes on chapter 9

1 Butterfield to Lord Heytesbury, 21 May 1875, Heytesbury Collection.
2 Notebooks 6 and 24.
3 Cathedral Library.
4 Specifications, Pinchbeck, 1862, Lincolnshire Record Office; *AAS*, (VII) 1863–4, pp. ix, lxxxvi (Caistor); Alec Clifton-Taylor, *The Pattern of English Building*, London, Batsford, 1962, p. 272 (for cob cottages).
5 I, chapter IV.
6 *B*, (21) 1863, p. 587; faculty, 1879, Northamptonshire Record Office.
7 *True Principles*, pp. 18, 45.
8 Whiteparish, faculty, 1869, Wiltshire Record Office.
9 St Mawgan rectory, Notebook 17.
10 (6) 1846, pp. 41–5.
11 I, chapter IV and p. 289 (Second Edition, 1858).
12 (14) 1856, p. 586.
13 *The Stones of Venice*, I, p. 273.
14 Butterfield to the Master, 19 September 1856, Balliol College archives.
15 *BN*, (5) 1859, p. 1033.
16 Rebuilding of the nave was not planned until May 1849, when the restoration had been in progress for some months; and work was stopped in 1852 after Edward Bastard's secession to Rome; the nave decorations date from 1863: faculty papers, Devon Record Office; *Transactions of the Exeter Diocesan Architectural Society*, IV, pp. 245–9; accnts.
17 p. 47.
18 *B*, (29) 1871, p. 491.
19 (1) 1842, p. 209, (6) 1846, pp. 98–101, and (8) 1847, pp. 90–2, 141–7.

20 *Ibid.*; and Butler, *op. cit.*, pp. 57–8. The church was built in 1848 and the design is at the Berkshire Record Office. All Saints' was therefore Butterfield's third brick building, Avington excluded.

21 Quoted by Stefan Muthesius.

22 (22) 1861, p. 317.

23 *Op. cit.*, p. 252.

24 *R.I.B.A. Journal*, (VII) 1900, p. 241.

25 *G*, February 1875.

26 *CB*, January 1863, p.17.

27 Butterfield to Rev. G. S. Holmes, 24 June 1870, Holme upon Spalding Moor chest.

28 'Art Cliques', *BN*, (12) 1865, p. 673.

29 *BA*, (12) 1879, p. 57; *B*, (22) 1864, p. 439; specification, 1858, Letcombe Bassett chest; *ILN*, (61) 1872, p. 393.

30 *E*, (12) 1851, p. 69.

31 Specification, Bodleian Library.

32 There is very little information of the spread of new methods, except for the fact that only machine grinding was in practical use by 1856 (*Journal of the Royal Society of Arts*, pp. 499–500). Mechanization was first introduced at Manchester in 1861, but in the south and south-east as late as 1937 hand-moulding remained the method of 298 out of 365 brickworks, in sharp contrast to a mere 86 out of 1097 brickworks in the rest of the country. (Marion Bowley, *Innovations in Building Materials*, London, Duckworth, 1960, pp. 64, 173.)

33 I, p. 168.

34 *G*, February 1875.

35 Butterfield to Philip Webb, 11 December 1869, *Architectural History*, (8) 1965, p. 55.

36 Hope to Henry Tritton, 6 August 1850, Tritton Collection.

37 p. 161.

38 *Early Victorian Architecture*, 1, p. 584.

39 *The Seven Lamps*, p. 126.

40 I.C.B.S. file 3434.

41 13 February 1854, Bodleian Library.

42 Metropolitan Buildings Office, Third Class Approvals, August 1849, Greater London Council Record Room.

43 Butterfield to secretary, 9 June 1863, I.C.B.S. file 6095.

44 *BN*, (3) 1857, p. 6.

45 *E*, (10) 1849, p. 66.

Daring and deceit reach their climax in Butterfield's roofs. If contemporary surveyors were anxious when they saw his slender walling, they were bewildered by some of his roofs. The Metropolitan surveyor only accepted the roofs at All Saints', which he thought 'very steep – that is to say badly constructed', because they were 'so stout and so well bolted together in every direction and stepped into the wall plates as to remove all possible doubts of their sufficiency'. When he came to the spire, however, whose abruptly steep outline reached a total height of over 210 feet, his critical surprise gave way to admiration of the ingenious wooden structure: the main timbers running up the outer angles, braced every fifteen feet by wrought iron ties, a central iron rod with radiating spokes at each level, and diagonal iron rods running from the outer edges at one level to the centre of the next.[1]

Deception, on the other hand, can also be found in roofs like that of All Saints' nave (157) which simulates the heaviness of stone in spite of its material; or still more clearly, in Butterfield's advice, when restoring Great Berkhamsted church in 1880, that the plain plaster roof of the north transept required modification: 'Some lines of wood applied, as was done in the nave ceiling, to represent rafters might be used here for relief.'[2] In other words, truthful structural expression is not an end in itself, but an aesthetic ideal; and where structure cannot be revealed, it must be shammed.

In the roof the dramatic expression of structure does not normally require such deceits; it is, on the contrary, the natural element for such display. Even in Butterfield's first work at Highbury Chapel (76), although there is no sense of massiveness in the thin walling, and the tall slender piers retain an almost Georgian gothic elegance, the roof is already a remarkable display of structural carpentry, steeply raftered, double-framed, secured by arched braces, a traceried collar, wall posts, and a massive crenellated wallplate. This particular form of roof, moreover, was one which Butterfield continued to use, with slight modifications, for many years; it occurs as late as 1872 in St Mary Stoke, Ipswich (77). There were in fact broadly five types of roof structure used by Butterfield: vaults, flat roofs, collar-braced,

75 St Barnabas
Rotherhithe under
demolition
(Gordon Barnes)

76 Highbury Chapel
interior

trussed-rafter and tie-beam roofs.

Vaults are by far the rarest type. At St Augustine's Canterbury, the library and chapel stand on vaulted undercrofts (78), largely because some evidence of medieval vaulting remained, including a wall shaft in the library undercroft.[3] Nevertheless these traces must have been fragmentary, for Butterfield's design is very closely related to the early thirteenth-century vaulted undercroft of the Archbishop's Palace at Lambeth (79): the wall corbels, the plain circular piers and their capitals, and the method of bringing the eight simply chamfered ribs down on to the capitals, is identical.[4] The only differences – both characteristic – are that Butterfield very slightly thickened the ribs and piers in proportion to the area of the vault, and filled the groins with a warm red brick instead of stone. Both vaults have unfortunately been whitewashed, and the library undercroft has also been split by partitions, but old photographs (taken when it was the college museum) show a triple-aisled room of great beauty, Cistercian rather than Benedictine in its pristine simplicity.

Butterfield's next occasion for vaulting was the chancel at All Saints'. The model is again English thirteenth-century work, in spite of the Italian and German elements in the general conception of the chancel: two bays of very simple cross-vaulting, with

77   St Mary Stoke church, roof

78 St Augustine's College Canterbury, library undercroft (St Augustine's College)

79 Lambeth Palace undercroft (National Monuments Record)

a ridge rib, transverse and diagonal ribs, as, for example, in the choir at Southwell. The ribs are thin, elegantly moulded, and rest on capitals and wall shafts which were closely based upon those at Warmington in Northamptonshire (80). The fact that the roof there (illustrated by Rickman) was a wooden vault of exactly this form no doubt encouraged Butterfield, who had to roof his nave in timber. The original groining, however, emphasized the contrast in materials, for the ribs were of a soft pink alabaster, and the groins filled with grey and white chalk. The effect was obscured by painting, against Butterfield's wishes, and he revealed it again – only to be re-covered in 1910 – when he restored the church in 1895.[5]

Three other vaults were constructed at the same time as All Saints', no doubt as by-products of the thought which it required. At St Matthias Stoke Newington the sanctuary vault was ribbed in stone, with groins of red and yellow brick; at Latton another pointed tunnel-vault is plastered; and at Sheen, he constructed an extraordinary vestry roof, again a tunnel, but very steep, with only transverse ribs, supporting what is in effect an inclined wall, so that the same solid dressed stone forms the external roof. Although there is a medieval precedent in the porch at Barnack, the constructional 'reality' at Sheen is characteristic of Butterfield: and the impracticality

80 Warmington church roof (Rickman, *Gothic Architecture*)

81 Keble College, chapel interior c.1900 (Starey Collection)

82 Rugby School, chapel roof

83 St Augustine's College Canterbury, kitchen roof

of this type of roof perhaps explains why he did not experiment much further with vaulting.

There are, in fact, only two vaults in his later work, and both take up old themes. At Keble College Chapel (81) the vault is a pointed tunnel similar to All Saints', but slightly less sharp, with clustered wall shafts brought down to the ground, so that the effect is much more static, the identity of each bay emphasized, and the eastward movement reduced. These qualities, together with the painted decoration of the chapel, and the emphatic horizontal thickening of the lower wall, make Butterfield's debt to the upper church of S. Francesco at Assisi (11) much clearer than it was at All Saints'.

Finally, at Rugby only the apse of the school chapel (82) is vaulted; but it is no doubt significant that it dates from 1872, when Butterfield was about to begin Keble Chapel. The Rugby vault is not itself interesting – another simple ribbed form – and mosaics added in 1882 now cover the constructional colour of its groins; but it is much more successfully related to the timber roof of the nave than at All Saints'. Instead of giving in each roof hints of the material of the other, a roof of mixed type is put between them under the chapel tower, a gaily painted flat wooden ceiling supported by four spectacular transverse arches and brilliantly side-lit by the windows high up between them.

Of Butterfield's flat timber roofs, which we have now reached, this is undeniably

84   St Augustine's College cloister (*Illustrated London News*, 1848)

the most impressive. Most of them are simply domestic roofs, occasionally enlivened by thin horizontal wooden ribs set in the plaster, a method used by Pugin which already appears at St Augustine's Canterbury (83, 84). In the college kitchen more substantial rafters were exposed, supported by a massive braced vertical strut, and there were also exposed rafters in the cloister, combined with stone cross-arches which anticipate the Rugby roof. There are two other interesting roofs in the Temple Reading Room of 1878 at Rugby (85, 289): in the ground floor triple shallow segmental brick arches run across the room, supported on soft pink and white pillars, while in the studio above a similar alternation of arch and horizontal is achieved by running broad flat sections from the dormer windows straight across a pointed roof, also panelled and plastered. Nor is it a coincidence that all the most interesting flat roofs occur at Canterbury and Rugby – any more than that Butterfield's vaults all occur within a few years: in each case development is a consistent variation of first concepts.

With the remainder of Butterfield's wooden roofs, something must first be said of his general method of construction. They are – like the flat roofs – all built with principals either of oak, usually from Memel or Quebec or, more commonly, of 'the best Memel Fir well seasoned, free from sap, shakes, large and unsound knots.' These were the best two structural timbers available in the period. A cheaper Christiana or Archangel pine was often used for floor battens, which were 'to be stacked in a dry place immediately upon signing the contract'. Where these timbers were left exposed,

85   Rugby School, Temple Art Room   **86**   Thurlaston school chapel, interior

they were either painted, often 'a brown oak colour', 'a good purple brown', or black; or, with the best woods, especially well knotted oak, oiled 'without any colouring mixture', or a 'good oil colour . . . flatted a dead white'; or lastly, with less good timber, 'carefully stained to a clear colour, with beer grounds, umber and terra sienna and varnished two coats'.[6] In constructing the roofs, the rafters and battens were nailed as well as notched, and the principal timbers were bolted with iron at both ridge and wall plate. In his choice of timber, and his use of nails and bolts, Butterfield thus followed the best contemporary rather than medieval precedent.

A few roofs of about 1850, such as Thurlaston, Alfington and Pinchbeck (86, 96), are further strengthened by iron ties. These may be later additions, but there can be no doubt of his interest in iron in this period, for the school and clergy house at All Saints' have cast-iron girders and brackets (87). Although their gothicization now seems incongruous, Gilbert Scott thought them 'the only successful instance I have seen of architecturalizing cast iron beams', so that the spectacular architectural use of girders at St Pancras owes something to Butterfield's influence.[7] In the 1850s the Ecclesiologists in general were sufficiently interested in the material to publish extraordinary designs for a complete church of iron in *Instrumenta Ecclesiastica* (88). Later, however, partly due to a general ebbing of public interest, and partly to Ruskin's furious opposition to its use, they abandoned the structural use of iron members. Butterfield's later attitude is revealed by a scornful letter to the vestry at

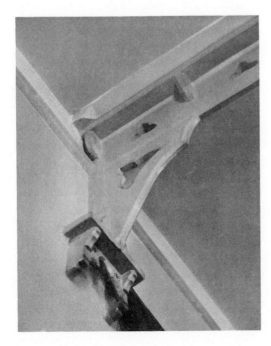

87 All Saints' Margaret Street clergy house, gothic girders

88 Iron church design by W.
Slater (*Instrumenta Ecclesiastica*)

Dundela, where a Belfast builder had suggested the use of iron ties to check the un-even settlement of the church tower: 'But where is the spreading which gives an excuse for such a recommendation? Where are his twelve strong iron tie bars to be placed? He does not say, and I cannot imagine. His mind is far from clear about it. As the movement in the masonry has been caused by a pressure downwards of the heavier walls, of what use can ties be? Iron ties are absurd under almost all circum-stances, as ties to masonry . . . Unless it is wished to injure the Tower by spending money which had much better be thrown into the sea, you will reject the idea of iron.'[8] Even so, Butterfield must have been grateful for the assistance of iron in securing some of the dramatic roofs which he conceived.

In his earlier buildings, Butterfield regarded the double-framed collar-braced roof as the finest form, and although rare after 1870, splendid examples occur as late as 1875 at Brookfield and 1888 at Perth (89, 90). There are several variations of the general type. At Highbury Chapel the horizontal collar is itself very prominent, because it is exceptionally low; and it is also quite prominent at Braishfield (107), where the braces are thin and straight, and in the library at St Augustine's (91), where there are both inclined struts and arched braces, both relatively slender. This last is unique in Butterfield's work, and is perhaps better described as a cruck roof; constructed like the mid-fourteenth-century Leicester Guildhall (92), but a spidery version, perhaps also influenced by the vast criss-cross timbers of late medieval barns.

More generally the straight rafters are contrasted with curved braces rising to the centre of the collar. Although it was structurally desirable, to stop the base of the roof spreading outwards, to start these braces below the wallplate on wall posts, unless the roof was very wide, or rose from the thin high walls of a clerestory, Butterfield pre-ferred a clear start to the roof at the top of the wall: as, for example, at Thurlaston or Waresley (86, 93). When braces sprang from wall posts, as at Wick and Abbotsley (94, 95), it was possible to vary the curve so that a wide face of timber was added to the wall post, or, higher up, to the collar. Again, additional braces could be added above the collar, as at Pinchbeck (96), so that the braces formed a primitive trefoil pattern.

Foliation, when attempted, was generally more elaborate. In the chapel at St Augustine's Butterfield used lace-like foils, lightly attached to the braces, as in the house of John Halle at Salisbury, which was much admired by Pugin; but normally he preferred the bolder foliation of the principals themselves, as in the Herefordshire roofs which he must have seen when at Worcester.[9] A charming early example is the porch at Llangorwen (97). From 1850 the motif is taken up strongly, first as a contrast against the straight rafters, and then much more boldly displayed against white alone, with curved windbraces usually added to carry the pattern over the plastered rafters. The effect clearly pleased Butterfield, for it was used at Belmont, Stickney, Gaer Hill

89 *above* St Mary Brookfield, interior

90 *above right* Perth Cathedral, nave

91 St Augustine's College Canterbury,
library roof (St Augustine's College)

(98) and Hammersmith in 1855–7, an unusual case of a complex design repeated with only the slightest modification.

One last variation in pattern in the collar-braced roof was favoured by Butterfield in the late 1850s (although in cheaper roofs, such as school rooms, it is quite frequent): the scissor-collar, formed by filling the triangular space between two crossed trusses, and often echoed by a similar triangular swelling of the wall braces. A characteristic smaller example was the school at Tattershall (99); the grandest was St Alban's Holborn (14). It is not, of course, a true collar, and the motif heralded Butterfield's shift away from collared roofs in the 1860s.

The first stage in this change was a refinement, so far unmentioned, which Butterfield introduced in most roofs after 1851.[10] Until then the roof rose in the normal medieval fashion, either directly from a broad wallplate, or more commonly from the outer edge of the wall, with a short vertical strut in line with the inner wall face rising to each rafter. Although this strut forms a visual link between roof and wall, there is

92 Leicester Guildhall (National Monuments Record)

93 *above* Waresley church, nave roof

94 *above right* Wick church, interior

95 Abbotsley church, roof

96 Pinchbeck Bars church, roof

97 Llangorwen church, porch roof

98 Gaer Hill church, roof

still an abrupt change of plane at the rafters; and so in 1851, at Huddersfield (100), Butterfield inclined the struts very slightly inwards, with the result that the wall plane is transformed by two subtle stages into the steep raftered roof. The whole spatial shape of the interior gains a new elegance at the same time. Although the motif is probably derived from the old palace at Hatfield (a brick building, which would have interested Butterfield at this date) its aesthetic possibilities were much more fully exploited by the longer struts at Huddersfield, and then very quickly transferred to a trussed-rafter roof at Langley (101).

Trussed-rafter roofs are strictly single-framed, that is, without longitudinal ties except at the ridge and wallplate. Consequently the rafters can spread outwards quite easily, and for this reason many of Butterfield's roofs of this type, especially the later examples, are in fact double-framed, with principals and wall posts interrupting the run of rafters. They are also unconventional in that, while some medieval roofs combined scissors braces with a collar, the horizontal collar rather than the pointed

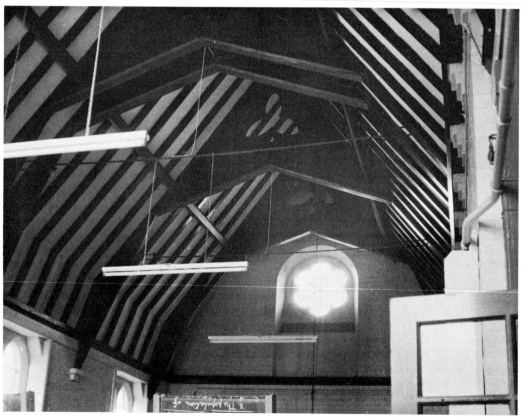

99   Tattershall school, interior

scissor usually formed the apex of the roof (102). Apart from some early examples at St Augustine's and at Ash near Canterbury, Butterfield's trussed roofs are invariably scissors-braced.

The visual attraction of the trussed-rafter roof is that it can provide a much more unified roof surface. The rafters are normally closely spaced, and their linear pattern continuous, unbroken by heavier principals, and reaching from wall to wall rather than soaring away to the infinity of a steep apex. When, as at Langley, the lowest struts are also inclined, and each section of the underside is of equal length, a perfectly even rhythm is achieved. Butterfield's early use of the roof form to cover oddly-shaped spaces like the Cumbrae Chapter house (103), and his avoidance of principals and wall posts until the late 1860s, confirm this quality; the only important exception, the cloister roof at Cumbrae (104), is another fascinating mixed type, in which the principals are closely spaced crucks, placed between the rafters, alternately paired and single, so that three close rhythms are interwoven.

100   Huddersfield St John, roof (National Monuments Record)

For the same reason, where a completely boarded roof was required, normally to provide a painted ceiling to the sanctuary, the six-sided roof provided an admirable shape. Butterfield used a diagonally ribbed ceiling of this type, which he discovered at Trumpington, at Merton College (348), and later at Babbacombe (105); and without diagonals at, for example, Langley and Balliol (106, 158). It is noticeable that the lowest section of these boarded roofs remains vertical until the later 1850s, possibly because they were less expressive of structure. This is also true of other boarded roofs, such as the collar-braced nave at Braishfield (107), a rare case of bare unpainted boarding, fixed diagonally, and also of the beautiful chancel cradle at Baldersby (36).

It is worth asking why Butterfield very rarely used the curved cradle, or wagon roof, the form of trussed-rafter in which all the braces are arched. It provides a perfect junction with the wall surface, together with absolute evenness. His noble open wagon roofs at Dorchester and Amesbury Abbeys show that he appreciated its

101   Langley church, nave roof

quality; but the wagon had disadvantages. Its very purity demanded a setting both plain and dignified: space, strong uninterrupted walls, and similar curves to the arcades, window heads and other arches. These conditions were rare in Butterfield's larger churches, and the wagon is not easily adapted to awkward circumstances. The open cradle, moreover, has no eastward linear direction, apart from its ridge. For these reasons he used the wagon only once in later years, at Ascot Priory Chapel, where for once the setting was perfectly appropriate (291).

The more adaptable trussed-rafter, on the other hand, became indispensable to Butterfield as his tastes changed in the late 1850s. We have seen how collar-braced roofs became exercises in black and white patterning. Trussed-rafters, particularly when plastered level with the rafter face, provided more delicate linear patterns: and at Winchester Hospital Chapel (108) he turned the inclined struts into a diagonal pattern of cross-bracing on the upper ceiling. The pattern is in fact non-structural, simply tacked onto the ceiling, and where there is a gap in the ceiling at the dormer

102 Long Stanton church, roof (Brandon, *Open Timber Roofs*)

103 Cumbrae College,
chapter house roof

104 Cumbrae College,
cloister

105 All Saints' Babbacombe church, chancel roof (National Monuments Record)

106 Langley church, chancel roof

107 Braishfield church, interior

108 Winchester Hospital, chapel roof

windows it carries on as a skeleton of flying ribs. It is used again, delightfully contrasted with the chancel screen, at Godmersham (109). Characteristically the church
at Dropmore (110), also designed in 1865, explores the same contrast with a collar-
braced roof and a heavier screen. Butterfield preferred the result at Godmersham, and
used lighter patterns with his later screens. The spaces between the lines are widened,
however, so that they usually enclose white squares, and the roof is clearly a ceiling
and no longer structurally deceptive. The later patterns are on the whole uninteresting
six- or four-sided grids. Three exceptions are the Salisbury Theological College
Chapel, where long diagonals form an attractive sanctuary cradling (111); the
pretty foliate chequer at Christleton (51); and Whiteparish (112), where the pattern
is brought down the underside of a turret staircase, swinging dramatically down the
roof slope, back over an arch, and down across the west window – an entertaining
display of structural gymnastics.

Nevertheless, it is undeniable that the characteristic late Butterfield roof, the low
four-sided linear grid, is both structurally and aesthetically much less interesting than
the steep raftered collar-braced roof of earlier years. Although the later roof was first
developed for chancels, it represents a general tendency; and gradually, especially
as Butterfield sought a continuous roof to both nave and chancel, it came to pre-

109 Godmersham church, roof and
screen

110 Dropmore church,
roof and screen

111 Salisbury Theological
College, chapel interior

112 Whiteparish church, roof and staircase

dominate. The general trend which allowed this victory is clearly revealed by the analysis of nave roof types below. Even where earlier forms are used, they are modified; the closely spaced trussed-rafter roof at Poulton, for example, is very low, although six-sided, and has wall posts (113); the Ascot cradle is round arched, rather than pointed (291); and the last high collar-braced roofs have emphatic wall posts brought down to the spandrels of the arcades (90). More commonly, they are ceiled or plastered, as at Rugby (52) and Enfield, so that the roofline is brought down to the arched braces of the principals. Butterfield's later experiments with flat roofs stem from the same aesthetic purpose; and so does his revival of the horizontal tie-beam roof, the last type which we have to consider.

Table 4

Nave Roofline Types

	1840–9	1850–9	1860–9	1870–9	1880–92	total
High	10	24	8	4	1	47
Low	—	—	8	12	11	31
% high	100	100	50	25	8	62

A few roofs up to 1850, such as West Lavington (114), and the reconstructions at Sessay and Kinwarton (173), use tie-beam roofs with king or queen posts. Ties then disappear until the mid-1860s. But from Manchester (115) onwards, they are usual in high roofs, and often emphasized by crenellation. At Rotherhithe the bold black patterns of the 1850s were recaptured with a tie and king post (75); and other, more conventional king posts occur, slender at Godmersham, and massive at Weston upon Trent (116, 117). Other variations are the flat panelled roof on arched braces at Ellough in Suffolk – a mongrel collar (118); and the mixed tie and hammerbeam of the nave at Rugby chapel, with its characteristically involved alternation. By far the most attractive tie-beam roof, however, is at Brigham in Cumberland, where gay painted patterns set off the foliated principals and posts (119).

So much, then, for the richly varied expression within Butterfield's roofs. We have yet to consider their external form. So far as materials go, this is relatively simple. The cheapest traditional material, thatch, was never used except in a colonial church at Victoria West, South Africa, and the restoration of a Suffolk church at Ringsfield (344); and the most expensive, lead, scarcely except at Keble Chapel (132). Usually, therefore, the choice lay between tiles and slates; and in most areas, as in his walls, Butterfield chose the best traditional material. Outside London, his brick buildings in the south-east are generally roofed in local tiles, often made from the same clay as the brick walls, and thus perfectly matched: red at Letcombe Bassett, with 'plain ridge tiles of local clay', for example, and at Trumpington a delightfully mottled Cambridgeshire blue, buff and pale yellow. Butterfield never extended the systematic patterning of his walls to the roof, which therefore always relies for its effect simply on good materials and a good shape. The tiles, secured by oak pegs to fir laths, were

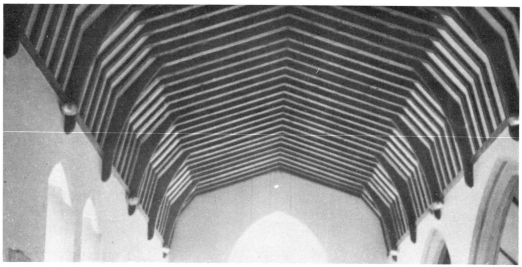

113   Poulton church, interior

'laid to a good lap', occasionally with mortar – 'under the hollow of the tile only', and always very slightly 'tilted against gables'.[11] Specially moulded plain tiles were used for valleys and hips, where the slight tilt gives a generous effect; and at the ridge there were normally plain bonnets. In churches, however, and also in some larger schools and houses, specially moulded crested dark Staffordshire tiles were used on the ridge. They were normally made by Mintons, and simply serrated or undulated, but the effect is complicated in most later buildings by interrupting them with plain tiles. Butterfield did not otherwise use decorated shapes in his tiles, apart from two houses of 1849 at Alfington (120) and Ogbourne St George where some of the walls

114 West Lavington church, interior

are tilehung with traditional undulated shapes; but this experiment was not repeated except in his last two farmhouses.

In stone districts the traditional material was again usually appropriate. In Wiltshire and the Cotswolds, Butterfield preferred the limestone roof tiles quarried at Stonesfield, which weather especially attractively; the little school at Poulton, its mossy tiles perfectly graded from eaves to ridge, is a delightful example (121). Further west and north there were excellent slates: blue-grey Delabole in Cornwall, the browner grey Willand Abbey slate north of Exeter, the range of Penrhyn greys in Wales, and the greenish grey Borrowdale slate in the north. Although always harder

115   Manchester St Cross church, interior

and sharper in effect than clay or limestone tiles, and generally of uniform size, without grading or tilting to the gables, Butterfield's slate roofs present yet another range of textures, never deliberately patterned, but sometimes delightfully blotched, elsewhere crisply uniform, just as the greys may be deep or silvery, or subtly tinged with blue or green (16, 333). Once again, the only variation is at the ridge, where he followed the normal method of using dark Staffordshire tiles, again, in the more important buildings, with ornamental cresting.

There were, however, many districts in which a local slate or tile was not easily available. The success of the Penrhyn quarries in north Wales had already broken

116 Godmersham church, nave roof

many of the traditional local boundaries before the end of the eighteenth century. The best Welsh slates were in fact not merely often cheaper, but technically superior, lighter, and making a closer fit. Provided the colour was good, and the design recognized their precise texture, they could be equally good-looking. Thus in Manchester and in London – where by the mid-nineteenth century tiles would have been an incongruous archaism – Butterfield invariably used slate roofs. Again, there were many districts where local stone could be had, but no stone tiles: Kent, for example, or north Somerset. Here his practice varied; there are yellowish white Brabourne tiles on Broad Street School at Canterbury, and warm red roofs at Axbridge; but in

117   Weston upon Trent church, roof

general, particularly in churches, Butterfield seems to have felt that stone walls demanded a slate roof.

A different difficulty was raised by districts where pantiles were the common material, such as Bristol, or eastern England. Pantiles had two serious disadvantages. Although making a lighter roof then ordinary tiles, because they were not double-lapped, they kept the rain out less well, so that even in the drier parts of the country they were not generally used for important buildings – even farmhouses often have ordinary tiles when their barns are pantiled; and in addition, pantiled roofs were traditionally of low pitch. These drawbacks explain why, apart from a terrace of

118 Ellough church, interior

about 1850 at Sessay (122), probably his first Yorkshire cottages, Butterfield avoided pantiles. Some of his Yorkshire brick buildings were roofed with ordinary tiles, but most were originally slated.

Price, as well as performance and appearance, was of course crucial to many choices of material. In Wiltshire, for example, limestone tiles were a luxury. At Heytesbury, although some parishioners would have preferred even ordinary tiles to Penrhyn slate, slate was significantly cheaper, and for such a large roof limestone tiles would have been out of the question.[12] At Keble, despite his general admiration of the buildings, Philip Webb thought the cheap slates used 'a real drawback': 'I

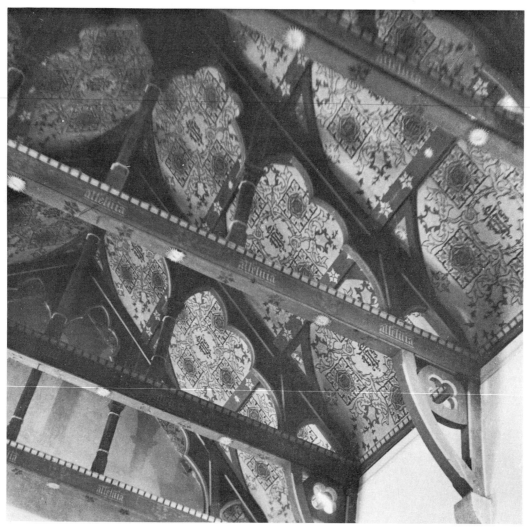

119   Brigham church, nave ceiling

cannot forgive you for using cold blue slates . . . You will most likely say that you had no money for grey Westmorland slates, and I shall say in answer, Tis a great pity that you hadn't.' He was right; Butterfield replied: 'I of course feel with you about the blue slates . . . The Committee was bent on economy and was composed of persons who did not I imagined care for the question of colour in slates, and I had not the courage, with further works in prospect for which I knew there was not enough money, to ask them for any extras of an artistic kind.' He had tried to so design the buildings to 'carry the eye somewhat away from the slating', and his modifications of the roofline in the later south quadrangle (71) show his continued anxiety to minimize

120 Alfington school and house, from the west

121 Poulton school

122 Sessay cottage terrace

the fault.[13] There is no doubt that Butterfield's cheaper slate roofs were chosen with reluctance. He would have supported a recent description of Borrowdale slate as 'the loveliest roofing slate in Britain, fine in grain and unforgettable for its green colour'.[14] Borrowdale must surely have supplied the exquisite silvery weathered roof at Cumbrae (270); and certainly Butterfield, in his last changes at All Saints' in 1895, replaced the original Welsh grey with Westmorland slate on the spire (I).

It is possible that the economic difficulty in obtaining a good-looking roof material where tiles were inappropriate contributed to the underlying change in Butterfield's roof form. His early roofs are all steep, their gables approximating to the equilateral triangle recommended by Pugin in *True Principles*.[15] From about 1860, even when the internal structure is a high collar-braced roof, the pitch is invariably lowered to forty-five degrees outside. Occasional experiments can be found with still lower pitches at Horton school, and even with flat roofs at Wraxall (123) and Monyash, although

123 Wraxall inn, flat roof

these cannot be authenticated, and are possibly not by Butterfield.[16] Certainly the use of a horizontal parapet to reduce the visible area of roof first occurs in the late 1860s, in the New Schools at Rugby (67).

Despite this fundamental change in pitch, there is an extraordinary continuity in the roof forms developed by Butterfield. From first to last his dominating interest is the continuous ridge line. In this he made an important contribution to the High Victorian style. The tendency towards a continuous ridge can be found in Pugin, if one compares the 'old English mansion' of *True Principles* in 1841 with the frontispiece to the *Apology* of 1843 (124, 125); and in the long dark ranges of student rooms at Maynooth College, begun in 1845, it was fully realized. Yet the great uninterrupted roofs of St Augustine's library and students' range at Canterbury are not only a little earlier than Maynooth, but a far bolder demonstration of the new principle (47, 168). Very likely Pugin would have seen them, for they were close to his home at Ramsgate;

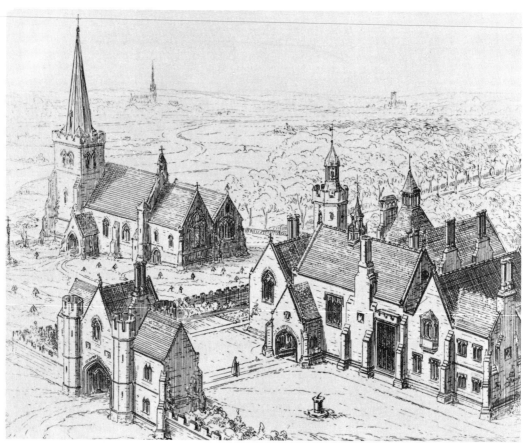

124   A.W.N. Pugin, church and manor house (*True Principles*)

and certainly they were noticed by other architects – Street, for example, still thought the 'great and unbroken length' of the dormitory range worth a special mention in 1853.[17] Meanwhile in *The Seven Lamps* Ruskin had proclaimed in 'The Lamp of Power' that 'a building, in order to show its magnitude, must be seen all at once. It would, perhaps, be better to say, must be bounded as much as possible by continuous lines'.[18] Butterfield's practice had thus become a High Victorian doctrine.

As such, it was as dramatic a reversal of early Victorian picturesque principle as was the assertion of the continuous wall plane. Pugin had argued in *True Principles* that 'an architect should exhibit his skill by turning the difficulties which occur in raising an elevation from *a convenient plan* into so many *picturesque beauties*; and this constitutes the great difference between the principles of classic and pointed domestic architecture. In the former *he would be compelled to devise expedients to conceal these irregularities*; in the latter *he has only to beautify them*'.[19] Since convenience, as we have seen, was

125 A.W.N. Pugin, frontispiece to *Apology*

126 Aston Cantlow schoolhouse

127 Cowick church, exterior

128 Wykeham church, exterior

129   *above left* Pollington church, exterior

130   *above right* Hensall church, exterior

131   Wantage cemetery chapel

132   *opposite* Keble College, chapel from the north

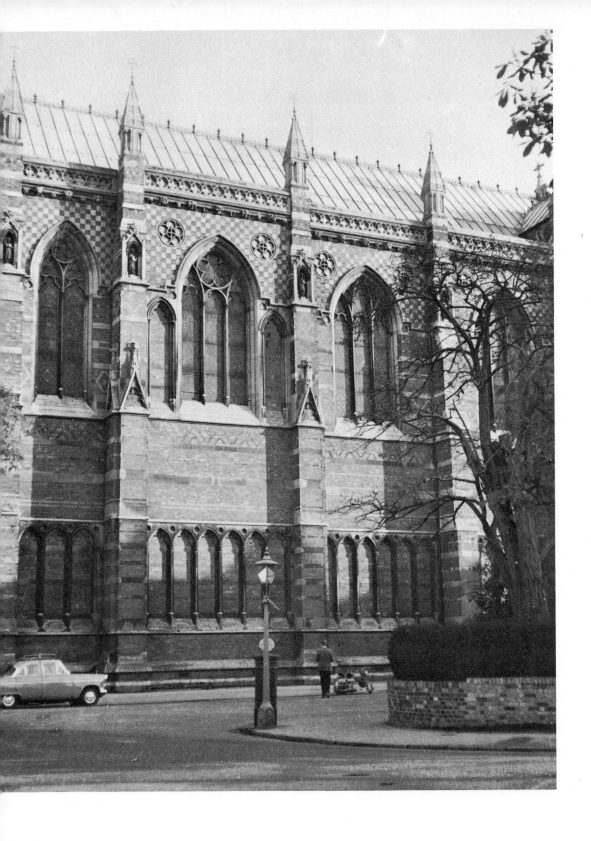

133 Northington schoolhouse, chimney and dormer

134 *below* Great Bookham, cottage pair

135 *below right* Wraxall inn, stable roofs

136 Yealmpton school

137 Pollington school

138 Alfington school and house, from the north

139 Hursley lodge

140 Pollington vicarage, exterior from
the south

141 Pollington vicarage, exterior from
the east

to a great extent an expression of social or spiritual hierarchy, its natural expression was to be a picturesque irregularity of scale directly related to the social function of the parts of the building. There is not doubt that Butterfield shared this view. At St Augustine's, we have noticed how he raised the principal's roof above that of the fellows (29); and the adjacent chapel roof, although no higher, is projected and emphasized by a gable; the refectory then recedes, and is followed by the lower long line of the dormitory range; and finally, the opposite side is crowned by the high ridge of the library. The same principle is observed in a looser group, like the village at Baldersby, rising in scale from almshouse to cottage, school to parsonage, and all overshadowed by the sheer steep church spire; or, in miniature, by the school at Aston Cantlow, where the roofline of the schoolmaster's cottage starts a little below the classroom gable, drops a few inches at the scullery, and finally, very distinctly, over the lean-to outhouse (126).

There were other difficulties to the continuous bounding line. Certain parts of buildings, such as stables, school cloakrooms, porches and church towers, could not have been incorporated within the main roofline without serious practical as well as symbolic disadvantages. In most buildings either lean-to roofs or variations in the ridge-level were thus essential. Chimneys also broke the skyline, and in many houses, especially with steep roofs, dormer windows were needed to light the upper floor, which would interrupt the eaves if not the ridge. Most fundamental of all was the

142 Bamford vicarage, exterior

143 Dropmore vicarage, exterior

fact that, unless pitched roofs were concealed – which would have denied both gothic precedent and principle – every ridge-line in one direction necessitated a gable face in the other. A gable was, by definition, the rupture of the horizontal bounding line. Moreover, in a building of any breadth, unless it was possible to use a gentler slope to the lower roofs, as over the aisles of a church, two ridges were almost essential. Contrasts were thus inevitable in all but the smallest building; and Butterfield, accepting their inevitability, used them as a picturesque foil to the continuous bounding line.

In general, the roofs of churches and chapels are relatively simple. The main ridge is first continuous at Thurlaston school chapel of 1849, and from then onwards Butterfield usually brought the chancel roof either right up to the nave ridge, or within a few inches of it. Aisles and vestry are nearly always lean-to, often brought very close below the nave eaves as at Cowick, or – despite a clerestory – at Wykeham (127, 128). Occasionally the nave roof continues over the aisles, the slope becoming less steep, as at Sessay (254); and at Pollington the whole south side is continuous (129). Hensall characteristically is a compromise between Cowick and Pollington, all three built in 1854: the nave is separate, but aisles, vestry and chancel continuous (130).

None of these roofs are absolutely uninterrupted, because they are broken by a west belfry, a chimney for the heating chamber, and a porch, placed at right angles so that its ridge neatly intersects the eaves of the main building. In two churches of the 1850s central rather than west towers separate nave from chancel, breaking the line; with dramatic effect at Milton, where the tower buttresses seem to paw the vestry blocking its move towards the nave (277). Later churches seem in general more complex in their roofline, with gabled organ chambers usual from the 1860s, and sometimes full transepts at right angles to the main roof. Nevertheless the long ridge is still there; it is simply closer to the parapet or eaves, because with a lower pitch less of the roof is seen, so that interruptions are more obvious. In his notes on his Clevedon church Butterfield particularly mentioned that 'the roof ridge is carried through at one level throughout the whole length of the church'.[20]

Perhaps the contrast is best put by two of Butterfield's very simplest roof shapes. The Wantage cemetery chapel roof of 1849, apart from a variation in the gable treatment (the west gable has a parapet) is a steep stone tile covering of perfect simplicity (131). The Keble College Chapel roof (132) is equally fine, a long strip of ridged and crested lead glistening above the pinnacles of the parapet. But at Wantage one is confronted by a surface; at Keble by lines. The change thus follows that of the internal roof structure.

The roof form of secular buildings is rarely as simple, and it is therefore more significantly affected by the treatment of the chimneys, the gable ends and dormer

144 Wykeham
vicarage,
outbuildings

windows. These motifs change as Butterfield's style evolves. Most of the chimneys are battered inwards in stages as they rise, but they vary from the earliest form, with one very pronounced batter and a slender stack, as at Coalpit Heath (6), to a hesitant threefold batter sometimes found in the 1860s, as at the charming flint school-house at Northington, or the restlessly patterned parsonage at Dropmore (133, 190). Generally wall stacks have a double and ridge stacks a single batter. A few chimneys of the middle years are absolutely vertical, beginning with the splendid ribbed chimneys of Milton Ernest (260); and at Great Bookham a strange high pair of cottages builds up with three levels of horizontal roof to a clear vertical central chimneystack (134). From the 1860s octagonal Tudor clusters are also used (139). At the top, where they have not been maimed or disfigured by the addition of chimneypots, the stacks are beautifully finished: moulded, sharp level, or battered and crested according to their type (16, 141, 313).

Dormers can either sit on the roof slope, as in some of the first examples in the 1840s (126), or rise through the eaves, with their face flush with the wall, as was Butterfield's normal practice. They can be formed by a lip of roof raised from the main surface, a method strikingly used at Pollington; or, more commonly, straight or hip gabled. The straight gable is the natural and earliest form, and occurs through-

out Butterfield's work, often bold in the 1850s, like the double dormers at Wykeham (144); later, sometimes a mere nibble at the eaves. The hip gable was, however, to Butterfield the most attractive form. It first occurs, small and rather timid, in the late 1840s, and at Cumbrae in 1849 it is used for main gable as well as for dormers (269). The hip gable remained from then onwards one of the most persistent motifs in Butterfield's work; and like the chimneystack, its subtle variations help to indicate the changes in his tastes. The first hip dormers, until 1855, are small, but rise well up above the eaves, and their hips are steep, generally steeper than the main roof. During the 1850s they tend to broaden and sink down, until the hip, lying parallel to the main roof surface, is often raised only a few inches above it (255). This severe form begins to give way, in the late 1850s, to two more complex shapes. The brow of the dormer had been either kept level, or if close to the eaves brought diagonally down to them; now, as in the Baldersby parsonage (34), or more simply at Northington (133), it is first brought down towards the eaves but then back into the roof horizontally – a fivefold instead of a single or a threefold line. In the second new form, the straight face of the dormer is changed to an angled bay, and its roof thus itself becomes fivefold. It is this last, most linear form, first used with brilliant effect to crown the rich south front of Milton Ernest Hall (261), which became Butterfield's usual type of hip gable from the late 1860s.

With main gables there is the same hesitant beginning, becoming bolder in the 1850s; but from the 1860s, because of the lower roof pitch, which makes a full hip a drastic motif, it is used much less often. Finally, towards 1880, in the barns at Ardingly and the stables at Wraxall, a double hip to a very short ridge appears, forming roof shapes like elongated pyramids of grand simplicity (38, 135).

The basic methods of assembling these motifs, in schools as in houses, are relatively simple. With schools, except for the rare single-room school like Letcombe Bassett, the problem was to provide for both large and small classrooms, outside cloakrooms, and very often also a master's cottage. The most drastic solution was to put the accommodation in a long line, adding lean-to roofs where necessary, and distinguishing the various parts by very subtle variations to an effectively continuous ridge-line. The attractive unfinished slate and stone school at Yealmpton was of this kind (136); and at Pollington (137) a brick school and master's cottage run end to end with five adjustments of level, pitch and eaves to mark the changes.[21] More commonly, however, Butterfield placed the cottage and smaller room at right angles to the main school room, keeping the main ridges at the same level, but providing each front with a combination of ridgeline and gable. The result could vary from the bare simplicity of Cowick to the intricacy of Baldersby (33, 62).

A third possibility, used in the group at Alfington (138), and rather less obviously in many pairs of cottages, was to build the roofs up to a rough pyramid, with a chimneystack normally forming the apex. At Alfington the ridge is stepped down in

146 Baldersby, agent's house

each direction as it runs outwards, and each front is thus composed of a series of gable ends. This method is also used in a later cottage at Hursley (139), but in such extreme forms it is rare; gables are almost always subsidiary to the horizontal, even in steep pairs like the Great Bookham cottages.

With terraces of cottages, Butterfield naturally used the horizontal ridge. Usually some very slight variation to the eaves, wall face or ridge distinguishes the cottages, but never sufficient to break the effect of continuity. Most houses, however, were more complex, and required more than one main ridge. The severest solution again appears in the 1850s: at Pollington the two ridges are parallel, the cross-ridge hidden between them, continuous ridges to north and south, twin gables east and west (140, 141). Although no later house is so unqualified, at Bamford the longer lower ridge is broken only by a central cross-gable (142). At Little Faringdon the front ridge is similarly broken, but the horizontal is reasserted by the second ridge behind, shorter but higher (48); while at Dropmore, again of the 1860s, double ridges at different levels interlock in each direction (143). As the designs become more complex, once again the criss-cross linear patterns seem to oust the original plain surfaces.

The more common solution with the larger house, as with the school, was to put the main roof ridges at right angles, forming an L shape with a combination of gables and horizontal on each front. Although the interlocking ridges could be extravagantly expressed in the elevations, as in the Baldersby parsonage (34), Butterfield usually preferred the simple statement: gothic at Coalpit Heath, absolutely plain at Pinchbeck and Hensall, elaborate but stern at Newbury (6, 19, 69, 74).

147 Alvechurch rectory, south front

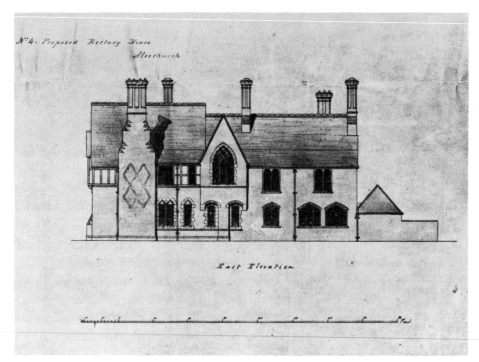

148 Alvechurch rectory, east elevation (Church Commissioners)

149 Alvechurch rectory, north elevation (Church Commissioners)

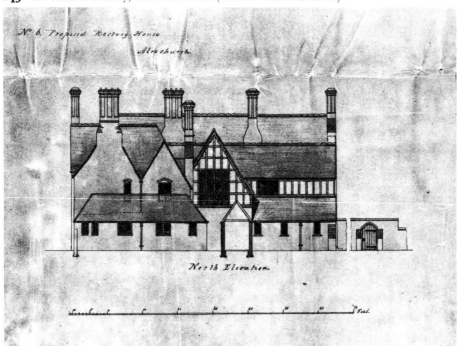

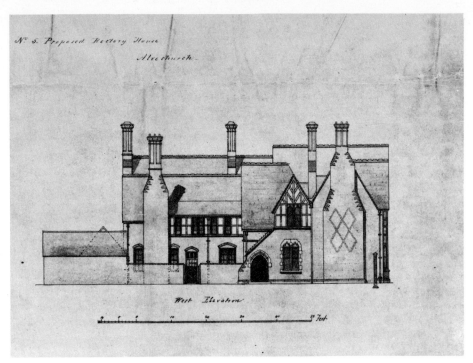

150 Alvechurch rectory, west elevation (Church Commissioners)

151 Alvechurch rectory, roof plan (Church Commissioners)

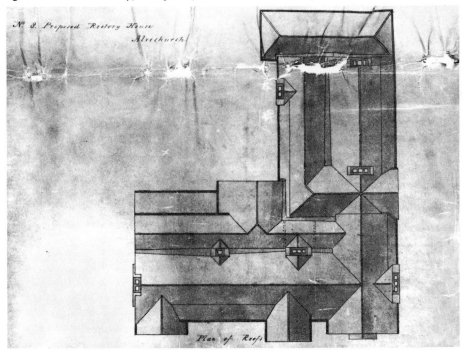

Finally, there were those houses too large to confine within the influence of a single dominant roof shape. For these, Butterfield would sometimes treat the main house severely, but turn its gables towards the stables and outbuildings, creating a sudden and fascinating pattern of triangles, as if its smooth sheet glass was shattered at the scullery. At Wykeham parsonage the outbuildings run in a long line, continuing the angle of the drive (144, 145); at the Baldersby agent's house they form a yard (146); and at St Mawgan, where the effect is much simpler, they follow the curve of the combe. Similarly at Milton Ernest Hall, where long ridge-lines face the park, the inevitable gables are turned towards the entrance courtyard, only revealed as the drive leaves the avenue, as if to mitigate the formality of arrival (258, 259, 260).

The Milton Ernest roofline was the richest that Butterfield has yet designed, but before the roof was on he had another, still more intricate, for Archdeacon Sandford at Alvechurch. 1855 was once again a turning point; for at Alvechurch, for the first time, the main roof surface is itself fragmented. It is, moreover, an extreme case, for later roofs, however linear in conception, are never so methodically broken except in outbuildings. The tangled roofs of the Keble servants' building, for example, are equivalent to the agent's yard at Baldersby, a deliberate foil to the continuous bounding line of the main roof. But at Alvechurch (147–150) even the main south front is fractured by three tall gables, patterned with herringbone half-timbering; the long east range is broken backed at the chapel; while the north and west sides, which face the drive, show altogether four high ridge levels, two lower levels for lean-to roofs and outhouses, and seven gable-ends. It is as if the entrance was intended to reveal to the visitor the full section and structure of the building, like a long fish that had been chopped and bent in half to reveal its guts and skeleton. But the analogy is false, for the plans show clearly that the Alvechurch roof is not a frank expression of structure, but an ornamental construction of great artificiality, requiring deep valleys which must be extremely difficult to keep clean and waterproof (151).

The pursuit of patterns begins here, technically and visually ruthless; and it is fortunate for Butterfield's reputation that, before he designed another house on this scale, he had developed the more sensitive linear method of the 1860s. Butterfield's roofs can all be compared, in some sense, to tents; but the great high tents of the 1840s are gradually tightened down, until they are closely folded over the buildings; and eventually they fly in fragments, leaving nothing but the lines of the ropes. It is at Alvechurch that the canvas splits, and the sight is harsh.

Notes on chapter 10

1 Metropolitan Buildings Office, Third Class Approvals, 1851–2, County Hall.

2 Report, 24 November 1880, Great Berkhamsted chest.

3 Boggis, *op. cit.*, p. 149.

4 *BE, London* (2), plate 2a.

5 *B*, (17) 1859, p. 376; *Church Times*, 25 September 1895.

6 Broad Street school specification, 1847, Canterbury Cathedral Library: Great Woolstone rectory, 1851, Bodleian Library; Alvechurch rectory, 1855, Church Commissioners.

7 *Remarks*, p. 108.

8 29 March 1888, Dundela chest.

9 *BE, Wiltshire*, p. 27 and plate 30b; *Herefordshire*, p. 36 and plate 34.

10 Pointed out to me by Stefan Muthesius.

11 Specification, 1849, Trumpington chest.

12 Butterfield to Lord Heytesbury, 22 March 1866, Heytesbury Collection.

13 Philip Webb to Butterfield, 27 November, and Butterfield to Webb, 11 December, 1869, *Architectural History*, 1965, pp. 54–5.

14 Clifton-Taylor, *op. cit.*, p. 171.

15 p. 11.

16 The original plan for Horton had neither house, nor low-pitched porch; the Wraxall roofs could be additions; and the Monyash porch a faithful restoration of a fourteenth-century original.

17 *E*, (141) 1853, p. 72.

18 p. 68.

19 p. 63.

20 R.S.S., *Complete Guide to Clevedon*. The notes on St John's were partly supplied by Butterfield and partly by Sir Arthur Elton: diaries, 30 May 1878.

21 The present texture is due to re-roofing of some parts. The small south cross-wing appears to be an addition, and the whole south side of the school has now been incorporated with a new building.

11 Colour

Butterfield described his work himself as 'largely dependent on, and connected with, coloured material. I should be sorry to see such works published unless that treatment could be done justice to'. Yet he has scarcely received such justice. The paper which quoted his letter introduced it with the statement that 'Butterfield like Burges seems to have had an insensitive eye for colour'.[1] From the very start his constructional colour at All Saints' and at Oxford was abused by a minority of critics, and in his later years, when High Victorian colour tastes had been generally abandoned, 'his views did not coincide with those even of his friends'.[2] At Keble College (71, XX) the walls which Butterfield himself intended to be 'gay' were at once dubbed 'the most approved "holy zebra" style', the 'startlingly contrasted colours . . . destroying all breadth and repose'.[3] According to his obituary in the *R.I.B.A. Journal* the buildings could 'only be properly appreciated upon a foggy day or in a photograph . . . The chapel interior is wracked by restlessness, and probably nothing but whitewash would exhibit its full dignity of design.'[4]

Clearly Oxford had not found 'the restfulness and strength, and sense of communion that come of quiet order, completeness and proportion', which Butterfield had intended in the chapel.[5] On the contrary, it became a habit of undergraduates and younger dons 'to break off on their afternoon walks in order to have a good laugh at the quadrangle'; and so loud was their laughter that when Sir Kenneth Clark wrote his pioneering reappraisal of *The Gothic Revival* in 1927, he could not find the confidence to write a chapter on Butterfield. It would have indeed required some nerve to refer with any respect to what Oxford opinion considered 'the ugliest building in the world', and at that time attributed to Ruskin with such confidence that Clark was called a liar at a public meeting for disagreeing. Yet even in the revised edition of 1950, his respect took a backhanded form: Butterfield was 'the first master of discordant polyphony'.[6] Summerson reacted to Butterfield's constructional colour in exactly the same way: 'These black bands are the Puritan answer to the sensuous beastliness of what we now call "texture" – they oppose sensibility.'[7]

Such responses reveal the continuing hold, even in criticism of the Gothic Revival, of classical instincts; of the divinity of whiteness proclaimed by Alberti, Palladio and the theorists of the Renaissance. Their belief in colourlessness was none the less powerful for being in conflict with most previous architectural tradition; so much so that in the mid-nineteenth century not merely constructional polychromy, but even pure red brick was thought a bold gesture. As late as 1871 the architect J. J. Stevenson defiantly called his plain red brick house in Bayswater quite simply 'Red House', just like William Morris a dozen years before at Bexley. If Londoners felt so strongly, no wonder that Keble College was too much for Oxford to accept.

A response of such persistence and authority is compelling. Even Nikolaus Pevsner, confronted by the soft dusty pink brickwork of All Saints' (I), saw instead the 'dark red brick' which the Butterfield tradition demanded.[8] It is hardly surprising that vicars of most Butterfield churches, rather than standing back to contemplate what may be a very prettily tiled sanctuary wall, hurriedly straighten the dowdy curtains hung to conceal them by a predecessor, muttering comparisons with public lavatories. Similarly, a painted roof or brick walls blackened by a hundred years of gas and candle smoke, and by dust circulated by the heating, will rarely be though worth cleaning. Whitewash is the instinctive suggestion, although its effect on any major Butterfield interior is disastrous, like an organ played with half the stops missing. Yet cleaning can effect an equal transformation, and one which Butterfield would have approved. His own last work was the cleaning of All Saints' in 1895, and it was cleaned again in 1960, with dramatic effect. A dismal brown and black interior, with touches of tarnished gilt and acrid green, suddenly became gay and glittering (X); cream and pink, with patches of black and warm yellow, and a few bright specks of green. Only the uncleaned walls now sound acid chords to 'The Glory of Ugliness'.

All Saints' is alas almost alone in its good fortune. Rugby Chapel and St Mary Brookfield have also been restored recently with sympathy. But of the other London interiors of coloured brick, St Alban's Holborn has been destroyed, St Augustine's Queen's Gate entirely whitewashed, and Woolwich and Hammersmith partly whitewashed. Outside London, Hitchin is darkened by excessive stained glass, and Manchester blackened by soot, so that only Baldersby, Alvechurch and Penarth effectively convey a major Butterfield colour scheme in brick. (XII, XIV). In the towns the brick exteriors have also suffered badly, but fortunately this is amply compensated by happy weathering in the countryside; and Butterfield's stone buildings, most of which are away from the big industrial cities, have also mellowed with time, and their rather softer interiors have been rarely mutilated. The gutting of Balliol Chapel – a typical Oxford gesture – is the one exception.

The impact of time has thus added further difficulties to the understanding of Butterfield's colour schemes, and especially to his best known brick buildings.

Butterfield's colour is for this reason far harder to discuss than his use of form. We can never know exactly how his buildings looked when they were opened; we can only be sure that the harsh patterns of contemporary black and white line drawings were a brutal reduction of their effect. One might as well assess the qualities of Turner's paintings from black and white prints in family magazines. There is moreover the added problem that Butterfield, unlike most painters, deliberately allowed for the weathering of his buildings, so that even if we were to see their original condition we should not know the final effect for which he hoped.

It must be conceded that in the towns Butterfield seriously miscalculated the effects of the smoke-laden air. He not only ignored the revolutionary experiments in glazed polychromy to counter atmospheric pollution which were advocated from the 1850s, but more foolishly he abandoned his original technique of broad contrasts of dark brick with stone washed white by rain (68), and introduced patterns in the brickwork itself. In the countryside, on the other hand, these patterns are almost always successful. At Ashwell a villager complained in 1860 that the new cottages 'were very convenient, but looked so hot-like',[9] but the brickwork has now mellowed perfectly; it glows, but no more than the Georgian cottages nearby (152).

Keble College, however, may never have looked as Butterfield conceived it. The chapel at its opening seemed a 'gaunt, barren pile of bricks and mortar, rising obtrusively in the very centre of a little rookery of lodging-houses', too much like a sliced veal pie for Oxford tastes. Even the friendly *Church Times* asked rhetorically, 'Was not Westminster Abbey once chalky-looking and raw?'[10] Within a dozen years

152 Ashwell, cottage pair

an unprejudiced eye might have noticed a considerable softening; in 1889, for example, a contributor to the *British Architect* wrote of the 'warmth and glow of the blazonry of colours [which] illustrate the POWER of Colour to ennoble architecture'.[11] Soon, however, grime from Oxford's chimneys would chill the warm blazonry, hardening its tones to suit the austere High Church reputation of the college itself, so that today it requires conscious effort to recapture the almost boisterous gaiety of its first years.

Nevertheless, there can be no doubt that the intention of the High Victorian revival of colour was the very reverse of puritanical austerity. 'We would have every inch glowing', declared the *Ecclesiologist* in 1845: 'Puritans . . . would have every inch colourless'[12] Butterfield himself wrote of the 'gay walls' of Keble, and of the 'warmth of tone' provided by contrasted materials in his church at Clevedon.[13] Others were more outspoken. To his friend William White, colour was an 'intense delight', 'a luxury upon which the eye can feast'; monochrome was a renunciation of worldly pleasure only appropriate to monastic asceticism (XXII). It was especially needed as a respite from the whirl of Victorian life. 'I am not pleading for the indiscriminate, inharmonious, strongly contrasted and fantastic colouring which earnest advocates for polychromy are sometimes supposed to delight in, but for the deep, full, rich, harmonious luxuriance which has the power of exhilarating while it soothes.'[14] In the same spirit Street complained of 'the puritanical uniformity of our coats and of all our garments', and John Francis Bentley (307) in an early letter asked: 'If Italy with all her sunny beauty and azure backgrounds requires nature's dyes, how much more cold and cheerless England?'[15]

Colour, in short, was a deliberate assault not upon the senses, but on the puritan spirit which starved them. It was an assertion of catholicism in a Protestant England, of luxury in the age of Gradgrind, of sensuous pleasures at a time of rigorous suppression. All Saints' and Keble, to Evangelical Victorian England, were red rags in a moral as much as a visual sense, and this was one reason for the hostility of much contemporary criticism. It required Ruskin, knowing the Evangelical mind from his parents, to justify constructional colour in terms which appealed to Protestant instincts. It was certainly untrue to suggest, he wrote in *The Stones of Venice*, that colour was a 'mere source of a sensual pleasure . . . None of us enough appreciate the nobleness and sacredness of colour . . . All good colour is in some degree pensive, the loveliest is melancholy, and the purest and most thoughtful minds are those which love colour the most'.[16] Ruskin satisfied his own audience and helped to make constructional colour into a middle-class fashion by the 1860s; yet in retrospect it seems more significant that the denial of its sensuousness was necessary.

We must, therefore, attempt an appraisal in the spirit which first stimulated the use of polychrome. We shall begin briefly with the exteriors, where the problem of weathering makes discussion inevitably inconclusive, and move to the interior, where fortunately some features, most notably tile and marble decoration, undoubtedly retain their original colouring virtually unchanged.

Butterfield's external walls and roofs were constructed, as we have seen, of traditional local materials: stones of delightful regional variety, slates, tiles and hand-made bricks. Many of them are finely coloured, none intrinsically unpleasant; and in most of Butterfield's buildings they are used with perfect simplicity. Stone is usually roofed with slate, or occasionally with a local tile, and its colour left to speak for itself: sometimes a rich brown or pink sandstone, a grey-blue slate, or a golden ironstone, but mostly grey or white. St Augustine's College, Canterbury, was already characteristic: 'green turf, grey flint, creamy Caen stone, and tiles of russet brown: nothing is gaudy, nothing is obtrusive, nothing jars upon the sight as in any way offensive.'[17] The Ruskinian colouring of Balliol Chapel (50), purple-pink and buff walls under a purple and sea-green slate roof, was altogether exceptional, not merely in being systematically banded, but in its fourfold colour contrast. Now that the walls are yellowed by grime it is impossible to see whether the scheme was in itself discordant, or merely too Italian for its setting. At any rate the experiment was not repeated.

The earlier brick buildings were equally simple, the only colour variation due to the slight natural differences of hand-made bricks. Roofs were sometimes of grey slate, more often of tile from the same local clay. From about 1855 a second phase begins with the introduction of stone banding and a small amount of diaper in darker bricks, motifs previously only found at All Saints' Margaret Street and St Thomas Leeds (73). Considered purely as a colour contrast the effect is still simple, and at this stage the patterns are slight and unobtrusive. Conversely, at the same time brick bands were first introduced into flint walls. Probably the first example was the school of 1856 at Great Bookham (53), which Philip Webb thought interesting enough to sketch, although the combination of relentless bands with half-timbered gables makes the intrinsically attractive texture harsh. Much more attractive was Aldbourne school (153) of 1857–8, where the spacing of the bands was subtly varied, the flint partly mixed with brick chips and brown stone, random fragments of stone scattered in the brickwork of the chimney, and the roof of beautifully weathered tile: its recent demolition was as unfortunate as it was unnecessary.

Diapers of blue or grey brick, bands of stone, and combinations with flint chequers and bands and half-timbered gables, all become much more common from the mid-1860s. Nearly all of Butterfield's later buildings, however small, are vigorously patterned in contrasted colours and materials. Without doubt these combinations are often restless, systematically reducing the simple earlier wall surfaces to patterns of intersecting lines; and this play of line and surface is difficult to unravel, so that to the unsympathetic eye it seems merely discordant. But the colours themselves are little changed, and the combinations restrained: red brick patterned with blue or

153 Aldbourne school

grey, or brown London stocks with flint and white stone. Woodwork was generally painted a dark brown, or sometimes with lighter bricks green; ironwork black. Even in such an elaborate design as the New Schools at Rugby (282) the colours are very simple: cream and buff, with a little weathered red. No doubt Rugby was in Halsey Ricardo's mind when he wrote of Butterfield's buildings – in 1900 cleaner than today: 'There is a give and take amongst them, especially in the matter of colour. The yellow brick borrows something of his neighbour's crimson, and flushes a tender coral or recalls the almond blossom in spring. The red . . . softens into purples and russets, with a high light of scarlet still gleaming here and there, the black headers show an iridescence of blue lustre, and in their grave way check the riot of colour,'[18] As a boy at Rugby Ricardo had looked at Butterfield's colour with fresh eyes, and found it charming; and his comment is fairer than the blind ridicule of Oxford dons.

So much for Butterfield's external use of colour. Colour within his buildings – apart from the occasional richly marbled fireplace in a larger house (154), and the college hall at Keble – is restricted to his churches. Even here, the fully coloured interior is far from typical. In two-thirds of Butterfield's churches, colour is confined to the floor, the font, and the sanctuary wall and window: all the rest is brown wood and white plaster. Constructional polychromatic interiors are in general in a minority, and the richer form of treatment is a rarity except in the 1860s.

The churches of the 1840s are the simplest. White walls, brown seats and dark roof timbers always set the tone. Even in the tiled floors, deep brown is the commonest colour, usually combined with dark blue, cream, black or emerald green. The chapel floors at St Augustine's and the Wantage cemetery chapel were entirely of this type, rich but sombre. More often yellow was introduced in the chancel, so that the effect lightened as the pattern moved eastwards. The chancel floor at Kinwarton is a charming pink and yellow; the east wall at Dorchester Abbey, blue and yellow tiles set in soft pink alabaster. There is little glass in these early interiors, although the original deep blue and red east window at Coalpit Heath survives; and at Kinwarton similar colours are the highlights to a fine grey window by O'Connor. Perhaps the supreme example of this first phase is the wonderfully light and creamy brown stone interior at Ottery St Mary (IX), where Butterfield picked out the medieval vaulting in blue, red and gold, and the windows glow with the same primary colours. But only at Wavendon is a whole church darkened by a series of rich red and blue windows. This last completed interior of the 1840s, with its blue chancel walls stencilled with gold fleur-de-lys, the ironwork picked out in red and green and the roof in gold, blue and red, is unique in its richness, and looks forward to the bold colour experiments of the next decade.

In most churches the change is shown only by details. A new font was designed for Ottery St Mary (VI), 'sumptuous and beautiful', a bowl of black, white and veined pink Devon marble set on dark and greenish shafts.[19] In a simple church like Cowick 'variety is given to the interior' by contrasting plaster with plain brick. At Ashwell the tiled floor and alabaster east wall are answered by a chancel roof picked out in orange and red, and at Langley (106) a white chancel roof is stencilled with red, black and green tendrils and monograms.[20] There are similar patterns on the floor, with a rich yellow added in the sanctuary. Contemporaries thought it 'the most brilliant colouring';[21] today one is more impressed by its vigorous simplicity. Nor is its fresh lightness an accident, for although Hardman glazed the whole church Butterfield told him to limit the dark colour to highlights: 'Keep the spots of *color* in the Langley grisaille bright and *strong* so as to sparkle like jewels on the grisaille surface . . . Remember that we *much* want light in all these windows.'[22] Colouring in the 1850s was intended to be bright and clear. Butterfield had turned his back on romantic gloom. Wavendon, and the unfinished scheme at Yealmpton, were the only interiors where it seems that darkness was deliberate.

This was true after 1850 of even the richer interiors. If stained glass was intended, Butterfield either confined it to east windows, or – as he planned at All Saints' –

154 Milton Ernest Hall, library chimneypiece

provided clear upper light from a clerestory. At Merton College Chapel (348) the great ribbed boarded roof, now sadly faded, was painted by John Hungerford Pollen with red, gold and dark brown ribs and wallplate, delicate angel medallions of paler red and blue, and twisting green tendrils of oak, vine and ivy; but he was careful to introduce as much white as possible in the upper parts 'to give lightness and brilliancy',[23] and in the new tiled floor Butterfield re-used many of the old white marble slabs. The *Building News* thought the result 'really lovely: the cold, gray, cheerless hue of plain marble being avoided on the one hand, and the danger of looking like a carpet, to which rich, unmixed encaustic tiles are liable, on the other.'[24]

155 Cumbrae College, chapel interior

There is something of the same balance in the colouring characteristic of the early 1850s – red, yellow and dark green rather than the earlier brown, yellow and blue. The interior at Cumbrae (155) is a beautiful example, high and cool, the white chancel walls set with big diamond tile patterns in green, black and dark red, the roof picked out with delicate fern leaves and wild roses. From the later 1850s Butterfield's colour schemes became warmer, and he relied more exclusively on red, pink and yellow. One of the last schemes in which green plays an equal part is Waresley (156), built in 1856, a fine last echo of Cumbrae, whose stone walls are inlaid with a thin dark pink trellis strung with diamonds of deep emerald, buff and leaf green.

Butterfield's original intention at All Saints' (X) must have been of this kind, although the tiling was much denser, and cream tiles rather than stone provided the background colour. Gerente's stained glass windows were intended to take up the same colours, and were based upon the splendid green and yellow Jesse window at Wells. But in fact the great west window was a disastrous failure, executed after Henri Gerente's death by his brother Alfred, badly drawn, garish yellow and 'cabbage green'. Butterfield wanted it altered, but Hope refused, and instead attacked the tile patterns, complaining that Butterfield had 'parricidally spoilt his own creation with the clown's dress, so spotty and spidery and flimsy it looks in a mass now that it is all done, and worst of all the Church looks so much smaller than it used to do with nothing but the solemn columns to give scale'. He preferred to hope that 'the 'raw slabs of glazed brick can be readily replaced'.[25] Similarly Butterfield quarrelled with Hope about the lighting of the church, and failed to secure the unpainted constructional polychromy which he wanted in the chancel vault. Moreover the church took many years to complete, so that in form as well as colour many of the details belong to Butterfield's later tastes and do not easily match the first intention. The tile paintings of the aisle walls and tower arch, for example, used the maroon and apple green of the 1870s and 1880s and at present clash with the crisper, more jewelled effect of the tiling over the arcades. Complete cleaning would lessen the contrasts, but even so there is no doubt that All Saints' suffered from its chequered history, and it will always require imagination to understand the scheme as Butterfield first conceived it, a brilliant reflection of the coloured interiors of Italy, of Assisi and Orvieto, which he wished to recapture in the cold monotony of Early Victorian London.

The essential effect can nevertheless be glimpsed on a bright summer day, or in the evening fully lit: the cooler cream and pink nave, with its patches of black and highlights of rich yellow and green, a prelude to the darker vaulted chancel and the gorgeous east wall, tiers of bright blue and red figures standing under great gilded crocketed canopies. It is unforgettable, as if suddenly an overwhelming and triumphant chorus of praise had broken the monotonous rumble of the streets. It is fresh, and undoubtedly naive, as might have been expected for an experiment of such unprecedented audacity. Eastlake rightly commented that 'the secret of knowing where to stop in decorative work had still to be acquired':[26] the circles, triangles and chevrons of colour which make up the tile surfaces are not yet organized to lead the eye in any consistent direction, so that they are dazzling, even bewildering. The capitals are of veined alabaster, of a texture which would not have been used for sculpture in later work, and the massive quality of the Aberdeen granite columns is denied by their deeply moulded clustered form (157). The innocence which Sir John Summerson sees in Butterfield is certainly evident at All Saints', obscuring to some extent 'that noble elegance which makes it, in some ways, the most moving building of the century'. There is indeed the element of wildness, of abandon, which was needed for Butterfield 'in All Saints', right in the heart of joyless London, . . . to deal his most tremendous blow'. But 'the contemptuous joy of distortion and distruction', the anti-sensual puritanism, the deliberate ugliness and aesthetic sadism which Summerson discerns, are in my view fundamental misunderstandings of the building. What we see here is not so much a sudden chasm, 'impenetrable and cold', but a moment of vivid enthusiasm, astonishing in its warmth and openness.[27]

Contemporary comment is, in the case of All Saints', particularly difficult to use because of the continuing dispute between Butterfield and his patron. The comments of the *Ecclesiologist* in particular were in part a display of personal irritation by Hope, who would have probably redecorated the whole interior under his own sole direction had he been given the opportunity. Nevertheless, it is worth citing the very thoughtful critical letter from 'F.A.M.' published by the *Builder*, which anticipates some of Summerson's words, but with a significantly different interpretation of the church. 'Until lately it has been considered as wrong, highly wrong,' it opens, 'to admit any but the coldest, most chilling conditions into attempts at decoration made in our churches. All colour, all precious materials, all evidence of delight or pleasure in the service of God, were considered as going back into mediaeval dimness and Romish superstition . . . Against our long-established parsimony and frigidity of decoration it stands as a magnificent protest.'[28]

Those who find All Saints' systematic only in its ugliness should look again at some of its details with these words in mind. The pulpit (XI), for example, although lumpish in form, is a triumphant display of the colour pageantry of rocks and marbles: Derbyshire fossil grey, autumn red Languedoc, warm Sienna, and cool Irish green, set on fat brawny pink granite columns which branch into waving seaweedy capitals. Even if one does not find this great piece of coloured sculpture beautiful, surely one can sense the happy enjoyment which produced it?

Or look at the floor of the church. It is one of the finest of the pavements for which Butterfield was justly renowned. The nave floor provides a bold simple prelude, a deep red background with a big white stone diaper and black checks, and clever triangle variations along the aisle. In the chancel the background becomes a sparkling white, with broad red strips and diaper and triangles of black and soft green. In front of the altar rails there are white, red and black zigzags at the sides and in the centre big diamond patterns lined with soft fossil grey marble, filled with yellow patterned tiles and a maze of tiny white triangles. The sanctuary floor is again more complex: big strips and diapers of fossil grey against a red background forming diamonds filled with patterned yellow, or black and white and red and green; and on the final step patterned tiles in blue and yellow and white and red tracery. The whole abstract sequence is of extraordinary quality.

156 Waresley church, chancel interior

157 All Saints' Margaret Street, interior from the east (*Country Life*)

All Saints' was the richest interior which Butterfield ever designed, and he was never to repeat tile patterns completely covering the wall surface in this fashion. The lost interior of Balliol Chapel (158) shared something of its elaboration in miniature, but his other experiments with constructional colour in the 1850s were by contrast modest. Yealmpton (IV), abandoned half-finished, was to have been white and grey, with a little soft red Devon marble and a series of frescoes. St Thomas's Leeds, however, built in 1850–2 and demolished after the Second World War, was by all accounts a more serious loss (73).

It was Butterfield's first complete brick interior, and its red brick walls were simply and strongly banded with white stone. According to Henry-Russell Hitchcock, who saw the church shortly before its demolition, the colours were 'exquisitely balanced', the main walls a light orange-pink with diapers in a pale blue-grey: 'Thus there was a harmony of tone which contrasted with the stridency of All Saints' both outside and in'.[29] A century earlier the *Ecclesiologist* had discerned in the church 'the hand of a master . . . Standing in a squalid waste, strewed with heaps of rubbish, St Thomas stands out unmistakeably a town church. Mr Butterfield always seems to build *con amore*, where there are extraordinary difficulties; and he succeeds with bricks better, in proportion, than with any other material'.[30]

The loss of St Thomas Leeds and Balliol means that of Butterfield's earlier fully polychromatic interiors, only Baldersby (36) now survives for comparison with All Saints'. Its subtle colouring is extremely impressive: a hard grey stone shell concealing an interior of soft pink brick, grey on the high wall above the chancel arch, set off by broad bands of white stone, and softly lit with glass by Wailes and O'Connor. Hitchcock thought it 'a delicate harmony of pink and grey-blue bricks, with accents of creamy stone', again in contrast to All Saints'.[31]

Equally attractive is the interior at Alvechurch (XII), designed immediately after the completion of Baldersby in 1857. It belongs, however, decidedly to the late- rather than the mid-1850s. The tones are all stronger: walls of glowing red brick set on tough buff and pink sandstone arcades and picked out with crisp clean white brick diaper and stone bands. The nave brickwork is linked across the old grey stone wall of the tower by two broad red brick bands, a superb colour contrast. The chancel is richer still, with the black and red pavement picking up yellow, and stained glass throwing strong red, pink and yellow light on the white and red walls (XIII).

Both pavement and glass were to be characteristic of Butterfield's work from the late 1850s. The chancel pavements of the 1860s are especially fine, the backgrounds red, divided by broad strips of white stone, and varied by delightful patterns of black and decorated yellow tiles. They add a touch of brilliance to churches otherwise scarcely memorable: Lyneham, for example, or Sudbury St Gregory with its intersecting arcs, or the human birds and lions' heads at Anstey.

158 Balliol College chapel, interior (George Davis)

159 Hitchin Holy Saviour, interior, early photograph (Hitchin Museum)

Stained glass of this period is less often successful. In the 1850s Butterfield was constantly asking Hardman to avoid the 'hot and glaring effect' of 'large masses of scarlet and yellow': 'blue must predominate and that a cold blue and not a purple. The mass of red in the tracery alarms me'. Some windows it is true are thought excessively blue from the start, and the deep cool blue is always intended as a background for spots of colour: deep red, 'good brown pink' and 'a good brown yellow' – 'the deep rich *orange* one finds for such purposes in old glass' rather than the 'straw coloured pale yellow' to which Hardman was instinctively inclined. After 1860, however, the windows tend to be much less blue in general effect, and Butterfield praises a window which 'glows with orange color.'[32] At the same time, owing to a quarrel with Hardman, Alexander Gibbs became Butterfield's stained glass maker. The change was undoubtedly unfortunate, for he was not an artist of the calibre of Hardman. Some of his windows are admirable: at Brigham, for example, a glittering series of the 1860s and 1870s, and again at Heytesbury, where they provide a perfect foil to Butterfield's dramatic black and red diagonal lines across the stone walls (XXI). But where sensitive, small scale work was required, Gibbs was rarely successful, and one regrets that Butterfield did not co-operate more often with Preedy, who designed the admirable glass at Alvechurch.

In the 1860s for the first time half of Butterfield's interiors were designed in constructional colour, and in these interiors his linear patterning reached its climax. It was matched by the inventiveness of his colour schemes. Very few of these interiors could be described as discordant in their colour. The small church at Dalton (356), which uses only red, black and white brick, is perhaps the most strident in effect, probably because of the contrast with the softer harmonies of its William Morris glass. Holy Saviour Hitchin (159), on the other hand, as far as one can perceive through the gloom of later stained glass, is a soft glow of buff and red, although Pevsner though it 'in every way a full-blooded example' of Butterfield's style.[33] At Horton (VIII) the exquisite semi-random patterning of hand-made Oxford grey bricks has been mentioned earlier; it is a pity that the glass is less sensitive. The two other small new interiors, Beech Hill and Dropmore, are a pair, both with brick and flint exteriors and strongly toned interiors of brick, light diaper and white stone bands, reaching a climax in the rich yellow, black and purply red tiling of the chancel. At Dropmore the colour is slightly different, a pinkish mauve, for once brilliantly matched by Gibbs' glass in red, pink, mauve, copper yellow and deep blue.

Of the four major interiors of the period, Manchester is a quite straightforward use of brick, while the much more ambitious St Alban's Holborn has been destroyed (14, 353). The boldness here seems, however, to have been restricted to the patterning, if contemporary comment is to be trusted. Pale brown stock bricks formed the general ground, with bands of white stone, red brick diapering, and terracotta wall

160　Mapledurham church,
chancel interior

161　Sedgeberrow church,
reredos and
altar frontal

I   All Saints' Margaret Street,
    exterior from the west

II   All Saints' Babbacombe, porch and spire

III   All Saints' Babbacombe, interior

IV   Yealmpton church, font

V   Letcombe Bassett church, interior

VI   Ottery St Mary church, font

VII   Hagnaby church, font

VIII   Horton church, exterior

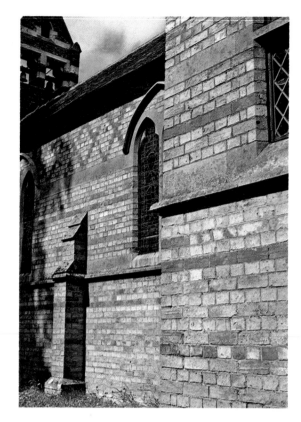

IX   Ottery St Mary church, interior

X   All Saints' Margaret Street, pulpit
    (Dennis Frone)

XI All Saints' Margaret Street,
     interior from the west (Dennis Frone)

XII   Alvechurch church, interior

XIII   All Saints' Babbacombe,
chancel floor

XIV St Augustine Penarth, interior XV All Saints' Babbacombe, font

XVI   All Saints'
Babbacombe, pulpit

XVII   Baverstock church,
wall tiles

XVIII   Keble College, chapel vault

XIX   Melbourne Cathedral, interior from tower gallery

XX Keble College, chapel from the south
quadrangle

XXI Heytesbury church, interior

XXII   Little Baddow rectory, by William White

XXIII   Liverpool University, by Alfred Waterhouse

XXIV   Alvechurch church,
       stained glass

XXV   All Saints' Margaret Street, altar frontal

shafts 'giving a warm tone to the colour of the building.'[34] The *Ecclesiologist* thought the painted east wall insufficiently powerful, softer even than the pink alabaster panels in which it was set; the roof a 'pale blue and feeble grey'; and the contrasted colours of the brickwork externally so ineffective that 'a few year's smoke will be almost sufficient to obliterate the traces of their existence.'[35] By High Victorian standards at any rate the scheme was far from strident.

At St Augustine's Penarth (XIV), crouched sea-grey on its headland above Cardiff harbour, the startling daring of the unexpected interior is undeniable: red brick walls, in fact quite soft and here and there orange-red or pink, but made extraordinarily vivid by the sharp white and black diapering, and in turn firmly contained by the broad irregular pink and cream stone of the bold simple arcading. The result is one of Butterfield's most majestic achievements, with a nobility which transcends the immediate shock of the materials: a harmony which is snatched from the very matter of discord.

Babbacombe (II, III), the second surviving masterpiece of the 1860s, is again concealed by a grey stone exterior. The nave here is more subdued, the marble columns light and dark veined browns, the outer walls reddish sandstone, the upper walls red and dark grey patterned in grey and buff. The rather sombre tones suddenly flare into brilliance with the marbles of the font and pulpit, rich yellow, black, dusty pink and gleaming white (XV, XVI). Beyond, in the rather lighter chancel, the harmonies are softer, and the broad marbled floor a wonderful composition of pinks, grey-blues, and buff, with highlights of black, sea-green and soft veined yellow (XIII). The whole sequence is of extraordinary beauty. Together Babbacombe and Penarth would alone establish the rare brilliance and subtlety of Butterfield's sense of colour.

On a simpler level there are also village churches which Butterfield restored at this time where the colour can be enchanting. At Mapledurham (160) and Letcombe Bassett (V), for example, the soft pink and white of the sanctuary wall above a tiled floor is delightfully sensitive. At Great Waldingfield the walls have randomly coloured fragments made of marbles collected, as an inscription records, 'in the ruins of the heathen temples of old Rome'. At Sedgeberrow (161) the wide aisleless interior, broken only by the tracery of a tall screen, has an east wall tiled with oriental splendour, its flamboyant patterned reredos crowned by a swaying row of ogee medieval canopies. Tadlow is another worthwhile restoration, well lit by jewelled blue-grey windows; a characteristic floor, delicate strips of pink and yellow on the sanctuary walls, and a delicious font of pinkish grey on a white base.

There were also painted interiors of the 1860s, although not one survives. Pennethorne's bare classical galleried Christ Church Albany Street was completely redecorated, the side walls with a dado of pink tiles, the middle section brown, and the uppermost part slate grey; pilasters a slightly lighter grey, with the spandrels of the

162 Winchester St Cross, chapel interior (*Builder*, 1865)

chancel arch a greyish red, and the imposts a warmer red; and the panelled ceiling grey, with ribs picked out in gold and blue.[36] The transformation earned the warm applause of John Seddon in a speech at the R.I.B.A.[37]

Butterfield's application of colouring to the great late Norman church of St Cross at Winchester (162) was much better known, and far less approved. The colours themselves were somewhat similar: Indian red, pink, blueish grey, pale green and a little black and gold. But there were not broad areas of colour, as at Christ Church Albany Street; columns and sculptures were richly coloured, but the main walls were white, covered by huge lines of trellis and imitation masonry. The original Norman interior may well have been quite as garish as this, for Butterfield accurately followed the surviving frescoed decoration in the south-east chapel, and the original architectural details are certainly coarse. But however crude the Norman masters may have been in their taste, Butterfield's decision to emulate them brought a storm of protest: it was denounced by William Morris as 'bedizenment' of a 'simple and majestic piece of early work', and even the sympathetic Bentley wrote that Butterfield had restored the decoration 'most shamefully . . . striped it from top to bottom with . . . patterns à la Tunbridge Wells ware.'[38] The fury of local antiquarians was indicated by the rough reception given to J. H. Parker's cautious comments at a meeting at Southampton: 'It appeared to him that the present colouring did not sufficiently bring out and emphasize the architectural forms of the choir – (hear, hear) – and the colours were, moreover, too brilliant – (hear, hear) – although they would, no doubt, tone down in time and improve in appearance . . . He thought, however, that too much fault had been found with it. (No, no.) At any rate, its intention was good, and the colour was much better than whitewash.'[39] In fact the contrary was probably true: not only was the patterning inferior to any scheme which Butterfield conceived free of his own imagination, but it had no chance of acceptance in a building which had become far grander with the mellowing effects of time and whitewash, gaining immeasurably from the simplicity and softness of old age.

St Cross was one of the buildings which gave Butterfield a reputation for devastating lack of sympathy in restoration work which was not, on the whole, deserved. In his restorations of the 1870s and 1880s colour was still quite frequently introduced, but generally with relative restraint: often no more than a tiled floor and a thin single line round the sanctuary wall. Barley, for example, gives an impression of grey and cold corn browns in spite of extensive constructional colour. From the late 1870s colours are generally softer, but the tile pavements rather more varied. The enchanting superimposed triangles and squares at Baverstock (XVII) are in yellow, red, black and a beautiful sea-blue; and there is the same blue at Ault Hucknall, with pink and yellow tiles and grey fossil marble.

Where the use of colour in these later restorations seems excessive, it is generally due to the use of mosaic work, as in the ornate chancel at West Deeping or the patterned south transept of 1878 at Ottery St Mary. At Dover Castle church (163) the neo-Norman mosaics are a startling miniature repetition of St Cross, although in a building largely dating from the reconstruction of 1860 it is a little easier to accept the great branching patterns on the chancel walls, and the colour itself is undoubtedly sensitive. The nave mosaics at West Tarring are also softly coloured, and the broad frieze is this time strongly reminiscent of Ravenna. The mosaics were in fact executed by Italian workmen and Butterfield had certainly spent many hours at St Mark's in Venice studying its motifs; but it seems that the men were attached to the workshop of Alexander Gibbs, and the mosaics generally have the same rather heavy-handed quality as his glass.[40]

It is the mosaics which dominate the interior of Keble College Chapel (81) and make it at first sight one of the least attractive of Butterfield's later displays of polychrome. Yet it is well worth a longer look. The chapel is treated as a single, vast space,

163 Dover Castle, St Mary sub Castro, mosaic decoration (J. G. Whorwell)

the whole effect concentrated on the outer surfaces. All the furniture is kept deliberately low: only dark long lines of seats, and a light open wrought metal pulpit and altar rails. The choir seats are pushed back to form a great open floorspace at the east end, paved in white and grey stone, with encaustic tile patterns in yellow, plum, emerald green and sea-green. These colours are taken up in the walls. The lowest stage is a bold wall arcade, the surface behind of glazed plum-coloured brick, with thin sea-green strips and broader bands of formalized mastic patterning set in stone-flowers, suns and tendrils. Next come the mosaics, rather softer in colour: green, pink, pale blue, a limp yellow, red and white. The colours seem in fact too soft for the strong archaic lines of the figures and their powerful architectural setting. Surely the white ground is especially mistaken?

Above the mosaics, however, the colouring reaches a superb climax (XVIII). Gibbs' windows are a complete success, light but glowing with scarlet, mauve, yellow and blue-greens. Between them in the upper walls the brick turns to a soft vermilion

164 Portsmouth St Michael, interior before demolition (National Monuments Record)

165 Belfast, Dundela St Mark, interior (D. S. Richardson)

red, crossed by grey and buff bands and light diapers, rising to chequer patterns high up under the vaults. At the springing of the vaulting the great grey wall shafts, which have risen from the lowest stage of the wall, give way to the enchantingly delicate pink and terracotta patterning of the ribs; the rhythm of the patterning quickening as the ribs cluster. Not only the ribs, but the entire surface of the vault is painted, with formalized patterns of jointing in broad zones of buff, sea-green and grey. Yet the result is not, as so often with this type of decoration, a maze of lines reducing the structure to a toy. In the Keble vaults the lines are kept deliberately soft, and it is the subtle colouring which prevails, modulating the clean lines of the vault. The effect is one of extraordinary freshness and freedom in contrast to the stronger shapes and tones of the lower walls; and, once discovered, the eye will return again and again to the strange beauty of this painted ceiling.

The interior of Keble Chapel, consecrated in 1876, was Butterfield's last master-piece in brick. Rugby School Chapel, with its tall simple columns of cream and pink sandstone softening the impact of the patterned brick walls, belongs to the early 1870s (290). St Augustine's Queen's Gate, whitewashed in the 1920s, is a serious loss, for the design was a fine development of Penarth (279). St Michael's Portsmouth, which belonged to the same group, has been demolished (164). St Mary Brookfield, again of the early 1870s, is a rather conservative but very attractive stock brick interior, with diaper and generous bands of red brick and white stone, and flecks of black (89). Finally, at Weybridge the tones are rather sharper, although effectively held by the cream and brown stonework. After Keble there is only Tottenham, where the elaborate tiling is unfortunately swamped by hotly coloured Gibbs glass; of the 1880s, Edmonton St Mary has been demolished, and the finely shaped nave of St Michael's Woolwich is lost in whitewash.

These late brick interiors were not, however, Butterfield's most important con-structional polychromy of the 1870s and 1880s. In the smaller churches there is a perceptible shift back to white plastered interiors, especially where the exterior was stone-faced; grey now always opens to white walls, although sometimes with a lower dado of dark tile. The stained glass by Gibbs also becomes in many windows noticeably paler. Similarly in the larger churches constructional colour more often comes from stone than brick. This was the period of the noble late sandstone churches, broadly banded in grey, pink, and white or cream: Rugby parish church, the convent chapel at Ascot, and the splendid Irish church of St Mark, Dundela (52, 165, 291). Without the flickering linear patterning of the 1860s the quietness of the colour is unquestioned.

The grandest of the sandstone interiors is not in England. Butterfield made the plans for Melbourne Cathedral (XIX) in 1878, and although he resigned in 1886 and neither the fittings nor the exterior were completed to his designs, at least the stone walls are his. He selected the stone from examples sent to England: Waurn Ponds,

Pyrmont and Barrabool. The banded stonework of the interior is superb, cream and grey, majestic and broad in detail. The roof is a fine dark brown local wood, and there are a few touches of soft red high up under the tower gallery. These are of plain tile, and the dado planned by Butterfield for the lower walls was to have been similarly restrained. The fussily patterned, green and orange tile dado actually executed is quite unsuitable, as indeed are most of the cathedral's fittings, but in spite of them Melbourne was Butterfield's final masterpiece. Certainly it is his noblest tribute to the Italian masters of constructional colour, for the inspiration of Siena is here, alone among Butterfield's buildings, immediately apparent. He kept a description of the cathedral printed just before its consecration, no doubt because it quietly pleased him. 'The effect is splendid rather than grand', the critic wrote, 'more suggestive of the grandeur of an emperor's palace than the chaste magnificence of a cathedral'.[41] Yet this was close to the very purpose of constructional colour: that splendour should not be the privilege of secular power alone. The critic could have been more generous, but he had grasped Butterfield's meaning.

166 Dropmore church, porch

Notes on chapter 11

1　Butterfield to M. B. Adams (28 December 1878) quoted *BN*, (78) 1900, p. 292.

2　*DNB*.

3　*B*, (28) 1870, p. 260; *BN*, (17) 1869, p. 284.

4　(VII) 1900, p. 245.

5　Butterfield to the Warden, 22 January 1873, Starey Collection.

6　Sir Kenneth Clark, *The Gothic Revival*, revised edition, Constable, 1950, pp. 3–5, 262–3.

7　*Heavenly Mansions*, p. 166.

8　*BE, London* (2), p. 326.

9　*E*, (21) 1860, p. 292.

10　*Daily Telegraph*, 27 April 1876; *Church Times*, 28 April 1876.

11　(32) 1889, p. 399.

12　'On Decorative Colour', (4) 1845, pp. 199–203.

13　R.S.S., *Complete Guide to Clevedon*: 'The roof is covered with tiles, which gives warmth of tone, and contrast pleasantly with the walls of the building. A similar effect of warmth is produced internally by the lower part of the walls in the nave and aisles being lined with red and other coloured Staffordshire tiles.'

14　See my 'The Writings of William White' in Sir John Summerson (ed.), *Architectural Writing in Britain*, London 1968.

15　G. E. Street, *Brick and Marble in the Middle Ages*, London 1855, p. 285; Bentley to Charles Hadfield, 15 December 1862, R.I.B.A.

16　*The Stones of Venice*, 2, pp. 144–5.

17　Boggis, *op. cit.*, p. 120.

18　*AR*, (7) 1900, p. 260.

19　*E*, (13) 1852, p. 87.

20　*B*, (12) 1854, p. 574.

21　*BN*, (2) 1856, p. 5.

22　Butterfield to John Hardman, 22 January and 4 April 1855, Hardman Collection.

23　*E*, (12) 1851, p. 297.

24　(2) 1856, p. 963.

25　*BN*, (5) 1859, p. 487; Law, *op. cit.*, p. 177; *E*, (16) 1855, p. 292.

26　*Op. cit.*, p. 254.

27　*Heavenly Mansions*, pp. 174–6.

28　*B*, (17) 1859, p. 364.

29　*Early Victorian Architecture*, *op. cit.*, p. 595.

30　*E*, (15) 1854, p. 59.

31　Henry-Russell Hitchcock, *Architecture: Nineteenth and Twentieth Centuries*, London, Penguin, 1958, p. 177.

32　Butterfield to Hardman, 18 March,　　and 16 October 1856, March 1857 and 9 May 1864.

33 *BE, Hertfordshire*, p. 134.

34 *CB*, April 1864.

35 (22) 1861, p. 317, and (24) 1863, pp. 114 and 147–8.

36 Notebook 13; plans, 1867, Christ Church chest.

37 *Transactions*, 1869–70, p. 138.

38 Philip Henderson (ed.), *Letters of William Morris to his Family and Friends*, London, Longmans, 1950, p. 129; Bentley to Hadfield, 24 September 1867, R.I.B.A.

39 *BN*, (23) 1872, p. 121.

40 Swinfen Harris, *op. cit., Church Times*, 28 April 1876; *G*, 26 April 1876.

41 *Daily Telegraph*, 9 October 1890.

12   Form: The Line

Line is one of the freest elements in architectural design, and hence one of the most revealing of taste. It may be subordinate to surface, as in Butterfield's earlier work, or the dominant element, as in his later buildings. His silhouettes varied from the long severe horizontal to the jagged outline of overlapping gables; and there are many other rooflines, such as steps, waves, or pure arcs of circles, which Butterfield chose not to use. Windows similarly can be outlined and divided with rectangles, triangles, single or double curves and circles; and all of these basic elements can be found, combined with a bewildering diversity, even within the range of English Middle Pointed architecture, so that historicism provided little explanation of Victorian choice of form. It is not coincidence that it was line – the 'bulgy curve' – which was one of the first hallmarks of the Victorian style to be identified by art historians.

This curve is essentially Early rather than High Victorian, although outside progressive circles it remained popular throughout the mid-nineteenth century. It can be found, not only in Victorian teapots, teaspoons and crinolines, but also in the Ecclesiological choice of Middle Pointed as the best phase of English gothic architecture. The reason is explicitly stated in a paper 'On the Study of Gothic Mouldings' given by Philip Freeman in 1844, who argues that the Decorated period 'may justly claim the title of Perfect Gothic', because it alone employs the waving double curve and the serpentine line, waving and winding at the same time. He cited as his authority the painter William Hogarth, who had called these two lines the archetypes of beauty and of grace in his *Analysis of Beauty*; the authority, that is, of classical rococo taste. It is a revealing reminder that choice of form does not depend upon choice of historical style. For this reason in what follows historical precedent will not be discussed: it will be sufficient to say even in the perplexing variety of window tracery, Butterfield's authority can almost invariably be found in late thirteenth- and early fourteenth-century English work.

In Butterfield's work of the 1840s a variety of linear forms is found which suggests a certain ambivalence in his taste. The double curve occurs not only in brilliant

253

reconstructions like the great east window of Dorchester Abbey (8) or the gates of St Augustine's Canterbury (167), but in the flamboyant transept windows at Perth, the reticulated tracery of the warden's study and cloister there (168), and the swaying details of the pulpit panel and bookrest at Ash (169). The pulpit panels at Canterbury Cathedral and at Sessay are approximate squares formed by four ogees, and the windows at Sessay are also mostly curvilinear (254). As late as 1850 he designed an astonishing undulating opening above a silhouetted arch at the Osnaburgh Street convent (170).

Nevertheless, there were signs from the first of the severer lines of the High Victorian phase which was to follow. Most important was the continuous horizontal roofline, which we have already considered at length. Characteristic of Butterfield throughout his life, it always provided a counter-emphasis to any flamboyant detailing. Inside St Augustine's moreover Butterfield's future taste was prophesied by the criss-cross patterning of the partitions in the library, and the tall narrow sharp-raftered corridor of the dormitory range, with lines of rectangular panelling vanishing to apparent infinity (171). Even in the reticulated windows of the cloister openings below, there was a clear limitation of the influence of the double curve, for the tracery was cut sharp by the line of the low containing arches – a telling detail which offended Ruskin, who fully shared the Early Victorian taste for the flowing line.[1]

More often Butterfield's ambivalence was expressed by developing other forms for decorative use. In woodwork he explored the possibilities of bold curved or straight triangular struts with foliated lower edges, as at Avington (172) or above the serving

167 St Augustine's College
Canterbury, gates

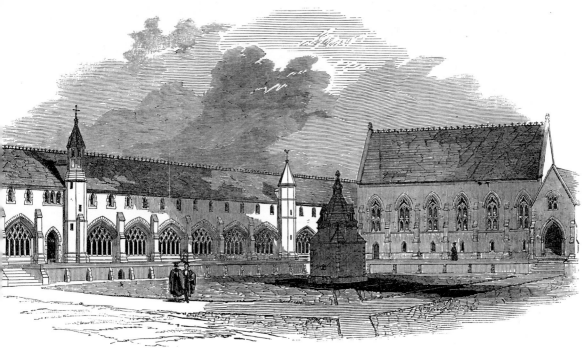

168 St Augustine's College, dormitory range and cloister (*Illustrated London News*, 1848)

169 Ash church, pulpit

170 St Saviour's Home, Osnaburgh Street, archway outside chapel

hatches at St Augustine's. At Kinwarton the rood cross itself stands on an ogee arch, but the frieze along the top of the screen is an ingenious grid of quatrefoils set between crosses in transparent squares (173). In pulpit panels by 1850 squares also provide a firm outline, even if the tracery forms still vary: a bold acute quatrefoil at Ashwell, triangular at Yealmpton, or still a hesitant ogee at West Lavington (174, 175).

Similarly, with window tracery the common plain form was either square-headed, or a level row of simple pointed or trefoiled lights, frequently cut as plate tracery without any mouldings (6). Even where richer tracery occurs, the ogee is generally avoided, sometimes by the use of simple Y-tracery or intersections, but more often by the use of circular forms. These vary from a mere trefoil or quatrefoil punched in the stone to the rich wheel windows of St Augustine's (29) and Perth Cathedral; but they have in common a certain self-containment inherent in the circle, so that they penetrate the wall surface with the least disturbance possible. This again anticipates the High Victorian style.

The moment of final ascendancy of the circle over the flowing line occurs in 1849. In the cloister at Cumbrae the sharp lines dividing the main openings carry straight over to the outer edge of the arch, as if to emphasize the absence of the expected curve; while in the chancel screen and refectory vertical uprights are carried right through without a break (155, 176). At West Lavington the chancel side windows have tracery heads in which the quatrefoils are set square rather than diagonally, and it was significant that the *Ecclesiologist* singled out this 'ungraceful' device among the 'stiff and quaint forms' and 'crochets of its author' which marred the beauty of the

171 St Augustine's
       College Canterbury,
       dormitory passage (St
       Augustine's College)

172 Avington church, stalls

173 Kinwarton church, interior and screen

174 Ashwell church, pulpit

175 West Lavington church, pulpit

176 Cumbrae College, cloister windows

177 St Matthias Stoke Newington, aisle window

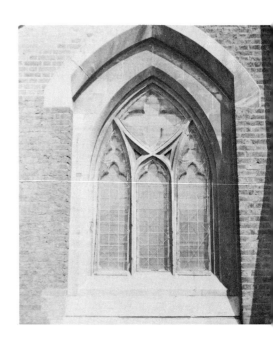

178 St Matthias Stoke Newington, aisle window

179 St Dunstan's Abbey, Plymouth, exterior from the west

180 Amesbury Abbey, altar rails

design. The window designs for St Matthias Stoke Newington (177, 178) also provoked strong protest in a letter from E. A. Freeman attacking 'one of the very worst designs I have seen for a long time'. He particularly disliked the round clerestory windows (abandoned in the second design), the 'depraved copy' of Dorchester in the west window, and the 'hideous tracery' of the aisle windows.[2] Everywhere the double curve is narrowly averted, and certainly in the aisle windows the powerful tightening of the elements is as ungainly as it is dramatic.

Such disturbing distortion is, however, unusual. The tracery at All Saints' (157), for example, is severe but elegant, above all in the side arches of the choir: triple arches clasping five circles, whose 'rich nobility' was justly noted by Gerard Manley Hopkins among others.[3] In the Wantage cemetery chapel a pure circle pierces the east wall, its cusping perfectly balanced (131). The three circles of the west window at Yealmpton are equally calm, especially in contrast to the slightly earlier east window; and at Plymouth is the most majestic of all Butterfield's triple wheel windows, bold, broad and almost motionless (179).

This balance and simplicity is characteristic of the early 1850s. Square and circle dominate; and even the gables are equilateral triangles. Furniture is sometimes reduced to the simplest horizontals and curves, like the altar rails at Amesbury (180). Wooden windows are square grids, like the big classroom window at Pollington (137), sometimes prettily decorated with cusping as at Alfington (138), or with splayed angles as in All Saints' clergy house. With stone tracery a two-light window is often headed by a broad cusped circle; the triple wheel window at Langley has a generous stability (181); and at Balliol Chapel the rather tighter tracery recalls the choir

181 Langley church, exterior from the east

arches at All Saints (50, 158). To apprehensive Oxford 'it was, indeed, no slight relief to see the beautifully chaste, and yet rich, tracery which he has employed in the windows of the present fabric, when we remember the prodigalities of ugliness which this architect has perpetrated . . .'[4]

After 1855, there are signs of change. The breadth and balance do not disappear altogether: the bold circles of the east wall at St Bees (182), for example, or the wheel windows at Winchester hospital or even Babbacombe, could easily belong to the early 1850s. The marble pulpit of All Saints' Margaret Street is inlaid with the circular discs which Butterfield first used in the Ottery font. But it is noticeable that in the pulpit the circles are no longer arranged symmetrically. At the same time the double curve reappears in the star headed west window at Etal, and the plain side windows at Belmont (183); soon also in a pulpit panel at Abbotsley (184), and an inner porch at Brigham. Nave bench ends, hitherto usually square-topped and only slightly chamfered, are sliced away to contrasted curves, spare and structural at Flitwick, ogee fronted at Belaugh, hunched at Bacton (185, 186). In the 1860s half the seats have rounded ends, most of them variations of the Bacton type, fascinating in their nervous line (369). Altar rails also become more intricate, the tracery of the gates varied from that at the sides, and often two rows of pattern laced together, as at Scottaw (187). A still stranger web of cusping clings to the strong outline of the screen at Dropmore (110). Everywhere one notices the bold trefoil outline of the early 1850s giving way to the richer cinquefoil. The sharply pointed multi-cusped vesica window, its vertical slit-eye the very antithesis to the open circle, first appears at

182   St Bees church, east wall

183 Belmont church, exterior

184 Abbotsley church, pulpit

185 Flitwick church, bench

Baldersby and the Duncombe Chapel at Waresley,[5] and this was the form which Butterfield was to choose for the chancel side windows at Babbacombe.

The disintegration of the square follows that of the circle. This is the time when, as we have seen, the roof-back is broken. Similarly, at St Alban's Holborn (225) the gable line of the great saddleback is bent, and the straight window heads of the clergy house are confused by striped keystones, relieving arches and even tracery piled up above them. The gabled churchyard gate at Brigham is triple-stepped, in striking contrast to the firm archway of the early 1850s to the grounds of Cumbrae College (188, 189). The stepped string course at Little Faringdon parsonage and the trembling chimney batter at Dropmore are equally typical of the new phase (48, 190). But its hallmark is the spreading use of diagonal diaper, filling more and more of the spaces previously left plain. Still subsidiary to the horizontal at Alvechurch, diaper becomes the dominant decorative motif at St Alban's Holborn (XII, 14); and in the 1860s it is the keynote of every major interior. Even in furniture, the diagonal criss-cross pattern fills the spandrels of the strongly arched pulpit panels at Chaddesley Corbett, or the desk at Broad Blunsdon (191, 192). It is hardly surprising that the spider's web of the nave walls at Babbacombe is echoed in the marbled pulpit (III, XVI).

Nevertheless, the diagonal line has a different role to that of the earlier square and circle, for its pattern is always essentially subsidiary to the main lines of the structure, giving way to horizontal bands, arches, or roof principals. This is why on the exterior the diaper is hesitant, restricted to a few carefully chosen zones of the wall, and

186 Belaugh church, bench

187 Scottaw church, altar rails

188 Brigham, churchyard archway

189 Cumbrae College, entrance gateway

190 Dropmore parsonage,
chimneystack

191 Chaddesley Corbett
church, pulpit

internally it is always either similarly restricted, or combined with very strong and simple architectural detail, or softened by the subtle colour tones. The impression given by contemporary engravings or by black and white photographs is for this reason often misleading. Even so, if one looks again at the engraving of St Alban's Holborn (14) the subordination of the diaper is apparent, for each of the seven zones above the chancel arch starts again from the point where it met the horizontal stone band, breaking the line of the diaper. Thus while the horizontals are continuous, the diagonals have a random quality, as Eastlake remarked, like the plumage of birds, although had he been more observant he would have scarcely argued that Butterfield had here discarded 'the *methodism* of ornament.'[6] System in Butterfield's ornament can always be found if one looks for it.

The nave at Babbacombe is again a case in point (III). We have seen how the ribbed diagonal web across the walls should be read as a play against the continuous wall surface behind it. Set within the wall surface is an apparently irregular and partial chequer of white stones inlaid with black patterns. Their half-sketched black and white lines form a third element, weaving behind the diagonal ribs, in Gerard Manley Hopkins' words, 'more by suggestion than outright, passing from one to the other'.[7] Hopkins, with his sense of line and instinctive search for the integrity of form, at once grasped a meaning which is easily missed. Yet the way in which Butterfield's mastic patterns are used is always a clue to his intention: circles to stabilize the horizontals, for example, or running tendrils picking up the spring of an arch. In the same way the seven-foiled blind medallions in the spandrels of the Babbacombe arches – another detail admired by Hopkins – lead the eye upwards towards the diagonals. The effect softens the meeting of web and arch. Had Butterfield wished to emphasize the mass of the loadbearing arch, he would have used a circle in the spandrel combined with simplified arch mouldings, as he had at Penarth (XIV).

Babbacombe is at first sight a powerful but a difficult interior. Pevsner found the surface treatment 'both fascinating and repelling',[8] and Hopkins himself felt its 'oddness at first outweighed the beauty'. But we should be in no doubt that beauty, if a strange beauty of contradiction resolved, echo and half-echo, was Butterfield's intention here. None of his own comments on Babbacombe survive, but fortunately we have his explanation of the patterning introduced in the chancel at Heytesbury (XXI). The thirteenth-century east wall there he regarded as a 'very graceful and refined triplet arrangement . . . The composition of this whole design is very dignified, and careful and perfect. No additions, except a shelf, have been made by me to the architectural lines of this East Wall'.[9] The architectural lines are thus distinguished from the patterning, which is assumed to be subordinate; its horizontals in fact give way to the upward thrust of the central lancet, and its diagonals link the lancets with the roof. Moreover, for the tiny horizontal lines sketched behind the black marble

192 Broad Blunsdon
church, desk

clustered shafts of the sanctuary piers, we have his meaning explicitly, for Lord
Heytesbury objected to them. Butterfield replied: 'I am sorry your Lordship does not
like the coloured lines on the columns at the east end. They are very simple and to my
eye so *very* characteristic that I should be very glad if you would sanction their being
done. They are a piece of old Heytesbury church which I much wish to perpetuate.
Those vertical lines on the columns *require* some horizontal ones for balance.'[10] Thus
just as the circle and square of the 1850s possessed the balance of self-sufficiency, so
the spreading later patterns explored the finer balance of interdependent line.

From the early 1870s the current again changes towards renewed simplicity. The
last brick churches showed the change least: Weybridge for example, both in its
patterns and in the multi-stepped support of the bell turret, is a conservative example
of the style of the 1860s. In Keble College Chapel (132) however, the diagonal almost
disappears internally, and in the later parts of the college, such as the dining hall, the
external patterning of the brickwork is at times strikingly horizontal. This is also true
of the later buildings at Rugby: the Chapel, Temple Reading Room, New Big
School, and the south end added to New Schools (193, 289, 290). Diaper and chequer
are still used, but less often than banding. In the sandstone interiors of the late 1870s
and 1880s, diapering plays no part at all; the constructional colouring is in broad
uninterrupted horizontal bands.

Window tracery shows no consistent development, but the very plain rose window at

193 Rugby School,
New Big Schools

194 Poulton church, stalls

Salisbury Theological College or the plate tracery of New Big School indicate a revived interest in the more elementary forms. Similarly, although furniture is frequently overladen by rich panelling and other decoration, the square is reasserted as the characteristic form for bench ends; and in some churches the choir stalls have plain rectangular grid fronts, a treatment which scarcely occurs except in the 1870s (194).

Occasionally in this last phase simplicity of line is entirely recaptured, as in the tall verticals of the triple openings to the chapel at Axbridge hospital, which allowed the patients in adjoining wards on each floor to hear the services (195). In many details, however, one finds only a coarsening of the line, as if Butterfield had failed to think his purpose through (196). There are also contrasts of thick and thin lines, or of scale, which have little apparent meaning, and seem more convincingly explained as signs of faltering imagination; and this would be scarcely surprising after forty years of perpetual invention. Nevertheless, if Butterfield's last linear patterns are a blend of boldness and intricacy often hard to accept, they can still astonish: the Dover Castle church mosaics, for example, or the writhing painted decoration at Harrow Weald (163, 197). In metalwork moreover he found a perfect final medium of expression. On door hinges or the spandrels of metal altar rails a leaf turns back across

195   St Michael's Home, Axbridge, chapel, openings to wards

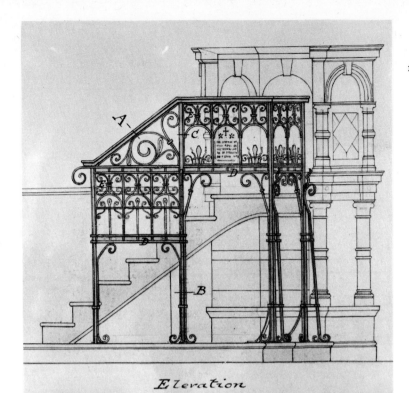

Elevation

196 Christ Church Albany
Street, pulpit design
(Christ Church chest)

197 Harrow Weald
church, nave decoration

272

198 Ardleigh church, altar rails

199 Coalpit Heath church,
door knocker

200 Rugby parish
church, altar rails

201 St Bees church,
chancel screen

its stalk in a sinuous line which anticipates *art nouveau*, although it can be traced back to the fresher flowing line of the 1840s, as in the charming decorative keyhole of the church door at Coalpit Heath (198, 199). *Art nouveau* is again foreshadowed in the rich stiff twisting altar rails at Rugby, combining iron, brass, painted colour and enamel (200). Finally, in the 1880s came the extraordinary metal screens: most ambitious of all at St Bees (201), a double tier of pierced and crenellated tracery supporting a great cross, around which giant seaweedy scrolls writhe and twine. It is very much a work of old age: graceless, in spite of the serpentine line, but in a real sense both terrible and pathetic.

Notes on chapter 12

1   See his plates in *The Seven Lamps*, London 1849.
2   (10) 1849, p. 68; (11) 1850, pp. 208–10.
3   *Notebooks and Papers of Gerard Manley Hopkins*, p. 248.
4   *BN*, (3) 1857, p. 6.
5   This chapel appears to be an afterthought, but it must belong to the late 1850s, for it does not appear in Butterfield's accounts.
6   *History of the Gothic Revival, op. cit.*, p. 257.
7   *Op. cit.*, pp. 254–5.
8   *BE, South Devon*, p. 292.
9   Notes supplied by Butterfield for Royal Archaeological Institute visit, August 1887, Heytesbury Collection.
10 Butterfield to Lord Heytesbury, 8 August 1867, *ibid.*

13   Form: The Mass

The massiveness so characteristic of High Victorian architecture reflected a fundamental move in European taste which affected not merely architecture. In dress,
for example (202), from the classic narrow line of the 1800s, the fashionable width of
skirt broadened decade by decade, until it reached a climax in the 1850s and 1860s
unrivalled in the last two hundred years.[1] The full-blown curves of mid-nineteenth-
century crinolines and teapots enclosed swollen volumes which are thus the counterpart to the short thick columns, the solid cylinder pulpits and fonts, the blunt round
apses and curved boarded ceilings of High Victorian churches (203). Once again
Ruskin spoke for the new instinct: 'The relative majesty of buildings', he wrote in
The Seven Lamps of Architecture, 'depends more on the weight and vigour of their
masses, than on any other attribute of their design.'[2]

Signs of this taste in Butterfield can be found already at Coalpit Heath. The stone
pulpit in the church is an octagon rising from a square base, its thick neck almost
buried by the encroaching volumes; while the lych-gate is a twin tunnel through a
solid mass of wall (204, 205). There are similar details in other early buildings: broad
buttresses, thick wall corbel and solid low stone walls for chancel screens (206). At
St Augustine's Canterbury the fireplaces have surrounds of simple white slabs of
stone, and the vicar's study at Wilmcote a chimneypiece of remarkable solidity (207).
Such features are exceptional, but clear anticipations of the 1850s.

Butterfield himself, however, did not fully develop this feeling for volume. It
reaches a climax in his work soon after 1849. The Wantage cemetery chapel, shorn
of buttresses, its entire walls thickening to meet the roof thrust, is 'gathered well
together' just as Ruskin wished.[3] At Osnaburgh Street the refectory chimneypiece
was of massive simplicity, punched with trefoils, a lintel shelf jutting out on four
elementary corbels (208). The tower at Wick, pyramid-capped and buttress-clasped,
was the most solid Butterfield ever built; and at Langley the spire is equally beautiful,
as if hewn from a single block (209, 210). At Sheen the vicarage (211, 212) is un-
equalled in its heaviness, the four great rolls where the garden bay squinches out to a

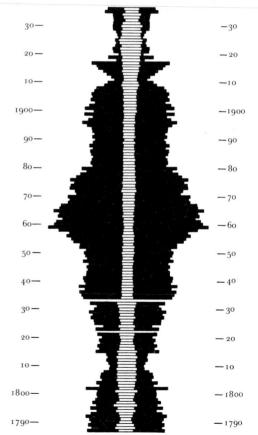

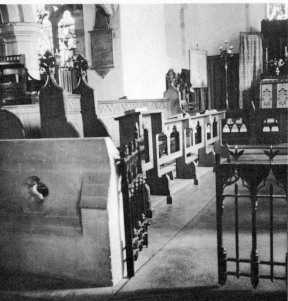

205 *above left* Coalpit Heath church, lychgate

206 *above right* Aston Cantlow church, chancel screen wall

207 *below left* Wilmcote parsonage, fireplace

208 *below right* St Saviour's Home, Osnaburgh Street, refectory fireplace

209 Wick church, tower

210 Langley church,
spire

211 Sheen parsonage, exterior from the west

212 Sheen parsonage, bay window

square almost sickeningly fat, particularly when compared with the stair turret at Winterborne Clenston which is probably the source of this motif. More attractive, and equally significant, is Butterfield's use of a circular stair turret at St Dunstan's Abbey, Plymouth, and his proposal for a cemetery chapel with a round nave (22, 213).

This exploration of the circular plan, however, proved momentary. Butterfield, probably alone of High Victorian architects, never wished to abandon the traditional English square east end; his only apse, at Rugby Chapel, was 'a case of necessity'.[4] From the early 1850s to the late 1870s the whole tendency of his design was the progressive reduction of mass to line. In this process the first stage is the square plan, the second the elongated rectangle and the polygon.

The tendency is not at once obvious. The pulpit at Amesbury (214) looks massive enough until one compares it with that at Coalpit Heath. Seen in isolation from the building to which they belong, the buttressed river wall at Milton Ernest and the thick stair turret at Waresley seem strikingly solid (215, 216). Already, however, the chimneypieces have wooden surrounds and the lych-gates are narrow and slender (154, 217); and soon the spreading feet of the porches will draw in, and the timbers become tauter and more slender (218, 219, 220). Bell turrets, square in the 1850s, similarly become octangonal, or fretted slabs eaten away by frilly detail like the west end at Blunsdon St Andrew (127, 221, 222); while the sheer upward square thrust of Baldersby and Bamford spires gives way to the uncertain pinnacles, parapet and lucarnes at Babbacombe and in the far finer unexecuted design for Brookfield (35, 223, 224, II).[5]

Opposite

213 *above left* St Dunstan's Abbey, Plymouth, exterior from the north

214 *above right* Amesbury Abbey, pulpit

215 *below* Milton Ernest Hall, buttressing

216 *left* Waresley church, stair turret

217 Milton church, lychgate

218 Milton church, porch

219 Godmersham church, porch

220 Milsted church, porch

221 Blunsdon St Andrew church, exterior from the west

222 Cape Town, St Saviour Claremont, bellcote (R. R. Langham-Carter)

223 Bamford church, spire

The dominance of line in the 1860s is such that pure composition in mass rarely occurs; the qualifying line is always present. At Babbacombe (III, XVI) the triple play of line and surface on the nave walls is repeated in the marble pulpit, whose three rows of pierced arcading are on three planes, the lower at a slightly different angle from the smaller central row, and the upper and outer row enclosing both of them. Hopkins thought it particularly 'beautiful, like a church or shrine'.[6] On a grander scale the volumes of the towering west transept and saddleback tower at St

224   St Mary Brookfield, spire design (I.C.B.S.)

Alban's Holborn (225) are brilliantly reduced by the broken line of the gable, the reduction of the stair turret from square to octagon, and the piercing of the main lower walls by slender windows of sharp tracery, including even the turret itself; although the window there is in fact blank. The still more remarkable tower of Rugby Chapel is here clearly anticipated.

The essential problem at Rugby (226) was to combine a polygonal apse with a square tower. Such juxtapositions always fascinated Butterfield: the pulpit at Coalpit

225 St Alban's Holborn, exterior

226 Rugby School, chapel exterior

Heath (204), for example, is an early exploration of the same theme. It can be found again in the slender vertical octagonals supporting chamfered square blocks in the porch at Bamford, but this time with the sharp clarity of the 1850s (227); while on the other hand the base to a wooden column at Mapledurham, triple chamfering of octagon to square and back to octagon again expresses the supreme linearity of the 1860s (228). Rugby Chapel has a little more body than this ghostly complex of intersecting angles, for its walls are largely of warm red brick. But this only makes the fracture of the volumes ·more dramatic: the flattening of the face of the apse, and double slope of its massive roof; the abrupt reduction of the square central tower to an octagon, and then to a stump of solid stone spire; the broad circle of tracery piercing the upper octagon; and the breaking of even the junction of square to octagon, and octagon to spire, by pinnacles, flying gargoyles, and tall belfry windows which penetrate the division of storeys. Yet just as internally the linear patterns play across the wall surface, but it remains behind them, essentially unbroken, so the massive High Victorian forms of the tower are still there, a tremendous silhouette against the sky, veiled, withdrawn, abstracted, and yet defiant.

Although nothing after Rugby Chapel has a comparable power, the reassertion of mass continues in Butterfield's last years. The spire at Rugby parish church is a

227 Bamford church, porch shafts

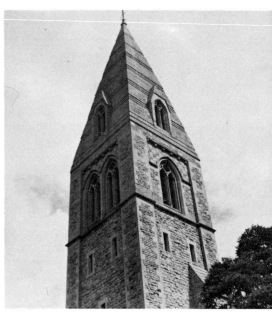

228 *left* Mapledurham church, pier base
229 *above* Enfield St Mary Magdalene, spire

noticeable simplification of Babbacombe, while Enfield is a square spire of the Bamford type, but slightly broader (229). Corbels in these last churches are sometimes as thick as those of the 1840s; a return to first motifs which repeats that of Butterfield's line. In mass, however, the failing of his invention is rather more marked. This becomes particularly clear if one traces his treatment of a single architectural element throughout his career. We shall choose two, one from structure and the other from fittings.

Of structural elements, the pier is undoubtedly the most natural medium for the expression of volume. The pier is the wall 'gathered up', in Ruskin's phrase, and its right material is solid blocks of stone: 'this gathering or concentration in form should, if possible, be the gathering or concentration in substance.'[7] Butterfield accepted this interpretation, and his piers invariably express the full integrity of the wall mass which they support. He also followed Ruskin in the forms which he chose. The Ecclesiologists in the 1840s had preferred the linear elegance of the clustered pier, or for simpler churches the neutral octagon; and these were the only forms which Butterfield used before 1850 (76). Ruskin, however, had little time for either octagon or cluster: squares and circles were 'the elements of utmost power', and the circle 'the best possible form of plan for a pier, from the beginning of time to the end of it.'[8] The change in Butterfield's choice followed at once. In the 1850s the circular column (61) is clearly the commonest form of pier (Table 5).

Table 5

Pier Types[9]

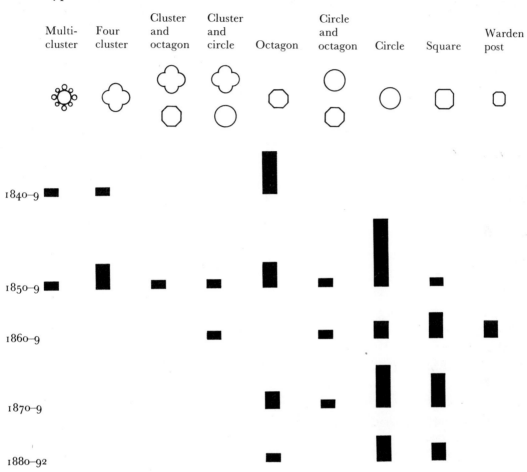

Multi-cluster	Four cluster	Cluster and octagon	Cluster and circle	Octagon	Circle and octagon	Circle	Square	Warden post

(chart rows by decade: 1840–9, 1850–9, 1860–9, 1870–9, 1880–92)

Butterfield's reaction against the circular pier at the end of the decade is indicated by the arcades at St Alban's Holborn, which revert to a sensitive multiclustered pier, less undercut than those at All Saints', but comparable in effect (14, 157). In the same church the mouldings of the arches, in many buildings of the 1850s a single plain chamfer, sometimes so slight as to leave the profile of the arch almost square, recovered some of the intricacy of the 1840s. 'They are just such pillars,' wrote the *Ecclesiologist*, 'as, in his happiest compositions, Carpenter would have been delighted to produce'.[10] The use of 'happiest' and 'delighted' here is significant, for one is tempted, looking for assaults on sensitivity, to interpret the piers and mouldings of the 1840s as hard and wiry rather than soft and subtle. All Saints', for example, would be less difficult to understand if its vivid constructional colour was strongly contained by bolder architectural forms, like those which Butterfield used at Penarth and Babbacombe (III, XIV); and these later choices suggest that the essentially elegant architectural structure at All Saints' was Early Victorian, and Butterfield innocent of the change which High Victorian colour would make in it. By the early 1860s, however, as taste turned against the bold simplicity of High Victorian detail, an elegance once innocent was re-evaluated in the light of experience. 'Mouldings are to soften the extreme bluntness of plain surfaces, but they must never appear to decrease the strength or massiveness', wrote Warington Taylor, then the manager of the William Morris firm, to the architect E. R. Robson. 'We say massive work is good, but so is light work with mouldings. The use of mouldings in this case is tenderness – not finickyness – to wit Butterfield'.[11] And again, in a letter to the *Building News* in 1865 he says: 'Nothing can surpass the supreme beauty of subtle curves, of light and shade, as found in English mouldings, and Mr Butterfield's churches in London are noble examples of this peculiar beauty. His mouldings are quite exquisite in tenderness and beauty. To dwell on them with the intention of seeking delicate curvature is an endless pleasure to the thoughtful mind.'[12] There is thus not necessarily any anti-sensual meaning in the reduction and veiling of the simpler building forms.

Nevertheless, Butterfield's piers in the 1860s retain a simplicity of a different kind. The typical form is now the square pillar, without capitals, but with a slight corner chamfer carried down from the edge of the arch (159). If the arch itself has broader mouldings these simply die into the surface of the pillar. The square pillar thus continues the wall uninterrupted to the ground, while the subtle chamfer gives the forms a linear edge: a perfect answer to Butterfield's requirements at this date. He also occasionally uses in the simplest churches, like Horton or Mapledurham, thin chamfered upright wooden posts. Here, by abolishing the wall itself, the solution is in complete linearity.

The final turn in Butterfield's taste is shown by the strong revival of the circular column in the 1870s, meeting his renewed desire for solidity (164). But it is at this point that his want of invention appears, for no new form of pier is found to suit his last buildings. He hesitates uncertainly between square and circle, and even revives the neutral octagon. One senses a drying up of the imagination; and this will be confirmed by his treatment of the font, which we must now consider.

Just as the column is the most natural structural expression of mass, so among fittings is the font. Always of stone, free-standing, raised on a pedestal, it is in fact by definition a pure piece of architectural sculpture. Butterfield's fonts reveal in fascinating sequence his attitude to line and volume.

The earliest fonts are all octagons, and the octagonal bowl was used by Butterfield

230 *above* Cautley church, font

231 *right* Wavendon church, font

with few exceptions throughout his career. It was the form recommended by the *Handbook of English Ecclesiology*; the order of preference, revealing of Early Victorian taste, was octagon, hexagon, circle and square.[13] There were, however, three variations used in the 1840s. The first and commonest was the octagon bowl and octagon stem, decorated by delicate tracery; at Coalpit Heath and Cautley the graceful Early Victorian flamboyant line (230). This type disappeared in the early 1850s. Secondly, the octagon bowl might be combined with a square base, the stem formed by intersecting chamfers like the neck of the pulpit at Coalpit Heath (204). Two attractive examples are at Wavendon and Alfington. This form was to be developed consistently for many years (231). Thirdly, there was the octagon bowl on four columns recommended in *Instrumenta Ecclesiastica* (232).[14] This design was not by Butterfield, but 'taken from the Church of All Saints', Great Barford, Bedfordshire', and probably the only case in which he himself used it without modification was the font at Hutton Buscel. Nevertheless, it is a combination of this type with a square base which produced the most astonishing font of the 1840s, in which Butterfield's brilliant originality in interweaving volumes is first revealed, at West Lavington (233). It is indeed an octagon on four columns; but the columns stand at the corners of the bowl instead of its sides, and the bowl rests on a square pillar placed diagonally on its square between the four columns, so that each face, of bowl, pillar and base, is turned

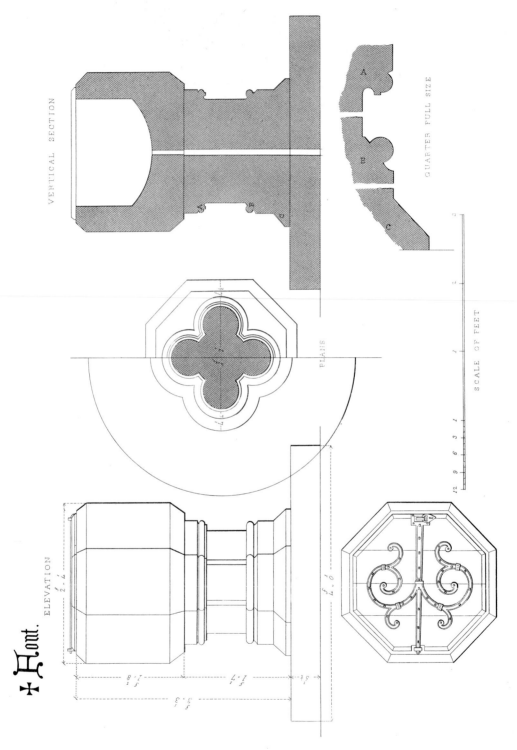

232 Font (*Instrumenta Ecclesiastica*)

233 West Lavington
church, font

to a slightly different angle. The effect is as fascinating as a transparent crystal.

West Lavington is also one of the first fonts in English marble. Colour makes its first full appearance in the massive glittering font at Ottery St Mary, which in form was closely modelled on its Norman predecessor (VI). It is revealing, however, to find that Butterfield never chose such simple massive shapes himself; his High Victorianism was from the first a controlled instinct. Even in the 1850s not a single full-blown circular font occurs. This reticence is most obvious in the richest marble fonts, whose colour gave them inherent warmth and body. At Yealmpton the rich dark bowl is quarried down to meet the paired octagonal columns of the stem (IV). At Baldersby the design is simpler, the bowl resting on eight circular columns, but the mouldings at the top and the base of the bowl provide incisive horizontals, and the shaftlines are carried up above the font itself by the slender ribbed cone of its cover (234). Finally, at All Saints' the font, designed in the late 1850s, has completely dissolved into lines, which chamfer a curved space for sculptured angels between the shafts, and cover the remaining faces with foiled webs of raised rib (235).

Among the simpler fonts there are a few more classic shapes. At Bamford there is even a solid grey marble cylinder, although arcaded and acutely tapered. At Wykeham (236) the octagon bowl stands on eight absolutely unornamented shafts, which melt into the base without a single moulding. Behind they join a central pillar, so that the

234 Baldersby church, font (Peter Burton)

235 All Saints' Margaret Street, font (*Building News*, 1859)

spaces between them are deep, soft shadows, the whole effect one of eerie dissolution. The font at Latton[15] is of equally astonishing purity, almost entirely horizontals and verticals, square base and square bowl on two levels, linked by an upright octagon (237).

More usually the forms of the 1840s are further explored. The least interesting was the octagon bowl and octagon stem, which was in fact soon abandoned. There are several octagons and squares with intersecting stems, such as the fonts at Ashwell with its splendid tall cover, and at Braishfield, where the stem's lines are traced across the bowl with trefoils of delightful simplicity (238, 239). A number of fonts also use versions of the *Instrumenta Ecclesiastica* design, with the shafts normally under the angles of the bowl. In two of these, contemporary with the All Saints' font, the projecting faces of the bowl are chamfered away; at Waresley by a simple trefoil, and at Ashford, where the bowl itself is incised with a criss-cross grid pattern, with a cinquefoil (240, 241).

These two fonts anticipate the most perfect form of the 1860s, when the trefoil chamfer of the octagon bowl is carried upwards from the intersecting lines of the stem. The purest example is at Wokingham (242). At Horton it is modified by a deep incised groove to mark off the bowl (243); and the same groove is also effectively

236 Wykeham church, font

Opposite

237 *left* Latton church, font

238 *right* Ashwell church, font

used in the older combination of octagon and squares at Tadlow. A final variation which Butterfield was to use in many of his later fonts was to carry the stem chamfer upwards as a plain sharp triangle, leaving the faces of the bowl like up-ended gables, and filling them with inset six-foiled vesica panels. This is the Godmersham type (244).

Versions of the *Instrumenta Ecclesiastica* form continue. The closest to the original is at Stibbard, varied only in its much more slender proportions (245). More often the sides of the bowl are unequal, as in the rich little marble font at Charlton, or there are eight rather than four columns as at Beech Hill (246). At Dropmore, in tune with the other sharp contrasts of the church, the blackish green, white and grey font combines both devices (247).

Finally, at Babbacombe a new type appears, one richly marbled cinquefoliate arcade pierced to reveal a second inner row (XV). It was a development of eight-shafted fonts like Baldersby (234), and earlier at Selly Oak the shafts were linked by canopied gables stretched across the faces of the bowl. Now, however, although the double arcading at Babbacombe was unique, the theme of veiling the surface of the bowl by outer arcading is pursued in a group of fonts of the late 1860s and early 1870s. The finest are at Whiteparish, where the play of surface is so sensitive that only

239   Braishfield church, font

240   Waresley church, font and bench end

241   Ashford church, font

242   Wokingham St Sebastian, font

243 Horton church, font

244 Godmersham church, font

245 Stibbard church, font

246 Beech Hill church, font

247 Dropmore church, font

248 Whiteparish church, font

249 Barley church, font

250 Morebath church, font

251 Netherhampton church, font

252 *left* Braunston church, font

253 *above* Kingsbury Holy Innocents, font

the thin line of canopy and the placing of the shafts flush with the bowl indicate the intention (248); and at Barley, where by contrast the font is a bold square, pierced by intersected circular arcading of noble elegance (249).

One font in the 1870s is equally original: the bowl at Morebath is a cluster of eight circles cut from a single piece, the larger volumes at the corners (250). Otherwise the fonts of the 1870s are either arcaded octagons, of which the most interesting is at Brookfield, or intersected squares and octagons. Colourless, the font at Netherhampton reduces the Godmersham type almost to transparent diagonal wire structure (251). Braunston, by contrast, is a delicious shape of pink and grey marble (252); and Hagnaby, also of 1879, is equally fine, with a big ochre yellow knob stuck to each face (VII).

Butterfield's sense of material was thus undiminished; and of the fonts of the 1880s the finest is undoubtedly another marble font of very similar type, at Ault Hucknall. Again, at Kingsbury (253) the Godmersham type is repeated in white stone, very slightly broader than at Netherhampton. But in form these fonts are almost identical repeats of earlier shapes. Nor do the shafted fonts show any more originality: Ardleigh, for example, is simply an inferior version of Whiteparish. If fonts are a fair indication, Butterfield's sense of form reaches a climax of imaginative invention in the 1850s and 1860s, and then dies away.

Notes on chapter 13

1 J. Richardson and A. L. Kroeber, 'Three Centuries of Women's Dress Fashions, A Quantitative Analysis', *Anthropological Records*, (V) 1949.

2 p. 91.

3 *Ibid.*, p. 70.

4 Swinfen Harris, *op. cit.*

5 The Brookfield design of 1870 is worth comparing with Street's spire at St Mary Magdalene Paddington, which was completed in 1873.

6 *Op. cit.*, pp. 254–5.

7 *The Stones of Venice*, I, vii.

8 *Ibid.*, and *The Seven Lamps*, p. 72.

9 Includes all *new* arcades (except Portsmouth); some rebuildings, such as Sessay, are excluded as doubtful.

10 (22) 1861, p. 322.

11 Warington Taylor to E. R. Robson, (7 and 9) n.d. c. 1865, Fitzwilliam Museum.

12 (12) 1865, pp. 17–18.

13 pp. 131–2.

14 Plate 44.

15 This font is not documented, but is closely related to the pulpit by Butterfield at Latton; it probably dates from the nave restoration of the late 1850s (*B* (19) 1861, p. 688).

When Butterfield came to put together the elements of the buildings which we have considered separately, he was not himself aware of the delight in awkwardness and 'coltish negligence', of the search for discord and ugliness, which modern critics have discerned in his work. He would have been astonished by Summerson's belief that he had 'no sense of composition', or Goodhart-Rendel's that 'his buildings never condescend to please, in fact they often seem intended to alarm.'[1] One finds quite the opposite intention expressed in his letters. He writes, for example, to Lord Heytesbury of the little church at Knook, which he was restoring, 'I have no doubt that Knook will make a remarkably pretty interior.'[2] Similarly, we have already seen how he conceived the patterned walls of Keble as 'gay', and the chapel as conveying 'quiet order, completeness and proportion'.

So anxious, indeed, was he to avoid any disharmonies in the chapel interior at Keble (81), that when the college accepted the gift, from the widow of Thomas Combe, of Holman Hunt's famous painting of the 'Light of the World', Butterfield strongly resisted the suggestion that it should be hung in the chapel. 'I am not so *very* much delighted about the "Light of the World" if it must be put in the Chapel,' he wrote to the Warden. 'Being a sentimental picture, it is much more appropriate in my judgement to some other room, such as the Library. I want the Chapel to be complete once for all in itself and not at the mercy of posterity, to be pieced and patched and adorned hereafter . . .' A year later the argument was still continuing, with the Gibbs family now drawn in, arguing 'that the picture and the mosaics are incongruous with one another', and that if it were hung in the chapel 'every surrounding colour will clash with it'.[3] Eventually the picture was hung in the library, although the college had its revenge later when a special chapel was built to contain it, thereby mauling the chapel exterior.

Moreover, in Butterfield's compositions we see not merely a search for harmony, a desire to please the eye, but also a conscious and systematic exploration of form. It might not be thought that for an architect working in the Puginist tradition of

304

picturesque rationalism any such system was necessary. 'An architect should exhibit his skill,' Pugin had written, 'by turning the difficulties which occur in raising an elevation from *a convenient plan* into so many *picturesque beauties*'.[4] Accidents, irregularities, surprising juxtapositions were to be welcomed rather than resisted. And certainly there are many details in Butterfield's work which spring from such an attitude: the cramped window at Balliol (50), for example, to which he felt not the least objection because there was 'such a good *reason*' for it, or the porch in the tiny constricted courtyard at All Saints', which he allowed – in Summerson's words – to 'collide grotesquely with the wall of the Clergy House.'[5] But to conclude from the detection of such details that accident and conflict is the essence of Butterfield's compositions is completely to misread his buildings. Gerard Manley Hopkins perhaps most clearly expressed the distinction between Butterfield's interpretation of the picturesque and its vulgarization when, in 1877, he wrote to Butterfield to thank him for sending a list of buildings, which he had asked for. These he would visit 'as chance puts me in the way. I hope you will long continue to work out your beautiful and original style. I do not think this generation will ever much admire it. They do not understand how to look at a Pointed building as a whole having a single form governing it throughout, which they *would* perhaps see in a Greek temple: they like it to be a sort of farmyard and medley of ricks and roofs and dovecots.'[6] It is in the sympathetic spirit of Hopkins, rather than with the jaundiced eye of most recent critics, that we are most likely to reach understanding of Butterfield's architectural composition.

Not that the difficulties of reaching an interpretation of any kind should be underestimated. We have very few comments on design from Butterfield which go beyond generalities. For example, we have no record of 'the shrewd deductions [which] he drew from . . . his careful diagnosis of the relative heights of towers and their relation to the buildings to which they belonged.'[7] Nor do we know how, in the privacy of his study, he worked out the first rough designs for his buildings. There is simply the information that he did not draw with a T-square, but with a two-foot rule and folding compasses.[8] This is itself interesting, for it suggests that he worked out proportions by a method of triangulation, such as had been used by the medieval master-builders. It has also been said that when designing tile patterns he would spend many hours juggling with actual tiles on the floor.[9] But apart from this we can only look at his architecture, approaching it through the aesthetic doctrines which Butterfield and his contemporaries professed.

We have already discussed several of these doctrines: the social notions of convenience and propriety which underlay the planning of buildings, and the distribution of ornament; the concern for 'reality' which led to the display of structure and materials; and the belief in gothic historicism, gradually shifting from relatively strict copyism to an eclecticism governed only by gothic principles. These doctrines were crucial in the selection of the elements to be composed. But in the process of composition itself, underlying them all, were the governing romantic principles of the picturesque and the sublime. Both followed from the discovery that buildings should be seen, not as isolated objects, but as part of a landscape. But they represented different moods. The picturesque scene would surprise the beholder, evoke his curiosity, through devices such as variety and irregularity, roughness and intricacy. The sublime on the other hand would evoke terror, like a black thunderstorm, or a bottomless chasm. Its attributes were held to be the reverse of the picturesque: vastness of height or length, smoothness, obscurity. These two moods were held to be the extremes, so that between them nicely judged, lay beauty. Beauty was thus regarded as essentially a classical concept, against which both the sublime and the picturesque should be understood as romantic reactions. It is hardly surprising that, conceived in this negative sense, it received less attention than the two newer categories.

The picturesque and the sublime were originally understood in the late eighteenth century as categories of scenery, but they were soon transferred to buildings, and both concepts influenced architecture throughout the nineteenth century. No longer was the ideal building symmetrical, capped by a straight horizontal parapet, approached axially, with proportions somewhere between a cube and a double cube. Instead,

254 Sessay church, exterior

very gradually, asymmetry, a varied silhouette, the diagonal view, and emphatic horizontality or verticality became the architect's aim. When Butterfield was beginning work in the 1840s the current of taste was still moving in this direction, and a general reaction towards more classical notions of beauty can hardly be discerned before the 1860s or 1870s.[10] It is therefore hardly surprising to find these romantic concepts remained fundamental to his architectural composition throughout his career, even though, as we shall see, he gradually moved away from the interpretation with which he began.

Butterfield's architecture in the 1840s is a picturesque style in which the heritage of an abandoned classicism can still be discerned. Coalpit Heath church and vicarage, or Sessay church, may be taken as typical examples (5, 6, 254). These small buildings are placed informally in the landscape and they are approached by paths which lead diagonally from little entrance archways towards the porch. They have irregular, although relatively simple, silhouettes, and each elevation is asymmetrical and distinctively varied from the other elevations. At the angles there is often a contrast between blank and windowed sections of wall. There is also, at Sessay and the Coalpit Heath vicarage, an astonishing variety in the tracery and the profiles of the mouldings of the windows. On the other hand, although there are variations of colour and texture, they are only slight; the buildings are still essentially monochrome, their materials reticent. It is also noticeable that the parts of the building seem like units put together in the classical method, even if they are in fact imperfect when separated. Certainly they convey little sense of organic unity or growth.

This is still more obvious within. The Ecclesiologists encouraged a certain degree of asymmetry internally, through the placing of the pulpit on the north side of the chancel arch, and the font near the (preferably south) entrance door. Nor did they believe it essential to balance one arcade with another: it was better 'to build one aisle as it ought to be, than to run up two cheaply'.[11] But Sessay has one aisle only because it is a rebuilding on an old plan. The Coalpit Heath interior is entirely axial, apart from the placing of the pulpit and the vestry doorway. Butterfield uses here what was to become a favourite device: the chancel arch is kept lower than the arcades, so that from the west end its apex seems to meet that of the east window. This relationship and the axiality are, however, the only links between the series of spaces, which are merely juxtaposed, opening to each other without any organic connection.

Similar qualities can be found in Butterfield's only major group of buildings from these early years, St Augustine's College, Canterbury (29, 47, 168). The chapel range, for example, is very much a juxtaposition of separate building units, and in this case each unit is itself virtually symmetrical. The long dormitory range is also divided by two matched staircase turrets into three apparently balanced sections. These buildings

w

are grouped round a courtyard, of which each range is different in character; while further variation is introduced by enclosing the fourth side only by a flint wall and a magnificent beech which had been specially protected during the building.[12] The informality is, however, carefully controlled by suggestions of axiality: the formal paths round the edge of the court, the little square pyramid-roofed stone conduit in the centre of the grass, the formal steps and terracing, the balanced height and projection of hall and library and the implied symmetry of the dormitory range. The picturesque is thus still playing with a classical sense of order, balance and completeness.

In one sense the second phase of Butterfield's design, beginning just before 1850, marks a heightening of picturesque variety, for this is the period in which he begins experimenting with constructional colour. Certainly brick churches like All Saints' or St Thomas Leeds, or even the little school at Alfington with its mixture of brick, half-timber and tilehanging, have far greater contrasts of texture and colour than any of his earlier buildings (73, 120, 138). Nevertheless it was not until the late 1850s that Butterfield turned to constructional polychromy in full earnest, and in the early 1850s his development was rather towards simplification than further variety. We have seen earlier how this was the period in which Butterfield favoured the classical line and form of the circle and the cylinder, the unifying continuous ridge-line, and the uninterrupted wall plane. For a brief moment he approached a High Victorian sense of volume. By the standards of the Early Victorian picturesque in the compact little cemetery chapel at Wantage, Butterfield achieved a classic unity (131). And although this building was unique in its lucid simplicity, Butterfield's small churches, schools and vicarages are a strikingly severe version of the picturesque: the straight wall face and level ridge which pull together Cowick school and Hensall vicarage, for example, or the great sharp-edged surfaces of their church roofs (19, 62, 127, 130). Similarly, within these smaller churches, although in several cases he now used an asymmetrical plan with only one aisle, a sense of spatial unity is now achieved by two means: the walls are linked to the roof by the subtle canting of the lowest stage of rafters first introduced at Huddersfield, and the nave to chancel by opening out the chancel arch and sometimes raising it on corbels, running the wall surface unbroken between the two parts of the church (101).

In plainer buildings, such as the single-cell school at Letcombe Bassett, or the long terraces of cottages at Kirby Maxloe and Braunston (255, 256), this phase seems to continue strongly to the end of the decade, only changes in the roofline and the introduction of wall patterning pointing to the style of the 1860s. With the larger church or house, on the other hand, the severity of the early 1850s made a far less obvious impact on the picturesque manner of composition. This was because of the number of elements and the degree of ornament, which could only be handled

255 Braunstone, cottage terrace

256 Kirby Maxloe, cottage terrace

according to picturesque principles. Sheen vicarage, for example, although massive, and boldly simplified in all its details, is clearly picturesque in its organization (211). The same is true of Milton Ernest Hall (258–261). Certainly the east front facing the avenue is severe, both ridge and wall surface uninterrupted, only a bay window and a restrained use of brick detail with the fine local stone introducing variety. But in the entrance front the silhouette is of broken ridges and three irregular gables, one of which merges into another; and although the wall plane is tight across the face of each gable, the parts recede and advance in six separate stages. A sense of balance is achieved by two means, both characteristic of picturesque composition. As one first approaches the front obliquely from the drive, it seems that the axis is at the taller central gable, with the projecting hipped main wing balanced by a projecting porch. But it soon appears that although there is a deep cleft in the front, the central gable is not at the back of it, but only slightly stepped back from the wing. The cleft thus marks a central axis with the two higher gables to the left; and to achieve an equilibrium the lower gable of the porch is now reinforced by a horizontal ridge line and roof surface to its right, an effect happily reinforced when a low wing was added in the 1900s. This balancing of verticals and horizontals is also used in the garden front. Although the essential form here is more compact, with a long horizontal bounding ridge, the wall surface itself is broken in a manner which looks forward to the 1860s. There are four sections to the front, each in itself symmetrical, with the two central sections the most elaborate. The most emphatic feature, however, is the tall projecting bay window of the section to the right of centre. This rises just sufficiently to break the main ridge, thus throwing the horizontal weight to the left, and this, together with the projection and gable of the outer left section, again secures an equilibrium. Once more, however, the effect changes as one moves to the angle: from the river bank below the garden the main ridge is scarcely visible, and instead the hipped lean-to scullery, bay gables and main roof gables build up to a powerful interlocking composition.

Inevitably, the organization is still more complex when we turn to the two major building groups of these years, Cumbrae College and All Saints' Margaret Street. It is in fact only when Cumbrae is compared with St Augustine's Canterbury that the tightening of the composition becomes obvious. It is not merely in the handling of details, such as the interlocking roofs of the chapel (262), the unbroken ridge-lines, the bold simplicity of the spire. The most dramatic change at Cumbrae is in the organization of the group as a whole in relation to the landscape.

Throughout his life Butterfield was concerned to present his buildings in a landscape setting: even Highbury Chapel was designed to stand among curved paths and shrubs.[13] He urged that the cheapest of chapels at Bursea required the planting of one or two yew trees: 'A building ought to have a few trees of its own'.[14] Where

ATTICS

FIRST FLOOR

GROUND FLOOR

BASEMENT

257 Milton Ernest Hall, plan (Starey Collection)

258 Milton Ernest Hall,
east front

259 Milton Ernest Hall,
approach to north
(entrance) front
(Colonel Hogg)

260 Milton Ernest Hall,
north front

261 Milton Ernest Hall,
south (garden) front

money was available, he was more ambitious. At Milton Ernest he paced the park
with Benjamin Starey, deciding where to plant copses to improve the vistas.[15] Even
for the relatively modest church and parsonage at Bamford, he designed not only a
garden (263), with a terraced lawn with flower beds in front of the house and syca-
mores behind, but spent a large sum in transplanting mature trees for the churchyard.[16]

Terraces and trees were the main elements in such designs for landscape. Terracing,
especially in front of a major building, was intended to be strongly architectural,
'kept at one dead level approached by steps . . . Its surface must not be frittered away
in flower-beds, but left in strong and severe lines.'[17] In the same spirit at Ottery St
Mary 'the old flower garden was done away with and in its place the slope was
terraced'.[18] Trees, on the other hand, were intended to introduce informality.
Butterfield would mix deciduous trees with yews and hollies. It is interesting to
notice that he valued evergreens not for their sombre associations, but because landscape was made 'very much more cheerful in winter by some good dark foliage . . .
I saw last autumn in Herefordshire an avenue of scotch firs and yews alternately of a
mile long and very old and handsome, and Herefordshire is full of yews everywhere,
to the great improvement of the scenery in winter.'[19] In a bleak open landscape, such
as Pinchbeck in the fens, or on the Yorkshire plain, Butterfield would usually group
his buildings within a grove of trees (264, 265). Baldersby village is a good example of
this technique. But where there were varied levels, he could exploit them brilliantly.
One thinks of St Mawgan rectory perched on the edge of the combe, approached

262   Cumbrae College, chapel roofs

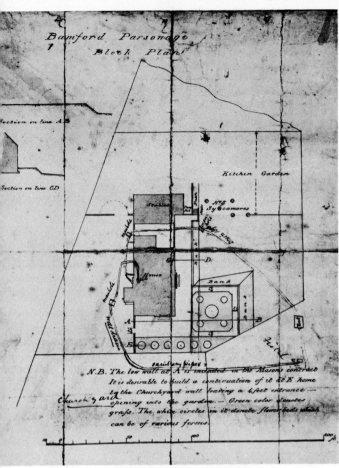

263 Bamford vicarage, garden plan
(Bamford chest)

264 *below left* Baldersby village

265 *below* Pinchbeck Bars church,
exterior

266 West Lavington parsonage, west (entrance) front

267 West Lavington parsonage, south front

either by a long drive hugging the slope, or by a steep path from the stream below (43); or the similar contrast at West Lavington (266, 267), where the carriage drive curves through tall trees to the first oblique view of the house, standing among lawns with a magnificent old beech, while the ground falls sharply from the adjacent church, so that the church path climbs a series of steep terraces from the corner of the lane.

Nowhere is Butterfield's sense of landscape more impressive than at Cumbrae (268). For the College of the Holy Spirit, founded in 1849 for 'the frequent celebration of Divine Service by a Collegiate Body under circumstances favourable to religious learning', a site of monastic isolation was chosen. It stands on a long low green island in the Clyde, hidden from the little town of Millport behind a thicket of trees and a long buttressed wall with heavy wooden gates under a stone arch (189). A wicket door opens to a path, which climbs through the wood. The college stands on grass terracing at the crest of the hill, so that the first glimpse of its spire from below exaggerates its height. The picturesque qualities of the buildings are at once obvious. Each main range stands at right angles to one of another character: the bare north roof surfaces of the church contrasted to the richer handling of the choristers' house, and the sheer verticality of the spire to the long roof of the canons' house (269, 270).

268 Cumbrae College, from the west (Valentine and Sons)

269 Cumbrae College, canons' range and chapel

270 Cumbrae College, choristers' range (Walter Kerr)

Equally, each separate elevation is asymmetrical. The choristers' house in particular is a brilliant composition, the roof brought down at each end with mansards and dormers, but hinged off centre on a grandly battered double chimney-breast, which encloses one of the windows as it rises. It is countered by a gothic door, tall staircase window and thin spirelet on the ridge. The irregularity at Cumbrae is in fact carefully controlled: the detail spare, the grey masonry wonderfully consistent, and the whole group tightly knit both by its plan and by its roofline. Instead of the loose enclosure of St Augustine's, the plan at Cumbrae is formal, a rough cruciform, the canons' and choristers' houses running along the slope, the cloister and refectory settled into the hill behind, and the chapel projected, facing the wide view of hills and estuary. The spire marks one axis, the balancing canons' and choristers' houses the other. The buildings are thus a close group, yet fully open to the landscape. Seen from the east, the college is unforgettable, the sharp thrust of the spire and the simply battered chimney-breasts playing against the long line of slate roofs and grey walls, and beyond, the distant mountain silhouette of Arran across the Clyde.

All Saints' equally needs to be understood in its setting: the town. Butterfield's concepts of town-planning are inevitably less clear than those of landscape, for he had little chance to develop them. His comments when the Metropolitan Board of Works threatened part of the Adelphi in 1866 are interesting, not merely for his admiration of that 'systematically planned block of buildings', but for his comments on street alignments. He criticized crescents and diagonal crossings resulting in houses 'running off in their ground plans to needle points' as causing 'a very great and needless amount of discomfort'. Streets in towns should not be laid out 'as if they were merely to run between hedges'. It was also important to keep them narrow, so as 'not to be too temptingly convenient' as a short cut from 'primary' traffic routes. Later Butterfield also gave some advice on the street plan of Bloomsbury.[20]

His only practical experience, however, was not in such densely urban problems, but in laying out the new seaside town at Hunstanton in Norfolk in 1861. The central area there follows his plan, a series of irregular triangular greens, with the Upper Green open to the sea. He provided plans for first, second and third class houses, and during the next two years spent some time examining proposals by local developers. At least one terrace of houses in the centre is a characteristic solid example of his style (271). All the buildings are relatively simple, and built of ginger brown local carrstone. Butterfield's scheme, according to a local directory, was to place the buildings 'singly or in groups, in masses of irregular form and size, interspersed with gardens and open spaces, so as to avoid to the utmost extent the air of chilling uniformity which is so conspicuous and disagreeable in some of our watering places. At the same time the bizarre and often hideous forms of building to be found in such places were rigidly excluded by the enforcement of a general similarity of style and material.' The Hunstanton plan was for a strictly controlled picturesque, and in fact it proved too strict for 'the natural craving for larger masses and more imposing arrangements' felt by Victorian seaside society. It was largely abandoned in the 1870s, when the north part of the town was developed with classical squares and terraces with the traditional seaside balconies and verandahs.[21]

It is thus important to remember that Butterfield's churches dominate their town settings, not so much because he wished to destroy the unity of the existing townscape, but rather because he believed that churches should be its focus. His one artisan terrace in London, four houses in St Michael's Street Paddington, could hardly be less assertive; they are as mean as any common builder's work. His town churches on the other hand, whether in relatively open situations as in Huddersfield and Manchester (58) or in cramped sites like All Saints' or St Alban's Holborn, almost always stand high above their surroundings. The Huddersfield spire reached 220 feet, All Saints' a few feet more. The main roofs were equally high, to provide the clerestory lighting which was essential in many town sites. Indeed while most of Butterfield's country churches have no clerestories, his town churches are all clerestoried, and some very grandly. Of Stoke Newington (7) the *Ecclesiologist* wrote, 'Mr

271   Hunstanton, St
         Edmund's Terrace

Butterfield resolved to make St Matthias a *town* church . . . Accordingly its huge clerestory, and high roof, and unusual gabled tower, stand out in marked contrast to the modern rows of houses which are rapidly rising round the site of the new church; arrest the eye at once . . .' Hence also the 'striking proportions' of the interior, the height to the ridge just half the total length, and one and a half times the total width of the church, and the great clerestory space above the relatively low arcades.[22]

The town church was therefore a special type evolved from both functional and symbolic needs. It was very much a concern of the Ecclesiologists at this time. It was in 1850, for example, that G. E. Street delivered his important paper 'On the Proper Characteristics of a Town Church' to the society. Yet there can hardly have been a more influential contribution to the discussion than the building of Butterfield's All Saints' Margaret Street. If his patron Beresford-Hope had dreamt of a building which would domineer 'over the haughty and Protestantized shopocracy',[23] surely his vision was realized? It is no coincidence that in this, the most dramatically vertical of all his buildings, the *Ecclesiologist* felt that Butterfield 'approached to the sublime of architecture'.[24]

Butterfield's achievement was a triumph over formidable difficulties (26, 272). He had little more than a hundred feet square in which to fit not only a church, but a choir school with dormitory, dining room, classrooms and kitchen, and a clergy house for the vicar, two curates and servants. At the back of the site the school and house would have been dark and inaccessible. Butterfield therefore pushed the church to the back of the site and brought the house and school to the street front, and by linking the two buildings at basement level he was able to open up a small entrance courtyard with a view of the church without running above the cornice and roofline of the existing Georgian street. The detailing of the street front is also sober, plain sash windows set in horizontal bands of darker brick, only the plain gables hinting of gothic. Behind them, as if independently, rides the noble twin-windowed smooth buttressed belfry stage of the tower and the astonishingly sheer slated spire.

The problem was how to relate these elements in the entrance. The juxtaposition of porch, school and tower base in the corner of the courtyard were not a difficulty *created* by Butterfield, as some of his critics would seem to imply; it would have been very difficult to have entered the church at any other point. Butterfield's solution was to focus attention on the great pinnacled buttress which rises, with a relief of the Annunciation on its face, from the outer south wall of the church. This leads the eye diagonally from the entrance archway towards the porch, and at the same time upwards, its emphatic verticality providing a relationship with the spire. At the same time, standing free above the aisle roof, it becomes the centre of a deeper space reaching back to the clerestory wall, and so mitigates the well-like constriction of the miniature courtyard.

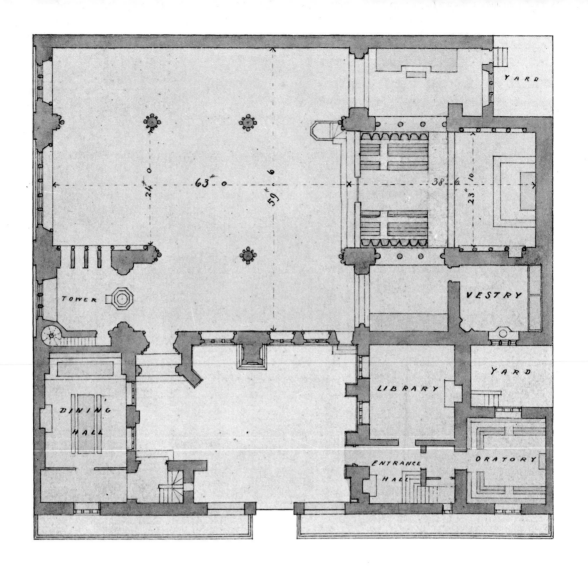

272 All Saints' Margaret Street, plan (Starey Collection)

Internally the small space is handled with equal brilliance (X, 157). The church was inevitably short, and this shortness was emphasized by the need for a blank east wall because of adjoining buildings. Rather than trying to minimize these difficulties, Butterfield exploited them. Three giant arches stride the nave; above them, to a third of their scale, runs the wall arcade of the clerestory and then the steep raftered roof. The chancel arch is also steep, but only a little above the height of the arcade, so that the sharp vaulting of the chancel rises into high shadow beyond. Although the actual shape of all these arches is nobly elegant, their cumulative effect is dynamic, telescoping the church and thrusting forward the great eastern reredos and the high patterned wall above the chancel arch. Moreover, while chancel and nave are distinct at roof level, their side walls are deliberately unified; the chancel arch rises from corbels and the string course above the arcades is continuous – a violation of the earlier Puginist doctrine that the parts of a church should be distinct both in plan and treatment. Through this deliberate foreshortening the interior is given its dramatic impression of height. It is difficult to understand why Professor Hitchcock regarded the plan of All Saints' as failing to generate 'any positive organization of spacial volumes'.[25] On the contrary, it is surely a masterpiece in exactly this sense?

It is worth emphasizing that where he had a free choice Butterfield never sought such unconventional spatial relationships. St Alban's Holborn (14) was certainly organized by the same method, although with a rather broader chancel, a lower arcade and a far grander clerestory. But at St Alban's the planning problem was very similar, a constricted site which again imposed a blank east wall. The solution was again original and impressive. The particular organization of these two interiors was, however unique. There are, moreover, a number of instances in which Butterfield expressly stated his belief in proportion. Keble Chapel has already been mentioned. There is also Heytesbury (XXI), where he wanted to avoid a tunnel-like effect: 'I think that a screen assists the proportions of such a very long and narrow Church as Heytesbury is.'[26] Perhaps most interesting is Balliol Chapel (158), where the college argued for several months on whether or not to lengthen or widen the chapel. Butterfield never 'ventured to suggest both extra length and extra width in the same plan' because the costs would have been too great. 'I should be very glad to have both. I think this would allow of making a perfect chapel'. Assuming this to be impossible, he proposed to widen and heighten the chapel, but keep within its old length. 'I felt that by giving the Chapel extra length and height, and the latter I feel must be given in any case, without extra width, we gain undesirable proportions.' The same disadvantage would follow from throwing the antechapel into the main space. He also resisted the extension of seating eastwards to encroach on the sanctuary. 'A considerable open space at the East end gives great dignity to the Chapel. I wish that space could have been larger.' And lastly, it is noticeable that he regards this internal proportion as more important than the exterior irregularities which resulted from it. He accepts the cramped north-west window, and welcomes the irregular new roofline. 'I really have not the least fear of the extra height of the Chapel above the library. I am sure it will give great life and effect of a good kind to the quadrangle'.[27]

'Life and effect' were of course typical attributes of the picturesque; and during the later 1850s they were to become increasingly prominent in Butterfield's work. Contrasts of texture and colour, variations in the wall plane, broken rooflines, recession and projection in plan, are now used not merely in large parsonages like Alvechurch (150) and Baldersby (34) – admittedly extreme cases – but also in smaller village churches like Waresley and Elerch (273, 274), and schools like Aldbourne, Castle Hill or Northington (133, 275). It is not until the 1860s, however, that these changes – initially somewhat disruptive – coalesce in a new style. Rather than attempting to analyse these harsh-patterned transitional buildings, it will therefore be more rewarding to turn to the new unity which Butterfield achieved in the 1860s.

This new unity is heralded by a return to a rather gaunt simplicity of shape in the Newbury parsonage (69) and St Cross church at Manchester, despite the fact that in both buildings the brickwork was strongly patterned and stone-banded (58, 115). Internally the Manchester church is a single space of noble proportions, its chancel

273 Waresley church, exterior

274 Elerch church, exterior

275 Castle Hill school and house

arch so broad and high that it defines nave and chancel without separating them. The double side arches of the choir are only a fraction higher than the nave arcades, and the upper level of windows is carried right round the church, the nave clerestory and west windows rising from the same moulded sill line as the choir clerestory and east window. The sill is also expressed as a continuous moulding externally, and only a coping marks the division of nave and chancel in the long slate roof. Nothing is allowed to challenge the long high main vessel of the church. A contemporary comment indicated how barren the exterior seemed to eyes trained in the picturesque tradition: 'Its outline is essentially modern. The details, with great costliness, are meagre to a degree, and the general proportions perverse and unsatisfactory. The tower . . . is a diminutive campanile . . . out of all proportion with the church.' The contrasts should have been emphasized by a 'more massive' steeple. Nor could the critic understand that Butterfield had not merely deliberately produced a light building rather than a massive one, but had emphasized this by the continuous linear patterning of the wall surfaces. His precedent-trained eye only observed that in the west gable there were 'three two-light windows, whose *acute* heads are surmounted at a considerable interval of plain masonry with *obtuse* arched labels – a freak that has the effect of disagreeably enhancing the weakness of the angles.'[28] Yet this particular detail had become an essential device in Butterfield's new system: watch, for example, how on the smooth brick surface of St Alban's Holborn clergy house (66) he plays with window heads, strainer arches and hoodmouldings of contrasting shapes, leading the eye upwards to the gables, but at the same time linking the horizontal bands which string the windows together. The apparently arbitrary lines have a clear purpose. Line, in fact, is the essence of the new style of the 1860s, as surface and volume had been of the previous decade.

The change runs through every type of building designed by Butterfield. The earlier plain solid brick cottages, for example, give way to the tall narrow Bookham design, or more commonly, to rich patterns of half-timbering (30, 134, 139). The strong simple shapes of a small stone church like Milton become at Elerch a complex series of broken spreading slopes (274, 277). Every surface is interrupted. Yet in spite of its complexity, its highly picturesque irregularity and asymmetry, Elerch church is tightly composed around its pyramid-capped central tower. The vestry wall, for example, although of three different eaves' heights, retains a continuous surface, and the middle roof section allows the east face of the tower to be extended like an arm over the vestry, while the upper roof section picks up the shapes of the tower cap and the porch. With a brick church like Horton the shapes are similar if less complex, because they are broken by colour patterns; and once again the contrast with the churches of the 1850s is abrupt (VIII, 276). But the most characteristic small churches of the 1860s are not in brick alone, but brick, flint and half-timbering, like Beech Hill or

276 Braishfield church, exterior

277 Milton church, exterior

Dropmore. Here, where the linear patterning is most insistent, the underlying shapes are the simplest: externally a long unbroken roofline, and within, a single space, the roof again unbroken, divided by a high open wooden screen (72, 110, 166).

In parsonages one again observes a tendency to tighten the shapes where the liveliest surface patterning is used. At Little Faringdon, for example, the surfaces are rougher, mouldings more frequent, window shapes more varied and the roof shapes looser than at Dropmore, where the house is a closely interlocked composition in brick, flint and half-timbering (48, 143). It is for this reason that, while the purest expression of Butterfield's style of the early 1850s was in his most unpretentious designs, in the 1860s the most elaborate and ambitious of his buildings are undoubtedly the most interesting.

The two finest church interiors of the later 1860s are at Penarth and Babbacombe. Both are concealed by long-roofed grey exteriors; Penarth (XIV) with its short saddleback tower high on the headland above Cardiff bay, Babbacombe also close to the sea, but in a gentler situation among trees and villas, with a delicate gossamer of buff, lead grey, steel blue and grey-green spread over its upper walls and tall fretted spire.[29] There is the same difference of mood in the richly coloured interiors. Penarth is altogether bolder, a broad clerestoried nave and short choir, its dense red brick walls criss-crossed with white and black patterns, and its stonework elementary cylinder and octagon blocks of pink and cream sandstone. The soft toned, strong stone arches at the same time harmonize the vivid brick colours and contain the insistent patterning, reasserting the massiveness of the walling. The broad stone bands and deep splays of the clerestory again emphasize the thickness of the wall, but the diapering reappears under the wallplate of the roof. The roof itself also expresses this linear play across elementary shapes, for it is all lines, closely-spaced rafters tilting over in six sections like a cage of wires, but at the same time providing a subtle continuation of the wall plane, and brought down by long wall posts.

At Babbacombe (III) the colours are all softer, 'a symphony in Devonshire marble and alabaster' as Halsey Ricardo put it;[30] and the forms are more delicate and also stranger than at Penarth. The church has another tight-raftered roof, but lower and flatter so that the whole interior seems longer, and the chancel is indeed planned with plenty of space at the altar steps. The lines of the nave walls and roof carry through to the chancel, so that although the broad chancel arch is relatively low it subdivides rather than separates the space. But the chancel arch, by echoing the low line of the roof, gives a sense of breadth as well as length, so that there is a slight ambiguity in the proportions of the interior. This ambiguity is taken up by the strange web of thin stone ribs which stretches over the face of the nave walls above the arcades and the chancel arch. In the chancel the theme is taken up again, and here twined up across the panelled roof. What is the meaning of this patterning?

Not much use can be made in this case of the concepts of the picturesque. It is not very helpful to notice that the patterning introduces intricacy or obscurity. It makes more sense, on the other hand, to relate it to the principles, not of the Gothic Revival, but of the original medieval gothic style.

Medieval gothic had developed through a gradual transformation of the romanesque.[31] Thus while the elements of romanesque seemed self-sufficient, in gothic they became interdependent. The forms and spaces of romanesque appeared to be added together, those of gothic to be subdivisions of a greater unity. Romanesque style had been characterized by its emphasis on structure; gothic in contrast developed texture. Now we have already seen how Butterfield himself moved from the addition of volumes and spaces to their subdivision, and from unqualified mass to a complex linear texture. Thus his general development was following the direction of gothic itself, although his starting point was very different. There were, moreover, other ways in which his patterning brought him closer to the spirit of gothic.

The medieval builders had eventually so reduced the mass of their arcades and clerestory walling that these ceased to be the decisive spatial boundaries of the main nave. Arcades and clerestory became a diaphanous structure, space flowing through them to the outer aisle walls, or beyond. Butterfield's walls are far from the transparency achieved by medieval gothic, but his diagonal patterning gives an illusion of depth, of light and shade, a suggestive echo of the crisp light arches standing out against the shadow of the aisle roofs. There were originally no clerestory lights above the ribbed wall, so that the web of ribs could be seen as a symbolic substitute for transparency. Butterfield's later interiors suggest that at Babbacombe he was moving towards the piercing of walls by spatial flow. In several of his smaller churches in the 1870s and 1880s (278) he repeated the scheme first used at Dropmore (110), nave and chancel a single space divided by a high open screen, under a continuous low network of rectilinear roof ribbing. In the small but high interior of St Clement's Finsbury the chancel arch was reduced to a high wooden beam at the wallplate, with a trefoil opening pierced through above. Still more significant, in the much larger St Augustine's Queen's Gate (279, 280), whose richly diapered brick interior developed other features such as the foliate arcade spandrels at Babbacombe, the wall above the chancel arch was penetrated by a double window through to the chancel, with a great cross rising from their tracery. The grandest stone church interiors of the 1870s, Dundela and Rugby, are similarly divided by great girder arches, open to the roof above (52, 165). Clevedon, before its alteration, was of the same type (281). It seems fair to conclude that the symbolic transparency of Babbacombe, and the spatial ambiguity which it gives to the interior, are deliberate.

The use of *diagonal* diapering as the characteristic motif of Butterfield's linear patterning again indicates that his development was following the direction of

278 *right* Foxham church, interior

279 *below* St Augustine Queen's Gate, interior from the west (Gordon Barnes)

Opposite

280 *above* St Augustine Queen's Gate, interior from the east (Gordon Barnes)

281 *below* Clevedon St John, interior in 1903 (Sir Arthur Elton)

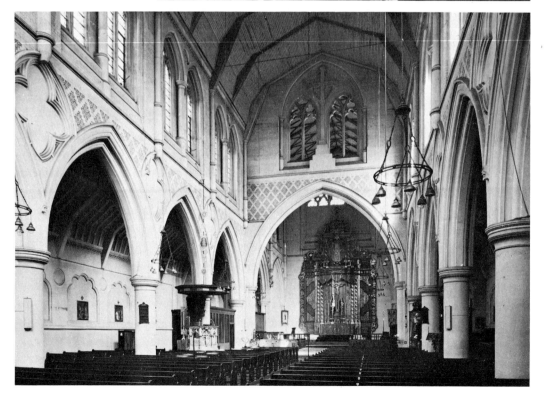

medieval gothic. It was through the use of diagonals that gothic had brought movement to the static romanesque style. Thus the inert dome or barrel vault had been
transformed by the transverse rib, a line of force running upwards and diagonally
across to the apex of the roof, at the same time a devious movement from bay to bay
and a clear upward thrust. Similarly the shapes of mouldings, such as those of the
piers between the bays, changed from the frontal romanesque cylinder to the angled,
diagonal gothic profile. The earlier angled profiles are keeled cylinders, or octagons;
in later gothic a complex cluster of mouldings forming a diagonal becomes more
common.

Butterfield did not make use of the diagonal in these characteristic forms, but he
developed substitutes. Thus he rarely used ribbed vaulting, and his favourite piers
were cylinders or slightly chamfered squares. Very occasionally he used clusters, but
without keeled profiles. On the other hand his wooden roofs are a consistent development towards linearity, and in the scissors-collar roofs of the late 1850s, and in a few
ribbed panelled roofs of the 1860s, he introduces diagonals (14, 109). But it is above
all in the wall diapers of his brickwork that the diagonal entered Butterfield's churches.
At Babbacombe, at the high point of his linear style, he transferred the diaper from
brickwork to stone ribbing. The strange wall web, both as rib and as diagonal, thus
symbolizes not merely gothic space, but gothic form.

Symbolizes; yet it is of course quite different from medieval gothic form, for two
reasons. Firstly, the rib is used here in a context which, even if precedents could be
cited, is far removed from its original context as a structural element in vaulting.
Now this raises an interesting problem. Victorian gothic was built up by transferences
of motifs, but usually by less daring innovations than this. It was Butterfield's willingness to use a motif in a startling and unexpected context, if for a good reason, which
explains most of the hostile comments which some contemporaries made on his work.
'We are no wholesale condemners of mannerism; we have no great prejudice against
the recognition of the individual artist by the individual work. But . . .' thundered the
Ecclesiologist against some wall arcading at Perth which offended the critic's sense of
historicist convention.[32] Yet by others such 'mannerism' was welcomed as essential
to the development of the gothic style. Of All Saints', for example, whose 'tower and
spire were of a shape and proportions which puzzled the antiquaries, scandalized the
architects, and sent unprofessional critics to their wit's end with amazement', Charles
Eastlake declared in his *History of the Gothic Revival*, 'The truth is that the design was a
bold and magnificent endeavour to shake off the trammels of antiquarian precedent,
which had long fettered the progress of the Revival, to create not a new style, but a
development of previous styles . . .'[33]

Seen in this light, Butterfield's 'mannerism' becomes simply a subjective reaction
in a critic who finds his development of gothic offensive. It is not a characteristic of

his style, but a typical although rather indiscriminate by-product in the uncomprehending spectator. There is a good deal of truth in this, for hostile criticism over
the last century has been very inconsistent and arbitrary in its selection of features
both for admiration and for attack. Much of it, moreover, has depended on in-
accurate observation.

Nevertheless, there is a second peculiarity about the Babbacombe ribbing which
might be more properly described as 'mannerist'. This is the fact that the diagonal
patterning is not an end in itself, but a foil to the wall plane behind it. It symbolizes
the dissolution of structure, but leaves the structure intact. Now this treatment is
quite characteristic of the linearity of the 1860s. Butterfield had not developed a new
style, but a play against the themes of the classic phase of the early 1850s. The
patterning only becomes comprehensible when one looks for the straight wall planes,
the sturdy piers, the stabilizing horizontals of the classic phase, to discover that they
are not abandoned, but rather veiled by the gossamer lines.

Butterfield's style of the 1860s is thus, like earlier 'mannerist' phases of architecture
in thirteenth-century England and sixteenth-century Italy, a play against a classic
ideal, and equally in each case the startling transfer of elements is essential to this
play. For this reason the treatment of detail in such phases is often, in a literal sense,
perverse. But the discovery of perverse details in no way implies the abandonment
of an overriding belief in harmony, or even elegance. John Shearman's recent study
Mannerism is a reminder that high skill, elegance and grace were essential attributes
of *maniera* in sixteenth-century Italy. But equally revealing is the realization that the
greatest of such skills was considered to be the conquest of *difficoltà*. It is this concept
which can account for the paradox that Butterfield, like Michelangelo in the sixteenth
century, used perverse and wilful detail in his search for a new architectural harmony.

The comparison between the two men is not as far-fetched as it might seem. There
are, for example, columns framing the Keble mosaics which are half-buried in the
wall, recalling in miniature the same device used by Michelangelo in his Laurentian
Library staircase. More important is the similar treatment which both have received
from critics. Vasari reads like a Renaissance Eastlake when he says of Michelangelo:
'This licence has encouraged others to imitate him, and new fantasies have appeared,
more like grotesques than regular ornament. Artists are perpetually indebted to
Michelangelo who loosed the chains and restraints that inhibited those who walked
along the common path.' And modern interpretations of Michelangelo have followed
a parallel path to those of Butterfield. Pevsner saw Michelangelo as an unsociable,
distrustful, deeply religious man, a fanatical worker, uncompromisingly proud; and
his architecture in the 1520s as austere, painful in detail, uncomfortable in proportion,
displaying 'conscious discordance all the way through'.[34] Shearman recognizes the
wilfulness, but suspects that 'to read such licence as conscious irrationality . . . may

well be a false projection backwards of a current aesthetic virtue.' He prefers to see the oddities as 'forms of *varietà* (to) relieve boredom', to notice the cool grace of the details, the exacting standard of execution, the overall movement and sense of mastery of form. 'It is fascinating, cerebral, and stimulates in the beholder the recondite pleasure of sharing the architect's erudition.'[35] A similar shift of emphasis will, I think, bring a clearer understanding of Butterfield.

The interior at Babbacombe is perhaps the clearest statement of 'mannerism' in Butterfield. Nevertheless it is possible to see similar qualities in his most ambitious exteriors of the 1860s and early 1870s. At Rugby, for example, the New Schools,

282 Rugby School, detail of New Schools

although jutting out into the town on a corner site and chamfered at the angle to help street traffic, are not composed into a picturesque silhouette to be seen from the diagonal viewpoint (67, 282). They present instead sections of smooth wall planes, crossed by regular rectilinear patterning, with the horizontal emphasis a little stronger than the vertical, and capped by a horizontal parapet. And behind the New Schools looms the ragged mass of the chapel tower (226), whose play of mass and line is still more clearly 'mannerist'; but a peculiarly High Victorian mannerism which here, in its tremendous height, in its Ruskinian 'savageness', also approaches the romantic sublime. In Ruskin's words, 'It is that strange *disquietude* of the Gothic spirit that is its greatness; that restlessness of the dreaming mind, that wanders hither and thither among the niches, and flickers feverishly around the pinnacles, and frets and fades in labyrinthic knots and shadows along wall and roof, and yet is not satisfied, nor shall be satisfied.'[36]

Rugby tower we have already considered in detail. We have also said something of the wall patterning at Keble, where, as in the New Schools, the wall plane remains intact behind the play of detail (71). But Keble College, as the largest group of buildings by Butterfield from this period, is worth looking at as a whole. There are certainly picturesque qualities in its composition, not only in the varied colour and texture, but in the asymmetry of the great quadrangle, and especially in the lively chequered dormers which break the roofline of the less formal south quadrangle. The use of trees here, and the dramatic glimpse of the chapel between the library and the gatehouse, are very much in the tradition of the picturesque (XX). So is the handling of the approach from the south, where Butterfield had the difficult problem of a very long frontage to a narrow slightly curving road with trees on the opposite side (283, 284, 285). He therefore broke up the front by a series of major and minor projecting gables, principally the warden's house at the corner, the gatehouse towards the centre, and a smaller block at the far end, with the east end of the chapel towering up behind it. The actual entrance to the college through the gatehouse is kept very low, a wide ribbed tunnel vault with white brick strips leading the eye inwards (286). And the great height of the chapel itself is undeniably romantic; its massive brick walls windowless until they rise above the parapets of the main ranges, only then breaking into stone chequering, pinnacles, and the whiteness of the long lead roof (132).

Once again, however, these picturesque qualities play on a regular structure (287). Everywhere it is the horizontals which dominate – the long rooflines, and the continuous stone bands and string courses. Except on one side of the south quadrangle, the buildings stand in tightly disciplined lines, and in spite of its asymmetry the main quadrangle is very formal. Its great sunken central lawn is crossed by two paths at right angles. To east and west are low ranges of rooms, with a slow alternating

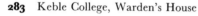

283 Keble College, Warden's House

284 Keble College, Parks Road (east) front, south end

rhythm of dormer and shallow porch. To the south are the hall and library under one great high roof, entered by a tall central porch, with similar regular window bays on each side. Finally, to the north stands the chapel, its entrance facing the hall door, but its main mass clearly off centre towards the east corner of the quadrangle. Here, instead of symmetry, Butterfield balanced its height by the long range running west-wards. The chapel itself repeats the same type of balance with its east transept as the principal axis. The minor transept is to the west, but the two great nave bays and windows are slightly wider than the two of the choir. This carefully controlled asymmetry is punctuated by the regular rhythm of tall pinnacled buttresses, and the strong horizontals of banding, eaves and uninterrupted ridgeline. Once again the picturesque detail operates upon a classic frame.

Keble College was Butterfield's last major group of buildings. Those which follow, such as St Michael's Hospital Axbridge in the late 1870s and the Gordon Boy's Home in the 1880s, are equally formal in their composition, although comparatively humble in detail. But Exeter School (288), an L shaped group building up to a grand six-storey corner tower, despite its simplified banding seems like a picturesque elaboration of Keble. It is in fact very difficult to see any consistent development in Butterfield's external composition in this final phase. The contrasts of texture and colour are generally bolder and simpler, but the grouping becomes looser and more picturesque. The inn at Wraxall (123, 135), for example, is as irregular as any group of the 1840s, while the rough textured, broken roofed chaplain's house at Axbridge (49) could well be mistaken for a parsonage of the late 1850s. Butterfield was now an

285 Keble College, Parks Road front, north end

286 Keble College, entrance

287 Keble College, plan

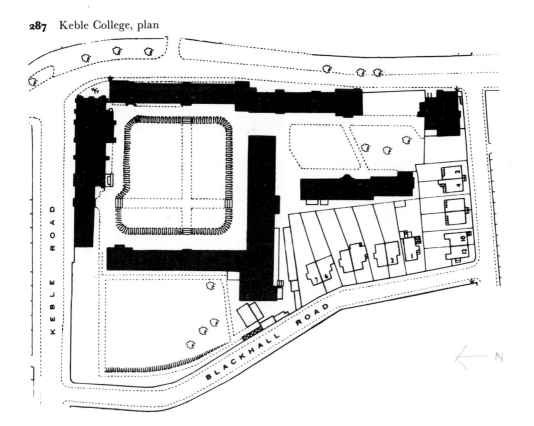

288 Exeter School, exterior

289 Rugby School, Temple Reading Room, interior

290 Rugby School, chapel interior

291 Ascot Priory, chapel interior (*R.I.B.A. Journal*, 1900)

old man, close to seventy, so that it would not be surprising to find him returning in somewhat random way to earlier themes.

Later interiors are more generally rewarding, because here the return to bolder, more simplified forms and colouring was well suited to Butterfield's continuing interest in spatial volumes. His most rewarding experiments in spatial interpenetration, the pierced chancel arches at Queen's Gate, Rugby and Dundela, date from the 1870s (52, 165, 279). The Temple Reading Room (289) at Rugby, with its two rows of slender triple segment arches, makes one of his most attractive smaller rooms, and the interior of the school chapel itself was a great open-centred cross, probably the most surprising space which he planned at any time (290). But whatever their plan, these later interiors develop a quieter dignity than those of the 1860s. This is true both of the grandeur of Rugby parish church, or the relative modesty of Enfield. Perhaps the calmest of all, as first finished, was the aisleless, cradle roofed, soft banded chapel at Ascot Priory (291). One feels in these last works that Butterfield was close to a final style which met his aesthetic ends without even superficial conflict. But this was not to be achieved; and so we are left with his 'mannerism', uncertain where it would have led.

Notes on chapter 14

1   Summerson, *op. cit.*, pp. 166, 168: H. S. Goodhart-Rendel, *R.I.B.A. Journal* (XXXI) 1924, p. 330.
2   Butterfield to Lord Heytesbury, 7 March 1876, Heytesbury Collection.
3   Butterfield to the Warden, 8 December 1872 and 5 January 1874, and H. H. Gibbs to the Warden, 26 January 1874, Starey Collection.
4   *True Principles*, p. 63.
5   *Op. cit.*, p. 166.
6   Gerard Manley Hopkins to Butterfield, 26 April 1877, Starey Collection.
7   *R.I.B.A. Journal*, (VII) 1900, pp. 247–8.
8   Redfern, *op. cit.*
9   Note on the reverse of floor design for St Thomas Leeds, Victoria & Albert Museum.
10   C. L. V. Meeks, 'Picturesque Eclecticism', *Art Bulletin*, 1950, pp. 226–35, is a stimulating (although too generalized) survey of the main tendencies.
11   *A Few Words to Church Builders*, Cambridge 1841, pp. 7, 21.
12   *Archaeologia Cantiana*, IV (1861), pp. 57–66.
13   Account from D. Baskerville, Highbury Chapel chest.
14   Butterfield to Rev. G. S. Holmes, 13 May 1870, Holme upon Spalding Moor chest.
15   Journal of B. H. Starey, 2 January 1856, Starey Collection.
16   £313: Bamford chest.
17   Westminster Hall, *The Times*, 2 December 1884.

18   Book of the Chanter's House, Coleridge Collection.

19   Butterfield to the Master, 13 December 1856, Balliol College archives.

20   *The Times*, 16 January and 1 May 1866. Accnts mention a 'Report on proposed extension of Tavistock St to Charlotte St', but this cannot be traced in the Bedford Estate archives.

21   Philip Wilson, *Hunstanton and Its Neighbourhood*, 5th edition, 1878, pp. 47–8.

22   (14) 1853, p. 267.

23   Law, *op. cit.*, p. 161.

24   Although the general tone of this article, probably inspired by Hope, was hostile: (20) 1859, p. 185.

25   *Early Victorian Architecture*, 1, p. 589.

26   Butterfield to Lord Heytesbury, 12 September 1865, Heytesbury Collection.

27   Butterfield to the Master, 12 June and 7 November 1854, Balliol College archives.

28   *BN* (18) 1870, p. 68.

29   Unfortunately a parapet and odd clerestory windows now break the sweep of nave and aisle roofs.

30   *R.I.B.A. Journal* (III) 1896, pp. 368–9.

31   See especially Paul Frankl, *The Gothic*, Princeton, 1960, and *Gothic Architecture*, London, Penguin, 1962.

32   (12) 1851, p. 28.

33   pp. 252–3.

34   *Outline of European Architecture*, Jubilee edition, London, Penguin, 1960, pp. 356, 368.

35   John Shearman, *Mannerism*, London, Penguin, 1967, pp. 17–22, 70–75.

36   *The Stones of Venice*, 2, pp. 154, 181.

Because the system of personal pupilage, rather than architectural schooling, was the mainstay of Victorian architectural training, some Victorian architects are as important for their pupils as for their own work. Gilbert Scott's large and busy office proved the nursery not only for his own distinguished sons, but for G. E. Street, William White and G. F. Bodley. Street himself handed down influence through assistants such as Edmund and John Sedding, Philip Webb and Norman Shaw. It was said by Shaw that 'Street would not let them design even a keyhole', delegating only mechanical work,[1] but it seems likely that Butterfield controlled his rather smaller office still more tightly than Street. This is the most convincing reason why his pupils and assistants proved on the whole undistinguished.

Butterfield's first pupil, Henry Woodyer, was undoubtedly the most interesting, for his architecture has much in common with Butterfield's In his first church of 1845 at Wyke (292) in Surrey the structural carpentry of the porch and pulpit is at once noticeable, and the wrapped-round corner buttresses of the slightly later south chapel. Woodyer's high raftered roofs, his tile floors, and his little west bellcotes perched on great western buttresses, give many of his simpler churches of the 1840s and 1850s an air of Butterfield. The richly frescoed interior of Highnam church, begun in 1847, was a polychromatic experiment only overshadowed by All Saints', and although the profuse details of the church show none of Butterfield's genius, there are significantly wilful details, such as a door hood squeezed against a buttress which is also pierced by a lancet window. The two men also shared an interest in brick architecture. Woodyer's picturesque little school at Bisley of 1846 in fact precedes any known brick design by Butterfield, and in the 1850s several buildings, some diapered, some bare and sheer like the long-roofed convent ranges at Clewer, some charming like the dormered brick and flint school at Shalford, recall Butterfield's work. It is in this kind of work too that the connection can still be strikingly close in the early 1860s. Shinfield school (293), a picturesque roof shape of varied slopes, dormers and lean-tos controlled by a long single ridge-line, is a clear example.

292 Wyke church, by Henry Woodyer, exterior

Still more interesting, however, is Woodyer's development of a mannered angularity, entirely his own in detail, and yet surely close in spirit to Butterfield. His windows become either lancet slits or tight late gothic tracery, gables and dormers acutely compressed, ironwork writhing with arrows and thorns (294). And as in Butterfield, there seems to be a deliberate play with earlier aesthetic attitudes. The expression of structure could hardly be less rational than at Woodley (295), where a sharp bellcote is clamped to a false gable by long thin suspended strips of buttress – except perhaps at St Anne's House, Clewer (296), whose tall tapering cylinder chimneyshafts hang by the eaves, as if to prove that even the sturdiest High Victorian forms can be disembodied.

Woodyer's motives in all this are another question. There seems to be mockery here of a kind which Butterfield did not display. Is this because the mannerisms are not so completely thought through? Or had Woodyer a strange sense of humour? Certainly he is not an easy character to assess. He was a doctor's son, an Oxford graduate, widowed after a brief marriage, tall and lean in appearance, deeply religious, and as shy of publicity as Butterfield. He was supported by the same well-educated earnest High Church patrons. But there was another side to Woodyer, rather more relaxed: his Bohemian clothes, and his decision to set up office in a Surrey farmhouse. Clearly he intended to enjoy himself; and indeed, when he found himself too formal in Surrey, he retreated to a Mediterranean yacht.[2] There is sufficient similarity between Butterfield and Woodyer to suggest that their architecture responds to common problems, and that both were highly sophisticated designers, but that in Woodyer conviction and ruthlessness gave way to an erudite, self-conscious wit.

293 Shinfield school, by Woodyer

294 Stratford St Mary church, ironwork, by Woodyer

295 Woodley church, exterior, by Woodyer

296 St Anne's House, Clewer, by Woodyer

How much Woodyer actually learnt from Butterfield and how much their influence was mutual is an open question, for according to one account he was Butterfield's pupil for only a few months,[3] and in any case there was very little work in the office before 1845. But there is still less known about his next pupils. To the Reverend William Lowder has been attributed the font at St Matthias Stoke Newington, St Paul's School Shadwell, and, incorrectly, his better-known brother's church, St Peter's London Docks. Presumably he spent most of his energies on his Cheshire parish.[4] It is said that Bishop Medley's son, Edward, who became a distinguished Gothic Revival architect in North America, worked in Butterfield's office between the ages of fifteen and eighteen in the early 1850s, but the story is uncertain;[5] while what happened to Thomas Wilson, undoubtedly Butterfield's assistant, who designed the brick and slate cemetery chapel at Farnborough in 1859, is a complete mystery.[6] Augustin Starey, who was articled to Butterfield in 1870, failed to make a living as an architect and became a clergyman. Galsworthy Davie, another pupil of the same years, made a more promising start, for he was awarded a Royal Academy scholarship in 1872, and was able to publish his *Architectural Studies in France*, dedicated to Butterfield, in 1876. Although one critic called them 'uninteresting and practically useless', the book served its purpose in bringing some commissions for houses from the West Brighton Estate Company and launched him on an undistinguished career.[7] Harry Redfern, who was sent to Butterfield by Woodyer shortly after Galsworthy Davie left, was a little more successful, for two of his Cambridge buildings have some merit, but they date from after 1918 and are not Butterfieldian in form. Finally there was T. W. Keates, who had served twenty years with Butterfield when he left to set up a small practice in Petersfield in 1882.[8]

Thus none of Butterfield's subsequent pupils had any of Woodyer's interest, nor had they even his closeness to Butterfield's style. It is curious that two more personal relationships apparently carried more influence. The first was with Frederick Preedy, who was a cousin of Henry le Strange and co-operated with Butterfield at Hunstanton. He also designed glass for Butterfield (XXIV) and frescoed the east end of St Alban's Holborn (353). His work has been mistaken for Butterfield's, and in the case of his severe stone-banded brick schools of the 1860s the likeness is very close.[9] There was also Butterfield's nephew, Richard Drew, who married Anne Starey in 1863. He started work as an architect in about 1860, after taking a university degree. His high raftered roofs, diapered brick walls, tile floors and open-back benches clearly show the influence of his uncle, and his church at Shaw in the Pennines is a quite powerful composition of slate roofs round a pyramid-capped tower. Whyteleafe, and St Peter's Leigham Court Road, are other characteristic churches, and he was responsible for several restorations in the 1860s and 1870s. He also designed a number of houses, including Horsegate House at Cuckfield, Shepton Beauchamp parsonage, and the demolished Leigh Park, Havant, for W. H. Stone, M.P. These have tall ribbed chimneys, hipped gables, staircases squeezed into angles and other Butterfieldian features. Unfortunately apart from Shepton Beauchamp they are better as engravings than in reality.[10] Butterfield's later style, which was the phase copied by Drew, did not make for easy imitation.

Thus not one of Butterfield's pupils or close associates became an architect of major importance. Even Woodyer had a relatively small, narrow practice, and only a minority of his buildings are of much interest. Butterfield's influence must be traced through other means than personal contact.

In the first phase of his career he held a peculiarly strong position as the effective editor of *Instrumenta Ecclesiastica* (15, 20, 22, 23, 88, 232). The first volume, published in parts between 1844 and 1847, contained mostly designs for metalwork, grave crosses, lecterns, font covers, church chests, chairs and so on. A few designs, notably the lych gates, were more architectural. Butterfield's clear, fresh, but at times awkward taste is already shown in most of his drawings, whether new designs or copies from old examples. The influence of this work upon church furnishings must have been very widespread, for it provided an invaluable reference work for High Church clergy. In the case of church plate, Butterfield himself supplied a very large number of variants to his designs, and can be fairly claimed to have dominated the field for at least a decade. The designs for grave crosses were used in modified forms for much longer – indeed, into the twentieth century. There are also instances of well-known architects, such as Gilbert Scott, precisely imitating the architectural designs, such as the church porch or the lych gates.[11] In short, *Instrumenta Ecclesiastica* was an influence at every level: upon patrons, architects, craftsmen and ecclesiastical furnishers. But so widespread an influence becomes very difficult to define, for thousands of objects can in one sense be referred back to *Instrumenta Ecclesiastica*. On the other hand, the more precise imitations survived longest where the book was least easily replaced: with craftsmen, like Keith the church plate maker or country suppliers of gravestones; or with the Anglican clergy in the colonies and America, where the English example had been followed precisely by the New York Ecclesiological Society.[12] In England other architects, having absorbed Ecclesiological principles (which were not of course Butterfield's invention) and observed these first models, were soon developing their own designs, and before long the most interesting work was not closely related to Butterfield. This second stage was marked by the decision in 1850 to take designs for the second volume from any quarter, although in fact most of the new designs for furniture were still his.[13]

Butterfield's architectural influence before 1849 was necessarily limited, for he had designed few buildings, and of these only St Augustine's College Canterbury was of much importance. Nevertheless, the architects working with the Ecclesiological

297 Christ Church Camberwell, parsonage, by Sir Gilbert Scott

298 Holy Trinity Halstead, exterior, by Scott

Society formed a close group in these years, and there is no doubt that there was much mutual influence between them – so much, in fact, that there was very little difference in style between them. Perhaps at this stage Butterfield absorbed more from others than he gave. This is certainly true of the two architects, the Roman Catholic Pugin and the Broad Church Scott, who stood at the edge of the group. Pugin's doctrines, his scholarly Middle Pointed architecture, his furnishings and decorations, were behind the whole achievement of the Ecclesiologists in the 1840s. Moreover we know that Butterfield was in touch with him, commissioned designs from him, and went to see his buildings.[14] Scott's contribution was also crucial, both in developing a High Victorian sense of volume, which can already be sensed in his churches at Camberwell and Halstead, and also in his boldly simplified gothic for parsonages, such as Smallwood and the house at Camberwell (297). The Halstead church (298) is still more remarkable in its use of brick arcades and brick dressings with flint walling, although this could possibly be a case of naivety rather than prescience. All these date from 1843–5, well before St Augustine's was completed (29, 168). Nevertheless, there was one feature of St Augustine's notices by contemporaries which was to be characteristic of advanced gothic work in the 1850s. This was the long, uninterrupted roofline of the dormitory range. Did they also observe the remarkable continuous wall planes of the warden's and fellows' residences, with their window traceries flush to the surface, unprotected by dripmoulds?

His commission for the Ecclesiological model church in Margaret Street made Butterfield almost immediately one of the major architects of the mid-century. All

Saints' was important above all because it showed that intelligent historicism need not be pedantic (I, X). It blended motifs, confined neither to England alone nor to the Middle Pointed phase of gothic, into a rational and original whole. And its progressiveness was shown not only in the sheer, simple shapes of the school and clergy house (26), but in their experimental use of cast-iron girders (87), and in the commissioning of frescoes for the church from a painter like William Dyce, well known for his connection with the government schools for industrial design. Dyce in fact was so much of a scientist that at one stage in his career he had abandoned painting for research in electro-magnetism. This rationality, which is such an important element in the originality of All Saints', explains why Butterfield's breaking of the fetters of precedent was so final. As George Edmund Street wrote in 1859, 'I cannot hesitate for an instant in allowing that this church is not only the most beautiful, but the most vigorous, thoughtful and original among them all.'[15]

Nor was it merely the freedom with which Butterfield handled gothic at All Saints' which impressed his fellow-architects. There was also one particular element in the design, constructional colouring, which was to be the hallmark of Victorian church gothic for at least twenty years. Constructional colour, it is true, can be found in a tentative form in a few earlier buildings, but its startling spread in the 1850s is certainly due to the combined influence of Ruskin's *Seven Lamps* and Butterfield's All Saints'. We have seen how the original plans and designs of All Saints' in the summer of 1849 had been, as Beresford-Hope wrote to his chief financial ally in the scheme, the banker Henry Tritton, in August 1850,

> on the supposition of its being merely built of common materials. Since then the aesthetic possibilities of different materials have become more and more clear, and the present scheme is that of a church whose character and beauty and effect of colour shall arise from *construction* and not from *superaddition*, namely that, the pillars shall be *made of granite*, and not pointed middle like those at St Barnabas (Pimlico), the diaper be an encrustation of tiles, and not the track of a paintbrush, and so on.[16]

The *Ecclesiologist* described the new plans as 'a practical example of what we are very anxious to see tested, viz., constructional polychrome'.[17] This was why long before the church was completed it had become one of the architectural sights of London.

As the test case of Ruskin's theory, All Saints' in a sense influenced all the innumerable examples of constructional colour which marked the remainder of the nineteenth century spreading gradually outwards to the furthest corners of European influence and downwards through the social layers of taste. And no doubt the ubiquitous bands and diapers owed a more particular debt to All Saints'. But of course these motifs were no more Butterfield's inventions than the doctrine of constructional polychromy, and there can be little doubt that they would have become popular without him. Certainly his aid was not needed to rediscover other patterns, such as William White's herringbones, or his variation of course widths by laying bricks on their sides – a device also used by Teulon in his Windsor Park cottages (299, 300). And in the use of grey and yellow brick patterns and polychromatic roof tiles it was Teulon, White and even minor architects like Joseph Peacock who led the way.

One reason for the rapid development of divergent personal styles of polychromy was that there were various ways of interpreting the new device. To Teulon (301, 302) and Peacock it was probably just picturesque ornamentation. Their architecture does not seem to be seriously worked out, and although Teulon had a real talent for picturesque composition he ran his busy office without close supervision. In 1853 he was asking Scott if he could recommend 'an intelligent trustworthy Assistant who could take up (from sketches) works generally and who is acquainted with practical details of Church work and can prepare them and exercise a wholesome influence over juniors'.[18] Perhaps it was this new assistant who introduced constructional colour to Teulon's work. Certainly the letter makes some of the inconsistencies of his detailing more understandable.

White was more thoughtful, indeed an architectural theorist of some interest.[19] Thus while remaining at heart a picturesque Puginist, he took account of High Victorian tendencies such as the continuous wall plane, and used his colouring in combination with simpler forms than Teulon. Butterfield was at the same time working out his own adaption to High Victorian aesthetics. There were many others, on the other hand, who responded to them more wholeheartedly, notably Street and in the 1860s James Brooks, whose Shoreditch churches reached a classic, full-blown simplicity (303, 304). In such architecture the colouring is normally handled in broader zones, closer to Ruskin's original Italian inspiration.

Among these more convinced High Victorians, Scott takes a place comparable to that of Teulon. Scott had undoubtedly sympathized with Thomas Stevens, the rector and squire of Bradfield, who 'got to employ the term "square abacus" as a moral adjective, used in the sense of manly, straightforward, real, honest and all cognate epithets, and "round abacus" for what was milder, "ogee" being used in the sense of mean, weak, dishonest, etc.'[20] Now he discovered in the Italian gothic recommended by Ruskin a 'certain squareness and horizontality of outline' which appealed to his taste. But Scott had not the time to fuse his earlier picturesque rationalism with these new interests in any thorough manner. He simply handed over 'rapid expressive sketches' to his assistants. This is one reason why Milton Ernest Hall, in spite of Butterfield's reservations, is a more convincing example of High Victorianism than Scott's much grander house at Kelham.[21]

299 Fenny Stratford church, herringbone brickwork, by William White

300 Windsor Park, cottages by Samuel Sanders Teulon

301 Burringham church, interior, by Teulon

302 Shadwell Park, stables and entrance front, by Teulon

303 Marston Maisey church, interior, by James Brooks

One of the most Butterfieldian of Scott's works in its details is his St Andrew's Leicester, which curiously dates from as late as 1860 (305). Was this the work of a young assistant who had newly discovered Butterfield's work? There is no doubt that constructional colour was still appealing to some of the most talented younger men in the 1860s and more than one began with a Butterfieldian phase. In the case of James Brooks this is shown by his splendid high-raftered first church in Mark Street.[22] Arthur Blomfield, bishop's son and Oxford graduate, later a conventional and prosperous church-builder, began with interesting combinations of coloured brick, wall planes and fat High Victorian detail. Jackfield of 1863 (306), with its notched dripmoulds interrupting the flush surface, invites comparison with Butterfield's mannerisms of the same date. G. F. Bodley's St Michael's Brighton, of 1858–61, is perhaps closer to Street than to Butterfield, but again represents a shortlived 'boyish antagonistic' spirit when he was 'tired of mouldings', as he later recalled.[23] In this phase, besides the similarities in general treatment and proportions, some of Bodley's detailing such as his roofs and his magnificent tiled pavements are distinctly Butterfieldian.[24]

Bodley's later work can also be compared with Butterfield's development. He became still better known than Butterfield for his adherence to a strict English Middle Pointed gothic style, so much so that his continuing interest in wall planes and his development of internal spatial unity are not at first obvious. Yet they give life to designs which in detail, however graceful, are undeniably conventional. One can understand the reflections on St John's Liverpool with which Eastlake concluded his *History of the Gothic Revival*: 'By dint of earnest study and endless experiments, by

304 *above left* St Chad Shoreditch, interior, by Brooks

305 *above right* St Andrew Leicester, exterior, by Sir Gilbert Scott

306 Jackfield church, window, by Sir Arthur Blomfield

help of theory and precept, by means of comparison and criticism, the grammar of an ancient art has been mastered. Shall we ever be able to pronounce its language – not in the measured accents of scholastic exercise, but fluently and familiarly as our mother-tongue?'

Bodley and Butterfield were both rather shy, religious men, working for similar patrons, professing similar architectural principles, and reacting in parallel ways to High Victorian taste. The differences between them are probably partly due to personality. Bodley was altogether gentler, with a strong dislike for the business side of his work, and in his early years he was much less sure of himself than Butterfield. Indeed his most revolutionary design, All Saints' Cambridge of 1862–4, which marked the return to English Middle Pointed, seems to have been forced upon him largely by the conservative taste of his Cambridge patrons, who still wanted something in the manner of the 1840s. The original design in 1860 had been made 'on the principle of getting effect by good proportion and a fair *elevation*, rather than by any rich and costly detail.' He made his first concession on grounds of cost. 'I shall be sorry to abandon the clerestory I confess. It gives the building the character of a *town* church which one desiderates. Economy must however be considered if £4000 is to cover all the expenses.' Argument then shifted to his proposal for an unbuttressed saddleback tower, rather than the more costly, elaborate spire demanded by his patrons. But again he showed little determination. 'However I will say no more and if it is desired I will remodel these plans so as to have a spire. I shall do so with great regret.' He produced two alternative designs. 'I confess I think the least expensive will be also the best – I mean the gabled tower. I fear our funds would not admit of a very lofty spire – and a poor small stone spire is a poor affair for a Town Church.' His patrons, however, stuck to their own opinions. He was not even able to persuade them to build right up to the street line. 'I am very strongly of opinion that it will be best to have the *north wall* kept well up to the side of the road. You will remember it is a *town* church.'[25] On reading these exchanges one realizes that the late Victorian return to historicism owed as much to declining courage as to increased sensitivity.

John Francis Bentley, the architect of Westminster Cathedral (307), was in this respect an interesting contrast. Like Butterfield he based his architecture on the examination of old buildings, but on principle rather than precedent, and he shared Butterfield's interest in materials and colour. Indeed a letter of the early 1860s shows him seeking an introduction to Butterfield, and his design shown at the Royal Academy in 1861 was described as 'an evident reminiscence of All Saints' Margaret Street'. Although later he returned to a stricter historicism, he was able to write in 1889 that 'in matters affecting work I don't change much. Twenty-five years and more ago I came to pretty strong conclusions and I don't think the moving fashions of the day produce any impression on me now.' Again, like Butterfield, he believed in an absolute control of the building process, and thought out all the detail of his work with great thoroughness. Westminster Cathedral, the masterpiece of his old age, was the last great triumph of constructional colour. 'I am not attempting a new style – that is impossible – but intend, as far as I am able, to develop the first phase of Christian architecture', he wrote in 1895. And again, in one of his last letters shortly before his death in 1902, one again senses the determination of a Butterfield: 'I have broken the backbone of that terrible superstition, that iron is necessary for large spans.'[26]

Butterfield's influence was not, of course, confined to church work. Among his contemporaries J. L. Pearson, for example, built a parsonage at Broomfleet in 1860 in which the spare brick diaper, the small-scale window frames and the complex hipped roof all suggest a close study of Butterfield's secular work. Bodley's parsonages of the 1860s at Burrington and Valley End, or parts of Bentley's Beaumont College of 1888, suggest his influence on younger architects (308, 309). This is all the more striking because, although contemporaries referred to Butterfield as the leader of the 'English or Farmhouse school',[27] scarcely any of his secular buildings were ever published by the architectural press. The chief exception is two schools published in

307 Westminster Cathedral, exterior, by John Francis Bentley (A. F. Kersting)

Instrumenta Ecclesiastica in 1856. Butterfield's secular work was thus only available to the few, like Philip Webb, who were prepared to seek it out in the countryside. Yet it may be because such knowledge was gleaned with difficulty that it was all the more carefully handed on. Certainly Butterfield's domestic work outlasted his churches as a source of active architectural influence.

The explanation lies in the career of Philip Webb. Although a pupil of Street, Webb's sketchbooks[28] prove his interest in Butterfield, for his was the only contemporary architecture which he drew. The style of Webb's earliest houses, Red House (310) for William Morris in 1859 and Benfleet Hall for the painter Spencer Stanhope, are first rate examples of the simplified brick style evolved for parsonages by Butterfield in the late 1840s, carrying to its logical conclusion the domestic gothic work of Pugin (311) and Scott. Butterfield's Ogbourne St Andrew, Alfington (138) and All Saints' clergy house (26) were the first examples, and thus represent a critical moment in English secular architecture: a crucial achievement comparable to All Saints' church itself. Street and White at once followed with their own personal variations. Before long versions of the Tractarian parsonage manner were being provided not only for

308 Beaumont College, by Bentley
(F. R. Yerbury)

309 Valley End parsonage, by G. F. Bodley

310 Red House, Bexley, by Philip Webb

Pre-Raphaelite artists like Webb's first patrons, but for dons in north Oxford and professionals in other suburbs elsewhere. Even in the hands of speculator-architects (312) it resulted in some quite attractive architecture in the 1860s.

Butterfield's cottage designs of the 1850s were another important application of the same style (313). There was considerable activity among mid-nineteenth-century landowners in providing improved cottages, and in some cases, such as the Bedford Estate around Woburn, a very utilitarian version of Tudor was already in use by 1850. A number of Ecclesiological architects, including Street and William Slater, undertook cottage work, and there was much discussion on how best to provide for morality, ventilation and other socially desirable qualities. Some of this literature indicates that mid-Victorian architects had information on the social behaviour of working-class tenants of a kind which had been lost by the mid-twentieth century: thus,

> The habits of the poor vary much in different places as to the occupation of
> their house; but in the midland and southern districts it is quite useless to
> provide a living-room independent of the kitchen. One family room, where
> the meals are cooked and eaten, and where the party gathers round the fire
> on a winter's evening, with a smaller scullery or wash-house at the back, and
> a pantry or larder with opening window, best meets the requirements of the
> ordinary labourer.

But if the result of such discussion was a widespread improvement in cottage planning, equally sensible elevations were much less common.[29] Butterfield's cottage groups were in this respect outstanding. They have the commonsense quality which at least one Ecclesiological champion of cottages had demanded, representing 'the rough, hand-to-mouth, manly character of cottage life. There is a symbolism of cottages as well as of churches.'[30]

Although it is by no means certain that Webb knew Butterfield's cottage work, his association with William Morris meant that the 'English or Farmhouse school' was still influential in the design of working-class housing in the early twentieth century. In the Morris circle Webb's debt to Butterfield was well remembered. Warington Taylor's letters of the 1860s express what was probably the common view of the group:

> We live in an age of railways, hence men think they must take the most
> prominent bits from every style and country. They forget that those peculiar
> types are expressive of feelings and sentiments foreign to this land . . . English
> Gothic is small as our landscape is small, it is sweet, picturesque, homely, farm
> yardish, Japanese, social, domestic – French is aspiring, grand, straining after
> the extraordinary . . . I think Ruskin ought to have dwelt more on England

311 Brewood priest's house, by A.W.N. Pugin

312 House in Canterbury Road, Oxford, by Frederick Codd

313 Butterwick, cottage pair (Gordon Barnes)

than Italy. Butterfield and Webb are English . . . No one save Butterfield and Webb has conceived an architecture suited to our times being a further development of what has gone before. All the rest of the British builders simply copy the old – late or early but copy it is.[31]

Still more remarkable is a letter from Webb himself in 1873 recommending Butterfield for the new Examination Schools as the 'one architect living who I think could do something which would not seriously hurt Oxford'.[32]

In the 1880s when Morris had become a socialist and a leader of the Arts and Crafts movement, these attitudes were handed on to younger architects, mostly in secular work – although including the most inventive church designer at the turn of the century, W. D. Caroë, to whom Butterfield, on his retirement, perceptively decided to give his drawings.[33] Of the others, Halsey Ricardo undoubtedly owed his interest in constructional colour to Butterfield if – as with Caroë – the results were very different. But perhaps the most notable was W. R. Lethaby, whose biography of Philip Webb very discerningly discussed Butterfield as a thinker and constructor, for whom gothic was a logical system rather than a set of cribs. Lethaby had in fact wished to work for Butterfield, and some of his later aphorisms indicate why. 'Notwithstanding all the names, there are only two modern styles of architecture: one in which the chimneys smoke, and the other in which they do not.'[34] In Lethaby's influential teaching the doctrines of gothic rationalism prepared the way for twentieth-century functionalism. The architecture which he and his friends produced remained however much closer to the style of Webb and Butterfield. Arthur Stansfield Dixon's Birmingham Guild of Handicraft is a fine example. Still more impressive is the early work of the London County Council, where some of the young assistants were friends of Webb.[35] The Millbank estate (314) of the 1890s was probably the finest public housing of its date in the world, and it set a standard which was still maintained – and indeed spreading to other parts of the country – into the 1920s.

The admirable standards of the London School Board also owed something to the same tradition, for its chief architect E. R. Robson had been a friend of Warington Taylor, who was pressing him to take up the Webb-Butterfield development of Queen Anne well before Norman Shaw's prettier version of the style became fashionable. Shaw's own admiration for Butterfield has moreover been recorded, and in the constructional colour and the wall planes beneath his elegant veneer one can sense why this was so.[36]

With the Queen Anne style Norman Shaw and his followers captured what had been the last strongholds of fashionable classical architecture, town housing and civic building. Outside Scotland, supporters of the classical style had contributed little to architectural development after 1850; its merits lay in the conservative maintenance of older standards of taste. Their movement was, however, in the same direction as High Victorian gothic, as the verticality and bold detailing of Cuthbert Brodrick's Leeds Town Hall or Barry's Halifax Town Hall indicate. This made them vulnerable, to gothic competition. Thus E. B. Lamb's Eye Town Hall of 1857, restlessly picturesque brick and flint Italian, precedes Barry's equally eclectic Halifax design. Subsequently the success of the Queen Anne fashion, which was equally an eclectic mixture of classical and gothic, practically drove classically trained architects from the field, with the strange result that the classical revival at the end of the century was led by former gothicists like Shaw himself and Edwin Lutyens.

This development indicated the remarkable High Victorian dominance of the gothic school as a whole rather than the influence of Butterfield himself, which could hardly be active so far from its origins. A more likely case of his influence among major secular architects would seem to be Waterhouse, whose dogged loyalty to High Victorian gothic showed none of Shaw's sensitivity to changing fashion. Waterhouse was in no sense a leader in the development of Victorian architectural style. His flair was for the technicalities of architecture, particularly for planning and costing. Bentley rightly observed that to compare Street with him was to match 'a jewel with

314 Millbank estate, by the London County Council

paste'.[37] His patrons, whether Jowett at Balliol, the Marquis of Westminster at Eaton Hall, or the city merchants at Manchester, would not have employed him if they were wanting bold aesthetic experiment, rather than efficient, large buildings in a worthy style. If Butterfield's patronage represented the doomed tradition of upper-class individualism at its best, Waterhouse anticipates the corporate patronage of the future at its worst. Yet although their situations span the extremes of mid-Victorian practice, Waterhouse by the end of his career had developed an architectural style which bears close comparison with that of Butterfield ten to twenty years earlier.

Waterhouse had no personal connection with Butterfield, nor at first did he admire his work. When he came down from Manchester in 1856 he noted first in his list of 'Things to see in London – All Saints Margaret Street'. But he found nothing there worth recording in his sketchbook; he was more interested in the designs he saw at the Architectural Association by Scott and Street, and by the more elaborate oddities of E. B. Lamb and George Truefitt. His own style until the late 1870s was clearly High Victorian, with bold detail, full volumes and straight wall surfaces. He took the details largely from his studies of French and Flemish gothic.[38] Even his first large-scale use of terracotta in the Natural History Museum of 1873–81 was still applied to High Victorian forms. It was by then more than ten years since the more progressive Gothic Revivalists had reacted against the excesses of High Victorian eclecticism which they had unleashed. It is true that Waterhouse, with his severe detail and rational planning, could not be accused of ignoring the need for formal rhythm in his facades, or allowing the 'piebald appearance' of indiscriminate poly-chrome, or 'the abuse of foliage . . . covering the building or object until it looks like a petrified arbour', 'spasmodic' string courses, 'barbaric' notchings, incessant chamfers or other details 'worked to death', of which William Burges was complaining in 1865.[39] Waterhouse was preserved from such faults by his Quaker sense of economy and discipline. It is interesting that the professional judges of the Manchester Town Hall competition chose his design on grounds of economy and efficiency rather than for its composition, which they thought rather barren. This however was in 1868. Even as late as 1879 his church at Reading consists of utterly sheer banded brick surfaces. When Waterhouse changed his style just before 1880 the one other major architect still working in the High Victorian gothic idiom was H. H. Richardson in the United States – whose clients were no doubt still better insulated from the change of taste than those of Waterhouse.

Waterhouse's style from the 1880s is associated with his numerous offices for Prudential Insurance, starting with their Holborn head office in 1878. Both the head office and its numerous provincial branches (315) are constructed in vitreous red brick and hard pink terracotta, both materials impervious to the weather, so that although the colours are not themselves harsh they completely lack softness in

315 Prudential Insurance, Liverpool, by Alfred Waterhouse (D. M. Wrightson)

texture. But the wall surfaces are enlivened not merely by the banding of the two materials, but by a rectilinear ribbing of attached wall shafts and string courses, which emphasizes the regular rhythm of the tightly grouped windows. Waterhouse retained his severe High Victorian detail and his fondness for a picturesque composition from the corner view, but the bold earlier shapes are now reduced to a grid of lines. Nor was this treatment confined to terracotta facades. Liverpool University for example (XXIII), of 1887–92, is of dark grey stone edged with glazed pink brick; to one side of the tall brick tower the horizontal bands of material run through the attached wall shafts, while to the other the vertical shafts are picked out in brick. Yet behind the insistent patterning the shape of the building, despite its size, is astonishingly simple – a continuous wall surface incorporating the tower and running straight into the curve of the corner. Waterhouse's later style, like Butterfield's, is a play with High Victorian ideals. But 'play' does not seem a very appropriate word in this case, for the mood of his buildings is very different. He had none of Butterfield's fertile invention. The same towers, windows, corbelled oriels appear again and again in his work. The two architects shared a technical mastery of building, an interest in constructional colour, and a belief in the development of a modern gothic style to meet modern needs. The architecture of both was highly rational and disciplined. But the system in Waterhouse was that of the bureaucratic organizations which he served – finance houses, city councils, museums and universities; Butterfield's logic was that of a lone spirit, questioning every detail of his experience.

Notes on chapter 15

1 Blomfield, *Shaw*, p. 16.
2 Redfern, *op. cit.*
3 *G*, 9 September 1896.
4 *A*, (7) 1872, 29; *BN*, (22) 1872, p. 44.
5 Information kindly given by Mr Douglas Scott Richardson.
6 *BN*, (5) 1859, p. 26.
7 *A*, (7) 1872, p. 270, *BA*, (9) 1878, p. 8, *BN* (30) 1876, p. 367 (33) 1877, pp. 521 and 534, (35) 1878, p. 156, (36) 1879, pp. 34 and 144, (39) 1880, p. 270, and (40) 1881, pp. 84–5.
8 *Who's Who in Architecture*, 1914. He designed a baroque-gabled stone Board School in St Peter's Street, Petersfield, and another in brick at Sheet, both nondescript.
9 E.g. Church Lench; or Quinton, *E*, (26) 1865, p. 317.
10 *BN*, (10) 1863, (16) 1869, p. 512, (19) 1870, p. 50, and (27) 1874, p. 460; *A*, (10) 1873, p. 174, and *B* (24) 1866 pp. 193–5.
11 E.g. Farncombe, *E* (8) 1847, p. 190.
12 *E*, (12) 1851, p. 220.
13 *E*, (11) 1850, p. 134.
14 E.g. while touring Staffordshire and Derbyshire with Beresford-Hope in 1849 he visited Alton Towers 'and went over the house'; Anne to Benjamin Starey, 24 August 1849, Starey Collection.
15 *B*, (17) 1859, p. 376.
16 A. J. B. Hope to Henry Tritton, 6 August 1850, Tritton Collection.
17 *E*, (10) 1850, p. 432.
18 S. S. Teulon to G. G. Scott, 15 March 1853, R.I.B.A.
19 See my 'The Writings of William White', Summerson (ed.), *Architectural Writing in Britain*.
20 *Recollections*, p. 155.
21 Mark Girouard, 'Kelham Hall', *Country Life*, 18 May 1967.
22 Later, respect was mutual: Butterfield wrote to William Starey on 6 March 1875 advising

him to ask Brooks for 'such an opinion of what the house (in Stoke Newington) would sell for as he could without going into it . . . He would do it me I think readily' (Starey Collection).

23 Basil Clarke, *Church Builders*, p. 209.

24 The proportions and roofs of his early interiors also deserve comparison with Butterfield's.

25 G. F. Bodley to Rev. W. Sharpe, 7 November and 3 December 1860, 21 February and 13 May 1861, All Saints' chest. See also *E*, (22) 1861, p. 124.

26 J. F. Bentley to Charles Hadfield, c. 1863, January 1889, 1 July 1895 and 13 January 1902, R.I.B.A.; *E*, (22) 1861, p. 163.

27 *BN*, (12) 1865, p. 657.

28 Brandon-Jones Collection.

29 'Labourers Homes', *Quarterly Review*, (107), 1860, pp. 267–97.

30 Rev. T. James, 'On Labourers' Cottages', *AAS*, (1) 1850–1, pp. 24–36; c.f. Nicholas Cooper, 'Housing the Victorian Poor', *Country Life*, 8 June 1967.

31 Warington Taylor to E. R. Robson, c. 1865 (25) and 27 October 1866, Fitzwilliam Museum.

32 Philip Webb to C. J. Faulkner, 26 May 1873, *Architectural History*, (8) 1965. But Webb's continuing sympathy with Butterfield is indicated not only by his admiration for Keble College, but also by the detailing of some of his own work, such as his house of 1868 at 19 Lincoln's Inn Fields.

33 Sketchbooks and working drawings of details, the latter now at the R.I.B.A. Butterfield had erased names on the drawings, so that until recently they were thought to be by Caroë. Caroë's architecture is a logical development of picturesque gothic and his originality has been criticized like Butterfield's. Goodhart-Rendel called his churches 'ugly and eccentric', 'piquant but naughty', etc.; but Pevsner describes them sympathetically as 'fanciful' (if restless), 'playful', 'cheerful', etc. (*BE, South Devon*, pp. 148, 231–2; *London* II, p. 267; *Middlesex*, p. 48). Caroë, son of a Danish consul in Liverpool, was a Cambridge graduate, and an authority on the Vikings. He was Architectural Association president in 1895 (*B* (154) 1938, p. 435).

34 *Philip Webb and his Work*, pp. 67–9.

35 E.g. J. M. Winmill, *Charles Canning Winmill*, London, Dent, 1946.

36 P. Ferriday (ed.), *Victorian Architecture*, London, Cape, 1965, p. 237 and pl. lxxxi–lxxxii.

37 Sketchbooks, Waterhouse Collection.

38 Bentley to Hadfield, c. 1863.

39 *Art Applied to Industry*, London 1865, pp. 109–20.

Like the Whig interpretation of history, nineteenth-century art criticism rested upon the notion of progress. To some minds indeed the two were inextricably linked. William Roscoe, the Liverpool merchant banker and notable early collector of Italian primitives, had written how

> From fair ITALIA's once-loved shore,
> (The land of Freedom now no more)
> Disdainful of each former seat,
> The ARTS, a lovely train, retreat:
> Still prospering under FREEDOM's eye,
> With her they bloom, with her they fly;
> And when the Power transferred her smile
> To ALBION's ever-grateful isle . . .

the Arts too migrated to the new land of freedom.[1] Such an explicit equation was rare, but there can be no doubt that the Victorians *expected* progress in the arts commensurate with their achievements in commerce and industry, and this was one reason for the vocal demand for a specific Victorian style in architecture. Even as late as 1891 Professor Kerr, reissuing James Fergusson's *History of the Modern Styles of Architecture* with lengthy depressed appendages on the decay of the classical tradition, instinctively headed his notes 'Progress since 1880', and so on. And in spite of his entirely different standards and cautious conclusion, Charles Eastlake's *History of the Gothic Revival* is a story of the rediscovery of an ancient art which closely follows the pattern of Vasari's famous account of the Renaissance.

Yet at the same time the more perceptive Gothic Revivalists were aware of a contradiction in their standards. There were, as Street remarked turning his back on the Palladian palaces of Vicenza, 'unhappily two views of art, two schools of artists – armies of men fighting against each other'; and the classicists had the advantage of possessing the traditions and rules of the majority school.[2] Gothic only won the battle

366

of styles in the 1850s through a direct assault on the classical harmonies. Ruskin, with his praise for the wilfulness of gothic, sometimes went as far as to urge the complete abandonment of rules: for example, 'It is impossible to be over quaint or angular in architectural colouring.'[3] Ruskin's young followers soon 'astonished their masters by talking of the Savageness of Northern Gothic, of the Intemperance of Curves, and the Laws of Foliation.'[4] It was in this spirit that Philip Webb praised 'the strength of what I've called barbaric', and loved 'a gaunt church', while William Morris to the end of his life felt joy 'to think of barbarism once more flooding the world'.[5]

Now there is no doubt that in the minds of Webb and Morris barbarism signified a fresh kind of beauty rather than deliberate ugliness and discord. Few men indeed were more constant in their efforts to bring beauty to a hostile environment. But even they were forced to express their tastes in negative anti-classical terms, which made them vulnerable to attack. To Norman Shaw's lighter taste, for example, Philip Webb was 'a very able man indeed, but with a strong liking for the ugly'.[6] And the *Ecclesiologist* warned Butterfield of similar tendencies in 1859:

> The architecture of All Saints answers to the earlier 'Prae-Raffaelitism' of the sister art, before its truthful principles had been exaggerated into their opposite errors. And curiously enough there is here to be observed the germ of the same dread of beauty, not to say the same deliberate preference of ugliness, which so characterizes in fuller development the later paintings of Mr Millais and his followers.[7]

The critic was here thinking of paintings such as Millais' *Blind Girl*, rather than the earlier angularity of *The Carpenter's Shop*, which makes the accusation of ugliness seem as vague as most such contemporary remarks were. But Millais' earlier work had provoked still angrier uncomprehending reactions. Charles Dickens found in *The Carpenter's Shop* nothing but the lowest depths of what is mean, odious, repulsive, and revolting.'[8] Cardinal Wiseman attacked the whole Pre-Raphaelite medievalist school of thought:

> What was the result of ignorance or unskilfulness we attribute to some mysterious influence or deep design. A few terms give sanction and authority to any outrageousness in form, anatomy, or position; to stiffness, hardness, meagreness, unexpressiveness – nay, to impossibilities in the present structure of the human frame. Feet twisted round, fingers in wrong order on the hand, heads inverted on their shoulders, distorted features, squinting eyes, grotesque postures, bodies stretched out as if taken from the rack, enormously elongated extremities, grimness of features . . . are not only allowed to pass current, but are published in the transactions of societies, are copied into stained glass, images, and prints, and

are called 'mystical', or 'symbolical', or 'conventional' forms and representations.[9]

The Gothic Revivalists had undoubtedly opened themselves to such criticism, and, more important, they had no effective answer to it. All their theory of symbols and conventions, of historicism and originality, still had to be fitted into a classical frame-work of ideals of beauty. This surely was one major reason for the swift reaction of the leading gothic architects against the tastes which they had themselves initiated in the 1850s. Burges's *Art Applied to Industry* is characteristic in suggesting the classic qualities of his own style (which he had not in fact changed significantly) by attacking the excesses of others. Ruskin also turned on the works of his followers, 'Frankenstein monsters of, indirectly, my own making'.[10] And an especially revealing incident – because the victim attempted to fight back – was the fate of Bassett Keeling. A former principal of the Leeds School of Art, Keeling was an intelligent but somewhat innocent follower of Ruskin and Street who made the mistake of applying their style to a music hall. After a series of savage attacks, he tried to defend himself, and the theoretical weakness of his position made his defence singularly inept.

> I may have been eccentric, but no one can accuse me of plagiarism. I claim
> to have produced an eclectic design, but it is eclecticism and not patchwork.
> I have taken Continental Gothic as my basis . . . I have avoided incongruities
> and discord . . . 'Tenderness and delicacy' I did not aim at, but it does not
> follow that I do not appreciate them . . . What I have wished to secure is general
> picturesqueness, and in detail piquancy and crispness.

One might think that Keeling was perfectly right in arguing that 'exhuberance' was the right mood for the Strand Music Hall. Nevertheless the incident lost him his reputation. His solecisms were thereafter mercilessly pursued, to the extent of dis-missing one church as an 'atrocious specimen of coxcombry'.[11] One can see the wisdom of men like Butterfield and Webb in avoiding publicity and remaining silent under attack.

The reaction to earlier critical standards in the 1860s removed the need for any reformulation of aesthetic ideals. The new orthodoxy was well expressed by Scott's pedestrian pupil J. T. Micklethwaite, who scornfully dismissed High Victorian vigour as mere vulgarity. 'The common symptoms of it in our churches are harshness, even to brutality, of general design, with studied ugliness and systematic exaggeration and distortion of details . . . "Go" is, in fact, architectural rant, and may be defined as the perpetual forcing into notice of the personality of the architect.'[12] The con-sequence was that even fifty years later, when another generation was re-evaluating his work of the 1850s, Butterfield's work bewildered critics. The enthusiastic Halsey

Ricardo confessed that his 'amazement at his power and the intensity of his romantic poetry of feeling increases as the years pass by'.[13] Nor could the less sympathetic Paul Waterhouse produce a more convincing argument than the lame assertion that Butterfield 'sometimes exhibited originality at the expense both of beauty and of traditional usage'.[14] And the rebate on his merits has generally continued on such emotive lines.

On the continent, however, there had been a renewal of interest in primitivism no doubt analogous to the development of cubism and expressionism in the 1900s, and in 1908 the art historian Wilhelm Worringer published his *Abstraction and Empathy*. Like many discussions of past history, it is equally revealing of its own epoch. Worringer in fact provided one of the best clues to the understanding of Victorian style.

Worringer launched a double attack on earlier historians of primitive art. First he rejected their assumption that it could be comprehended, like works of art in the classical European tradition, through empathy – that is, through the spectator's projection of his own personality into the object, and consequent feelings of mutual identification and sympathy. Primitive art was not ineffective realism. It was intended to be abstract, distant, self-sufficient.

Secondly, he challenged their materialistic explanations of its development. It was rather the expression of the essential insecurity of man, of his 'spiritual dread of space' in a hostile universe. Primitive peoples were 'dominated by an immense need for tranquillity'. Hence their desire 'to wrest the object of the external world out of its natural context, . . . to purify it of all its dependence upon life'. But this basic insecurity could be tempered by the development of social tradition and organization, and by scientific and technical knowledge. Hence the paradox that 'the style most perfect in its regularity, the style of the highest abstraction, most strict in all its exclusion of life, is peculiar to peoples at their most primitive cultural level . . . Increasing spiritual mastery of the outside world and habituation to it mean a blunting and a dimming of this instinct'.

Worringer was not however postulating a simple progression from abstraction to realism. He recognized at once that there could be spiritual dread, a realization of the insignificance of the individual, *after* knowledge, as in the case of oriental civilizations. He also regarded north European art as a complex problem, the reaction of a more primitive people whose experience was of a 'harsh and unyielding nature' to doctrines and art forms originating in the Mediterranean, distorting them through 'the restless searching and striving after knowledge, all the inner disharmony', which he later tried to explain more fully in his *Form in Gothic*. There were in fact few pure cases of either abstraction or empathy; most art was the result of a dialectic between them consequent on 'the religion and outlook on life of the people in question'. Thus even the classic realism of Greece or the Renaissance was an extreme rather than an unqualified expression of a confident, rational spirit.

Naturalism and abstraction were nevertheless the two theoretical extremes, and each had its own perfect forms. And although in practice these forms were most clearly revealed by ornament, in which 'the artistic volition of a people finds its purest and most unobscured expression', they could also be discerned in architecture. Natural material volumes could be abstracted by the loss of texture or colour, and by reduction to mere planes or lines.

Clearly these concepts are much less simple when applied to specific periods. Indeed the one major attempt to develop them into a general sociology of art, Sorokin's *Social and Cultural Dynamics*, while interesting for its development of the contrasting types of society which might produce abstract or naturalistic art, is totally confused in its practical criticism of architecture. It is not however relevant to the present discussion to consider whether the same laws of analysis apply to pre-industrial art and to Victorian architecture. There can be no dispute either that twentieth-century art and architecture have tended strongly towards abstraction; or that the mid-Victorian situation was by contrast one of extraordinary confusion, of a battle between realistic and conventional ornament, between texture and planarity, between mass and line. Thus wall architecture, display of materials, constructional colour and the High Victorian delight in solid volume all speak of empathy, of proud material confidence; but equally clearly the qualifying abstractions, the linear patterning and sheer planar surfaces, tell of an intrusive spiritual anxiety, the inexorable price of progress. Worringer's formal polarities indicate a fundamental lack of direction in the High Victorian style, which is one reason why it was so shortlived and so diverse in its expression. One is left with increased admiration of Butterfield's formal solution to the dilemma of style.

Alternatively – and not necessarily incompatibly – the conventional ornament of High Victorian architecture, the restless linearity of diaper and banding, perhaps even the sheer wall planes, could be seen as signs of the future, pioneering experiments in a transitional period. But the first modern architects did not recognize this parentage, and preferred to prove their descent from the conservative utilitarian classical tradition of engineering. This was because abstraction in the twentieth century has one major element which certainly did not contribute to High Victorian style. This is its deliberate avoidance of the social language of architecture. It has repudiated not merely the association of particular styles with particular building types, but also the use of ornament to indicate status, and even traditional formal distinctions between elements such as doors and windows. There are perfectly good reasons for complaints that modern schools are indistinguishable from factories, or that there is no way of telling (except perhaps by some makeshift signs) where is the way through a wall of glass. The International Style was the product of professional architects who did not expect to be understood by the public. Nor did they require this understanding, for their patrons were either large industrial or municipal corporations prepared to allow their designers to set their own standards, or middle-class men who respected the mystique of fellow-professionals. The more demanding old upper-class patrons were significantly absent from their clientele.[15] Moreover their reputation was made not by the recommendation of these patrons, but by the approval of professional architectural criticism. It was thus possible for architectural style to concentrate exclusively on the means rather than the end of building, on the technical problems of structure, materials and spatial planning. Communication with an audience, if not disclaimed, was not to be won by concession. Certainly such social communication was no longer, as with almost all architecture in the past, a major consideration of the designer. In this sense the modern architect is as isolated from the public by his style as the painter or the poet.

On the other hand, this social abstraction does not necessarily imply the formal aesthetic abstraction of Worringer's theory. It happens that the International Style, evolved during the cataclysmic social upheaval and world warfare of the early twentieth century, had both qualities. Since 1945 there has been a strong recovery of interest in texture and volume, and in verticality in the place of the classical sense of proportion of the earlier phase, so that the formal situation is now again thoroughly confused. The revival of interest in Victorian architecture is of course itself part of this trend. But what is the cause of it all? Increased competition causing individualistic mannerism? Certainly architects in private practice have generally led the change, but public architecture has followed as swiftly as economics allow. Or is it the expression of a more confident, less Puritanical era?

Exactly the same questions can be asked of High Victorian style. The materialist explanation is certainly arguable. Mid-Victorian England, with the exception of late nineteenth-century America whose architectural style followed a similar course, was probably the most competitive and individualistic of all advanced societies. The sheer pace of technical and social change was itself unprecedented. Architects had to adapt during a life's work to changes on every side: to new building techniques and materials, to the transition from building craftsmen to contractors, to the growth of middle-class patronage, to the need to design a series of new building types for an industrializing and urbanizing population, and to bewildering reassessments and discoveries in architectural history. The coherence of architectural style gave way, like that of a language overwhelmed by a rush of new words and concepts. At the same time the rapid expansion of the scarcely organized architectural profession meant that it was inundated by untrained impostors. Victorian architects had bitter personal experience of unrestrained competition, and their stylistic individualism was a necessary part of the struggle of each for survival. Equally, in a society in which the gulf in standards of living between rich and poor had never been so wide, they could not but express these harsh social contrasts in their style; for apart from stylistic convention, the unequal distribution of resources for different building types made this inevitable. The extraordinarily acute contrasts of High Victorian style, its vociferous personal mannerism and its lack of aesthetic direction, were thus the anarchical consequences of unbridled private enterprise.

This view is not implausible. It is difficult to believe that the industrial revolution did not have some effect of this kind, and it emphasizes the response of architects to a general situation rather than blaming the rise of specific ill-educated new clients. While it can be shown that as patrons industrialists were relatively conservative rather than initiators of fashion, there can be no doubt of the indirect impact of their business activity in the expansion and transformation of the building industry. We have already seen how Butterfield's style reflected his need to control every detail of the building process. Surely these less precise aspects of the architect's situation left their mark?

On the other hand, this lack of precision is itself disconcerting. One cannot distinguish individual architects by arguing that some faced more competition than others, so that the argument cannot be tested in detail. Worringer's spiritual interpretation does not eliminate the economic situation as one explanation of High Victorian style, but it has the advantage that it can be applied to individual architects as well as to the general spirit of the age itself.

Amazed by the suddenness of the change they saw around them, the mid-Victorians were a generation torn between unprecedented optimism and disorientated despair. There was justice in Macaulay's claim that the English had become

> the greatest and most highly civilised people that ever the world saw, have spread their dominion over every quarter of the globe . . . have created a maritime power which would annihilate in a quarter of an hour the navies of Tyre, Athens, Carthage, Venice and Genoa together, have carried the science of healing, the means of locomotion and correspondence, every mechanical art, every manufacture, every thing that promotes the convenience of life, to a perfection which our ancestors would have thought magical.

But there were others for whom the turbulent growth of towns and population, the vague fear of some general social upheaval like those on the continent, the personal exhortations 'to push on, to climb vigorously upon the slippery slopes of the social ladder', the new speed of travel and the cut and thrust of business, were a price hard to accept. 'We are whirled about, and hotted around, and rung up as if we were all parcels, booking clerks, or office boys'. And still more serious to many was the collapse of traditional Protestant religious doctrines in the face of biblical and scientific scholarship, producing that great consciousness of doubt weighing, in Huxley's phrase, 'like a nightmare' upon many of the best minds of the age.[16] It is this deep confusion in the Victorian spirit which, more than any other single factor, helps one to understand the unresolved conflict in Victorian style.

Consider for a moment the impact of this spiritual dilemma on the Victorian home. As other traditions were eroded, the Victorians clung more strongly to the traditions of family life, emphasizing its hierarchy and its ritual. The family album and the family magazine, morning prayers and evening readings from the classics, Sunday church and the annual seaside holiday, all served to emphasize the solidarity of the family community. In the household of William Gibbs, the donor of Keble College Chapel, there were services conducted twice daily by a family chaplain in the great gothic house chapel, and their dual meaning was made clear by 'the distinct and emphatic reading of the Lessons by the master of the family and his genial, cheerful, cordial "Good Morning" or "Good Night" before the small congregation dispersed.'[17] It was in the family that the Victorian professional or business man could find compensation for the inhumanities of competitive life. 'When we come home, we lay aside our mask and drop our tools, and are no longer lawyers, sailors, soldiers, statesmen, clergymen, but only men. We fall again into our most human relations . . . We cease the struggle in the race of the world, and give our hearts leave and leisure to love.' Here too was a refuge from doubt. 'To the skirts of human love I have clung, and I cling blindly', wrote J. A. Symonds. 'But all else is chaos.' Ruskin summed up the common attitude well when he wrote, 'This is the true nature of home – it is the place of Peace; the shelter, not only from all injury, but from all terror, doubt, and division.'[18]

At the centre of the idealized Victorian family was the mother, 'The Angel in the House'. She was expected to be the embodiment of all its virtues, and above all of its moral purity. Hence the exaggeration of the feminine heart at the expense of the feminine mind, the emphasis on purity of conversation, the expurgated editions of the classics. Yet this process was carried so far that femininity was itself spiritualized. F. W. Robertson recalled how, to a child, 'woman was a sacred dream, of which I would not talk. Marriage was a degradation . . . The beings that floated before me, robed in vestures more delicate than mine, were beings of another order. The thought of one of them becoming mine was not rapture but pain . . .'[19] And is not this same attitude the explanation for Victorian fashion, with its exceptionally persistent trends, and its exaggerated feminine curves of crinolines and bustles converging on wasp-waists of astounding fragility? Human forms full-blown, and yet, by the same process, ethereal?

Within the framework of fashion, whether in dress or architecture, there is ample scope for the expression of individual personality. This is not always easy to interpret, for only a minority are bold enough to use this opportunity. But there are individual examples which will support a general interpretation of High Victorian style as the expression, very often simultaneously, of material optimism and spiritual disquiet.

Let us take first the most consistently substantial of all Victorian architects, William Burges (316, 317).[20] We find him the embodiment of optimism, a jovial Bohemian figure with a zest for company (including that of children, birds and animals), apparently untroubled by religious or moral problems. He never allowed his enthusiastic scholarship to dim his sense of paradox and absurdity. 'Burges loved the amenities and sunshine of Mediaeval Art' rather than 'its austerities and clouds'.[21] No doubt the 'singular boyishness and playful disposition' which he kept to the end of his life (he died with his parrot at his bedside) was assisted by the special character of his architectural practice.[22] Burges was not for ever chasing to keep up with his work like so many of his contemporaries. He did not need to, for he had no family to eat away his ample private income. Consequently, although he executed little more than twenty commissions in twenty-six years, he had the funds to build an artist's palace for himself in Melbury Road, one of the most fashionable streets in Kensington. Moreover he found sympathetic patrons, particularly in the aristocracy. They in-

316   Castell Coch, by
William Burges
(*Country Life*)

cluded the somewhat eccentric Marquis of Ripon, who as a young man had been a
Christian Socialist, claiming descent from Oliver Cromwell and asking working men
to call him plain Jack Robinson. At this stage he treated monarchy and aristocracy
as 'dead dogs'.[23] Later he succeeded to Studley Royal, and became a Roman Catholic
and viceroy of India. Equally unusual was the Marquis of Bute, another convert to
Roman Catholicism, and probably the richest man in England. The income from his
estates, which included Cardiff Docks, was recorded by the *New Domesday Book* of
1875 as over £230,000 a year. He was a reserved, scholarly man who found in
building 'my chief pleasure' in life. He commissioned his first fantasy castle at Cardiff
from Burges while an Oxford undergraduate. At his second, Castell Coch, 'gleefully
equipped by Burges with drawbridge, portcullis, holes for boiling oil and so on', the
Marquis served his guests Welsh wine grown on the hill slopes below. 'The whole
building exudes a pride in the weight and power of stone'.[24] With their elephantine
zest, their luxuriant and witty detail, these castles represent High Victorian style at
its most exuberant. Nor would it be easy to find a bolder use of solid matter than
Burges's pulpit at Cork Cathedral.

The castles date from the late 1860s and the 1870s. So does some of the poetry of
Gerard Manley Hopkins. Yet here we find an entirely different mood, of deep
seriousness and spiritual loneliness. Hopkins transformed gothic rhythm through his
searching realism; his verse, like his vision, rings with 'Pied Beauty'.

> All things counter, original, spare, strange;
>   Whatever is fickle, freckled (who knows how?) . . .

Moreover he watches men in exactly the same way; for example, 'Harry Ploughman':

> Hard as hurdle arms, with a broth of goldish flue
> Breathed round; the rack of ribs; the scooped flank; lank
> Rope-over thigh; knee-nave; and barrelled shank –
>   Head and foot, shoulder and shank . . .

Hopkins' metaphor is here explicitly architectural, and in these lines one can sense
vividly what he admired in a church like Babbacombe. 'And that virtue of originality
that men so strain after is not newness', Butterfield had noted from Ruskin, 'It is only
genuineness; it all depends on this single glorious faculty of getting to the spring of
things, and working out from that . . . There is reciprocal action between the intensity
of moral feeling and the power of imagination, for on the one hand those who have
the keenest sympathy are those who look closest and pierce deepest and hold securest;
and on the other those who have pierced and seen the melancholy deeps of things are
filled with the most intense passion and gentleness of sympathy. I suppose the chief
bar to the action of the imagination, and stop to all greatness, in this present age of

ours, is its mean and shallow love of jest . . .' And although Victorian originality was
less confined than Ruskin wished, he had identified the mood which dominated the
imagination of both Hopkins and Butterfield.

Hopkins was entirely unrecognized as a poet in his lifetime. He had rejected the
world for the religious life, and his superiors decided against the publication of his
poetry. As an architect, Butterfield was by contrast deeply involved in Victorian
social and economic life. He had to be able to handle builders, tradesmen and patrons,
and his buildings were designed for day to day use. Careful not to expand his practice
beyond what he could control, he imposed the strict discipline of realism on all his
work. But equally his style bears the mark of his persistent thinking, his religious
passion, and the courage of his isolation. It required a determination which Bodley,
for example, lacked, to continued developing a style when fashion had turned against it.

No doubt there were always some who, like Halsey Ricardo, found Butterfield's
architecture could 'compel one to shout and cry at the same moment'.[25] But of the
majority Hopkins himself was probably correct when he wrote to Butterfield, 'I do
not think this generation will ever much admire it. They do not know how to look
at a Pointed building as a whole having a single form governing it throughout . . .
And very few people seem to care for pure beauty of line, at least till they are taught

317 Cork Cathedral,
pulpit, by William
Burges (Charles
Handley-Read)

to.'[26] Even a friend and supporter like Coleridge became very qualified in his enthusiasm. When Butterfield was reconstructing his London house in 1868 he thought the general scheme 'very beautiful and convenient', but he only gave way under protest to the 'fantastic Butterfieldian wall-paper' which was proposed for the dining-room. 'I see we shall have to put up with the "worms", which in time, I dare say, we shall get to endure, perhaps even to like'.[27] Among others there was a good deal of outright mockery and abuse, such as Oxford jesting at the streaky bacon and holy zebra styles, and the Rugby *Meteor*'s campaign against the 'destructive' buildings which 'disfigured' the school close.[28] Yet it is just those features of Butterfield's work which these young hearties chose to deride, which make his buildings so representative of their age. For no other architect so consistently explored both the *material expressiveness* of wall architecture, and its *discipline* through wall planes; and, at the same time, through colour, the triumphant joy of *faith*, and through line and pattern, the *insecurity* of an age of doubt and change.

Probably unpopularity did not concern Butterfield greatly; it was the accepted fate of men of principle. But the rejection of religious doctrine itself which he witnessed was another matter. He felt it all the more intensely because he was starved of personal affection. Living alone, he lacked the consolation to which Matthew Arnold turned, confused by the infinite, despairing sound of the sea on 'Dover Beach':

> The sea of faith
> Was once, too, at the full, and round earth's shore
> Lay like the folds of a bright girdle furled,
>   But now I only hear
> Its melancholy, long, withdrawing roar,
>   Retreating to the breath
> Of the night-wind down the vast edges drear
> And naked shingles of the world.
>
>   Ah, love, let us be true
> To one another . . .

It is because this anxiety was so fundamental to the mid-nineteenth century, and equally to Butterfield himself, that his work could represent the spirit of his age at a deeper level than is usual with architecture. In most periods, convention is strong enough to muffle any clear statement. High Victorian style was confused, but because it was also the product of a rare moment of aesthetic freedom, it was able to speak both the confidence and the fear of the first industrial nation at the height of its power. This is why it is the most challenging of all English architectural styles and, at its best, great architecture.

Notes on chapter 16

1   John Willett, *Art in the City*, London, Methuen, 1967, pp. 24–5.

2   G. E. Street, *Brick and Marble in the Middle Ages*, London 1855, p. 109.

3   *The Seven Lamps*, p. 130.

4   Eastlake, *op. cit.*, p. 278.

5   Lethaby, *op. cit.*, pp. 24 and 130; *Letters of William Morris*, p. 236.

6   Lethaby, *op. cit.*, p. 75.

7   (20) 1859, p. 185.

8   *Household Words*, (1) 1850, p. 265.

9   *B*, (11) 1853, p. 649.

10 E. T. Cooke and A. Wedderburn, *The Works of John Ruskin*, London 1903–12, X, p. 11.

11 *A*, (36) 1886, p. 294; *BN*, (11) 1864, p. 864, and (17) 1869, p. 121.

12 *Modern Parish Churches*, London 1874, p. 264.

13 *A*, (83) 1910, p. 147.

14 *DNB*.

15 With the assistance of Mrs Elspeth Burrows, I have listed the patrons of the houses built in Britain in the International Style up to 1939 and published in the *Architectural Review*. Scholars and educationists account for ten, architects and their relatives for six, other artists, designers and writers for six, and other professionals and businessmen for eleven. There are no other significant groups and the old aristocracy is entirely unrepresented.

16 Houghton, *op. cit.*, pp. 39 (Macaulay), 187 (Froude), 7, and 71 (Huxley).

17 *G*, 7 April 1875.

18 Houghton, *op. cit.*, pp. 345–6 (Froude), 389 (Symonds) and 343 (Ruskin).

19 *Ibid.*, p. 355.

20 Charles Handley-Read, 'William Burges', in Ferriday (ed.), *Victorian Architecture*, pp. 187–220.

21 Robert Kerr in James Fergusson, *History of the Modern Style of Architecture*, London 1891, p. 145.

22 R. P. Pullan, 'The Works of the Late William Burges', *R.I.B.A. Transactions*, 1881–2, pp. 183–95.

23 N. C. Masterman, *John Malcolm Ludlow*, Cambridge 1963, pp. 136 and 146.

24 Mark Girouard, 'Cardiff Castle' and 'Castell Coch', *Country Life*, 13 and 20 April 1961 and 10 and 17 May 1962.

25 *A*, (83) 1910, p. 147.

26 Gerard Manley Hopkins to Butterfield, 26 April 1877, Starey Collection.

27 Coleridge, *op. cit.*, 2, p. 158.

28 25 May 1871 and 5 March 1872.

Part Two

The second part of this book consists in a survey of Butterfield's work, and since his original buildings have been the central concern of the first part, there is little which needs to be added here to the documented catalogue which follows in Chapter 19. A few comments on each of the groups of building types will suffice.

CHURCHES and CHAPELS are in one respect the most varied type of all, for they range from full cathedrals to temporary chapels and chapel schools. This is reflected in the astonishing variations of cost. The cheapest on record are Charlton (56) (£200) and Bursea (4) (£350), although it would be interesting to have the price of the mud-floored thatched colonial church at Victoria West, South Africa. Butterfield was probably more skilled in cheap church building than any of his well known contemporaries; Wokingham, for instance, was given him when Blomfield had not seen his way to cut his designs to the avilable funds. At the other extreme, Melbourne (XIX) was estimated to cost £100,000, All Saints' (X) £70,000, Keble College Chapel (132) £40,000, Rugby church (52) about £25,000 and Dundela (165) £14,000.

Plans very to some extent according to type, and not merely in the provision of ancillary features such as cloakrooms in a chapel school or chapter rooms for a cathedral. With churches, the absence of one or both aisles is invariably an economy (322, 323). With chapels, on the other hand, it was Butterfield's universal practice, however grand and costly they were to be (28). The presence of a clerestory is generally reserved to denote the town church type, in contrast to the lower un-clerestoried country church. Cathedrals are distinguished by their towers and transepts.

Churches and chapels have either a bellcote or a single tower or spire, placed either at the west end, or at the south-west corner forming an entrance porch at the same time, or sometimes centrally between nave and chancel. This last position did not necessitate a cruciform plan, and was used in some small churches such as Milton and Elerch without either aisles or transepts (274, 277). At Stoke Newington (7) the aisles are simply carried through to the east end of the tower. When he provided

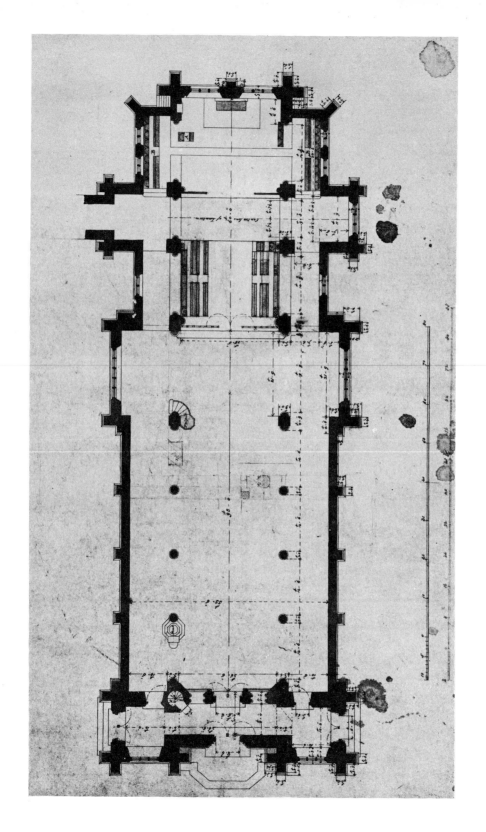

318 Adelaide Cathedral, plan (Messrs Woods, Bagot, Laybourne-Smith and Irwin)

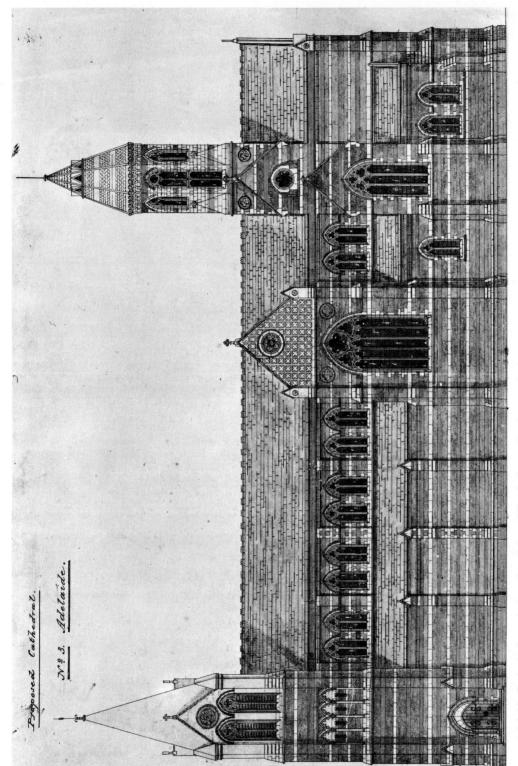

Proposed Cathedral.

Nº 3. Adelaide.

319 Adelaide Cathedral, south elevation (Messrs Woods, Bagot, Laybourne-Smith and Irwin)

320 *above* Adelaide Cathedral, exterior

321 *below* Melbourne Cathedral, plan (R.I.B.A.)

322 *opposite above* Braishfield church, plan (Starey Collection)

323 *opposite below* Coalpit Heath church, plan (R.I.B.A.)

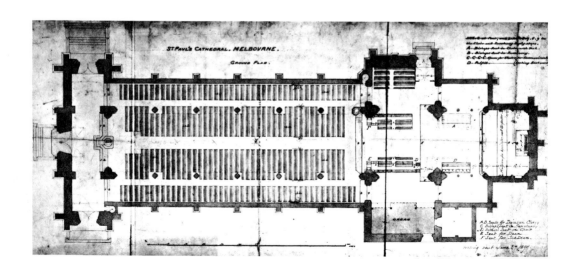

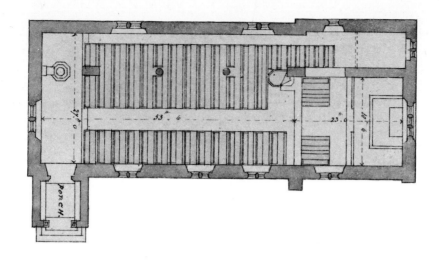

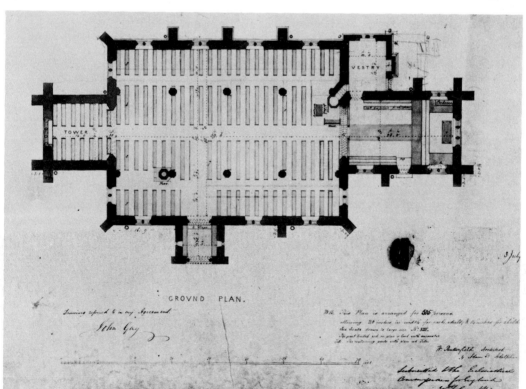

GROVND PLAN.

transeptal roof lighting over the nave at Leeds (73) he did not extend it over the aisles, and the device was condemned by the *Ecclesiologist*: 'we can see neither use nor propriety in such an arrangement: it is simply odd'.[1] For a church of cathedral character, on the other hand, a cruciform arrangement was essential. Both of Butterfield's first cathedral plans, for Perth and Adelaide, provided short high transepts which did not project beyond the line of the aisles. At Perth they were to be combined with two west spires, at Adelaide with a low pyramidal crossing tower.

At St Alban's Holborn (324) there are similar transepts abutting the west tower,

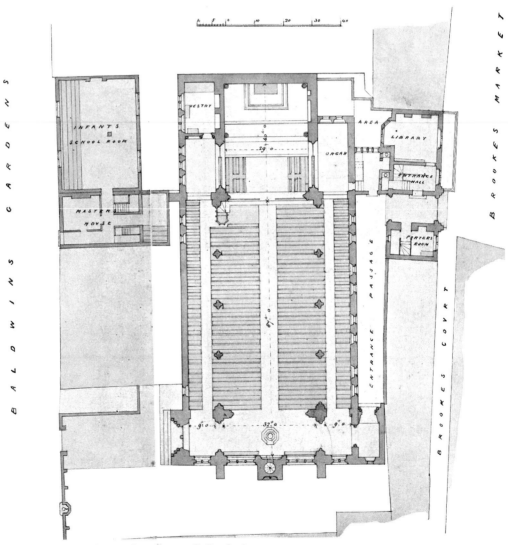

324   St Alban's Holborn, plan (Starey Collection)

and forming an entrance space within, but transepts of any kind are rare in Butterfield's churches between 1850 and 1865. Then a distinctive cruciform group follows, including major churches of all types. Babbacombe, a country type, was originally designed with two low projecting transepts, although only one was built. Rugby, Portsmouth and Clevedon were cruciform town churches, at least externally. At Keble College Chapel the west bay forms miniature transepts (70), and at Rugby School Chapel the great central congregational space is formed by double transepts, with the choir placed below the great octagonal lantern tower (290, 325).

The form of the Rugby lantern appears earlier in Butterfield's second plans for Adelaide Cathedral (226, 318, 319). His drawings of 1868–9 show an elaborate double cross plan. There is a western narthex under the two stumpy west spires. The nave is lit only by a clerestory, but it opens to a great transeptal space with five-light windows. These broad transepts rise to the full height of the long roof ridge. The choir transepts are lower and narrower, but project further, and a high cross-gable echoes their shape, building up to the central octagonal lantern. The cathedral was not executed by Butterfield, and the plans were modified in many ways: the constructional colour eliminated, the west spires enriched, nave aisle windows and transept introduced, and later an apse added. Nevertheless the external effect (320) is highly successful, for the triple transeptal gables and the contrast of spires and lantern give not only variety, but through their progression in scale an illusion of cathedral size. This illusion is not maintained internally, where the lantern cannot be seen from the choir, and the architectural treatment as a whole is surprisingly light. The plastered walls are shown in Butterfield's drawings.

Butterfield's final cathedral design was for Melbourne, in 1877 (321). This was on the grand scale both without and within, with single transepts only, western saddleback towers, and a great central octagonal tower and spire. Although the difficulties of superintending a cathedral building in Australia again proved insuperable, so that the fittings and later the spires were completed to other designs, the interior is his finest realization of the cathedral type. A triforium is provided by the wall arcading between the arcade and high clerestory, the scale is further emphasized by its broad colouring, and the giant arches to the western narthex and at the crossing rise almost to the roof, so that they mark a single immense space.

There are other features of Butterfield's planning common to all church types (272, 322–326). From quite early he always provided, where possible, an entrance space at the west end. In chapels this was formally distinguished as an antechapel, and at Balliol Butterfield threatened to resign if asked to depart from this 'received universal ground plan of a College chapel'.[2] His cathedrals have a western narthex under the towers, and a few parish churches, such as Hammersmith, were designed with an external western narthex. At Auckland this was said to be locally necessary as 'a

B*

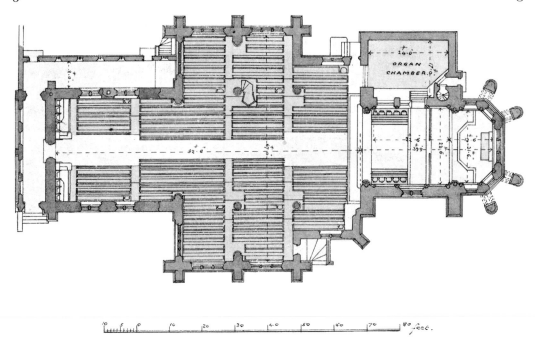

325   Rugby School chapel, plan (Starey Collection)

326   St Augustine Queen's Gate, plan (Starey Collection)

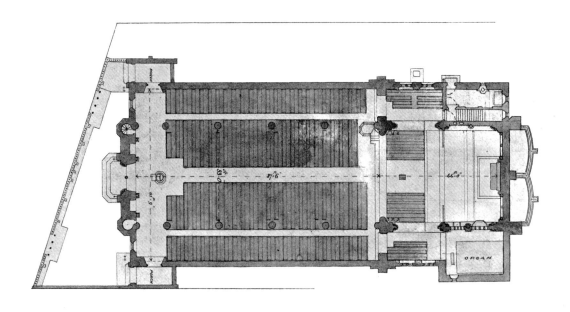

guard against the violence of the wind'.[3] Normally, however, he placed the porches at the western side bay of the nave, and quite often he made the last bay of the nave slightly shorter and higher. The western space was convenient for processions as well as latecomers. But it was a feature of Butterfield's plans at first disapproved by the Ecclesiologists: 'I had to persist in it against their criticisms. But I could not endure the cutting a congregation in two by a porch halfway up the side.'[4]

Butterfield's chancels are square ended. The one exception, Rugby School Chapel, was 'a case of necessity' owing to the confined situation. He apparently regarded the splendid apse of Norwich Cathedral as 'a piece of Norman extravagance' and not an English precedent.[5] More justly, he criticized the typical Victorian apse as 'a square end, minus the angles, i.e. a square end spoilt, while an old apse was a square end plus the apse – a very different thing'.[6]

There was no provision in Butterfield's churches of a side chapel with an altar for daily services. This can be found in churches by Brooks and Pearson, and is now common practice. The absence of an altar explains the lean-to character of Butterfield's church aisles.

> Mr Butterfield is so strongly convinced that every gable implies an altar, that, as it is well known, he will not even build gabled chancel-aisles; and that in cases like the communication between the nave-aisles and chancel-aisles of All Saints, Margaret Street, he has designed a half-arch, still further to emphasize the fact. This is pushing the principle to an extreme.[7]

It has certainly provided subsequent difficulties in the liturgical use of some of Butterfield's churches.

Another criticism which can be found very early is that his churches were acoustically unsatisfactory. It was said that from the back of St Alban's Holborn there was 'a ceaseless conflict between the sound and its echo which is destructive of all harmony . . . I could scarcely hear a single syllable distinctly.'[8] Keble College Chapel was described similarly. These were of course unusually tall buildings and the fault does not seem to be common, although there were no accurate methods of acoustic calculation in the period.

Certainly Butterfield wanted voices to be clearly audible in his buildings. This was one reason for his peculiar feud against organists. As early as 1861 he was writing to Sir William Heathcote, the Warden of Winchester College, 'I do trust Dr Wesley may not be listened to about the organ. It is a pity he is the organist. A building of that size requires a very moderate organ. If the boys would but sing and respond, one might almost say it required no organ.'[9] Later the tone became somewhat obsessive: 'I am afraid I think that organs are being much overdone in our churches nowadays. The organist becomes a too important person, &c, &c, &c. I need not enlarge. We are running into a great and growing danger . . .'[10] Sir Arthur Elton found to his surprise that Butterfield greatly disliked the famous organ-builder Willis. 'He could not work with him, an utterly impracticable disobliging man, who set at naught everything in the church except the organ.'[11] Butterfield showed his attitude by providing 'organ rooms' rather than 'organ chambers' in his church plans, carefully avoiding any implication of dignity. The practical consequence of all this was that the organ was never given prominence in a Butterfield church, and in some cases its position has been found distinctly unsatisfactory.

The idiosyncrasies of Butterfield's church planning should not, however, be emphasized. In general he conformed closely to the standards established by the Ecclesiologists: the parish church with its nave and aisles, font close to the door, pulpit on the north side of the chancel arch, nave porch, and chancel containing the choir stalls and the altar on raised steps. It is only with the occasional opportunity to design a new building type, such as the cemetery chapel or the chapel school, that his inventiveness becomes apparent.

In planning CONVENTS and COLLEGES there were fewer traditional solutions available. Butterfield designed two convents, both in 1850. That at Osnaburgh Street London has been demolished (170, 208). It was for the Sisterhood of the Holy Cross, founded in 1845, which had until then occupied two houses in Regent's Park. The work of the sisters included home visiting, a Ragged School, an orphanage for girls, and a refuge for destitute women. They were supported by Pusey, who provided for most of the cost of the new building. It was begun in September 1850, the first Anglican convent to be built since the Reformation, and completed in 1852.

It was a stock brick building, more interesting for its firm gothic detail than for its general appearance. As first planned, there was a three-storey street front, the attic storey with dormers, with cellars below, and a large coped and battered chimney. The plans only show the ground floor, so that it is not clear how the upper rooms were first used; later they became hospital wards. On the ground floor there was a large traceried arch, leading to the garden; a refectory and parlour, and the main entrance with a porter's room and a 'waiting room for the poor'. The refectory and parlour had stone fireplaces, and beautifully simple wooden shutters and panelling. A slightly lower range ran along the north side of the garden, with a staircase in the angle, and probably originally a cloister on the ground floor. This range contained another panelled room, work and school rooms, and a 'room for cutting out work', although all these were later altered. There were cells for the sisters above, opening off a central corridor. On the east side of the garden the buildings were more substantial: a chapel, a miniature ambulatory with chamfered stone panelling, and a community room with a steep-roofed bay window. There was an infirmary above, with a window opening into the chapel. Servant girls slept in the attics. The whole building was so cut about in later years, both outside and inside, that it is far from clear how successfully Butterfield had organized this irregular plan.

At Plymouth (179, 213) the site was less confined, but there was less money, and the plans were changed during the building. St Dunstan's Abbey was built for the Devonport Society, a nursing sisterhood founded by Lydia Sellon during the cholera epidemic of 1849. There was the same diversity of activities as at Osnaburgh Street – a soup kitchen and dispensary for the poor, various night and day schools, a printing workshop, a home for old sailors, a girls' orphanage and a home in which destitute women were trained as domestic servants. Not all these activities were to be housed in the new buildings, but the plans were ambitious, for a long range along the street front and wings at each end, containing large kitchens, dormitories, dining rooms, a bakehouse and so on. The foundation stone was laid with considerable ceremony in October 1850, an occasion only marred by the local ultra-Protestant mob, which broke in, pelted the sisters and clergy with potatoes, and devoured the ale. But almost at once it seems that the plans were changed, and only one wing was built, containing cells, a garden room, and a fortress-like tower with the refectory and community room. The refectory was very soon converted into a chapel, and its splendid wheel window inserted. The original plans for a cloister and chapel were never executed, but it seems that the gatehouse (with a room specially kept for Pusey) was added in about 1860. A large number of schoolrooms were also added, but their crude masonry and detailing contrast so poorly with the beautiful random coursing of Butterfield's buildings that it seems unlikely that he was concerned with them. The original fragment is one of his most attractive early works.

In 1856, as a result of their co-operation in sending a party of nursing sisters out to the Crimean war, the two sisterhoods amalgamated, with Lydia Sellon as Mother Superior. She planned the joint Society of the Most Holy Trinity in three parts; Sisters of Mercy at Devonport, Sisters of Charity at Osnaburgh Street, and an enclosed order of nuns of the Love of Jesus, dedicated to continuous prayer, for whom a site was found at Ascot in 1860. It is interesting that the buildings here were designed by Buckeridge rather than by Butterfield. Later, however, he was responsible for the chapel (291), which was built in 1885–6. This fine transeptal building has been described earlier. Ascot Priory soon became the strongest of the three sections of the Society, and the other activities were eventually abandoned. Osnaburgh Street became a hospital in 1864, and Devonport a school in 1906.

Apart from a plain stone novitiate wing built for the Wantage Sisterhood in 1878, there are no other recorded designs for convents by Butterfield. There are, however, several collegiate buildings of a comparable character which he designed for men. His first major commission was indeed for the missionary college of St Augustine's College, built in 1844–8 (29, 168). Before its completion, Butterfield designed schemes

327 Seminaire de St
Paul, Ambato-
haranana
(Bishop
O' Ferrall)

for colleges attached to the missionary cathedrals of Perth and Adelaide, although neither was executed. With them must be linked the noble College of the Holy Spirit on the Isle of Cumbrae in Scotland, built in 1849–51 (269, 270). These buildings share the characteristic features of the convent designs: chapel, cloister (104), refectory, corridors of cells (171), even the infirmary window looking into the chapel, may be found in most of them.

Other collegiate buildings follow the conventual type much less closely, even though two of them were theological colleges. The most surprising is the Seminaire de Saint Paul at Ambatoharanana, remotely situated among the mountains of central Madagascar (327). The college building, completed in 1890, is two-storeyed, with a vast library above, four classrooms below, a teak verandah along two sides, and a great pyramidal tower at one end. At the opposite end, standing separately, is the chapel of 1882, with a more slender pyramidal bellcote, and tiny, elaborate windows. The execution of these windows by local craftsmen, and the primitive, regular blocks of Imerina sandstone, gives a curiously African flavour to an otherwise very English design. Only the small windows and the verandah suggest a colonial college. The scheme, however, was never completed, and it may be that this odd group represents a fragment of a specific tropical type of design conceived by Butterfield.

The second theological college, at Salisbury, is only partly by Butterfield, for the main building is a fine late seventeenth-century brick house. Butterfield's first addition was an L shaped range of student's accommodation at the back, quite a simple three-storey design in flint and brick. Corridors run down the side of each range, opening to the students' rooms. Each set contains a study, with a fireplace, and a small bedroom.

328 Keble College, a staircase

329 Keble College, plan of cloister block (R.I.B.A.)

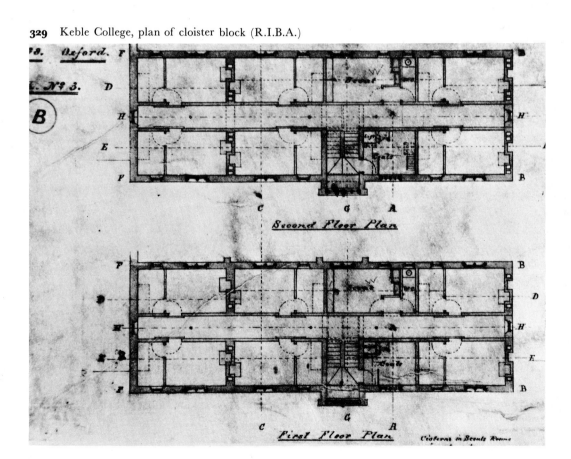

A lift was provided for coals. This building was completed in 1876, and after an interval Butterfield added the short high chapel, built on top of a small library, and consecrated in 1881 (111). The chapel interior is attractive, but outside it intrudes unhappily on the old house.[12] Butterfield's plain stone library of 1863 at St Bees should also be mentioned, for this was provided for the Theological College which then occupied the priory buildings.

The Salisbury College can be compared with the much more important work at Keble College, which Butterfield had designed in 1867. The same spirit of economy can be seen in the two-room sets for undergraduates, strung along both sides of a central corridor, with a provision of servants' rooms distinctly meagre by Oxford standards (71, 328, 329). This was because Keble undergraduates did not expect to be served breakfast and lunch privately in their own rooms. At intervals there are also sets for fellows. The bare, brick-walled access staircases, with half-landings daringly crossing clear of the tall windows, are a particularly impressive feature. Contemporaries also noticed the equipment of the servants' rooms with 'sinks, cistern, range, etc, with lifts for coal from the cellars in the basement, and with other modern conveniences calculated to save trouble'.[13]

The first ranges in the north quadrangle were built in 1868–70, with a temporary hall and chapel, and part of the west side of the south quadrangle followed in 1872–3. William Gibbs had by then decided to pay for the chapel, so that this was built in 1873–6 to a larger scale than first intended. The hall and library range followed in 1875–8, and apart from a small block added to the north side in 1955, the main quadrangle was then complete. The south quadrangle, however, was never properly enclosed, for after most of the east side had been built in 1874–5 it was decided to use the end site for the ambitious Warden's House. This was built in 1876–7. Finally, in 1879–83, the bursary block was added to the buildings of the west side of the south quadrangle. The total cost was about £150,000, of which £80,000 was spent on the hall, library and chapel. Enough has already been said of the composition of these buildings and of the great chapel interior; but it should be added that the interiors of the library and hall are scarcely less ambitious: approached by a splendid broad staircase, the first richly timbered, the second with patterned brick walls, a painted ceiling and Gibbs glass.

Butterfield's other Oxford college buildings were the chapel at Balliol of 1854–7 (50), and the reconstruction at Merton College which he started in 1849. This included the addition of a short new block of rooms facing Christ Church Meadow, designed around the traditional Oxford staircase and constructed in rough local stone. 'The use of bands of coloured stone' was avoided at the request of the fellows.[14] It is difficult to understand why this building, which appears from old photographs to be simply detailed, with big ribbed ridge chimneys and a massive bay window, and in any case replaced the nondescript outbuildings which had previously obscured the library, was locally thought to have 'spoiled the most beautiful view in Oxford'.[15] In deference to local opinion it has since been cut down and refaced in an unpleasant stone, and it is widely asserted in justification that Butterfield's exterior was in brick – in fact used only internally, in the well managed staircases.

Colleges lead naturally to SCHOOLS, for although the typical Butterfield school is a small parish day school, he designed a number of secondary and boarding school buildings. The first were in London. The choir school at All Saints' (26), with dormitories, a master's study and bedroom, a classroom and a fine refectory brilliantly fitted on four floors into the constricted site, was built with the church in 1849–53, although not in use until 1860. At the same time Butterfield built 'a library, cloister, and oratory, of red brick, in the simplest and cheapest way', for St Andrew's College at Harrow Weald.[16] This was a school at which poor boys 'were boarded and received the education of gentlemen free of charge', but it was without endowment, and indeed Edward Munro, who ran it, was in continual financial difficulty, and it was closed before he moved to Leeds in 1860.[17] Beresford-Hope characteristically claimed that Munro had '*swindled* him out of £7500'.[18] Sir Walter St John's School in Battersea (68) was a much sounder institution, and although the buildings which Butterfield designed for it have been much altered they are still in use. At the south end was the headmaster's house, and at the north, entered by a double archway from the street and an external staircase in the courtyard, were three small classrooms, the headmaster's room, and two long school rooms, planned on two floors, with the long rooms at right angles to the main street front. An old photograph shows the lower school room in 1913, by then divided by a screen, packed with rows of boys (330). The smaller rooms are less well lit than is usual in Butterfield's schools. In 1862 he also designed new buildings for Highgate School, but this scheme was eventually abandoned.[19]

Another important design, for the rebuilding of Exeter Girls' High School in 1878, was also apparently abandoned owing to financial difficulties. But the Exeter Grammar School plans of the same date were carried out, with a chapel added in 1885–6 (288). The main buildings are L shaped, in red brick with broad stone bands. At the angle is an impressive six-storey tower, containing rooms for the masters and matron. Classrooms are in the main north wing, facing east, with a corridor on the west side, and studies on the floor above opening from a corridor like monastic cells, and then on the second floor dormitories, and servants' rooms in the attic. The studies and dormitories are lit by rows of lancet windows. In the lower west wing are the kitchens and a dining hall. The plan allowed for the addition of a great school room to the east of the tower, but this was not in fact designed. There have been other additions, but the original buildings remain the most complete boarding school scheme which

330 Sir Walter St John's School, Battersea, schoolroom (Sir Walter St John's School)

Butterfield carried out. He added a red brick wing to King Alfred's Grammar School at Wantage in 1872–3, containing a dormitory and dining hall, and also a dormitory wing at St Mary's School again in Wantage in 1874, but these are both minor works. Nor is the Gordon Boys' School at Bisley of much interest, for although the original design of 1885 was by Butterfield it was executed gradually, and has been much altered in recent years. The earliest buildings were the miniature brick barrack room dormitories, ranged along the parade ground, and at the edge of the grounds the hospital, commandant's and staff officer's houses, and two cottages, all in brick and roughcast. Here – as at St Mary's School – Butterfield charged no fee.

Much better known, although again not complete new schemes, are Butterfield's designs for Winchester College and Rugby School. His work at Winchester consisted in the restoration of the chapel and alterations to provide more seating, and the conversion of the 'bare workhouse-like fabric of New Commoners', built in 1839, into 'an Elizabethan chateau' containing classrooms and a library.[20] At the opening of Moberly Court, as it became, in 1870, Butterfield was said to have 'made a silk purse out of a sow's ear'.[21] The building has since been degothicized. He also provided a report in 1875 for the adaptation of the medieval quadrangles to provide better bedrooms and studies for the boys, new earth closets, and other improvements, requiring no significant changes in the appearance of the buildings, 'but a mass of minute alteration and cutting about'.[22] These works are more revealing of his attitude to the restoration of older buildings than to school design. He was frequently employed by the College from 1857 until 1881.

At Rugby, where Butterfield was active for a still longer period, he had more scope, although even here the original school buildings and chapel greatly influenced the shape of his work. His first commission, which immediately followed the appointment of Frederick Temple as headmaster in 1858, was for a window in the old chapel. This was followed by a racquet court in 1860, and a 'fives court on the Eton plan', both of which were later replaced. He made drawings for a sick room in 1861, but this was not executed, and C. F. Penrose was employed instead. But in 1867 Temple commissioned him to design the New Schools (67), and stuck to his designs in spite of the requests of the School Trustees for 'greater congruity at least in colour with the old buildings'.[23] This classroom block, an L shape linking the Old School with the original chapel, was completed in 1870. The Trustees then sanctioned Butterfield's plans for extending the chapel (226, 290), which once again they did not finance, 'without expressing any opinion of the architectural character of the plans submitted'.[24] Finished in 1872, the chapel forms a quadrangle with the New Schools. The old white brick chapel remained as its nave until 1897, when this in turn was rebuilt by T. G. Jackson.

These are undoubtedly Butterfield's masterpieces at Rugby, and together they dominate the school, but they by no means exhausted Butterfield's contribution to its atmosphere. Round the edge of the school close are the cricket pavilion of 1869, now converted into a store; the gymnasium of 1872, utilitarian at the sides but with one end 'just like a Methodist chapel with a belfry', as the *Meteor* remarked;[25] a swimming bath of 1875–6, relatively modest; and racquet courts of 1880, with impressively simple, large double arches to a gallery. Further out are more buildings, which again show Butterfield's changing style: Kilbracken House in Barby Road, a master's boarding house built for J. W. J. Vecqueray in 1865–7, elaborately patterned with diapers and sharp raised ribs in the Keble manner; the quieter Temple Reading Room of 1878–9, with high dormers lighting the Art Museum on its upper floor (85, 289); and the broad banded, spreading New Big School of 1884–5 (193). In addition, Butterfield had designed a small fever cottage in 1878, and carried out minor alterations to several houses. He reconstructed the chapel spire in stone instead of slate and added the apse mosaics in 1882, and he completed the New Schools with three further classrooms and a cloister next to the chapel in 1884. Most of these buildings seem to be infected by the original restlessness of the New Schools, and being scattered about the grounds they lack the coherence of Butterfield's work in a similar style at Keble. Thus although the best Rugby buildings are outstanding, and several represent building types unique in his work, as a group they are undoubtedly indigestible.

The characteristic simplicity of Butterfield's parish schools is in complete contrast (331). In style only Baldersby (33), and the second school in Margaret Street, could be called ambitious, although an unusually ornate effect also results from the use of half-timbering at Great Bookham (53), Hellidon and Kirby Maxloe. Excepting the late 1850s, the typical school is of plain stone or brick with little or no patterning. Not that they were intended to be meagre. The *Ecclesiologist*, in an important article on school design in January 1847, argued that a school should be 'the prettiest building in the village, next to the church'. It emphasized the depressing effect of utilitarian designs on 'those children who are used to the sight of factories, and see schools built in humble imitation of them'. Care should be taken with all the details and the fittings ('the commonest utensil may be pretty in its way'), the interiors patterned with 'good and real' wallpapers, and the outside embellished by 'roses, jessamines, or Virginia creepers'.

The article also laid down that all the rooms should be if possible on the ground floor, lofty, with 'clear, but not too dazzling light', and an equable temperature. It advocated a separate roof for the school room and the master's house, a class room at right angles, and lean-to cloak- and hat-rooms. These amenities are provided in all Butterfield's schools, although the picturesque symbolism of the roof shapes was less strictly observed in his designs after 1850. Ample light is provided, sometimes by the use of large wooden grid windows. The school plans are all varied arrangements of a basic set of elements: large school room, small class room, porch, hat- and cloak-rooms, and lavatories. In the very smallest school, such as Letcombe Bassett (332), there was only a single school-room, while in the largest, such as Stoke Newington, there would be a complete duplication of provision for boys and girls. But the usual arrangement was to separate only the cloak-rooms, lavatories and yards, and to divide the large room by a curtain. Butterfield's first surviving school plan, for East Farleigh, was in fact quite typical (331).

The treatment of the earliest schools, up to 1850, is essentially picturesque, with simple gothic detail. Aston Cantlow is the most complete example, with its rustic cottage for the schoolmaster attached (126). The group at Alfington is still more attractive, but larger, probably because the house was intended for the curate (138). The next group, of the early 1850s, is the most severely simplified of all, with plain, flush wall surfaces, relying for effect on their tall battered chimneybreasts and well-shaped roofs. Cowick (62) and Pollington (137) are the masterpieces in brick, far bolder than the designs which Butterfield had published in *Instrumenta Ecclesiastica*. In stone, Wykeham, Hutton Buscel (333) and Langley have a few gothic details, but are equally successful. Yealmpton is a fragment east of the church, never completed because of the secession to Rome of Butterfield's patron (136).

A more highly textured group follows in the late 1850s. The richest of these have been mentioned, but the plainer examples, particularly Aldbourne (153) and Trumpington, are still very rewarding. Castle Hill, Northington and Tattershall, the best of the rather simpler group of about 1860, are similar in combining good shapes with attractive strongly textured materials (42, 133, 275). The boxy patterned shapes

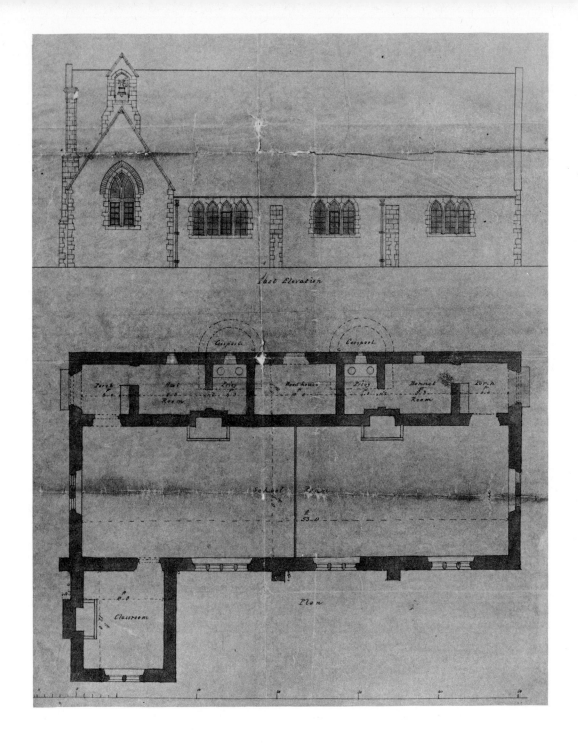

331 East Farleigh school, design (Kent Record Office)

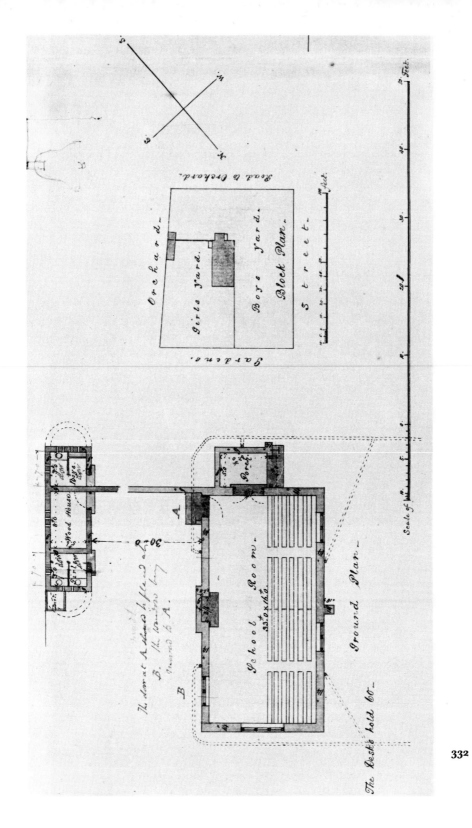

332 Letcombe Bassett school plan (Berkshire Record Office)

of the 1860s are only represented by Horton, which was of the same varied bricks as the church, and Hellidon, a much more sensitive use of half-timbering than in the late 1850s. The last schools are much simpler, but with the exception of the delightful Cotswold stone school at Poulton (121), they are of the least interest.

Attached to many of these schools (and listed with them in the catalogue) were HOUSES for the schoolmasters, and in several cases the original plans for them survive. They are thus the smallest house type of which this is so. The typical arrangement is that published in *Instrumenta Ecclesiastica* (20), with the door opening to a lobby with the staircase in front, the sitting room to one side, and the kitchen to the other. At the end of the kitchen are a small pantry and larder, but in some plans these are placed at the side. The staircase leads to two, or sometimes three bedrooms. All the rooms are small, but there is no wasted circulation space, particularly since the lobby and staircase assist the socially desirable separation of functions in the house. Tattershall, Aldbourne (153) and Trumpington provide typical examples. In style, the houses generally follow the school, but with still simpler detailing. In a few cases, such as the very early vernacular cottage at Aston Cantlow (126), or the plain late flint and brick house at Shaw, this means that they are the most rewarding part of the design. Both in plan and style, they are a valuable help in interpreting Butterfield's less well documented designs for working class cottages.

The importance of his remarkable ESTATE HOUSING for the Dawnay family in the 1850s has already been emphasized. Up to 1859, this can only be identified by

333 Hutton Buscel school (Peter Burton)

stylistic attributions, but the sequence is probably roughly as follows. Just west of Sessay church is a brown-red brick terrace (122), with thick ridge chimneys, a pantiled roof and elementary gabled door surrounds. The ridge is level. There is another similar terrace at Ruston, which has all its casement windows complete, but doorhoods added. Also at Sessay are two single cottages and a small house, hip roofed in tile, with timber framing to the gables, and rather high dormers flush faced with the wall, with level eaves. All these can be dated to about 1850. Next, around 1855, follow the earlier, plain brick cottages at Baldersby, at the edge of the village group (31). The dormers are of the same type, but a little lower in the roof. One pair is symmetrical, hip-gabled, with a brilliant variation of roof shapes over a tight rectangular plan; the other has matched front windows, but a buttressed porch with a bedroom storey above at one end, while at the other end the entrance is tucked behind a projecting room, and the second bedroom forms a projecting gable at the back. A third pair, closely related to these two, is at Butterwick (313). Its plan is staggered, as if two half versions of the first Baldersby pair had been put together with their corners overlapping. It has a buttressed porch, and a combination of sash and casement windows which is almost entirely original, for the variations are repeated on each side.

Although most of these cottages are composed in a complex picturesque manner, all of them, largely because of their straightforward detailing and materials, convey an impression of rough simplicity. This is also true of the Ashwell cottages, which date from the late 1850s (152). There are two pairs of the symmetrical Baldersby type,

presenting different sides to the lane, and differing from the original in their fine sash windows and their band of diaper and brick-on-edge moulding. Next to them is an L shaped terrace of four cottages, again with a touch of diaper, good sash windows, and plain chimney-breasts (334). It is surprising to discover that the plan, including the disposition of chimneys, the combination of a porch with an external staircase, and the projection of the roof slope at one corner like a raised flap, is exactly the same as the terrace at Baldersby west of the church (30, 335). But the detail at Baldersby is self-consciously gothic, with stone bands, mullioned pointed windows, and small buttress walls used to produce contrived, twisting movements at the angles. Fortunately this group, which represents a turning point in Butterfield's cottage style, can be dated to 1859. The rather simpler, large pair in old Baldersby village, which again has some gothic windows, is probably slightly earlier (336). Butterfield's last works for the Dawnays, a stepped terrace of four and a tall pair at Great Bookham, revert to the straightforward plainness of his earlier cottages, although now in the attenuated manner of the 1860s (134).

Meanwhile Butterfield had designed two very successful cottage groups for the Winstanley estate outside Leicester. These are again of brick, with very slight touches of diaper. The earliest, probably of 1857–8, are three pairs in Braunstone Lane, of which two are closely modelled on the symmetrical pair at Baldersby, while the third is irregular. The long terrace facing the green followed in 1859 (255). The irregular rhythm of low dormers is particularly attractive. Almost at once, a second terrace was begun at Kirby Maxloe, this time L shaped, with the eaves broken by gabled dormers

334 *opposite page* Ashwell, cottage terrace

335 *left* Baldersby, terrace of banded cottages

(63, 256). The crisp simplicity is astonishing, and the group could well be mistaken for cottage housing of the 1920s.

Butterfield also designed an attractive hipped cottage at Milton Ernest in 1859, and an unidentified group for Lord Ashburton in 1861. His remaining cottages are disappointing, and after 1865 surprisingly scarce. His lodges at Hursley for Sir William Heathcote (139) and his later cottages at Milton Ernest are elaborate exercises in half-timbering. The cottages for the Gibbs at College Farm, Ardingly, and near the Home Farm at Aldenham House represent the less agitated manner of 1878–9, but the stiffer half-timbering is still less attractive. Finally, there are the nondescript town terrace adjoining St Michael Star Street, Paddington, also for the Gibbs, and a lodge at Fulham Palace.

At Ashwell and Baldersby (32) the Dawnays provided village almshouses, probably in 1858–9. Both are single-storied half-timbered ranges, perhaps inspired by Christ's Hospital, Abingdon. The detailing is much bolder than in the group at Heckfield, built for Lord Eversley in 1861–3. Butterfield also restored older almshouses at Sackville College, East Grinstead, St Nicholas' Hospital, Salisbury, and St Cross, Winchester.

336 Baldersby old village, cottage pair

Turning now to housing designed for the middle and upper classes, it will be best to begin with his country PARSONAGES, for these are his most representative medium sized house type. There are altogether some twenty-five, and they present a complete spectrum of the development of his style. The earliest, picturesque gothic of Coalpit Heath (6) and Wilmcote is succeeded by the first non-historicist vernacular houses, brick at Ogbourne and Great Woolstone (337), brick and flint at Avington (55), stone at West Lavington (266), and stone and roughcast at Pinchbeck Bars (74). The bold severity of the early 1850s follows, the stone houses at Sheen (211) and Wykeham (144, 145) grand and ambitious, the brick houses at Hensall, Cowick and Pollington of unprecedented, free simplicity (19, 140). Alvechurch and Baldersby represent the turning point of 1855–7 towards heightened contrast, broken forms and patterning (34,150). The smaller houses at St Mawgan (43) and Charlton on the other hand remain relatively simple, and so are the rather bald boxy houses of the early 1860s at Newbury (69) and Bamford (142). Linear patterning then reached its climax in the brick, flint and timber of Dropmore (143), the stone of Little Faringdon (48), and the brick of Hitchin and Baldock (64). The last house at Enfield is typically indecisive, a plain shape heavily textured. The phase after 1870 is poorly represented, although a number of OTHER HOUSES designed by Butterfield in this period are comparable: the splendidly patterned and ribbed Warden's House (283) at Keble in 1877, the rock-textured Axbridge chaplain's house (49) probably in 1878, and the nondescript brick and roughcast officers' houses at the Gordon Boys' School probably in the 1880s. Earlier, there is also the hip-roofed, stone-banded and diapered brick agent's house of 1850, by the main road at Baldersby (146).

Beneath their varied elevations, the planning of the PARSONAGES is remarkably consistent (337, 338). Butterfield believed, with the *Ecclesiologist*, that 'the exterior ought to be adapted to the requirements of the internal arrangements, instead of the latter being made to accommodate, and in a manner *pack into*, a preconceived uniform shell.'[26] The basic shape was nearly always a rectangle, although in some cases the kitchen parts projected at right angles, forming an L-shape; or a coach house might be used to half-enclose the entrance in a similar way. The porch, most often on the north side, opened to a small hall. The arrangement at Bamford, where the main staircase is boldly projected without supports from the inner wall of the hall, forming an ample space, was exceptional, although as an economy in several small houses the stairs rose from the hall. But there was no set place for stairs; they were often close to the kitchen, and in one case, at Great Woolstone, entirely separate from the hall, and accessible only from the kitchen or the dining room. The study, on the other hand, was almost invariably next to the entrance, and next to it, facing south, the drawing room; and then the dining room, again most frequently facing south, although there was more variation here. The kitchen, adjacent to the dining room, was given the least attrac-

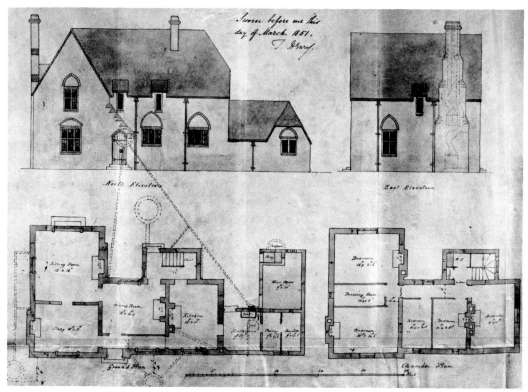

337 Great Woolstone parsonage, plan & elevation (Bodleian Library)

338 Bamford parsonage, plan (Bamford chest)

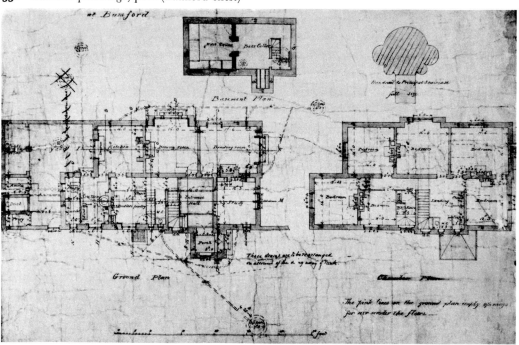

tive outlook. Much of course depended upon the particular site, and the patron's preferences and purse. In most respects Bamford may be taken as a typical arrangement; an informal, asymmetrical plan, but with no arbitrary irregularities.

The medium-sized town house is less well represented, but the clergy houses at Burleigh Street (65), Margaret Street (26) and Holborn (66) are examples of housing work of this type. All three exemplify Butterfield's ingenious planning on tight sites, and in the first two he broke the regular streetline to achieve this. The Holborn clergy house was unusual in providing flats for a housekeeper and four bachelors, with a communal dining room. At Queen's Gate the undistinguished parsonage has no street front, and the other London parsonages are detached.

OTHER HOUSES of this type which survive include only the terrace at Hunstanton (271). His remodelling schemes, which have all disappeared, included 1 Sussex Place for the Coleridges, 8 St James' Square for the Earl of Carnarvon, London House in the same square for the Bishop of London, 16 Princes Gardens for J. D. Chambers and work in Belgrave Square for Viscountess Downe.[27] There are thus no large town houses by Butterfield.

Butterfield's two substantial country houses have fortunately survived. It is not perhaps surprising, when the scale of Alvechurch parsonage (21) is recalled, to find that the planning principles at Milton Ernest Hall are similar to those used in the parsonages (257). The chief difference is that the porches lead into a spacious staircase hall, lit by upper gothic windows, with the landing a stone slab cantilevered from the wall. This device is crucial, for even here there is no space wasted. The main rooms are planned so that they open to the east and south, facing the gardens. The servant's hall, unusually for the nineteenth century, shares this privilege.

Milton Ernest is in fact Butterfield's only complete country house. He was also responsible for minor alterations at Trafalgar House, Highclere, Aldenham House, Audley End and Fulham Palace.[28] More important, however, in 1880–3 he almost completely reconstructed the Chanter's House (then known as Heath's Court) at Ottery St Mary for Lord Coleridge, at a cost of £16,724. The main rooms of the old house were kept, but refaced externally in brick and half-timber, and the kitchen converted into a new entrance hall. All the service buildings to the north were rebuilt, the low outbuildings dominated by a long half-timbered range, with big ridge chimneys. The most important addition, however, was the west wing, with a conservatory and tall bay-windowed library of the ground floor, and ample new bedrooms above. Internally, the house is full of Butterfield detail, from a metal wall lamp and a gabled pendulum clock to the great kitchen dressers. Brown panelling, warm red walls and quatrefoiled cast-iron radiators painted red and green, line the upper passages. The lowest part of the staircase, wooden and light, has been replaced, but the upper stairs remain. They are of stone from the half-landing, with red, blue and yellow tiled walls, approached through an archway, with more arches to the landing and windows high up – a dramatic, effective arrangement. The top floors are reached by a second wooden staircase, three-sided, springing across a window, with elegant balustered rails in light and dark woods. But the finest room is undoubtedly the library (339), built to house Coleridge's 18,000 books. It is a high room, lit from one side by bay windows at each end with a linking band of upper windows above the books. The plainish bookcases form bays between the tall bay windows and along the opposite wall, and this wall has more shelves above a wooden gallery. The brown of bound books and the dark panelled end walls set off splendidly the white marble busts, the framed crayon cartoons and the noble marble slab fireplaces caught in the light of the end bays.

Butterfield's OTHER BUILDINGS are a miscellaneous group.

Below the church at Sessay a small stone BRIDGE (340) with a massive ribbed arch, buttressing, and the Downe arms in an ogee-headed panel, crosses the stream. It is more likely to be by Butterfield than to be a genuine medieval bridge. The influence of Pugin's rib-vaulted railway bridge designs is apparent.[29] It probably dates from 1847–50.

Butterfield designed a WATERMILL (39) at Milton Ernest in 1856, on the Ouse a mile below the hall. This fine simple brick building has been mentioned earlier. He also designed FARM BUILDINGS at the mill, and at the hall and the Home Farm. These are very straightforward stone walled buildings with brick quoins, and include an attractive pyramid roofed dovecote. Much later, in 1879, he reconstructed two farms for Henry Gibbs. At Aldenham the Home Farm is on its own in the park, approached down a lime avenue. The open courtyard of brick barns is mid-nineteenth century, but at one corner Butterfield added a brightly textured bailiff's house, with vivid diapered brick and half-timbered upper walls, partly tilehung. More half-timbering was introduced into the barn gables at the same time. Behind the house is a brick dairy, treated like a pyramidal dovecote, with a delightful wrought iron weathervane. It is altogether an enchanting group, particularly for so late in his work.[30] College Farm at Ardingly (38) is rather larger, with a complete yard enclosed by long ranges of barns, brick walled on a stone base, with amply roofed, buttressed openings. The farmhouse is of brick, partly tilehung, but seems to have been altered. Next to it is a charming stable with a triple row of hip dormers, and at the back a steep-roofed octagonal pigeon house. There is also a big brick-buttressed open wagon house. It is again an admirable group.

Two other commissions were for the Tyntesfield branch of the Gibbs family. In 1880–1 Butterfield designed the VILLAGE INN at Wraxall (123, 135), including the coach houses, inn sign, bar, tap room, cider cellar and a village club house. They form an irregular group in rough stone, the main entrance to the bars and hotel bedrooms

339 Chanter's House,
Ottery St Mary,
library

340 Sessay bridge

341 Office of the Society for the Propagation of the Gospel (*Builder*, 1871)

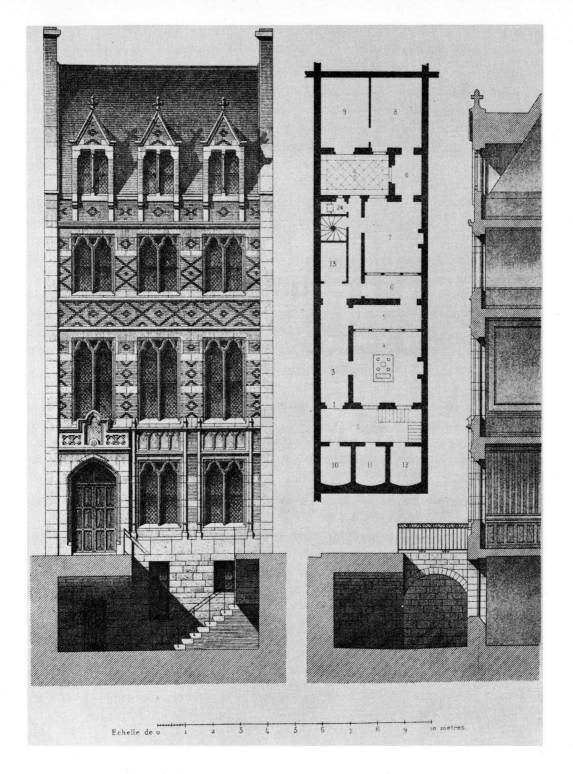

342 The same, adapted by Viollet-le-Duc (*Building News*, 1877)

through a buttressed porch, a garden on the hill slope behind, big-roofed stables to one side, and the partly half-timbered club hall to the other. Behind the club is a caretaker's house, with a remarkably interesting flat-roofed squared front to the side lane. The club hall has a timbered roof, but the bar fittings are disappointing. It is pleasanter to drink one's cider in the garden.

More characteristic in purpose is the HOSPITAL which Butterfield built for Mrs William Gibbs at Axbridge in 1878. It was a convalescent home for tuberculosis patients, managed by sisters from St Peter's Kilburn. Patients had to pay their own maintenance. St Michael's Home (as it is now called) is a range of stone buildings set high up in wooded parkland. The original group consisted of a central chapel, with two floors of wards north and south of it. At the end of each ward was a triple shuttered opening to the chapel, which allowed the weaker patients to hear services from their beds (195). Along the west side of the chapel and wards a glazed traceried corridor runs at each floor level, providing an internal sun gallery. At the ends, two wings project westwards, the northern with rooms for the sisters, the southern with dayrooms for the patients, and kitchens on a lower floor level, which is made possible by the slope of the hill. This southern wing was extended to the south in 1882, so that the visitor is now first confronted with this L shaped lower portion. The general effect of these buildings is reticent, but the park also contains lodge cottages and an elaborate stone and half-timbered chaplain's house, presumably all of the same period. St Michael's was Butterfield's second hospital design, and is of less importance than the Royal Hampshire County Hospital of 1863–8 at Winchester, which has been fully discussed earlier.

Finally, there was Butterfield's one London OFFICE (341), built in 1869–71 in Duke (later Delahay) Street for the Society for the Propagation of the Gospel. It has been demolished, but a marble fireplace from it survives in the Society's present Tufton Street library. It was an interesting brick elevation with a doorhead and chapel window breaking the diaper patterns, and Viollet-le-Duc thought it sufficiently striking to persuade Butterfield to lend him the working drawings, so that he could adapt it into one of his *Habitations Modernes* (342).[31] It is odd that this office should thus provide the one example of direct Butterfieldian influence on his major European contemporaries.

Notes on chapter 17

1   *E*, (15) 1854, p. 60.
2   Butterfield to the Master, 12 June 1854, Balliol College archives.
3   *E*, (19) 1858, p. 91.
4   *A*, (63) 1900, p. 195.
5   Swinfen Harris, *op. cit.*
6   *A*, (63) 1900, p. 226.
7   *E*, (25) 1864, p. 150.
8   *BN*, (14) 1867, p. 746.
9   23 May 1861, Winchester College archives.
10 Butterfield to Rev. G. Hales, 1 February 1892, Ardleigh chest.
11 Diaries, 25 July 1877.
12 Swinfen Harris, *op. cit.*
13 *A*, (4) 1870, p. 12.
14 Register, 10 June 1862, Merton College archives.
15 J. Wells, *Oxford and Its Colleges*, revised edition, London 1923, p. 75; c.f. a subsequent assertion that it 'was formerly one of the great eyesores of Oxford' and has been 'civilised at great expense and with much skill', C. Hobhouse, *Oxford*, London 1939, p. 12. Hobhouse also thought 'Henry' Butterfield's work at Balliol to be 'actively poisonous'.
16 *E*, (13) 1852, p. 300.
17 *DNB*.
18 N. Woodard to Henry Tritton, 18 April 1853, Tritton Collection.
19 Minutes of Governors' Meetings, 14 April 1877 and 4 May 1878. It was to be on the Cricket Field site. Butterfield was invited to prepare new plans for a master's house and boarding house in 1877, but this commission was withdrawn because cost limits imposed by the Charity Commissioners (£10,000) made it 'inappropriate to request an architect of Mr Butterfield's eminence to undertake to carry the scheme in that limited form into effect'. He was replaced by Porter, the school surveyor.
20 Winchester College Archaeological Society, *Winchester College, its History, Buildings and Customs*, 1926, p. 139.
21 *Wykehamist*, October 1870, pp. 2–3.
22 40106, Winchester College archives.
23 J. Hope Simpson, *Rugby Since Arnold*, London, Macmillan, 1967, pp. 46–8.
24 *Ibid.*, p. 73.
25 16 May 1872.
26 (2) 1843, pp. 146–7.
27 Coleridge, *op. cit.*, 2, p. 158; accnts; 1868, 1863, 1885–91, 1861 and 1861 respectively.
28 Accnts; the balustrade at Trafalgar is his (1859); the Music Room doorcases and fireplace and the hall pavement at Highclere (1863; illustrated in *Country Life*, 13 August 1959, p. 21); the fountain at Fulham (1886) and the reconstructed kitchens at Audley

End (1882). He installed heating at Highclere and gas at Fulham.

29   *Apology*, plate III.

30   The older barns were demolished late in 1968, so that the group is now much less attractive.

31   *BN*, (39) 1877, p. 314.

Butterfield's restoration work was chiefly in churches. His first principle was to make the building sound and efficient. Pre-restoration prints of church interiors now appear, through mere rarity, extraordinarily picturesque, and one would be thankful if more had been spared the attentions of the nineteenth century. But it must be remembered that such buildings were very often suffering from serious damp, subsidence and other structural defects due to years of insufficient attention. Equally serious was their invariable unsuitability for the performance of the Anglican liturgy along the lines advocated by the Oxford Movement, which is in fact common practice today. For both reasons, unless the buildings were to be abandoned extensive work was inevitable.

Butterfield brought both structure and arrangements to a new standard. He underpinned the walls where necessary, inserted damp courses, provided dry flooring, re-using old stone where available and ventilating the wooden floors with air bricks, and dug away earth so that the ground level outside was not above the airbricks and damp courses. Gutters and drains, including a cesspool for the font, were put in order. Heating was installed, and a vestry or organ chamber added if required, normally on the north side of the chancel. Similarly a porch was provided to the nave door. In the nave the old box pews were either cut down to a reasonable height or replaced by new benches. The font was moved to a position near the entrance, and the pulpit, which had normally stood across the chancel arch, to its north side. Where there was no medieval or good later font or pulpit, Butterfield would supply a new one to his own design. The chancel would normally need more drastic alteration, for very few had the necessary fittings: an altar, approached by steps, choir stalls and either altar rails or a choir screen would be installed. The Royal Arms, the Commandments, and the various wall tablets would be removed, the tablets being refixed elsewhere in the church, and very frequently the sanctuary roof would be replaced, or at least painted up. Hatpegs would be removed from both nave and chancel, for it was thought more reverent to put hats on the floor. Finally, all galleries were cleared out, chiefly because gallery seating made kneeling, facing eastwards, and administration of the communion in the sanctuary extremely difficult.

All these changes were simply demanded for the functional efficiency of the building. But there was a second purpose in restoration work. An aesthetic as well as a structural and liturgical standard must be achieved. There were two stages in this. Firstly the building must be examined to discover the stages of its development during the Middle Ages, so that the design as a whole, or the contributions of different periods, could be best re-established. Butterfield's approach to this problem was, for his time, conservative. He rarely attempted to reduce a building to a single period. On the other hand, he wished each element in the design to speak clearly. The stonework and timber was cleaned, broken mouldings and sills were renewed, and blocked windows were reopened. Tracery and other details patched by brick were renewed in stone. Whitewash – at Milton Ernest twenty-five coats – was scraped from the walls, but Butterfield did not expose undressed stonework; plastering was always renewed. The floor level was adjusted to the level of the pier bases, which were often found buried below it. The tower arch, normally blocked by a gallery, was opened up to its full height. Low plaster ceilings were taken out to reveal the original high medieval roofs, or if none survived a new open roof would be designed.

In all this work Butterfield took the greatest care that nothing ancient should be needlessly lost. 'Carefully protect all stones which have inscriptions on them or which have had brasses', reads a typical specification. 'Carefully protect the font and cover, and all monuments . . . The work is to be made good to the old joints . . . As far as possible leave the existing red colors upon the columns'.[1] And old materials were to be treated with equal care. When rebuilding the chapel tower at Winchester College (40), for example, Butterfield wrote that he intended that the reconstruction 'should on principle reuse as much of the old work as possible in the reconstruction'. On closer examination he found the mouldings and surface

> more decayed than I had expected. Stones which looked in good condition
> peeled off when touched with a penknife, and mouldings which looked sound,
> crumbled between my thumb and finger. A great deal of new external work
> will be necessary. A few more years would put the surface of the Tower in a
> far worse state than it is now. I should carefully save and reuse every old
> moulding and surface stone which is at all likely to last, even though it may be
> in some respects in an imperfect state.[2]

Such a conservative attitude was well ahead of most opinion in the early 1860s. It was to be another fifteen years before William Morris began his campaign against the whole concept of the restoration rather than mere repair of ancient buildings. And Butterfield's practice even anticipated the most famous of Morris's doctrines, 'anti-scrape'. Speaking at a meeting in 1865, William White attacked what he believed 'to be one of the most dangerous and destructive elements in church restoration, that infatuated desire for refined, clear, new finished sharp surface . . . That it is perfectly unnecessary is shown by Mr Butterfield's restoration of the tower of Winchester College, where he replaced stones in their old position and the colour of that slightly brushed over perfectly harmonized with the new stone work. He [White] believed that no tool, no scraper, no instrument whatever, ought to be used for the surface of old work, harder than a common clothes-brush'.[3]

There are admittedly some buildings where Butterfield seems to have failed to protect frescoes, brasses, tiles or other old features. But it is quite clear that this was never because he did not care about them. It was very difficult to convey to Victorian builders the necessary reverence for warn fragments of the past. An anxious letter to Lord Heytesbury shows Butterfield's difficulties well.

I trust that Mr Coombs has not laid open the timbers of these Knook church roofs to these rains without some tarpauling over them. Old timbers must not be exposed in such a manner as they suck in so much wet. I feel sure that *with care* these roofs will do, with the amount of repair which is specified for them in the contract. But they will require most careful protection and handling. If Mr Coombs makes up his mind to this and dismisses from his mind all thoughts of a new roof, all will be right. A part only of each roof should be uncovered to the weather at any one time, and even for such part tarpaulings should be provided. Mr C must nurse them in the most careful manner, repairing each rafter as best suits the case of each.[4]

There was, however, a second stage in the aesthetic restoration of a building, in which Butterfield showed none of this cautious conservatism. All unnecessary post-Reformation excrescences were removed, unless they were of a high standard of design. The same was true of internal fittings. It must be emphasized that Butterfield's approach to such classical features was undeniably discriminating. A good carved Jacobean pulpit, or altar rails with turned balusters, or high quality panelling would be treated with respect. In a number of churches he preserved whole sets of seventeenth-century woodwork in his rearrangements. Here again he was in advance of his time. But he did not see any value in cheap deal box pews and wainscoting, or in ramshackle box three-decker pulpits, for these had none of the picturesque value to the nineteenth-century eye which they now possess. Decent wooden pews would be cut down to a reasonable height, but the rest would be thrown out with the hat-pegs, and new designs supplied in their place. Where architectural features needed to be supplied and there was no medieval work to follow, Butterfield would again design new work in his own style.

A mediocre structure might be completely transformed by this process. At Winchester St Michael (345) the reconstruction can be seen halted unfinished, about to devour the wide plaster-ceiled nave. But virtual rebuilding on this scale was exceptional. The interior at Great Alne, for example, although completely refitted and with a new aisle added by Butterfield, still has great charm, chiefly due to the massive roofbeams exposed by the restoration (343). Similarly there are many exteriors like Letcombe Bassett where Butterfield's nicely scaled additions and sense of texture add rather than detract from the interest of the building (346). Butterfield's restoration work was systematic, but respected the oddities of a building: the thatched roof at Ringsfield, for example, with a classical monument breaking through its eaves, and the random variation of window levels and mouldings (344). Moreover with major buildings, such as Dorchester (8) or Amesbury Abbeys, his reconstruction of the fabric was so sensitive and careful that few now realize the state of ruin to which the building had fallen.

All this is of course quite contrary to Butterfield's later reputation, as expressed somewhat self-righteously by the *R.I.B.A. Journal* in 1900: 'We are wrapt in wonder that he could appreciate so much and spare so little. He despised the insipid and empty renovations of Scott, [and] he was altogether blind to the tender and scholarly respect and delicate abstention of Pearson . . . We can regret for our own sake and for his reputation's that he was ever called in to deal with a single ancient fabric.'[5] There is no doubt standards were by then changing, largely due to the influence of William Morris, and the less cautious attitudes of the mid-century were under attack. Butterfield was identified with those attitudes largely due to a small number of celebrated cases in which his work had been attacked. These we shall shortly discuss. But even if one takes the worst interpretation of these cases, one could hardly regret that he was ever called in to deal with a single ancient fabric. Who would now be aware, for example, that Butterfield had spent £10,000 on saving the structure of St Mary's Warwick? Dorchester (8) and Amesbury, where he faithfully reconstituted outstanding medieval designs, and contributed his own fine furnishings, have been mentioned. Ottery St Mary is a similar case (IX). One could add other smaller, but equally attractive churches, such as the romanesque Chaddesley Corbett, or the late gothic Dinton or Tattershall. St Mary Rotherhithe is a classical church restored by Butterfield, still full of charm, and there are many lesser examples like Great Alne, or St Mildred's Canterbury.[6] With such buildings there can be little dispute that Butterfield handed them on to the future enhanced rather than damaged.

There are other buildings where one's attitude must depend upon an assessment of Butterfield's positive contribution. At Wavendon or Kinwarton (173) it is the wood-work and glass of the 1840s rather than the medieval work which gives the church its character. At Tadlow, Letcombe Bassett (V) and Mapledurham (160) the interiors

343 Great Alne church, interior

344 Ringsfield church, exterior

345 Winchester St Michael, interior

346 Letcombe Bassett church, exterior

are memorable for Butterfield's coloured marble work of the 1860s; at Godmersham for his elegant roof and screen (109); at Sedgeberrow (161) for the gaudy tiling of the sanctuary. At Brigham the elegant metalwork and gaily painted roof contrast delightfully with the older architecture. Milsted (220) is a church made distinctive by Butterfield's woodwork of the 1870s, while Baverstock (359), Hagnaby (VII) and Ault Hucknall have splendid marble and tile designs from his last years. All these buildings have a clearly Victorian atmosphere, but the new work is itself of high quality and sets off well what remains of the old, especially since the Victorian work has gained a period charm of its own.

On the other hand one might list perhaps some twenty smaller buildings where Butterfield's mark is all too clear, yet undistinguished. Stickney is a case from the 1840s; St Mawgan, Millbrook and Flitwick from the 1850s; Castle Eaton, St Edmund Lombard Street and perhaps Great Waldingfield from the 1860s. But up to 1870 these are far outnumbered by the successful restorations. Butterfield's last years of restoration, the years of Cliffe Pypard, West Deeping, Winterborne Monkton, Abbots Kerswell and Hadstock, are undoubtedly the worst.[7] As his imagination failed, so his restoration work became obtrusive and unrewarding.

So much for the general picture. We must now examine a number of special cases. The first is that of the seventeenth- and eighteenth-century London churches which Butterfield rearranged. His rearrangements here have been very severely criticized. Nevertheless, what is remarkable is not that he adapted classical churches to the new liturgical needs, but that he respected their architectural character. This was so from the first example, St Paul's Shadwell, of 1848. Butterfield never attempted to gothicize or Byzantinize classical churches, like Scott, Street or Teulon; he was prepared to change them without imposing his own aesthetic tastes upon them. He would even preserve old woodwork, such as gallery fronts, where the new arrangements made it redundant, so that there was no permanent loss of any value. Yet what was considered conservative and cautious in the 1850s and 1860s has seemed outrageous to the neo-Georgian tastes of the twentieth century. At St Clement's Eastcheap it has been said that Butterfield 'tore out' the pews, destroyed the gallery, 'plonked' the organ in the aisle, built altar steps with 'staring black and white paving', and 'tore apart the lovely triple altarpiece, flinging the two wings of the triptych on to side walls and leaving the centre mean and pointless where it is. And last of all, his rage collapsed, he put stained glass in the windows so dark that nobody could see what he had done'.[8] This account is largely correct except that the pews were simply cut down and partly realigned, but the implied sadistic assault on the beauties of a classical building is quite unjustified. Butterfield never attacked old work in a spirit of rage. One can find evidence of sorrow: at Ottery St Mary, for example, he found the modern 'coping of the choir painful', and noted that it should be altered.[9] He simply looked at buildings from the standpoint of his own time. One could hardly expect his attitude to Wren or Gibbs, however respectful, to be one of unqualified admiration.

The second group which must be mentioned consists of three medieval parish churches of high architectural quality, where Butterfield's work has again been criticized. Friskney in Lincolnshire is late gothic. Paul Waterhouse cited it as an example of Butterfield's 'unsympathetic attention to old churches', and Bumpus asserted that 'he would have swept away the fine screenwork merely because it interfered with his scheme', and the 'he erected a would-be Perpendicular aisle which exhibits his want of sympathy and scholarship in dealing with the later developments of English Gothic.'[10] There is, however, no evidence in the faculty documents that Butterfield proposed to destroy the medieval screenwork, and it would have been entirely uncharacteristic for him to do so. Nor is it easy to see what is outrageous in his quietly detailed aisle design. New aisles were needed because very little survived of the old, and the arcades were leaning dangerously outwards. Butterfield set them upright, and retained the old nave roof and the fine woodwork in a beautifully mellowed state. His restoration was regarded at the time as careful and conservative, and Friskney remains 'one of the most rewarding of the Marshland churches'.[11]

The second church, St Bees, was a late Norman priory chapel with a thirteenth-century chancel, which suffered seriously after the priory's dissolution; the roofs were stripped, and the tower, clerestory and aisle walls collapsed. It was patched up in the seventeenth century as the parish church, except for the chancel, which remained unroofed until it became the Theological College hall in 1817. The College also took over the south transept as a lecture room, walling it off from the rest of the church. There was yet another wall across the nave. The architectural effect of the interior was thus completely lost. Butterfield wished to recover the whole for the church, but was only allowed to take one bay of the chancel, and for this reason he designed a new boldly arcaded east wall (182). He opened up the rest of the church, providing a new lecture hall for the college to the south, and he rebuilt the aisles and tower in an early gothic style, giving the tower a distinctive pyramid cap which has since been removed. There is no doubt that the result was a great enhancement in the architectural quality of the building, which for three hundred years had been completely obscured. Much more controversial, however, is the wrought iron screen (201) which he added much later, in 1886. It is, as Sir Nikolaus Pevsner has recently said, 'an outstandingly good piece'.[12] But it is the most striking feature of the interior, and undeniably strange. It is not surprising that reactions to it have always been strong, and often very hostile.

Heytesbury (XXI) is a somewhat similar case, a large thirteenth-century church which Butterfield found divided up, the transepts walled off, a huge mahogany pew separating the nave from the chancel, and the chancel aisles destroyed. Once again the 'undeniable grandeur'[13] of the interior was recovered by Butterfield, who opened up the whole church, widening the west arch of the central tower, and provided chancel aisles. But he also filled the windows with stained glass, and decorated the upper chancel walls with thin grey and red criss-cross lines. Thus the effect is as much Victorian as medieval. In its own way it is extraordinarily attractive.

The three remaining restorations have acquired a special notoriety through the traditional persecution of Butterfield's memory at Oxford and at Winchester. At Oxford Butterfield began work on Merton College Chapel in 1849 (347, 348). Until 1840 this noble late thirteenth-century building had been fitted up with plain panelling, stalls and a fine screen by Wren, but led by two Tractarian fellows, James Hope-Scott and John Hungerford Pollen, the college decided in 1842 to start stripping the classical woodwork as the first stage in the restoration of the original design. Some of the woodwork was given to the new High Church school at Radley. At this stage the college was using Edward Blore as its architect. Butterfield's restoration work completed this process. Although one may well regret that the screen was dismantled (it has now been replaced), the new work was in most other ways an improvement. The new roof, splendidly painted by Pollen, was far better integrated with the walls than the old; the sanctuary was cleared of its jumble of monuments (which were replaced in the antechapel) and the altar raised on spacious steps; the sedilia were fully reconstructed; a rich tile pavement and vigorously designed stalls were provided. The only eccentricity was the font with its enormous suspended cover, which was in the antechapel. It is easy to see why the chapel restoration, which was completed in 1853, was enthusiastically admired by contemporaries, even if it has since been allowed to fade sadly.

An interval followed during which Butterfield only designed a few details for the chapel, such as a gable cross and gas lighting. Then, in 1860, came his most controversial work for the college. Following the decisions of 1853–4 to open its fellowships to laymen and to all branches of learning, and to increase undergraduate numbers, the college urgently needed to build new accommodation. A confused struggle ensued, during which it was at one stage resolved 'that the College is agreed to the entire destruction (if necessary) of Mob Quadrangle'.[14] The same meeting, however, rejected 'the alteration of the Library proposed by Mr Butterfield'. This was on 21 May 1861. A few weeks later rumours of the proposal were published, and produced a storm of protest in antiquarian circles, particularly in the Oxford Architectural Society. It emerged that 'the idea of removing Mob Quad was not of [Butterfield's] suggestion', and his plan required the rebuilding of one wing of the library on a new alignment, but no actual destruction.[15] On the other hand, Mob Quad, as a quadrangle, would have been quite transformed, with the new rooms filling its south side. It was an ingenious plan, and in some ways extremely progressive; but the blindness to the importance of the old buildings as a group, rather than individually, was a fatal defect. Fortunately the antiquarian protests persuaded the college to change its mind and build on a new site. Butterfield, however, became the scapegoat for a proposal which he had not suggested, and had in fact tried to modify in its effect.

At Winchester Butterfield had a double connection. He acted as architect to both the College and the Hospital of St Cross from the late 1850s until after 1880. It is to his credit that each of these two outstanding groups of medieval buildings remains largely unspoilt. At St Cross, in spite of forty-five years of repairs and minor alterations under his supervision, Butterfield's hand is only obvious in the chapel (162). Even here it is less obvious now that the painted decoration has been removed. His fittings are excellent. The one serious fault is the harsh finish to some of the re-carved work in the sanctuary, although the oddity of much of the detail is not Butterfield's invention, but closely follows the original late Norman design.

At Winchester College, as at Merton, Butterfield has become a scapegoat where he may well, in fact, have been a restraining influence. He was first called on in 1858 to suggest a suitable form for the Crimean Memorial. Butterfield 'walked over the place' with some of the masters and 'at once struck out the thought' of placing it in the porch to the west of the chapel.[16] This is a remarkably unobtrusive situation. Three years later he was again asked to advise on a memorial, to two Wardens of the college. The most likely proposals had been for a standing monument, or for restoration work in the chapel. Butterfield

> looked at the College with a view to the separate Memorial. I do not think it would stand well within such small quadrangles. It would injure the scale of the surrounding buildings I should fear – Such a Monument should generally be, as it is at Oxford and Waltham, in some open space . . . I do not think that the College buildings would gain in effect by an addition to this kind. It would injure in my own opinion their present quiet simplicity and would look foreign to them. The longer I considered it the more I felt that the Chapel buildings will admit a memorial better than any other part of the College.[17]

As a result, Butterfield rebuilt the chapel tower (40). He found it 'in a most uncomfortable state, cracked in all directions, with its windows, and arches blocked up, and its walls tied by irons, under a false idea of giving it strength. It is in fact in the nature of a ruin in the very centre of the College. Its bells are never rung, but only sounded'.[18] We have already seen the care which he took in this reconstruction. He made some slight alterations to the design, changing the pinnacles (which were not original) and giving the belfry a little more height. Internally he moved a window, so that the dark vestry bay next to the tower could be used for extra seating, and he introduced a marble column and inscription. The font was moved from under the

347 Merton College chapel, before restoration (Merton College)

348 Merton College chapel, after restoration (Merton College)

tower to the old vestry, again to provide more seating for the increased number of boys in the school.

Butterfield's next work for the college, the Moberly Library, was the conversion of a plain brick block of 1839. The work here was completed in 1870. Four years later it was decided to proceed with the chapel restoration. Gilbert Scott was first consulted, but withdrew when he realized that Butterfield had already been acting as architect to the college. He had in fact prepared notes in 1858. Among his comments he wrote, 'put ornamental wainscotting at the west end which is now at the east and restore the stone reredos'.[19] And later, in 1861, he had written to Sir William Heathcote, 'I really see no difficulty in leaving that boarding and carving of Grinlin Gibbons. I think I have said as much to the late Warden. I am no fanatic in matters of that kind.'[20] There is thus little doubt that the removal of the panelling, for which Butterfield has been violently criticized, was not due to his insistence. In fact the college resolved specifically to include the alteration of the panelling in April 1874, so that Butterfield must have left the question open. Another later notebook is also revealing, for the builder is instructed to 'relay brasses carefully'. The loss of the brasses has therefore been wrongly attributed to Butterfield's lack of interest in their fate. It has also been incorrectly said that in restoring the reredos Butterfield destroyed the evidence of its original design. This is not so; it was in fact 'scrupulously restored', and the old parts can certainly be distinguished from the new.[21] The last criticism has been of Butterfield's alignment of the seating in the chapel, which has since been altered. Altogether the subsequent attacks on his restoration of the chapel seem to be excessively indignant.

His remaining work for Winchester College was slight, and consisted chiefly in proposing minor internal rearrangements, and in watching the state of the buildings, pasting paper bands across cracks to record movements in the structure. He seems to have been more patient than the authorities, who had inserted 'a very useless iron girder'.[22] Eventually, in 1882, he resigned his connection with the college when they refused to support his view on the positioning of the copies of the lost brasses, which were being laid in the chapel. It is appropriate, and indicative of the care which he took with an old building, that he resigned over a question of liturgical archaeology.

Notes on chapter 18

1   Pinchbeck, Lincolnshire Record Office.
2   Butterfield to Sir William Heathcote, 1 and 17 June 1861, Winchester College archives.
3   *E*, (26) 1865, p. 249.
4   19 July 1875, Heytesbury Collection.
5   (VII) 1900, p. 242.
6   Other good examples are Abbotsley, Avington, Caistor, Hewelsfield, Latton, Mattingley, Sudbury St Gregory, Trumpington and York St Mary Castlegate.
7   Other unsympathetic examples are Cheddar, Dover Castle church, Morebath, Sparsholt, and the London churches, St Paul Covent Garden, St Clement Eastcheap and St Mary Woolnoth.
8   E. and W. Young, *Old London Churches*, London, Faber, 1956, p. 78.
9   Notebook 6.
10 *DNB*; *R.I.B.A. Journal* (VII) 1900, p. 246.
11 *CB*, July 1879; *BE, Lincolnshire*, p. 238.
12 *BE, Cumberland and Westmorland*, p. 184.
13 *BE, Wiltshire*, p. 237.
14 College Register, 21 May 1861.
15 *B* (19) 1861, p. 552; *E* (22) 1861, p. 218.
16 G. Moberly to Sir William Heathcote, 23 May 1861, Winchester College archives.
17 Butterfield to Heathcote, 1 June 1861, *ibid*.
18 *Ibid*.
19 Notebook 19.
20 Butterfield to Heathcote, 23 May 1861, Winchester College archives.
21 *BE, Hampshire*, p. 701.
22 Butterfield to J. D. Davenport, 10 July 1876, Winchester College archives.

This list is divided into nine groups, each arranged chronologically, with principal documentation, costs where known, the building material, older parts incorporated and subsequent alterations. Churches have two aisles unless stated otherwise. Exceptionally small or large parsonages are noted. Fittings are not listed, except in the case of restoration work, where the details are of parts newly designed rather than repaired or reconstructed. T signifies tiled flooring, F a font, B benches, seats or stalls, P a pulpit, S a screen, and R altar rails. It is hoped that the documentation in this section is sufficiently full for a medievalist to identify exactly how Butterfield altered the buildings which he restored. His notebooks contain especially valuable information of this kind.

In addition to the drawings listed, there is also in the Starey Collection a book of 'Plans of New Churches designed & erected by W. Butterfield', which includes all the churches listed, except Highbury Chapel, Cautley, Charlton, Sessay, Wantage workhouse chapel, Alfington, Pinchbeck Bars, Thurlaston, Wantage cemetery chapel, Alvechurch, Gaer Hill, Amesbury cemetery chapel, Pitt, Penrhyncoch, Bursea, Ipswich, Victoria West, Salisbury Theological College chapel, Page Green and Woolwich.

Churches and chapels

Gillingham, Dorset; 1837; competition entry, *Somerset and Dorset Notes and Queries*, XV, 1917. Not executed.

Highbury Congregational Chapel, Bristol, 1842–3; correspondence and accounts, £2119, chest. Stone. Chancel, tower and SE rooms added.

Swindon St Mark, 1843; competition entry (Highbury chest). Not executed.

Coalpit Heath, 1844–5; I.C.B.S. file 3434, £1900; *B*, (3) 1845, p. 549; *E*, (3) 1844, p. 113; drawings, R.I.B.A. Stone. Chancel refitted.

Cautley, 1845–7; I.C.B.S. file 3652; accounts, c £1000, chest; vestry added 1858–60, specification, &c, chest. Stone, aisleless. Refitted.

Adelaide Cathedral; *E*, (8) 1847, p. 141, brick, not executed. Butterfield's second plans (1868–9) in stone, 'somewhat modified' (*B*, (28) 1870, p. 74) by E. J. Woods of Adelaide (whose successors have Butterfield's drawings), built 1869–78; see my account in *Country Life*, forthcoming; Butterfield's font and reredos, accnts, 1878–80. Apse added.

Charlton, Berkshire, 1847–8; *Life and Letters of W. J. Butler*, pp. 57–8, £200; drawings, Berkshire Record Office. Brick, aisleless. Rebuilt.

Perth Cathedral, 1847–90; *E*, (8) 1847, p. 138 and (12) 1851, p. 24; A. J. B. Hope, *English Cathedrals of the Nineteenth Century*, London 1861; drawings, Victoria & Albert Museum; choir 1849–51; nave to modified designs 1887–90, accnts, £5528. Stone. Choir refitted.

Sessay, rebuilding, 1847–8; old parts probably include arcade (T. Whellan, *History and Topography of the City of York and the North Riding of Yorkshire*, Beverley 1857–9, II, pp. 332–3). Stone, south aisle only.

Epping; *B* (6) 1848, p. 274, c £6000; not executed.

Wantage Workhouse chapel, 1848–50; Wantage Parish Diaries, Berkshire Record Office. Stone, aisleless. Demolished.

Alfington, 1849; 'a temporary church', Butterfield to J. Hardman, 1851, Hardman Collection; belfry and vestry 1879–83, accnts. Brick and roughcast, aisleless.

Cumbrae College chapel, 1849–51; *B*, (9) 1851, p. 533; *E*, (20) 1859, p. 379; desk drawing, Starey Collection. Consecrated as the Cathedral of the Isles, *Buteman*, 6 May 1876. Stone; aisleless.

Leeds St Thomas, nave, 1849–52; *B*, (10) 1852, p. 103; *E*, (15) 1854, p. 59; chancel 1890–3, accnts, £1454; drawings, R.I.B.A., Starey Collection and Victoria & Albert Museum. Brick. Demolished.

London, All Saints' Margaret Street, 1849–59; c £70,000, *BN*, (5) 1859, p. 488; see my account in *Architectural History*, (8) 1965, pp. 73–94; also, restoration 1893–5, £3178, correspondence, chest. Brick.

London, St Matthias Stoke Newington, 1849–53; I.C.B.S. file 4436, £7975; *E*, (11) 1850, pp. 54, 142, 209, 233, and (14) 1853, p. 267; Bumpus, *London Churches*, 2, p. 211; drawings, Starey Collection. Brick. Refitted after bomb damage.

Pinchbeck Bars, 1849–50; *E*, (11) 1850, p. 187. Stone; north aisle only.

Thurlaston school chapel, 1849; *E*, (9) 1849, p. 321; Francis White, *Gazetteer of Warwickshire*, 1850, p. 665, £1000. Brick; aisleless.

Wantage cemetery chapel, 1849–50; parish diaries, Berkshire Record Office. Stone; aisleless. Recently demolished.

West Lavington, Sussex, 1849–50; *E*, (10) 1849, p. 67. Stone.

Huddersfield St John, 1851–3; Mark Richardson, *St John's Bayhall, 1853–1903*, Huddersfield public library; drawings, Victoria & Albert Museum. Stone.

Liverpool; *E*, (13) 1852, p. 283, and (15) 1854, p. 262. Not executed.

Balne: see Pollington.

Cowick, 1853–4; *B*, (11) 1853, p. 470, and (12) 1854, pp. 574 and 609. Brick.

Hensall, 1853–4; *B*, (11) 1853, p. 470, and (12) 1854, pp. 574 and 609. Brick.

Lincoln, St Anne's Bedehouse chapel, 1853–4; *B*, (12) 1854, pp. 185 and 549; *E*, (15) 1854, p. 355. Brick; aisleless.

Pollington, 1853–4; *B*, (11) 1853, p. 470, and (12) 1854, pp. 574 and 609. Brick. Roof altered.

Wykeham, Yorkshire, 1853–4; *B*, (12) 1854, p. 609. Stone.

Braishfield, 1854–5; Eastlake, *op. cit.*, p. 256; *Romsey Register*, March 1855. Brick; north aisle only.

Langley, Kent, 1854–5; *B*, (13) 1855, p. 610; *BN*, (2) 1856, p. 5. Old plan. Stone; north aisle only.

Milton, Oxfordshire, 1854–6; diocesan surveyor's reports, Bodleian Library; *B*, (14) 1856, p. 461, and (15) 1857, p. 709. Stone; aisleless.

Oxford, Balliol College chapel, 1854–7; correspondence, college archives; *E*, (17) 1856, p. 432, (19) 1858, p. 241, and (22) 1861, p. 22; *BN*, (3) 1857, p. 6; *B*, (14) 1856, p. 586, and (17) 1859, p. 402; drawings, Starey Collection and Victoria & Albert Museum. Stone; aisleless. Refitted. The seats now at Duloe, Cornwall.

Baldersby, 1855–7; *B*, (15) 1857, pp. 583 and 613; lychgate drawing, R.I.B.A. Stone, brick interior.

Belmont, Durham, 1855–7; I.C.B.S. file 4897, £1260. Stone; aisleless. Refitted, porch added.

Waresley, 1855–7; I.C.B.S. file 4958, £2288; *B*, (15) 1857, p. 452. Stone; north aisle only.

Ashford, Middlesex, 1856–8; I.C.B.S. file 5157; drawings and vestry minutes, chest; tower 1865, accnts. Stone.

Bamford, 1856–60; accnts, £2117; buildings accounts, etc. chest; gateway drawing, R.I.B.A.; *B*, (18) 1860, p. 708. Stone; north aisle only.

Etal, 1856–8; *DNB*. Stone; aisleless, but with south chapel.

Alvechurch, rebuilding, 1857–61; accnts, £2972; *E*, (22) 1861, p. 409; *BN*, (7) 1861, p. 842. Old plan, tower, arcades, north aisle and east window. Stone, brick interior.

Gaer Hill, 1857–8; *B*, (15) 1857, p. 613. Stone; aisleless.

London, St John Hammersmith, 1857–9; *E*, (19) 1858, p. 341, and (20) 1859, p. 323; *Short Account of the New District Church of St John*, 1858, Hammersmith public library; tower 1879–82, accnts; unexecuted screen design 1890, Starey Collection. Brick.

Amesbury cemetery chapel, 1858–60; accnts, £933; *B*, (18) 1860, p. 141. Brick and stone; aisleless.

Auckland St Matthew; *E*, (19) 1858, p. 91. Stone. Not executed.

London, Battersea Training College chapel, 1858; *E*, (19) 1858, p. 340; Thomas Adkins, *History of St John's College, Battersea*, London 1906. Brick; aisleless. Demolished.

Pitt school chapel, 1858; £800, Rev. J. F. Moor, *Memorials of the Rev. John Keble*, Winchester 1866, pp. 145–8. Brick and flint; aisleless.

London, St Alban Holborn, 1859–62; accnts, £18,055, including clergy house; *E*, (22), p. 317, (24) 1863, p. 147; *ILN*, (43) 1863, p. 60; *B*, (20) 1862, pp. 442–3, and (21) 1863, p. 157; *BN*, (7) 1861, p. 46 and (10) 1863, pp. 432–3; *CB*, January 1863 and April 1864; Bumpus, *London Churches*, 2, pp. 267 and 275. Brick. Bombed, and internally reconstructed to a new design.

Newbury St John, 1859–60; I.C.B.S. file 5456, c £5000; drawings, R.I.B.A.; *B*, (18) 1860, p. 500. Brick; north aisle only. Demolished.

Manchester, St Cross Clayton, 1862–6; accnts, £10,172; *BN*, (18) 1870, p. 68. Brick.

Penrhyncoch school chapel, 1862–4; accnts, £423. Demolished.

Aberystwyth St Mary, 1863–6; accnts, £2212. Stone.

Emery Down, 1863–4; accnts, £1160; *B*, (22) 1864, p. 438. Brick, aisleless.

Hitchin Holy Saviour, 1863–6; accnts, £3040, aisles 1880–3, £1642; building accounts &c, chest; *B* (23) 1865, p. 417. Brick.

Dropmore, 1864–6; accnts, £1364. Brick and flint, aisleless. North transept an addition, 1877.

London, Fulham Palace chapel, 1864–7; accnts, £1849; *BN*, (14) 1867, p. 270; drawing, Starey Collection. Brick, aisleless.

Penarth St Augustine, 1864–6; accnts, £7550; correspondence, Plymouth Estate Collection, Glamorgan Record Office; *B*, (24) 1866, p. 749; *BN*, (13) 1866, p. 618. Stone and brick.

Rangemore, 1864–8; accnts, £4932. Stone, aisleless. South aisle and chancel are additions.

Wokingham St Sebastian, 1864–5; accnts, £755; 'parish record', chest; *B*, (22) 1864, p. 942. Brick; north aisle only. Refitted, belfry and porch added.

Babbacombe All Saints', 1865–74; accnts, nave 1865–7, and remainder 1872–4, c £10,000; drawings, Victoria & Albert Museum, Starey Collection, R.I.B.A. and chest; *BN*, (12) 1865, p. 926, (14) 1867, p. 800, and (25) 1873, p. 552. Stone.

Elerch, 1865–8; accnts, £1520. Stone; aisleless.

Beech Hill, 1866–7; accnts, c £4000; *B*, (24) 1866, p. 749, and (25) 1867, p. 809; north aisle, *ILN*, (63) 1873, p. 383. Brick and flint; north aisle only.

Bursea chapel, 1867–72; correspondence, Holme upon Spalding Moor chest, £350. Brick, aisleless.

Highway, 1867; faculty and plans, Wiltshire Record Office, *B* (25), 1867, p. 738 Old screen and other bits. Stone, aisleless. Disused.

Horton, Oxfordshire, 1867–8; accnts, c £1200. Brick, aisleless.

Dalton, Yorkshire, 1868; D.N.B.; accnts, c £2000; drawing, Starey Collection. Brick, aisleless.

London, St Mary Brookfield, 1869–75; I.C.B.S. file 7137, nave c £6400; *BN*, (29) 1875, p. 241; *A*, (30) 1883, p. 93. Brick. Chancel added by G. E. Street, spire not executed.

Ipswich, St Mary Stoke, 1870–2; accnts, £2000; faculty, Norfolk Record Office. Old church incorporated as north aisle. Stone and flint.

Lamphlugh, rebuilding, 1870; accnts, c £2000. Old chancel arch and other parts. Stone, aisleless.

London, St Augustine Queen's Gate, 1870–77; accnts, screens and decorations 1886–91; drawings, Victoria & Albert Museum, Starey Collection and R.I.B.A.; *A*, (6) 1871, p. 244, (19) 1878, pp. 234–5, and (38) 1887, pp. 73–4, Brick. Interior whitewashed, chancel refitted.

London, St Barnabas Rotherhithe, 1870–2; accnts, c £3500; *ILN*, (60) 1872, p. 16; *BN*, (22) 1872, p. 532. Brick. Demolished.

Rugby School chapel, 1870–2; c £7000; see under schools.

Barley, rebuilding, 1871–3; accnts, c £5000; *B*, (30) 1872, p. 551. Old tower arcades. Stone and flint.

Chipping Barnet, 1871–5; accnts, c £15,000, fittings etc. 1878–85. Old church incorporated as double north aisle. Stone and flint.

Portsmouth St Michael, 1872–92; accnts, transepts and chancel 1886–92, £5626; *BN*, (23) 1872, p. 331. Stone, Demolished.

Poulton, Gloucestershire, 1872–3; accnts, c £1500; I.C.B.S. file 7513; *B*, (31) 1873, p. 473. Old chancel windows. Stone; north aisle only.

Oxford, Keble College chapel, 1873–6; c £40,000; see below.

Victoria West, Cape Province, South Africa, 1873; *Cape Church Monthly and Parish Record*, March 1893. Brick; aisleless. Thatch replaced by iron.

Weybridge St Michael, 1873–5; accnts, c £4000; I.C.B.S. file 7616; drawings, Victoria & Albert Museum. Brick.

Christleton, 1874–8; accnts, c £7000, reredos 1893; correspondence and plans, Cheshire Record Office; some drawings, Starey Collection and R.I.B.A. Old tower. Stone.

Clevedon St John, 1875–8; £4800, diaries of Sir Arthur Elton; *Complete Guide to Clevedon*; some drawings, R.I.B.A.; *BN*, (31) 1876, p. 380. Stone. Due to subsidence, stone arch unfortunately replaced with girder and iron screen by C. S. Hare: *Clevedon Mercury*, 9 October 1909. Reredos removed.

Rugby St Andrew, 1875–96; first plan 1870, main work 1877–9, restoration committee minutes, Warwickshire Record Office; tower 1894–6, accnts, £8222 (remainder, c £17,000); drawings, Starey Collection, Victoria & Albert Museum and R.I.B.A.; *BN*, (37 1879, p. 561; *B*, (35) 1877, p. 721, and (37) 1879, p. 1358; C. G. Richards, *The Story of St Andrew's*, Rugby 1959. Old tower and north aisle incorporated as outer north aisle. Stone.

Belfast, St Mark Dundela, 1876–91; accnts, nave 1876–8, chancel 1889–91, c £14,000; drawings, R.I.B.A.; vestry minutes, correspondence and drawings, chest and Starey Collection; *BN*, (31) 1876, p. 428. Stone.

Netherhampton, 1876–7; faculty and plans, Wiltshire Record Office; *BN* (33) 1877, p. 91, £1900. Old tower. Stone; south aisle only.

Tottenham All Hallows, rebuilding, 1876–7; accnts, c £3000. Old tower, arcades, north aisle, south porch. Brick.

Dublin, St Columba's College chapel, 1877–80; accnts, £6000; *BN*, (39) 1880, p. 312; *Columban Annual*, 1933. Old fittings incorporated. Stone, aiseless. Antechapel screen has been removed.

Melbourne Cathedral, 1877–91; accnts, resigned 1886; drawings, R.I.B.A.; correspondence and drawings, chest, c £100,000; *BA*, (13) 1880, p. 309; *BN*, (36) 1879, pp. 536, 630, and (39) 1880, pp. 64, 113; *AR*, (3) 1898, pp. 100–3; *Daily Telegraph*, 9 October 1890; Clarke, *Anglican Cathedrals Outside the British Isles*; my own account forthcoming in *Country Life*. Internal fittings and spires not to Butterfield's designs.

Leslie House chapel, 1879; accnts. Not executed.

London, St Clement City Road, 1879–80; accnts, £9091; *B*, (42) 1882, p. 220–2. Brick; north aisle only. Demolished.

Enfield, St Mary Magdalene, 1881–3; accnts, c £10,000, drawings, Starey Collection; *BN*, (45) 1883, p. 147. Stone. Chancel decorated to Buckeridge's designs, 1897; screen added 1898.

Salisbury, Theological College chapel, 1881: see below.

Ambatoharanana, Madagascar, 1882; drawings, Victoria & Albert Museum; Prayer Union for the Church in Madagascar, *Occasional papers*, 5; £6000. Stone.

Chislehurst, 1882; accnts, c £400. Temporary church. Demolished.

Edmonton, St Mary Fore Street, 1883–5; accnts, £5647; drawings, Starey Collection and Victoria & Albert Museum. Stone and brick. Demolished.

Kingsbury, Holy Innocents, 1883–4; accnts, £2180. Brick.

Southampton St Barnabas, 1883, accnts. Not executed.

Tottenham, Page Green Mission Room, 1883–4; accnts, £2377; interior photograph in William Starey's album. Demolished.

Ascot Priory chapel, 1885–6; drawings, R.I.B.A.; Williams, *Sellon*, p. 270. Stone. Incorporates earlier neo-Norman nave, not by Butterfield.

Caterham Guards chapel, 1885–7; accnts, £6812; some drawings, Starey Collection and R.I.B.A. Brick and stone.

Exeter Grammar School chapel, 1885–7; £1981; see below.

London, St Michael Borgard Road, Woolwich, 1887–90; accnts, £5759, nave only; drawings, Victoria & Albert Museum. Incorporated chancel of 1875 by J. W. Walter. Brick. One aisle not built, the other recent; whitewashed.

Bournemouth St Augustine, 1891–2; accnts, £5285; drawings, Starey Collection and drawings, R.I.B.A. Stone. South-east addition.

Convents and colleges

Canterbury, St Augustine's College, 1844–8, 1860–1 and 1872–3; *Archaeologia Cantiana*, (IV) 1861, pp. 57–66; R. J. E. Boggis, *History of St Augustine's College, Canterbury*, Canterbury 1907; G. F. Maclear, *St Augustine's Canterbury*, London 1888; Henry Bailey, *Twenty-five Years at St Augustine's*, Canterbury 1873; *St Augustine's College Papers*; *ILN*, (13) 1848, p. 5; *E*, (9) 1848, p. 1; *B*, (3) 1845, p. 370, (4) 1846, pp. 34 and 522, and (6) 1848, p. 161. Native wing added 1860–2, accnts £2507, and Notebook 18; Maclear Library 1872–3, accnts c £600. Desk drawing, c 1880, Starey Collection. Gatehouse and parts of chapel range and library foundations mediaeval. Flint and stone. Cloister recently converted and tracery altered and library roof concealed.

Adelaide Cathedral college; *E*, (8) 1847, p. 141. Brick. Not executed.

Perth Cathedral college; *E*, (8) 1847, p. 138. Not executed.

Cumbrae College, 1844–51; *B*, (9) 1851, p. 533; *E*, (20) 1859, p. 379; plan, Starey Collection. Stone. New provost's house, accnts 1877, not executed.

London, Osnaburgh Street, St Saviour's Home, 1850; Metropolitan Buildings Act Third Class Approvals, September 1850, County Hall; Williams, *Sellon*, pp. 25, 97–101. Brick.

Plymouth, St Dunstan's Abbey, 1850–c 1860; Sister Margaret Teresa, *The History of St Dunstan's Abbey School*, Plymouth 1929; Williams, *Sellon*, pp. 89, 115, 139, 205; Margaret Goodman, *Sisterhoods in the Church of England*, London 1863, p. 118. Stone.

Oxford, Merton College, Grove Building, 1860–3; accnts, c £8000; register, college archives; *E*, (22) 1861, p. 218; *B*, (20) 1862, p. 863; *ILN*, (45) 1864, pp. 480–2. Stone.

St Bees, Theological Library, 1863; accnts, £1312. Stone.

Oxford, Keble College, 1867–83; accnts, c £150,000; correspondence, Milton Ernest Collection, Keble College, and Gibbs Collection, City of London Guildhall; drawings, R.I.B.A. and Starey Collection; *ILN*, (68) 1876, p. 415, (69) 1876, p. 205, (72) 1878, pp. 417–18; *A*, (I) 1869, p. 287, (3) 1870, p. 322, (4) 1870, p. 12, (8) 1872, p. 42, (19) 1878, p. 267, (28) 1882, p. 253, and (38) 1887, p. 364; *BA*, (5) 1876, p. 222, and (32) 1889, p. 399; *B*, (28) 1870, p. 260, (32) 1874, p. 977, (34) 1876, pp. 402 and 495, and (43) 1882, p. 536; *BN*, (17) 1869, p. 284, (25) 1873, p. 422, and (41) 1881, p. 324; *G*, 27 January and February 1875; *G*, *Standard* and *Morning Post*, 26 April 1876, *Daily Telegraph*, 27 April 1876, *Church Times* and *The Times*, 28 April 1876, *Church Bells* and *Saturday Review*, 29 April 1876. Brick. Chapel S chapel and NW range added.

Salisbury Theological College, new wing and chapel, 1875–81; *BN*, (31) 1876, p. 222. Flint and brick.

Wantage, St Mary's Convent novitiate wing, 1878; *DNB*. Stone.

Ambatoharanana, Madagascar, Seminaire de Saint Paul, library and lecture rooms, 1887–90, £2200; accnts, *Madagascar Times*, 8 February 1890, and information from Rev. K. J. Benzies and Bishop R. S. M. O'Ferrall. Chapel, 1882, see above. Stone.

Ascot Priory chapel, 1885–6, see above. Stone.

Secondary and boarding schools

London, All Saints' Choir School, Margaret Street, 1849–60: see All Saints' church. Brick.

Harrow Weald, St Andrew's College, 1852; *E*, (13) 1852, p. 300. Brick. Demolished.

Winchester College, 1857–82: see restorations.

London, Battersea, Sir Walter St John's School, 1858; accnts, £4021; minutes, contract and accounts, and *Sir Walter St John's School, Souvenir of the Building, A.D. 1913*, kindly shown me by Mr F. T. Smallwood. Brick. Much altered, except front.

Rugby School, 1858–84; accnts; *Meteor*, from 1867; J. Hope Simpson, *Rugby Since Arnold*, London 1967; *ILN*, (41) 1862, p. 544, and (61) 1872, pp. 393–4; drawings for chapel, swimming bath and gymnasium, R.I.B.A. and for New Big School and Temple Reading Room, Starey Collection. First racquet court, 1860, £1930, demolished. Fives court, 1860, £235, demolished. Sick room, 1861, not executed. Kilbracken House, 1865–7, £5842, somewhat altered. Cricket pavilion, 1869, £900, converted into store. New Schools, 1867–70, £5000. Chapel, 1870–2, probably £7000; apse mosaics and reconstruction of spire in stone, 1882. Gymnasium, 1872, £3500. Swimming bath, 1875–6, £2500. Fever cottage, 1878, £964, demolished. Temple Reading Room, 1878–9, £8000. Second racquet court, 1880, £1171. New Big Schools, cloister and south end of New Schools, 1884–5, £8302. Brick.

Highgate School, 1862; accnts; Minutes of Governors' Meetings. Not executed.

Wantage, King Alfred's Grammar School, 1872–3, dormitory and dining hall; accnts, c £900. Brick.

Wantage, St Mary's School, dormitory wing 1874; *DNB*. Brick and timber. Altered. Sir Nikolaus Pevsner kindly informs me that, according to a school jubilee pamphlet, since lost, Butterfield made plans in 1874 for a school room, music room, dormitory and chapel.

Exeter Grammar School, 1877–87; accnts, main building £13,568, north wing and chapel, 1885–7, £1981; drawings, Victoria & Albert Museum; *B*, (37) 1879, p. 980, and *BA*, (12) 1879, p. 57. Brick.

Exeter Girls' High School, 1878; accnts. Not executed.

Gordon Boys' Home, from 1885; *BN*, (53) 1887, p. 671. Brick. Altered.

Parish schools and school houses

Jedburgh and house; *E*, (4) 1845, p. 143. Stone. Enlarged 1854, much altered 1934.

Wilmcote; attribution only; sketch and contract, 1845, Wilmcote scrapbook, Shakespeare's Birthplace Library; £339. Stone. Only NW angle remains.

East Farleigh and house; *E*, (5) 1846, p. 159, and (7), 1847, p. 4; school plans, Kent Record Office. Stone. Demolished.

Canterbury, Broad Street, 1847–8; contract, Canterbury Cathedral Library, £2217. Stone. Wing altered.

Aston Cantlow and house; 1847–8, school register, Warwick Record Office; *E*, (8) 1848, p. 259. Stone. NE wing added.

Sessay and house; attribution only; 1848, T. Whellan, *History and Topography of the City of York and North Riding of Yorkshire*, Beverley 1857–9, II, p. 333. Stone.

London, St Matthias Stoke Newington; *E*, (11) 1850, p. 145; plans, Metropolitan Buildings Act Third Class Approvals, August 1849, County Hall. Brick. Somewhat altered.

Alfington and (clergy?) house; attribution only; dated 1850; early sketch in church. Brick, half-timber and tilehanging. Restored recently.

Yealmpton and house; 1852, *Transactions of the Exeter Diocesan Architectural Society*, (IV) 1852, p. 249. Stone. Incomplete, converted into a house.

Cowick and house; *B*, (12) 1854, p. 574. Brick. Addition, and some windows altered.

Hensall and house; *B*, (12) 1854, p. 574. Brick and roughcast. Much altered.

Pollington and house; *B*, (12) 1854, p. 574. Brick. New school recently added to south side.

Wykeham, Yorkshire and house; *B*, (12) 1854, p. 609. Stone.

Hutton Buscel and house; attribution only; 1854, T. Bulmer, *History and Directory of North Yorkshire*, Preston 1890. Stone.

Langley, Kent, and house; c 1855; attribution only. Stone and timber.

Alvechurch and house; *BN*, (2) 1856, p. 569; plans, Worcestershire Record Office; accnts, new house 1859–65, £280. Brick. School much altered.

Cape Town, Lady Grey School, 1856; cathedral records. Stone. Demolished 1875.

Great Bookham and house; 1856–8, Webb sketchbooks. Brick, flint and half-timber. Large addition.

Kirby Maxloe; *B*, (15) 1857, p. 377. Brick and half-timber. Converted into house.

Baldersby and house; *B*, (15) 1857, p. 613. Stone and half-timber.

Trumpington, house only; c 1857; plans, Cambridgeshire Record Office. Brick and timber.

Aldbourne and house; opened 1858; plans, Wiltshire Record Office. Brick and flint. Demolished.

Charlton, by Downton, Wiltshire; accnts, 1857–8, £440. Brick.

Letcombe Bassett; *B*, (17) 1859, p. 7, £350; specification, chest; plans, Berkshire Record Office. Brick.

Castle Hill, Devon, and house; accnts, 1859–64, £940; drawings, Starey Collection. Stone.

Northington and house; accnts, 1860. Brick and flint. School much altered by conversion into a house.

Tattershall and house; accnts, 1860–2, £700; plans, Lincolnshire Record Office. Brick. Small addition.

St Mawgan; accnts, 1863, £350. Stone.

Horton; c 1868; plans, Oxfordshire Record Office. Brick. Demolished.

London, All Saints' Margaret Street; accnts, 1870; drawings, R.I.B.A. Brick.

Hellidon; attribution only; c 1870, F. Whellan, *History, Topography and Directory of Northampton-shire*, London 1874, p. 421. Stone, brick and timber.

Poulton; accnts, 1873, c £450. Stone. Two minor additions.

Dinton, Wiltshire; 1873–5; restoration papers, chest; plans, Wiltshire Record Office. Brick.

London, St Clement's, City Road; accnts, 1875. Demolished.

Shaw, Berkshire, and house; *B*, (34) 1876, p. 63, £1300; accnts, 1876, and 1883–5, house, £448. Brick and flint.

Wraxall; accnts, 1879–81, £1616. Stone. Additions.

Rugby, Bath Street; accnts, 1881–4, £1550. Brick.

Estate housing

Sessay, terrace and two cottage pairs, c 1850; attribution only. Brick.

Ruston, terrace, c 1850; attribution only. Brick.

Baldersby, two cottage pairs, c 1855. Brick.

Butterwick, cottage pair, c 1855; attribution only. Brick.

Baldersby, almshouse, c 1858; *B*, (15) 1857, p. 613. Half-timber.

Baldersby old village, cottage pair, c 1858. Brick.

Ashwell, almshouse, two pairs and L terrace, c 1858; *BN*, (6) 1860, p. 767; *E*, (21) 1860, p. 292. Brick, almshouse partly half-timber.

Braunstone, Leicester, three cottage pairs, c 1858. Brick.

Gaer Hill, two cottage pairs and schoolhouse, c 1858; attribution only. Stone with brick quoins, now rendered.

Baldersby, L terrace; 1859, accnts, £207 each. Brick.

Braunstone, terrace; 1859, accnts, £231 each. Brick.

Milton Ernest, cottage in village street; 1859, accnts, £259; also 'correcting and overlooking cottage to south of the park'. Brick.

Kirby Maxloe, terrace; 1859, accnts, £233 each. Brick.

Heckfield, almshouse; 1859–63, accnts, £944. Brick and half-timber.

Northington, cottages; 1861, accnts. Not identified.

Hursley, Home Farm Lodge; 1863, accnts. Brick and half-timber.

Great Bookham, terrace and cottage pair, Leatherhead Road; 1864–6, accnts, £309 each. Brick.

Hursley, Church Lodge; 1866, accnts. Brick and half-timber.

Milton Ernest, cottage pair at south end of village; 1867, Journal of Benjamin Starey, Starey Collection. Brick and half-timber.

Aldenham, cottage pair near Home Farm; 1878–9, accnts, £420 each. Brick and half-timber.

Ardingly, cottage pair at College Farm; 1878–9, accnts. Incorporates former farmhouse. Brick and half-timber.

Axbridge, St Michael's Home, lodge, c 1878; drawings, Starey Collection. Stone and half-timber.

Paddington, houses next to vestry of St Michael Star Street; 1878–80, accnts, £1105 each. Brick.

Fulham Palace lodge; 1892, accnts, £584; correspondence, Church Commissioners. Brick and half-timber.

Parsonages

Coalpit Heath; *E*, (4) 1845, p. 189. Stone. NE corner added 1863 by W. Robertson, Mortgage plans, Gloucester Record Office.

Wilmcote, 1846–7; contract, £942, Wilmcote scrapbook, Shakespeare's Birthplace Library. Stone. Additions to south and west.

Ogbourne St Andrew; Rev. J. Bliss to chapter clerk, 2 June 1848, St George's Windsor archives. Brick and tilehanging. Now Tresco House, on main road.

Avington, Berkshire, 1849; mortgage plans, Bodleian Library. Incorporates an older cottage. Flint, stone and brick. Small. Now cottages, opposite church.

Pinchbeck Bars, 1849–50; conveyance and outline plan, Lincolnshire Record Office; attribution only. Stone and roughcast. SE angle altered.

London, All Saints' Clergy House, 1849–53: see All Saints' church. Brick.

West Lavington, Sussex, c 1850; attribution only. Stone.

Great Woolstone, 1851; plans and specification, £630, Bodleian Library. Brick. Only SE corner remains; large addition c 1875.

Sheen, Derbyshire; *B*, (10) 1852, p. 516; *E*, (15) 1854, p. 155. Stone. Large.

Cowick; *B*, (12) 1854, p. 574. Brick. Smallish. Recently marred by demolition of porch and alteration of windows and coach house.

Hensall; *B*, (12) 1854, p. 574. Brick. Smallish. Recently restored, and link to coach house demolished.

Pollington; *B*, (12) 1854, p. 574. Brick. Smallish. S side recently rendered.

Wykeham, Yorkshire; *B*, (12) 1854, p. 609. Stone.

Alvechurch, 1855; plans and specification, Church Commissioners. Brick and half-timber. Large.

Bowness, Westmorland (not Cumberland); *E*, (17) 1856, p. 312. Stone. Not executed.

Baldersby; *B*, (15) 1857, p. 613. Stone and half-timber.

St Mawgan; c 1858, Notebook 17. Stone.

London, St Matthias Stoke Newington, 1858–63; accnts, £1500. Demolished.

London, St Alban's Holborn clergy house, 1859–63: see above. Brick.

London, St Michael Burleigh Street, 1859–60; parish ratebooks and Middlesex Land Register 1857/7/160, Mr P. A. Bezodis of the Survey of London kindly informs me; *A*, (25) 1881, p. 65. Brick.

Charlton, by Downton, Wiltshire; 1860–2, accnts, £887. Brick. Smallish.

Newbury St John, 1861–7; accnts, £2650. Brick. East end recently demolished.

Bamford, 1862; accnts, £1557; plans and specifications, chest. Stone.

Llanbadarn, 1864; accnts. Not executed.

London, St John Hammersmith, 1864–6; accnts, £1902. Brick.

Hitchin, Holy Saviour, 1865–6; accnts, £3385. Brick. Large. Demolished.

Dropmore, 1866; accnts, £1495. Brick, flint and timber.

Twickenham, 1866; accnts. Not executed.

Little Faringdon, 1867–9; accnts, £1750. Stone.

Beech Hill, c 1870 'proposed'; *ILN*, (51) 1867, p. 451; addition of hall and stairs, accnts, 1883–4. Brick.

Baldock, 1870–3; accnts, c £2400. Brick.

London, St Augustine's Queen's Gate, 1877–84; accnts, £2345. Brick.

Enfield, St Mary Magdalene, 1882; accnts. Stone.

Rochester, houses for canons and cathedral verger, 1884; accnts. Not executed.

Other houses

Sessay, small house in village street, c 1850; attribution only. Brick and timber.

Milton Ernest Hall, 1853–6; £12,167, accnts, and Journal of Benjamin Starey, Starey Collection; Mark Girouard, *Country Life*, 23 October 1969; drawings, Starey Collection and Victoria & Albert Museum. Stone.

Milton Ernest Home Farm house, 1859; accnts. Largely rebuilt.

Hunstanton, first, second and third class houses, 1861–3; accnts. Probably St Edmund's Terrace and perhaps other housing near Upper Green. Stone.

Baldersby, agent's house on main road, 1860; accnts, £1623. Brick. The windows recently spoilt by the removal of mullions, and the roof crudely pantiled.

Keble College, Warden's House, 1877: see above. Brick.

Axbridge, St Michael's Home, chaplain's house, c 1878; drawings, Starey Collection. Stone and half-timber.

Ottery St Mary, The Chanter's House, formerly Heath's Court, 1880–3; accnts, £16,724; plans, and 'The Book of the Chanter's House', Coleridge Collection. Incorporates older house on south side. Brick and half-timber. Upper south front since tilehung.

Bisley, officers' houses at Gordon Boys' School, from c 1885: see schools. Roughcast, brick and tilehanging.

Ardingly, College Farm house, 1878–81: see below. Brick and tilehanging.

Other buildings

Sessay bridge, c 1850; attribution only. Stone.

Milton Mill, Bedfordshire, and farm buildings, 1856–7; Journal of Benjamin Starey, Starey Collection, £1500. Brick.

Milton Ernest Hall farm buildings, 1859; accnts, £940; Journal of Benjamin Starey. Brick and flint.

Winchester, Royal Hampshire County Hospital, 1863–8; c £29,000; accnts; building committee minutes and accounts, report of sub-committee on drainage, and governors' reports, Hampshire Record Office; Nightingale Collection, British Museum; E. T. Cook, *Life of Florence Nightingale*, London 1913; B, (21) 1863, p. 833. Brick. Many small additions.

London, Offices for Society for the Propagation of the Gospel, Duke (later Delahay) Street; B, (29) 1871, p. 866; BN, (32) 1877, p. 314. Brick. Demolished.

Oxford Union Society additions; accnts, and A, (5) 1871, p. 282. Not executed.

Axbridge, St Michael's Hospital; BA, (10) 1878, p. 155; accnts, addition of wing, 1882; drawings, Starey Collection. Stone.

Ardingly, College Farm, barns, dairy, duck house, pigeon house and bailiff's house, 1878–81; accnts, £9555. Brick, half-timber, stone and tilehanging.

Aldenham, Home Farm, dairy and remodelling of bailiff's house, 1879–81; accnts, £1251. Brick, half-timber and tilehanging.

Wraxall, Battle Axes Inn and club house; 1880–1, accnts, £8719. Stone and half-timber.

Restorations, alterations and completions

Canterbury, St Augustine's College, 1844–73: see above.

Eton College chapel, B, (3) 1845, p. 275. Competition entry, not executed.

Hellidon, 1845–7 and 1867–8; Notebook 18; I.C.B.S. file 3759; E, (4) 1845, p. 142 and (5) 1846, p. 126; new roof, vestry, F, B, P. North aisle and reredos, B, (26) 1868, p. 120; BN, (15) 1868, p. 133; faculty, Northamptonshire Record Office.

Little Rissington, *E*, (4) 1845, p. 141; new porch, roofs, T, B, ? P.

Wilby, *E*, (4) 1845, p. 141. Not executed.

Ash, 1846–?; *E*, (7) 1847, p. 37; new north porch, east and west windows, T, B, P.

Dorchester, 1846–53; correspondence and accounts, Oxford Architectural and Historical Society; Notebook 11; *E*, (4) 1845, p. 219, (5) 1846, pp. 24, 161, 193, 259, (6) 1846, pp. 38, 228, (7) 1847, p. 145, (8) 1847, p. 43, (12) 1851, p. 61, and (15) 1854, pp. 145 and 180; *B*, (4) 1846, pp. 250, 273, (10) 1852, pp. 141, 407, and (11) 1853, p. 408; chancel roof, B, P, S. Nave and chapels restored by Scott, etc, *BN*, (6) 1860, p. 418.

Horfield, 1846–7; faculty, Bristol Record Office; petition, chest; *E*, (7) 1847, p. 37; *Bristol Mirror*; new aisles, porch, nave roof and additions to chancel. Since much enlarged, and chancel rebuilt.

King's Lynn, St Nicholas, plan, watermarked 1846, Norfolk Record Office. Not executed.

St David's Cathedral, 1846; John Murray, *Handbook to the Cathedrals of Wales*, London 1873, p. 111; T. F. Bumpus, *Cathedrals of England and Wales*, London 1906, 3, p. 195; chapter accounts, National Library of Wales; north transept window.

Kinwarton, 1847–50; *B*, (5) 1847, p. 605; new porch, belfry, T, B, P, S, organ case.

London, Christ Church Hoxton, *E*, (8) 1847, p. 117, and (9) 1849, pp. 335, 378 and 399; B, P. Demolished.

Ogbourne St Andrew, 1847–9; Notebook 8; baptismal register, Wiltshire Record Office; chancel arch, lynchnoscopes in tower, T, B, P, R, reredos.

Sessay, 1847–8: see above.

Thanington, 1847–8; *E*, (7) 1847, p. 37; F, P. Much later work by others.

East Grinstead, Sackville College, 1848–50; J. M. Neale, *History of Sackville College*, London 1854; *ILN*, (16) 1850, p. 210; new well-house, hall fittings, chapel roof and east wall decorations, T, B, S.

Fredericton Cathedral, 1848–53; Phoebe Stanton, *The Gothic Revival and American Church Architecture*, 1968, ch. IV; *E*, (8) 1847, pp. 109, 361–3, (10) 1849, p. 192 and (13) 1852, pp. 279 and 295; *ILN*, (14) 1849, p. 276; drawings, Fredericton; alteration of design by Frank Wills, whose nave was executed, and completion of chancel with high roof and central instead of transeptal spires; T, B.

London, St Paul's Shadwell, 1848–9; *E*, (8) 1848, p. 322, (9) 1849, p. 378 and (10) 1849, p. 72; new vestries, reredos, decorations.

Wavendon, 1848–9; Notebook 8; *B*, (7) 1849, p. 449; *E*, (9) 1849, p. 391; new porch, vestry, roofs, T, font cover, B, S, R.

Yealmpton, 1848–9; Notebook 8; faculty and correspondence, Devon Record Office; *Transactions of the Exeter Diocesan Architectural Society*, (IV) 1852, pp. 245–9; largely rebuilt except south-east chapel, but piecemeal, as it had been hoped to preserve the nave; T, F, B, P, R. Aisle decorations 1863, accnts. Tower since added.

Harrow Weald, 1849–52; *E*, (6) 1846, p. 75, chancel by Harrison; (10) 1849, p. 66, nave and aisles and F; accnts, 1889–92, and drawings, R.I.B.A. and Victoria & Albert Museum, tower, west doorway, north aisle, organ chamber, vestry, nave roof, mosaics, T, B, P.

Hathersage, 1849–52; Notebook 6; faculty, etc, chest; *E*, (15) 1854, p. 357; *B*, (10) 1852, p. 284, £1575; new roofs, T, B, P, R.

Llangorwen, 1849; *E*, (9) 1849, p. 382, and (11) 1850, p. 210; addition of bellcote and porch.

London, St Mark Westminster; *E*, (9) 1849, p. 332; Notebook 13. Demolished.

Ottery St Mary, 1849–50; Notebook 6; faculty, Devon Record Office; *B*, (8) 1850, p. 262; *E*, (13) 1852, pp. 79–88; T, F, B; Lady Chapel restoration at the same time by Woodyer. South transept, accnts 1878, £1000; *B*, (36) 1878, p. 1051.

Oxford, Merton College, 1849–63; register, college archives; *E*, (10) 1849, p. 73, (12) 1851, p. 297, (14) 1853, p. 301, and (22) 1861, pp. 218, 252 and 261; *B*, (7) 1849, p. 562, (19) 1861, p. 552; *BN*, (2) 1856, p. 963, (7) 1861, p. 538; *The Times*, 28 June 1861; *ILN*, (45) 1864, pp. 480–2; J. R. L. Highfield, 'Merton College Chapel', *Oxoniensia* (XXIV), 1959; T, F, B, S (last now at Elham, Kent).

Trumpington, 1849–54; correspondence and specification, chest; Notebook 8; *B*, (12) 1854, p. 86; *E*, (18) 1857, p. 197, (19) 1858, p. 67; T, B, reredos. Nave roof, accnts 1877, c £2800; *B*, (35) 1877, p. 647.

Wick, Gloucestershire, 1849–50; I.C.B.S. file 3617; completion of church started in 1845 by Charles Dyer; lychgate, tower, buttresses, roofs, F, B, P, S, R.

Ashwell, 1850–1; *AAS*, (1) 1850–1, p. xiii; *E*, (21) 1860, p. 292; *BN*, (6) 1860, p. 767; new roofs, T, F, B, P, S.

Aston Cantlow, 1850; vestry minutes, Warwickshire Record Office, £560; new porch, B, S, R.

Chirton, Wiltshire, 1850; Notebook 8; faculty, chest; new porch roof and door, T, B, P. Chancel since refitted.

Clehonger, 1850; Notebook 6; new porch, B.

Stickney, 1850–2; *E*, (11) 1850, p. 187; *AAS*, (1) 1850–1, p. xlvi, (2) 1852–3, p. lvi, (3) 1854–6, p. cix; new chancel, aisles, clerestory, roofs, T, F, B, R – in fact only old arcades and tower left.

Buckland-in-the-Moor, c 1850; Notebook 6. Not executed.

Church Lench, c 1850; Notebook 6. Not executed.

Burnham Overy, c 1850; Notebook 8. Not executed.

Chipping Campden, c 1850; Notebook 8. Not executed.

Crick, Northamptonshire, c 1850; Notebook 8. Not executed.

Dittisham, Devon, c 1850; Notebook 8. Not executed.

Foulsham, c 1850; Notebook 8. Not executed.

St Clear, Cornwall, c 1850; Notebook 8. Not executed.

Wooburn, Buckinghamshire, c 1850; Notebook 8; *ILN*, (56) 1870, p. 76; T, F. Not 1868–9, as *BE*.

Great Mongeham, 1851–61; *E*, (15) 1854, p. 435, (16) 1855, p. 66; accnts, 1860–1; drawings, Starey Collection. New porch, south aisle, roofs, T, F, B, P, S, R.

Amesbury, 1852–3; Notebook 17; faculty and plans, Wiltshire Record Office, £3219; specification, chest; *B*, (11) 1853, p. 761; chancel roof, east, west and some south windows, T, B, P, R.

Cubbington, 1852; *B*, (10) 1852, p. 308; chancel only, T, B, P, R.

Feckenham, 1852; faculty and plan, Worcestershire Record Office; *B*, (10) 1852, p. 407; new porch, roofs, B, R.

Sheen, 1852; Law, *op. cit.*; Notebook 17; faculty, and *Notes Illustrative of the Parish of Sheen*, chest; *E*, (15) 1854, p. 153; *B*, (10) 1852, p. 516; completion of church by Burleigh; new vestry, G, ?F, ?P.

Highclere, 1853; accnts. Not executed.

Marlston, 1853–5; Notebook 17; new porch, windows, T, B, G. Chancel since rebuilt.

South Kelsey, 1853; *AAS*, (2) 1852–3, p. lvi; plans by Butterfield 'not carried out in all their details'. Since restored by Hodgson Fowler.

Stoke d'Abernon, 1853; Notebook 17; building accounts, chest; *E*, (14) 1853, pp. 219, 300; minor chancel work. Later heavily restored by others; *Surrey Archaeological Collections*, XX, pp. 81–9; 1866 faculty, London County Hall.

Hutton Buscel, 1854–5; *BE*; new north aisle, roofs, F, B, R.

Limber Magna, 1854–64; accnts; *AAS*, (5) 1859–60, p. XX; T, B, R. More work by others.

Lower Heyford, 1854; *B*, (37) 1879, p. 1019. Nave only; much subsequent work by E. F. Law.

Salisbury, St Nicholas' Hospital, 1854–70; Wordsworth, *St Nicholas' Hospital*, chapel £1158; new rooms, etc. 1862–70, £2267; accnts; *B*, (12) 1854, p. 449; new ranges, chapel roof, B.

Sudbury St Peter, 1854–8; Notebook 17; *B*, (13) 1855, p. 522; *ILN*, (31) 1857, p. 261; *BN*, (4) 1858, p. 1083; *E*, (20) 1859, p. 75; T, B, P. Chancel since refitted.

Pinchbeck, 1855–64; *B*, (13) 1855, p. 593; accnts, second stage, £3199; faculty and plans, Lincolnshire Record Office; *CB*, October 1864; new vestry, east wall, chancel roof, T, B, P (altered 1915), S, churchyard archway.

Tadlow, 1855–74; accnts; correspondence and accounts, chest; new porch, roofs, T, F, B, R.

Arley, c 1855; Notebook 17. Not executed.

Swaffham, c 1855; Notebook 17. Not executed.

Caistor, 1856–63; accnts, £1153; faculty, Lincolnshire Record Office; P.B.G. Binnall, *Caistor*, Gloucester 1960; *AAS*, (7) 1863–4, pp. ix, lxxxvi; *BN*, (6) 1860, p. 980, (10) 1863, p. 302; *B*, (21) 1863, p. 282; chancel, accnts 1873, c £500; new roofs, T, F, B, P. Furniture recently painted.

Cape Town Cathedral, 1856–71; Clarke, *Anglican Cathedrals Outside the British Isles*; vestry minutes, cathedral archives; accnts, 1862–71, c £1600; B, reredos, &c. Rebuilt; only the Bishop Gray Memorial Cross remains (R. R. Langham-Carter, *Africana Notes and News*, June 1966).

London, St John Drury Lane, 1856–80; *E*, (17) 1856, p. 428; accnts; F. Demolished, except vestry.

Neen Sollars, 1856–7; accnts, c £1000; new chancel, porch, roofs, T, F, P.

St Mawgan, 1856–63; Notebook 17; accnts, £2013; lych gate drawing, R.I.B.A.; *E*, (17) 1856, p. 233; lych gate, T, B, R.

Alvechurch, 1857–61; see above.

Ampfield, 1857; Notebook 13; minor repairs.

High Legh chapel of the Blessed Virgin Mary, 1857; accnts; correspondence and accounts, John Rylands Library; R. Richards, 'The Chapels . . . at High Legh', *Transactions of the Historic Society of Lancashire and Cheshire*, (101) 1949, pp. 97–136; T, B. Since heavily restored by Oldrid Scott.

Lawshall, 1857; *B* (15) 1857, p. 464; new vestry, chancel roof, T, B, P.

Millbrook, 1857–8; *B*, (16) 1858, p. 649; *E*, (20) 1859, p. 291; new porch, chancel roof, B. Since refitted.

Winchester College, 1857–82; accnts; Notebooks 19 and 25; minutes, correspondence and accounts, college archives; Winchester College Archaeological Society, *Winchester College, Its History, Buildings and Customs*, 1926; *Wykehamist*, from 1866; *ILN*, (33) 1858, p. 521; *B*, (21) 1863, p. 557; *BN*, (10) 1863, p. 594; stall drawing, Starey Collection; Crimea Memorial, T, B (now at Binstead, Isle of Wight), R. Chapel since completely refitted.

Barton, c 1857; Notebook 13. Not identified.

London, St Bartholomew Moor Lane, c 1857; Notebook 13. Demolished.

Market Lavington, Wiltshire, c 1857; Notebook 13; parish officer's proceedings, Wiltshire Record Office. Not executed.

Colkirk, 1858–62; *History of Colkirk Church*, Cambridge 1960; *CB*, April 1863; T, B, P, R. Subsequent restoration and enlargement by others.

Flitwick, 1858–67; J. L. Ward Petley, *Flitwick*, n.d. c 1900; *AAS*, (9) 1867–8, p. xlix; new north aisle, vestry, chancel roof, T, B, R.

Latton, 1858–63; accnts, £650; *B*, (19) 1861, p. 688; new chancel, transept, porch, ?F, B, P, R.

Lavendon, 1858–9; accnts, £730; *B*, (17) 1859, p. 766; new chancel roof, T, B.

London, St Philip Granville Square, 1858–61; accnts, £763; *E*, (21) 1860, p. 262; *BN*, (6) 1860, p. 43; T, F, B, P. Demolished.

Milton Ernest, 1858–65; accnts, £1430; *B*, (23) 1865, p. 929; new chancel, T, B, P, S.

St Bees, 1858–87; Notebook 17; accnts, nave roof 1872 (c £800), aisle roofs 1879 (£905), screen 1886–7; pulpit drawing, Starey Collection; new tower cap, east wall, aisles, T, B, P, S.

Winchester St Cross, 1858–93; accnts; Notebook 24; drawings, R.I.B.A. and Victoria & Albert Museum; *B*, (22) 1864, p. 320, (23) 1865, pp. 763–5; *BN*, (12) 1865, pp. 670, 688; *ILN*, (47) 1865, pp. 481, 485–6; chapel decorations T, B, R.

Yazor old church, 1858–60; accnts, £550. Conversion of disused transept to chapel.

Bacton, Suffolk, 1859–65; accnts, £1926; *B*, (18) 1860, p. 353, (22) 1864, p. 782; T, B, P, R.

Belaugh, 1859–60; accnts; ?B, ?P, ?R.

Great Alne, 1859; accnts, £400; *AAS*, (5) 1859–60, p. xcix; new north aisle, T, B, P, R.

Great Bookham, 1859–85; B. G. Skinner, *St Nicholas Church Great Bookham*, Leatherhead 1957; *E*, (20) 1859, p. 78, south-east chapel; accnts, chancel roof 1872, remainder 1881–8; new vestry, chancel roof, B, P, R.

Port Elizabeth, South Africa, 1859; accnts; vestry minutes, chest; A. T. Wirgman and C. E. Mayo, *Collegiate Church and Parish of St Mary, Port Elizabeth*, London 1925; realignment with new sanctuary and nave, B. Since rebuilt and refitted.

St Columb, 1859; accnts; *B*, (18) 1860, p. 382; plan to convert into Cornish cathedral, with new choir. Not executed.

Standlynch chapel, 1859–66; accnts; Notebook 19; new porch, roofs, churchyard cross.

Chiddingfold, c 1860; Notebook 9. Not executed.

Northington, 1860–2; accnts; Notebook 24; drawings, R.I.B.A.; new porch, vestry, B, P. Since rebuilt.

Sudbury St Gregory, 1860–3; Notebook 25; correspondence and faculty, West Suffolk Record Office; *BN*, (9) 1862, p. 403; *CB*, April 1863; light fittings, T, B, P (since removed), R.

Woodborough, Wiltshire, 1860; accnts. Not executed.

Abbotsley, 1861–2; accnts, £520; Notebook 17; *CB*, January 1862; new chancel, porch, nave roof, T, B, P, R.

Canterbury St Mildred, 1861; accnts, £1000; *BN*, (7) 1861, p. 1009; *CB*, January 1862; T, B.

Castle Eaton, 1861–3; accnts, £850; Notebook 24; new chancel roof, T, B, R.

Chaddesley Corbett, 1861–4; accnts, £1621, and 1878–9, £348; faculty, Worcestershire Record Office; *B*, (21) 1863, pp. 412, 587; *BN*, (10) 1863, p. 401, (11) 1864, p. 432; new roofs, T, B, P, R.

Letcombe Bassett, 1861–2; accnts, c £800; Notebook 24; *BN*, (9) 1862, p. 383; T, B, P, R, reredos.

Marston Morteyne, 1861–2; accnts, £1286; Notebook 25; nave only, T, B, P.

Selly Oak, 1861; accnts; *BN*, (7) 1861, p. 770; F only.

Stibbard, 1861–3; accnts, £577; Notebook 25; *CB*, January 1864; new porch, T, F, B, R.

Portsea Holy Trinity, c 1861; Notebook 25. Demolished.

St John's, c 1861; Notebook 24. Not identified.

Bremhill, 1862–3; accnts; tower memorial.

Holt, 1862–4 and 1886–7; accnts, £720, and 1886–7, chancel roof; *BN* (11) 1864, p. 409; new chancel roof, B, P.

Llanafan, 1862–7; accnts, £1005; specification, National Library of Wales; new west end, bellcote, porch, east wall, roofs, F, B, P, R, reredos.

Llanbadarn, 1862; accnts; Notebook 24. Not executed.

Lyneham, 1862–5; accnts, £2297; faculty and plans, Wiltshire Record Office; *BN*, (11) 1864, p. 330; new chancel, roofs, T, B, P, R.

Mapledurham, 1862–4; accnts, £1170; plans, correspondence and account, chest; faculty, Bodleian Library; *B*, (21) 1863, p. 759; *BN* (10) 1863, p. 770; new tower cap, porch, vestry, wooden arcade, T, B, P, R, reredos.

Aldbourne, 1863–7; accnts, £1216; restoration committee notebooks and faculty and plans, Wiltshire Record Office; *CB*, April 1868; T, B, S.

Brigham, 1863–76; accnts, nave 1863–6, £1800, chancel 1876, c £3500; vestry minutes, accounts and faculty, chest; drawing for wall decoration, Starey Collection; *B*, (23) 1865, p. 753; new gateway, tower cap, south and east walls, roof painting, T, B, P, S.

Charlton by Downton, Wiltshire, 1863; accnts; F.

Great Waldingfield, 1863–7; accnts, £556; new chancel, T, P, R, wall marbling.

Hewelsfield, 1863–7; accnts, c £1300; *B*, (22) 1864, p. 299; *CB*, October 1864; new lych gate, roofs, T, B, P, R.

London, St Edmund King and Martyr, Lombard Street, 1863–80; accnts, £1652; faculty, Guildhall; *ILN*, (46) 1865, p. 83, (78) 1881, p. 34; *E*, (28) 1867, p. 233. Rearrangement and decoration (since removed).

Preston Plucknett, 1863; accnts, £276; R.

Tattershall, 1863–5; accnts, £486; T, B, R.

Wootton, Northamptonshire, 1863–5; accnts, £1130; faculty, Northamptonshire Record Office; *B*, (23) 1865, p. 161; *BN*, (12) 1865, p. 144; new porch, chancel arches (in order to extend chancel into nave), T, F, B, P.

Yedingham, 1863–4; accnts, £295; *B*, (21) 1863, p. 796; new chancel only, B, R.

Blunsdon St Andrew, 1864–75; accnts; *B*, (26) 1868, p. 120; *BN*, (15) 1868, pp. 133, 152; largely rebuilt, T, B, P, R.

Daventry, 1864–6; accnts, £900; extra bay to chancel. Since refitted.

Godmersham, 1864–6; accnts, c £2000; *CB*, October 1865; *ILN*, (49) 1866, p. 251; new south aisle, porch, transept, organ chamber, roof, F, B, P, S.

Rougham, Suffolk, 1864–5; accnts, £288; repairs to roof only.

Heytesbury, 1865–7; accnts, £4902; correspondence and accounts, Heytesbury Collection; faculty and plans, Wiltshire Record Office; *B*, (23) 1865, p. 666, (24) 1866, pp. 52, 258, (25) 1867, p. 738; *BN*, (13) 1866, p. 32; new south porch, aisles, T, F, B, R.

Hyde, Winchester, 1865; accnts; drawings, Starey Collection. Not executed.

London, St Michael Paternoster Royal, 1865–6; accnts, £1082; vestry minutes and faculty, Guildhall; *BN*, (13) 1866, p. 537; *ILN*, (49) 1866, p. 31; F. Gutted.

Rownhams, 1865–9; accnts. Probably repairs only.

Battle, St Mary, 1866–9; accnts, c £5000; *B*, (27) 1869, p. 572; *BN*, (17) 1869, p. 19; chancel roof, T, B, P.

Great Budworth, 1866; accnts; B.

London, Christ Church Albany Street, 1866–85; accnts, 1867, c £2200, 1879–80 redecoration £884, 1884 pulpit, etc.; Notebooks 13 and 18; faculty, Guildhall; drawings etc., Starey Collection and chest; *E*, (28) 1867, p. 233; *BN*, (13) 1868, p. 505; decorations, T, B, P, S, alteration to font.

Highway, 1867; see above.

Mattingley, 1867–9; accnts, c £900; F, B, P, R.

Sedgeberrow, 1867–8; accnts, c £1500; *AAS*, (VIII) 1865–6, p. xi, (IX) 1867–8, p. cxiii; *B*, (26) 1868, p. 497; *BN*, (15) 1868, p. 474; drawing, Starey Collection; new spire, B, P, R, reredos.

Bromham, 1868–9; accnts, c £1200; *B*, (27) 1869, p. 431; new north chapel, chancel roof, B, P, R.

Great Berkhamsted, 1866–88; accnts; report, accounts, &c, chest; *ILN*, (52) 1868, p. 299; *B*, (29) 1871, pp. 311, 491; *BN*, (20) 1871, p. 306; *A*, (5) 1871, p. 212; new walling, gallery narthex, T, F, B, R.

York, St Mary Castlegate, 1868–70; accnts, c £4000; faculty and plans, Borthwick Institute; *B*, (26) 1868, p. 218; largely new chancel and north aisle, T, B, P, S.

Anstey, 1869–72; faculty, specification, etc., Hertfordshire Record Office; *B*, (27) 1869, p. 992, (30) 1872, p. 352; *BN*, (22) 1872, p. 362; T, B, P, R.

Bristol Mayor's Chapel, 1869–70; accnts; Finance Committee minutes, Bristol Record Office, £347. Much restoration since.

Hastings All Saints', 1869–70; accnts, c £5000, and 1888–9, reredos and decorations, £289; *ILN*, (57) 1870, p. 494; *B*, (28) 1870, pp. 950–1; *A*, (1) 1869, p. 158, (4) 1870, p. 190; drawing, Starey Collection, new west wall decoration, vestry, nave roof, T, B, P, R.

Tamworth, 1869–71; accnts, c £3000; Notebook 18; some drawings, R.I.B.A.; *A*, (3) 1870, p. 248; *B*, (29) 1871, pp. 193, 931; T, B, P, G. Much earlier and later work by others.

Whiteparish, 1869–70; accnts, c £2000; faculty, Wiltshire Record Office; W. B. Swayne, *Parson's Pleasure*, London 1934; new belfry, aisles, nave roof, porch, F, B, P.

Broad Blunsdon, 1870; *BN*, (19) 1870, p. 455; *ILN*, (57) 1870, p. 614; new organ chamber, T, B.

Ipswich, St Mary Stoke, 1870–2; see above.

London, St Leonard Shoreditch, 1870–1; accnts, c £2000; Notebook 9; faculty, Guildhall; T, B, S.

Barley, 1871–3; see above.

Cheddar, 1871–3; faculty, Wells Diocesan Office; *BN*, (23) 1872, p. 152 (c £2000), (24) 1873, p. 548; *B*, (31) 1873, p. 413; *A*, (9) 1873, p. 255; T, B, R.

Chipping Barnet, 1871–5; see above.

London, St Clement Eastcheap, 1871–90; accnts, c £4000; Notebook 19; vestry minutes and accounts and faculty, Guildhall; *ILN*, (60) 1872, p. 151; *A*, (7) 1872, p. 85; *B*, (30) 1872, p. 153; *BN*, (22) 1872, p. 224; *Athenaeum*, 17 March 1877; T, B.

London, St Paul Covent Garden, 1871–2; accnts, c £1500; faculty, Guildhall; *BN*, (21) 1871, p. 238, (22) 1872, p. 532; F.

Marton, Cheshire, 1871–2 and 1894; accnts, c £2000; faculties, Cheshire Record Office; *B*, (30) 1872, p. 152; *BN*, (22) 1872, p. 183; chancel aisle and tower walls, T, F, B, R; 1894, skylights and east window.

Purton, 1871–2; accnts, c £2500; specification, accounts, &c, chest; faculty, Bristol Record Office; *B*, (30) 1872, p. 972; *ILN*, (61) 1872, p. 467; T, B.

Bombay Cathedral, 1872; drawings, Starey Collection; T.

Haughton-le-Skerne, 1872–5; accnts. Not executed.

Hastings St Clement, 1872–6; accnts, c £5000; some drawings, Starey Collection and R.I.B.A.; *B*, (30) 1872, p. 894; *BN*, (23) 1872, p. 331; T, B, P.

London, St James Curtain Road, Shoreditch, 1872; accnts. Demolished.

London, St Thomas Regent Street, 1872; accnts, c £800. T, B.

Milstead, Kent, 1872–3; accnts, c £1500; some drawings, R.I.B.A.; *B*, (30) 1872, p. 412; new porch, T, B, P, R.

Poulton, 1872–3; see above.

Romsey Abbey, 1872; accnts. Not executed.

St Buryan, 1872–6; accnts, c £2800; *B*, (30) 1872, p. 1034; *BA*, (26) 1887, p. 477; T, B, R.

Weston upon Trent, Staffordshire, 1872; accnts, c £4000; *B*, (30) 1872, p. 472; new vestry, porch, nave roof, B.

Cape Town, St Saviour Claremont, 1873–81; vestry minutes, chest; *G*, 13 and 27 October 1875; new bellcote and west end of nave.

Cliffe Pypard, 1873–4; accnts, c £1800; faculty and plans, Wiltshire Record Office; *ILN*, (65) 1874, p. 150; new chancel roof, T, B, R, reredos.

Dinton, Wiltshire, 1873–5; accnts, c £2000; report, &c, chest; new vestry, porch, roofs, T, P, R.

Saffron Walden, 1873–8; accnts, c £1200; *B*, (31) 1873, p. 253; repairs only?

Braunston, Northamptonshire, 1874–81; accnts, c £700; Notebook 18; faculties, chest; *B*, (37) 1879, p. 894; T, F, B, S.

Christleton, 1874–8; see above.

Knook, 1874–6; accnts, c £900; correspondence, Heytesbury Collection; faculty and plans, Wiltshire Record Office; *ILN*, (68) 1876, p. 467. New vestry, south and east walls, T, F, B, P, R.

London, Christ Church Endell Street, 1874–7; Bumpus, *London Churches*, 2, p. 74; faculty, Guildhall. Demolished.

London, St Mary Rotherhithe, 1874–89; accnts; *BN*, (27) 1874, p. 182; *ILN*, (69) 1876, p. 451; T, S.

Morebath, 1874–5; accnts, c £2000; new roofs, T, F, B, P, R.

West Deeping, 1874–7; accnts, c £1000; faculty, Lincolnshire Record Office; *BN*, (32) 1877, p. 159; new vestry, T, B, R, reredos.

West Harnham, Wiltshire, 1874; accnts, c £1200; faculty, Wiltshire Record Office; *A*, (11) 1874, p. 81; new porch, east and west walls, roof, T, B, P, R.

Balsham, 1875–8; report, chest; *B*, (33) 1875, p. 869; T, B, screen heightened; perhaps P, R; previous and subsequent work by others.

Exeter Bishop's Palace, 1875–82; accnts, chapel £1366; J. D. Chanter, *The Bishop's Palace*, London 1932; *BA*, (12) 1878, p. 196. Gutted.

London, St Mary Woolnoth, 1875–6; vestry minutes and building accounts (£1147) and faculty, Guildhall; *A*, (15) 1876, p. 187, (19) 1878, p. 217; *Athenaeum*, 17 March 1877; T, F.

Rugby St Andrew, 1875–96; see above.

Shaw, 1875–8; drawings, Victoria & Albert Museum and Starey Collection; *BN*, (35) 1878, p. 172; new chancel, T, B, P. Since frescoed.

Ashton Keynes, 1876–8; accnts; report, chest; *B*, (35) 1877, p. 795; chancel arch widened, roof painted, T, B, P, S, R.

Netherhampton, 1876–7; see above.

Tottenham All Hallows, 1876–7; see above.

Belbroughton, 1877; accnts. Not executed.

Bexhill, 1877–9; accnts, c £5000; faculty and plans, West Sussex Record Office; new chancel, aisle, porch, B. Since refitted.

Blandford Forum, 1877; accnts; new chancel. Not executed.

Wantage, 1877–81; accnts, £1335; *B*, (40) 1881, p. 491; new west bay of nave.

Winterborne Monkton, 1877–9; accnts, c £2000; building accounts, chest; faculty and plans, Wiltshire Record Office; *BN*, (35) 1878, p. 253; new chancel, vestry, T, B, R.

Ardleigh, 1878–84; see above.

Buckland by Dover, Kent, 1878–82; accnts, £1731; *B*, (39) 1879, p. 468; old photograph, National Monuments Record; nave extended westwards, T, F, B, S. Earlier chancel work by others; Butterfield's wooden screen replaced in 1898 by the present metal screen, designed by a local ironworker (parish council minutes).

Dodford, 1878–80; accnts, £905; faculty, Northamptonshire Record Office; nave only, new roof, T, B.

Friskney, 1878–9; accnts, c £3500; faculty and plans, Lincolnshire Record Office; *CB*, July 1879; new aisle roofs, T, B, R.

Sparsholt, 1878–83; accnts, £2183; correspondence, etc, chest; new tower cap, roofs, porch, arcade, T, B, R.

Chiseldon, 1879; accnts. Not executed.

Colabah St John, India, 1879–84; accnts, £580; drawings, Starey Collection; new reredos, Afghan War Memorial mosaics, T, B, S.

Hagnaby, 1879–81; accnts, £294; F, B.

London, St Peter le Poor, 1879–82; accnts. Not executed.

Winchester St Michael, 1879–82; accnts, £2129; drawings, R.I.B.A., Starey Collection and Victoria & Albert Museum; *A*, (24) 1880, p. 56, (28) 1882, p. 220; new porch, chancel, vestry, T, B, R.

Baverstock, 1880–2; accnts, £982; largely rebuilt, T, B, P, S, R.

Ellough, 1880–2; accnts, c £1000; chancel only, new roof, organ chamber, T, B, P, reredos.

London, Holy Trinity Bedford Row, 1880–1; accnts; faculty, Guildhall. Demolished.

London, St Paul Bunhill Row, 1880–4; accnts, £1734. Demolished.

London, St Philip Dalston, 1880–2; accnts, £363, and font, 1889; faculty, Guildhall. Demolished.

Stratford-on-Avon, 1880–1; accnts; *A*, (25) 1881, p. 298. Not executed.

Abbots Kerswell, 1881–3; accnts, £1419; faculty and plans, Devon Record Office; T, B, P, R.

Hadstock, 1881–7; accnts, £1923; chancel rebuilt, new roof, T, B, P, R.

London, St Mary Haggerston, 1881–4; accnts. Demolished.

Rochester Cathedral, 1881–3; accnts, £378; minor repairs.

Heath, Derbyshire, 1882–6; accnts; T, S.

West Tarring, 1882–6; *CB*, January 1886; mosaics.

Arley, 1883; accnts; Notebook 17. Not executed.

Ringsfield, 1883–4; accnts, £2229; some drawings, R.I.B.A.; new roofs, T, B, R.
Waltham-on-the-Wolds, 1883; accnts; S.

Warwick St Mary, 1883–6; accnts, c £10,000; T. Kemp, *History of Warwick and Its People*, c 1900; *A*, (31) 1884, p. 149; *BN*, (50) 1886, p. 561; drawing, Starey Collection; T, B, reredos.

Cardiff St Andrew, 1884–6; accnts, £2365; faculty and plans, National Library of Wales; new transepts, vestries, B, T.

Colchester, St Helen's chapel, 1884–6; accnts, £457; J. H. Round, *St Helen's Chapel, Colchester*; *BN*, (51) 1886, p. 181; largely rebuilt.

Hopesay, 1884–6; accnts, £426; chancel only, new roof, T, B, R.

London, St John Smith Square, 1884; accnts, £926; faculty, Guildhall; *B*, (47) 1884, p. 876; B. Gutted.

London, St Mary Magdalen and St Gregory by Paul, 1884; Notebook 13; *B*, (46) 1884, p. 45. Demolished.

Monyash, 1884–7; accnts, £2420; new roofs, ? south porch, T, B, P, S, R.

Winchester St Peter, 1884; accnts. Not executed.

Ault Hucknall, 1885–8; accnts, £2714; drawings, Starey Collection; T, F, B, P, R.

Biggleswade, 1885–8; accnts, £361; new vestry and chancel roof.

Sunningdale, 1885; accnts. Not executed.

Burley, 1886–7; accnts, £1526; faculty, chest; *B*, (52) 1887, p. 165; *BN*, (52) 1887, p. 35; new chancel, T, F, B.

Shirley, Southampton, 1886; accnts. Not executed.

Dover Castle church, 1888–9; accnts, £2104; drawings. Starey Collection; new vestry, T, B, R, wall decorations.

Letheringsett, 1888–90; accnts, £1358; drawings, R.I.B.A.; new porch.

Teversall, 1888; accnts. Not executed.

Little Faringdon, 1889; May Morris, *William Morris, Artist, Writer, Socialist*, Oxford 1936, I, p. 161. Not executed.

Copythorne, 1890–2; accnts, £1545; new chancel.

London, St Paul Rotherhithe, 1892–3; accnts, £342. Demolished.

London, St Giles in the Fields, 1895; drawings, Victoria & Albert Museum, for new vestry, extension of sanctuary, F, B; only minor work executed.

Puttenham, not dated; Notebook 11. Not executed.

Beddington, not dated; Notebook 18. Not executed.

Chartham, not dated; Notebook 18. Not executed.

Upper Winchendon, not dated; Notebook 18. Not executed.

Probable misattributions

Ascot Priory hospital (by Buckeridge, *E*, (25) 1864, p. 49).

Belmont parsonage (by Walton and Robson, *E*, (23) 1862, p. 66) and school (by Austin and Johnson, 1870, plans, Durham Record Office).

Belvidere church, Cape Province, South Africa (stylistically improbable).

Bletchingley east window (*BE*; but by Pearson, *Surrey Archaeological Collections*, (V) 1892, pp. 227–232, and restoration committee minutes, chest).

Brasted church.

Broad Blunsdon parsonage (probably by Christian, as Poulton).

Cambridge, Jesus College (misreading by *DNB* of *B*, (78) 1900, p. 202).

Cranleigh, 'harsh restoration', transepts and porch, 1846 (*BE*; but the transepts are however of 1864–5, and the restoration, to judge from *E*, 1846, p. 86, unlikely to be Butterfield's).

Danby chancel and vicarage (*BE*; but style atypical and no contemporary attribution as for plate in *E*, (8) 1848, p. 261).

Driffield, Gloucestershire, restoration (*BE*; influenced by Butterfield, and glass perhaps his, but remainder unlikely).

East Farleigh school (*BE*, 'aggressively high . . . jagged gable'. This, however, is a replacement of Butterfield's school: see above).

East Garston restoration.

Eton church (Eastlake, *op. cit.*, p. 256; probably a confusion with the chapel restoration scheme).

Exeter Choir School (*BE*; but the present building was built for an archdeacon in 1870 and is stylistically unlikely to be by Butterfield; the Cathedral archives show that the previous building was not his).

Ford restoration, Northumberland (*E*, (22) 1861, p. 151; but in fact by Dobson).

Gunthorpe Hall.

Highworth (references indicate Blunsdon).

Horfield Barracks chapel (*BE*; but the parish church was used for this purpose until 1847).

Hunstanton Hall, west wing (style shows Butterfield's influence; probably Preedy).

Hursley church (Harrison).

Llangorwen church (Underwood, building accounts, chest).

London, All Saints' Highgate (Blomfield).

London, St James Moore Park Road (*B*, (35) 1877, p. 745; but in fact by Darbyshire and Christian).

Mears Ashby restoration and parsonage (*BE;* but by Buckeridge, *E*, (21) 1860, pp. 259, 262). 259, 262).

Newbury, St Nicholas' school (*BE*; but by Woodyer, *B*, (18) 1860, p. 500).

Poulton parsonage (*BN*, (37) 1879, p. 512; but by Christian, plans, Church Commissioners).

Rochester, King's School House (*BE*; 'determinedly cranky', 'vice-like grip' and 'grinding contrasts of colour and texture'. Nevertheless, undocumented and stylistically improbable).

Stratfieldsaye (references indicate Beech Hill).

Walsall St Mary (*A*, (31) 1884, p. 149; but this is a misprint for Warwick).

Wavedon parsonage (*BE*; but by Ferrey, plans, Bodleian Library).

Wilmcote church (see Chapter 4, note 9).

Wisborough Green restoration, 1867 (*BE*, from *Little Guide*, but stylistically improbable).

These are here treated as ancillary to architecture, as they were indeed conceived. The limitations of this method must however be stated. I have not collected references to glass in Butterfield's buildings which was inserted without his documented supervision, nor searched for undocumented plate, embroidery or wallpaper designs. Fuller studies of Butterfield's stained glass, metalwork and perhaps his wooden furniture, placing his techniques and designs in relation to work in the same field rather than in architecture, would produce different interpretations and further material. However each would demand a separate monograph, and I have preferred to consider them in this volume in relation to Butterfield's central and I believe supreme activity, architecture.

Sculpture

The *Ecclesiologist*, contrasting the profusion of Street's St James's Westminster with the discipline of Butterfield's St Alban's Holborn, remarked on the complete absence of carving, even of leafage, in Butterfield's church. He was certainly exceptional in his repudiation of the rich naturalistic sculpture favoured by most High Victorian architects. And in particular it was observed that 'Mr Butterfield . . . with that severity which forms so conspicuous an element in his artistic character, has always been shy of the sculptured human figure.'[1] Indeed, the Annunciation at All Saints' and the canopied saints at Keble are unique in his work. This abstinence runs right through his work. Capitals and corbels, for example, are generally absolutely plain, or very occasionally boldly fluted. In the whole of his architecture there are less than a dozen cases of the use of sculpture, and all of them are restricted to a few places: generally the corbels at the chancel arch, a band of foliage round the sanctuary wall, or external gargoyles. There is more carving in fittings, especially fonts, but it is almost without exception severely formalized in character. Even in monumental sculpture he rarely allowed the carver more than a foliated cross on a coped stone.[2]

453

A few of Butterfield's sculptors have been recorded. As one would expect, he relied on reputable London firms. In the Dorchester Abbey restoration most of the sculpture of the east window was by White of Pimlico, but two figures were carved by Thomas of London, presumably the John Thomas who was then responsible, under Pugin, for the sculptural decoration at the Houses of Parliament.[3] 'White the Carver' appears again at Balliol.[4] At Keble some of the chapel drawings are signed by Field, Poole and Sons who (later as Henry Poole and Sons and then as M. J. Bayne and Co, but with Hubert Poole manager) executed several monuments for Butterfield, as well as reredoses, the Christleton pulpit and the Tadlow font. On the other hand another Keble drawing, for the hall staircase oriel pinnacles, is annotated 'Mr Smith to make model'.[5] The authorship of the sculpture at All Saints' Margaret Street (X, 157) is only a little less anonymous, having been executed by the large building firm of George Myers. At Ottery St Mary, however, the Flaxmanesque plaques in the library were the work of Frederick Thrupp; at Dundela there are wooden roof angels by Smith of Clapham, who could also be the Keble Smith; and a number of fonts, pulpits and reredoses came from the well known workshop of Thomas Earp.[6]

If Earp's work for Butterfield is disappointing, this may be because he was allowed none of the freedom that, for example, G. E. Street gave him. We know that Butterfield provided 'full sized drawings for the sculpture' of the reredos at St Mary's Warwick,[7] and in the surviving drawings the sculpture is drawn with sensitivity, but

349 Heckfield church, tablet to Lady Eversley

350 St Matthias Stoke Newington, capital

351 West Lavington church,
capitals

352 Teversham church, Early
English capital

precise clarity. His method is also shown by his close supervision of White at Balliol (158). Butterfield came down specially 'to set the carver to work. He had prepared his models under my eye here before he left town, and we marked them out on the stone. I shall be down again on the 24th, to see his progress.'[8] There was little room here for Ruskinian expression of the craftsman's personality. And it follows that the style of Butterfield's sculpture is very consistent. Apart from the uncharacteristic, slightly florid font of 1851 in Merton College Chapel, it is always strongly and simply modelled in the severe, rich style of early gothic. Several times, first at All Saints' and Stoke Newington (350), later at Keble and Dundela, Butterfield closely followed the stiff twisting foliage corbels at Warmington in Northamptonshire, which were also chosen by Owen Jones as models in his famous *Grammar of Ornament*. The result could hardly be very imaginative – although there is sometimes life half-hidden in the leaves – but it achieved a classic dignity. The sculpture at All Saints', it was observed, was 'impossible too highly to praise. There is a masculine breadth of treatment and vigour not often found in modern works. Seen from across the nave, every stroke of the chisel tells.'[9]

There is however one building in which Butterfield produced foliage sculpture of real imaginative power. One senses that in the early 1850s, as in so much of his design, he was experimenting. There is the unsuccessful font at Merton, and also, perhaps under his direction, the use at Sheen of 'natural models, the flowers and foliage of the neighbourhood', for the chancel capitals.[10] Much more remarkable, however, are the two contrasting pairs of corbels at West Lavington (351). The arcade stops are of ferns, a fragile, crinkled, delicate surface of fronds with black shadows in the cracks between them. They have the quality of an early Victorian steel engraving rather than of sculpture. The chancel corbels on the other hand could hardly be more solid or stylized, fronds again, but a seaweedy swirl chiselled in grey marble. The surface itself is in bolder relief, but with no deep undercutting, and the details are much rougher, so that the reality is the sculpture itself rather than its subject. If these corbels date, like the church, from 1850, they are a remarkable forecast of High Victorian vigour and sense of material in sculpture. They are not mentioned in contemporary descriptions of the church. Nevertheless, they are almost certainly original, for they bear an uncanny resemblance to two Early English corbels at Teversham, near Cambridge (352). Butterfield's notebooks show that he was sketching at Teversham church in about 1844.[11]

Notes

1 (22) 1861, p. 321.

2 Butterfield objected to railed-off tombs in which 'the heavenly family is lost in that of the earthly one', just as he disapproved of 'the enclosure of members of the same family within a pew' (Butterfield to Mrs Keble, 19 August 1866, Keble College). Apart from tomb chests, he designed the headstones in *Instrumenta Ecclesiastica*; a few memorial crosses (notably the stone Bishop Gray Memorial Column of 1873–6 at Cape Town, drawings, Starey Collection – R. R. Langham Carter, *Africana Notes and News*, June 1966; and the brick Patteson Cross of 1873 at Ottery St Mary – *ILN*, (63) 1873, p. 263); brasses (to Anna Maria Hanbury at Babbacombe, 1877 – drawing, Starey Collection – and Guy Cuthbert Dawnay at Sessay, 1889 – rubbings, R.I.B.A.); and some wall tablets (Heathcote's at Hursley dark and weighty, 1885 – drawings, Starey Collection – and Lady Eversley's at Heckfield (349) elegant, like a bracelet on lace diaper, 1862 – accnts). They are inscribed in uncial lettering.

3 Restoration accounts, 1846, Oxford Architectural and Historical Society.

4 Butterfield to the Master, 16 June 1857, Balliol College archives.

5 R.I.B.A.; restoration accounts, Tadlow chest.

6 Chanter's House rebuilding plans, 1881–2, Coleridge Collection; specification, 1890, Dundela chest. By Earp, Battle pulpit (*B*, (27) 1869, p. 572), Brookfield font, 1875 (drawing, R.I.B.A.), St Augustine Queen's Gate pulpit, 1876, Christ Church Albany Street pulpit, 1882–5, and Warwick St Mary reredos 1886 (drawings, Starey Collection).

7 Accnts, 1886.

8 Butterfield to the Master, 13 January 1857, Balliol College archives.

9 *B*, (17) 1859, p. 365.

10 *E*, (15) 1854, p. 154.

11 Notebook 11; *E*, (3) 1844, p. 134.

Wall painting and mosaics

Painted decoration is not very common in Butterfield's architecture. There are about a dozen painted roofs, including the splendid vaults at Ottery (IX) (1849) and Keble (XVIII) (1876), but mostly wooden ceilings picked out with formalized flowers, stars and monograms, especially attractively at Langley (106) (1855) and Brigham (119) (1865). Occasionally this kind of painting was brought down onto the walls, as at Wavendon (1849), and also in the notorious chancel decorations of St Cross, Winchester (162) (1865). The pseudo-constructional decoration here was exceptional. So are a few later schemes for which Butterfield's responsibility is not certain: the chancels at West Deeping, Ardleigh and Enfield, all rich and dark combinations of painting with constructional colour.[1]

These paintings were executed by a variety of artists, ranging from village craftsmen at Brigham (119) to a fellow of the college, John Hungerford Pollen, at Merton
(348). In most cases Butterfield must have supervised the work closely. His accounts
record 'fullsized cartoons for the painters' for chancel decorations at Bournemouth
(1893), and at Barnet (1880) he went 'to meet Standish for the reredos painting'
(which was on tiles) and charged for 'superintendance of the picture'.[2] Pollen, however, must have been allowed considerable freedom, and the same is true of the
artists who executed the two most remarkable series of wall paintings in Butterfield's
churches, the great reredos walls at All Saints' Margaret Street and St Alban's
Holborn.

At All Saints' (X) Butterfield had in fact little direct contact with the painter,
William Dyce. It was Beresford-Hope who persuaded Dyce to undertake the frescoes
('a piece of success unlooked for and surprising') and then corresponded with him
about the choice of subjects and the degree of conventionalism or naturalism appropriate in their treatment. Indeed Dyce's decoration of the chancel vaulting conflicted
with Butterfield's wishes. On the other hand the original scheme, including the nave
frescoes by J. C. Horsley which were not executed because of the change of plan to
constructional colour, must have been approved by Butterfield, and, since Dyce's
frescoes deteriorated quickly and are now covered by Comper's substitutes, it is
inevitably the original conception which is most interesting. In the 1840s Prince
Albert had introduced to England the revival of the medieval Italian technique of
fresco painting, which had begun with the German Nazarene school of painters some
thirty years previously. Butterfield, with his interest in Pugin's work as well as in
Italian painting, must have been aware of the resulting frescoes in the Palace of
Westminster, to which both Dyce and Horsley had contributed. Moreover, also in
1849, he may have independently suggested the most distinguished of the Nazarenes,
Overbeck, as the artist for the altar painting at St Thomas's Leeds, although Beresford-
Hope later bought the painting when the church would not pay for it. But in 1849
Hope seemed surprised to discover 'this little knot of painters who have gone back to
the old models, and with whom we have had so little communication. No doubt they
must have thought us narrow-minded prigs for not having found them out'.[3] It therefore seems most likely that the triple tier of glowing red, blue and gold saints, so
boldly catholic a culmination to a Protestant church, was Butterfield's suggestion.

Certainly he repeated the idea at St Alban's Holborn (353), where the east wall
was 'painted in party colours by the water-glass process, like Mr Maclise's frescoes at
the Houses of Parliament, on stone columns rubbed with lime which had been
quickening for twenty years'.[4] The paintings were once again given a strong architectural setting, but instead of the canopied niches of All Saints' there was a big bare
grid dividing the flat wall face into rectangular spaces. Butterfield also chose a painter

353 St Alban's Holborn, east wall, from an early photograph (Gordon Barnes)

whom he knew was able to respond to an architectural situation, Henry Styleman le Strange, squire of Hunstanton and close friend of the great collector Gambier Parry. Le Strange was already at work on his magnificent nave roof at Ely. At St Alban's Holborn, however, he had not completed the cartoons before his death, and although the executed paintings by Preedy followed his designs they were destroyed during the Second World War. Further comment is thus impossible.

Nor is it easy to assess the paintings which Butterfield eventually designed for the nave of All Saints' – the north wall in 1876, the west wall in about 1887 and the tower wall in about 1891. The first was apparently designed by Butterfield himself, painted on tiles by Alexander Gibbs and executed by Henry Poole and Sons. Their big figures are stiffly outlined in pale buff, apple green, reds and blues. Butterfield had been wiser in earlier work to delegate figure designing to artists with more feeling for it than himself. Nevertheless, the 'series of beautiful tile paintings' was welcomed by the *Building News:* 'The drawing of the figures exhibits almost a classic grace, and the drapery is simple and architectural in character. We also like the mellow colouring

. . .'[5] It is possible to look at the paintings in this spirit, even if without much conviction of their quality.

At the same time Butterfield had also developed an interest in another form of permanent mural decoration, mosaic work. He had apparently at some stage studied the mosaics of St Mark's, Venice.[6] His earliest use of the medium was a panel of the Adoration at Fulham Palace chapel in 1867, which was executed by Salviati with the help of Gibbs. An attractive small fragment remains. There are similar small mosaics by Salviati in the chancel at Babbacombe.[7] The Keble mosaic work completed in 1876 was much more ambitious (81). It was the first large-scale mosaic made in England during the period, and if its combination of stiff drawing and rather pallid colouring is not attractive it still remains an important experiment. Gibbs was sent by Butterfield to Venice, where he recruited a chemist and craftsmen, who were brought back to operate a furnace specially built for the purpose in England, 'the numerous designs and cartoons being executed under the artist's own hand'. All were inevitably 'under the immediate superintendance' of Butterfield.[8]

Italian workmen were also said to have worked on the West Tarring mosaics of 1885, where Butterfield's design is closer to the Byzantine spirit of St Mark's, and consequently more acceptable. But his last mosaics are idiosyncratic patterns probably executed by English firms, although the makers of the writhing decorations at Dover Castle Church (163) (1888) are unrecorded. The thin patterning at Ottery (1878) was made by Simpson of Westminster; the formalized scrollwork at Harrow Weald (197) (1890), the Christleton and Leeds reredos panels (1893–6) and the rather prettier decoration at Dundela (1890) by Minton. Butterfield's accounts record the 'fullsized drawings' for Harrow Weald, and those for Dover survive, with notes on the colour in his own hand.[9] Although all these mosaics are of some interest, none was really successful in exploiting the decorative qualities of the material.

Notes

1   At West Deeping the painting was 'mainly under the supervision of the rector' and the builder (*BN*, (32) 1877, p. 159) and is not shown in Butterfield's drawings (Faculty Book, Lincoln Record Office); at Ardleigh Butterfield recommended the addition of ceiling painting and coloured tile mosaic in the sanctuary, but resigned the commission (Butterfield to Rev. G. Hales, 28 December 1891 and 12 March 1892, Ardleigh chest); at Enfield the rich red and gold paintings were also a later addition, the roof, according to an inscription, at the cost of Philip Twells in 1897, to designs by Buckeridge.

2   Accnts.

3   Law, *op. cit.*, p. 164; A. J. B. Hope to W. Dyce, 22 November 1851 and 10 April 1852, Aberdeen Art Gallery.

4   *ILN*, (43) 1863, p. 60.

5 (31) 1876, p. 303. On the other hand Bumpus thought the tile paintings of 1889–91 at St Augustine's Queen's Gate merely 'puerile' (*London Churches*, 2, p. 308).

6 Swinfen Harris, *op. cit.*

7 *BN*, (14) 1867, p. 270 and (25) 1873, p. 552.

8 *B*, (34) 1876, p. 495; *Church Times*, 28 April 1876.

9 *CB*, January 1886; *B*, (36) 1878, p. 1051; accnts; specification, Dundela chest; drawings for Leeds, Christleton, Dover, and the Keble Annunciation, Starey Collection. There was also a mosaic at Portsmouth, above the chancel arch (164).

Stained glass

We shall not need to set out Butterfield's changing tastes in colour or his understanding of the need for good natural light in buildings, for these have been discussed earlier. Our chief concern will be with his relationship with his stained glass artists. There are a dozen in all, and they run as follows.

Until the late 1840s Butterfield used Thomas Willement, then close to the end of his distinguished career and undoubtedly the most eminent stained glass artist of the early 19th century. He was an antiquary, heraldic scholar, artist to the crown, and a minor Kentish landowner.

In the 1850s Butterfield gave most of his stained glass to three artists: Willement's pupil Michael O'Connor, who had returned to England in 1842 after running his own business in Dublin, and had then executed the outstandingly good glass designed by Pugin for St Saviour's Leeds; John Hardman of Birmingham, who was Pugin's closest collaborator from 1837 until Pugin died in 1852, and continued in the same spirit to produce glass and metalwork of a high standard for many years afterwards; and William Wailes of Newcastle, who also produced some admirable glass for Pugin in the late 1840s. Butterfield also experimented very briefly with the French artist Henri Gerente, who had restored the glass at the Sainte-Chapelle and designed windows at Ely Cathedral, with Ward and Nixon; and at the end of the decade with the new firm of Clayton and Bell, and with Frederick Preedy, much less known, who also had a small architectural practice.

In the 1860s there was a sharp turn away from these highly reputable Puginist designers. O'Connor's sight had failed and Butterfield made only brief use of his son Arthur; Clayton and Bell were not taken up in spite of their rapidly growing reputation; Wailes was given very much less work; and Hardman, who had quarrelled with Butterfield, almost none. The two outstanding progressive firms, James Powell and William Morris, were scarcely employed by Butterfield, nor were the best makers of a more High Victorian taste, such as Lavers and Barraud or Heaton and Butler. The last firm, it is true, was not infrequently employed by Butterfield from the 1870s. But the only maker whom Butterfield consistently supported from 1860 onwards was

Alexander Gibbs. In 1860 he was not well known, and although some of the glass he produced for Butterfield has real merit, at no time do Gibbs' windows rise to the quality of the best work of his rivals.

In spite of this later reliance on an essentially mediocre artist, worthwhile glass can be found scattered over a wide period of Butterfield's activity. From the first phase only two minor windows by Willement survive, although the glowing reds of their angels and vine patterning show his mastery as a glass designer.

O'Connor was less reliable than his master, and Butterfield thought his first work for him at Dorchester 'very bad'.[2] It is not clear which glass this was, although another letter shows that Butterfield was more concerned to make sure that the old glass was put back into the east window: 'While people are on all hands putting new stained glass into churches it is hard to find them grudge the restoration of some glass which is far superior to present designs.'[3] Even later at Sheen O'Connor and his son were, according to Beresford-Hope, 'very bumptious . . . and Butterfield has to be down upon them continually'.[4] The Sheen glass is undistinguished grisaille, much less successful than the clerestory glass at All Saints', also by O'Connor, where the cold grey wheel patterns are vigorously leaded, and speckled with violet and red.

Most of O'Connor's remaining windows are figure designs, and they include the rich set at Wavendon, dark blue and red, with purple and gold and green. More often, however, Butterfield wished to avoid such a darkening of the church. In the Crucifixion window of 1847 at Kinwarton the rich red, purple-blue and burnt gold of the figures and tall canopies stand against a sad grey ground. This is a very moving and beautiful design, outstanding for its date. The figures are wooden, and clearly did not satisfy Butterfield, who got Dyce to draw cartoons based on designs by Taddeo Gaddi and Perugino for the windows at Christ Church Hoxton. These windows have gone, but the self-consciously primitive south-east window of 1857 at All Saints' does not suggest that pre-Raphaelitizing influences helped O'Connor, even if Butterfield was pleased by the change.[5] His son Arthur continued to develop the same type of design, using figures taken from Perugino against a grey ground of Powell's glass in his aisle windows at Stoke Newington. It is unfortunate that this controversial window has also been destroyed.

The same difficulty makes it impossible to comment on Clayton and Bell's work for Butterfield, or Ward and Nixon's or Gerente's, for no windows survive in any case. With Gerente's glass at All Saints', this was because Butterfield disliked its 'cabbage green' and garish yellow tints himself, and later replaced it with glass by Gibbs.[6] Wailes' important windows have also suffered badly. From the 1850s, there is nothing significant except at Hursley, and even there the glass had been put in with the assistance of Dyce, Copley Fielding and William Richmond before Keble secured Butterfield's help. He found that the background colours of the windows varied from 'most agreeable and grey and silvery' to a dingy chocolate, and some of the colours were already disintegrating with exposure to the weather. As to the east window, he was not satisfied 'until the third essay had been made; two, which were finished, and placed, were removed to make way for it. It is but justice to Mr Wailes . . . to say that he submitted to his judgement with perfect good temper.'[7] At Balliol, where Wailes' east window has been replaced, there was the same difficulty of matching. Butterfield wanted a design which harmonized with the older Flemish glass, but at the same time wished to keep up 'the banded character of the walls . . . We must have the best window which has yet been done'. He proposed to superintend 'every stage of the work', going with him to inspect and copy old examples in various places, planning the design himself, and then inspecting Wailes drawing to 'correct it carefully and harmonise the colouring'. He also proposed, 'instead of following the usual plan of putting up the whole window at once, to put up a part at a time and judge of it before proceeding'.[8] Perhaps it was his too easy willingness to accept correction which explains the lack of a distinctive quality in his glass for Butterfield. The Ampfield windows are acceptable, but like the Tamworth window, and the fine Adam and Eve west window at St Cross, they are hardly distinguishable from Gibbs' work. Another window at Weston upon Trent might be taken for Hardman's. Unlike O'Connor or Hardman, Wailes seemed to have little artistic personality.

With Hardman, as their correspondence shows, Butterfield was able at first to establish a good working relationship. Altogether Butterfield gave him some fifty commissions. He visited him frequently in Birmingham to see the progress of the works; in 1860, for example, more than five times during the year. The two men appear to have become friends, for beside business they discussed politics, plans for the Birmingham Oratory ('Italian by Viollet le Duc'), and after Pugin's death the plans for a testimonial to him. Pugin himself designed the windows at Alfington, Grazeley, and two at Ottery, and he may have had a hand in others, for these four designs are very like the remainder, and Butterfield was no less willing to comment: 'I hope that the figure of our Lord is a more full front figure than shewn in the sketch. I mentioned this as a point to Mr Pugin'. He was also frank enough to discuss minor devices for wooing patrons – 'Be particular that the trademan's window is directed to Mr Digby as they like it to appear independent' – or on another occasion, by producing a sketch 'more finished and less spotty than you are in the habit of making, as the persons who have to decide on it are not much versed in these things.' But the main purpose of both visits and correspondence was to correct the designs. While in Birmingham, according to a note on a letter, he would annotate the drawings: 'Several little changes are to be found marked on the cartoons which Mr B thinks it important should be adopted, such as the crockets and pinnacles are made bolder, small balls of colour introduced into the cusping . . .' and so on.[9]

The letters themselves are full of such detailed comment. Butterfield suggests models for the designs and offers to send a print of the Mock Homage by Fra Angelico. He sends another print for Langley: 'Lazarus might be a little more distinctly evident as from the grave. Fra Angelico gives him swathed like a mummy'. On a Sudbury design he remarks, 'I *do* most thoroughly like Fra Angelico's manly way of treating the circumcision without any false delicacy as I think. But as many people might object to this, I think you might arrange for the priest's hand to fall so as *a little* to cover the naked figure.' And the details are to follow the same authorities: 'I think that the drapery of our Lord's figure should be simpler, more like the simplicity of line of Giotto or Fra Angelico.'[10]

Apart from questions of propriety, the patrons' wishes affected the type of design chosen through expense. 'What can we do for £60, the sum I have got put at my disposal for the purpose. The design is full of figures which is of course an expense.' There were also frequently problems in fitting a subject into the window shape, and getting correct proportions between the various figures. 'I return your sketch for Yeldham. The angels and St John's emblem at the bottom are out of scale and too small. The panels for these angels should be as large and important as those of the elders above. The emblems of the evangelists are all somewhat small. These like the centre figure should be striking features. Our Lord's figure can go up higher and the canopies of the elders be got rid of and rearranged.' But the paramount problem was in 'keeping everything as clear and distinct and admitting as much light as possible'.[11]

In the early years, Hardman often satisfied Butterfield on this point. He thought the 'delicate treatment' of the Ottery windows, with their clear pale blue, pink and red, 'exceedingly beautiful'. The West Lavington windows are also successful, white grounds picked out with bright spots of red, blue, yellow and a little green and bronze. Gradually, however, differences of opinion emerged. Butterfield asked Hardman at Blickling to 'draw this window boldly. Using lines of some strength and avoiding soft shadows. Remember . . . the *principles* of *early* glass which are the only principles for *all time*.' At Langley he regarded the window tracery as 'almost Early English. I don't see the use of putting late ogee forms into the glass, nor canopies at all, especially flamboyant ones. Let us be geometrical and throw in all the grisaille we can. We *want light* and contrast.' Later he was irritated by Hardman's 'highly sentimental' treatment of the Last Judgment, with angels bestowing crowns rather than the apostles enthroned. 'There is abundant precedent for everything good or bad in all times', he comments somewhat inconsistently. More seriously, during 1855 and 1856 he found Hardman less willing to concede the changes he demanded. Over Sudbury window, for example, he emphasized the need for

a good deal of distinctiveness about it, crockets relieved on black ground, etc, and the legends under figures on black grounds. I still feel a great objection to this kind of canopy unless you can give it great strength by outline and black. Wiry lines on grisaille do not produce good effect in a large window and a large church. The fault I generally notice in your work is deficiency of effect for want of strength and force. The details when examined are beautiful but the lines of the features etc are not nearly bold and broad enough and then it is too even an effect throughout the window.

Over the next window for the church Butterfield realized that Hardman's designer John Powell was deliberately delaying ('he defends a treatment which I consider should be most carefully avoided') and the glass was put up without his approval of the cartoons. 'I laid such great stress on strength and force that I am quite unable to account for the appearance of the window . . . I must defer the third window and the Yealmpton design till I see whether you quite understand me in this one.'[12]

No doubt it would have been wiser for Butterfield to have accepted a parting with Hardman at this point. One can see at Langley, Great Yeldham and especially at Blickling, how Butterfield was struggling towards a new vividness in glass, a freshness in design, hampered by Hardman's instincts. But he accepted the Sudbury window when it had been altered, and continued to ask for others. Then in September 1859 Butterfield commissioned Hardman to design an Entombment window for Rugby School Chapel, which was to face another window which Hardman had made earlier, without Butterfield's supervision, in his normal rather Germanic late gothic manner, with delicate shadowed detail. Butterfield as usual wished the colour to be clear and 'the window to be bold in both lines and lead'. He rejected the first arrangement of the figures, suggesting an alternative more 'in accordance with the old painters' way'. Of the second sketch he thought 'the figure of our Lord wants composing. The head and arms might be stiffer and more persons engaged in depositing the body into the grave . . . And I think the women in the background rather belong to another subject.' On being pressed, he allowed the women, 'but as no good woman ever wailed with her hands in the air in the way one of these is doing, I shall be glad if you will quiet her attitude a little.'[13] The design was then approved, and at the end of 1860 it was arranged for Butterfield to see the completed window.

There was a pause, and then the storm broke. Hardman wrote to explain 'that if the design had been entrusted to us to carry out unfettered we are confident that we should have produced such a work as would have pleased you', and that the difficulty was Butterfield's anti-historicist view 'that all good of every period and character may be used to produce an effect wished'. Butterfield wrote in fury that 'the window in its present state is absolutely useless . . . It has been executed in direct contradiction to my wishes. I have always said that I must have early line relief and that stippling and shadowing of the ordinary late character was quite out of the question . . . And you have in return given me a window of the very *latest and worst* character.' Hardman tried to explain. 'The difficulty is this. That we are asked by you to carry out a design which *we* supplied in a manner which was not intended by the Artist who made it, and to produce a result which we should not approve of when accomplished . . . If this was a mere question of trade, and our artistic credit not concerned, it would be simple enough.' This defence simply irritated Butterfield further: 'You write as if I had not interfered in the first small design . . . You said nothing then about your Artist's feelings being injured. If you had done so, the matter would have come to an end . . . It has been a case of quiet resistance on your part throughout. Had it been an open and consistent resistance, I should have understood it all at once, and should not have wasted your or my time in the contest . . . That which I have asked for is nothing new or whimsical, but merely that the rules of the best treatment of glass should be observed.'[14]

Hardman tried again: 'No doubt you did, and we are always happy to do our best to carry out any of your wishes we can comply with *consistently* . . . As we stated in our last letter we cannot get rid of the responsibility of any windows we may execute and we cannot help feeling that you treat us very hardly having regard to our respective positions.' Butterfield, however, was adamant: 'I do not think you are improving your own case by this correspondence . . . It is a question of honour, which has nothing to do specially with stained glass. It is a question of ordinary fair dealing.' Nor was he impressed by Hardman's subsequent offer 'to *begin again*' from a fresh sketch, if the artist could be left 'free from continual restraint and changes during the progress of the work . . . We want to be trusted by you as we are trusted by all other architects to do our part – the artistic one'. To Butterfield there was 'no need for a fresh sketch. The original design has been approved and I only wish it carried out in the way I have all along described to you.'[15] And indeed, three years later, after more recrimination, the window was eventually put up in an acceptable if not ideal state. Its lines are clear and its colour glitters, but there is no spirit in the design. Standing in marked contrast to the unfettered Hardman window opposite, it is easy to see why the argument was so heated. The dispute is equally revealing of the growing demand in the nineteenth century among artists of all sorts for a recognizable personal manner, which was undermining the gothic ideal of architecture as the mother of the arts.

The point is emphasized by Butterfield's comparative willingness to compromise when he found an equally obstinate patron. At Clevedon Sir Arthur Elton first rejected his proposal for 'rows of figures of Apostles and Prophets . . . We are resolved to be rebellious on this point'. Subjects were then agreed, and Butterfield's first designs accepted. Later, however, Butterfield had second thoughts, and told Sir

Arthur that he intended 'to bring an altered design of window. I wrote . . . and regretted any *material change*.' Some days later 'Butterfield called and showed the altered design. Better in some respects than I feared, but on the whole objectionable. He went to the Church and Bessie and I followed him afterwards. She pleaded for the old design being entirely preserved except the undoubted improvement of the two figures Mary and Elizabeth being on the same level. Butterfield was very kind and amenable, and Bessie obtained all she wanted.' Nor was this the end to the interference of these strongminded patrons, for they insisted on inspecting the glass before it was put in the church. 'Bessie and I drove to Heaton Butler and Bayne. Dear Bessie did not approve of the pink tone of the window in memory of dear Minnie. She was *right*. Butler says it was Butterfield's doing but he believes he would give way: he had indicated as much. So Butler will cause the colouring and shading to be strengthened.'[16] In short, Butterfield was prepared to respect an independence of taste in his patrons which he found quite unacceptable in his artists.

One is left with little surprise that, after his dispute with Hardman, Butterfield turned to inferior artists. Three of his churches have glass by William Morris, but there is no evidence that he either suggested the artists or directly supervised the designs for these windows. This glass is, as might be expected, of very high quality. So, however, are a few windows of the late 1860s by Lavers and Barraud, in which Butterfield was more closely involved. The Blunsdon St Andrew south-east window is especially attractive, with its deep blue and green backgrounds, conventionalized trees, and fierce faced chain-mailed kneeling knights (354). The windows of the usually more

354   Blunsdon St Andrew,
stained glass by
Lavers and Barraud

distinguished firm of James Powell are also few, but unremarkable, and so are all but one of those which can be identified by Heaton, Butler and Bayne. The exception is the great west window at Berkhamsted, stiff but dramatic scenes in strong colours – inky blue, blackish green, madder and scarlet. It is unfortunate that there is no documentation for the middle south aisle window of 1891 at Heytesbury, which is in memory of Butterfield's patron and friend, Lord Heytesbury. It seems likely that Butterfield was consulted about it, and it has all the firmness of line which he demanded; but there are other qualities, such as the use of black with deep purple and scarlet, and the wonderful hierarchical dignity of the design, which strongly recall Heaton and Butler's finest windows of the 1860s.

Compared with any of these firms, neither Preedy nor Gibbs are of major reputation. In the case of Preedy, this was because he designed relatively few windows. His architecture suggests that he had a close sympathy for Butterfield's work, and his Alvechurch windows (XXIV) are particularly notable for their bold patchwork effect of reds, pinks and warm yellows, firmly leaded, with even the lettering in bands of alternate colour.

Gibbs' quality was always uneven. Too often his windows of the 1860s and 1870s give an impression of mechanically crude drawing, and their hot red and burnt sienna tones clash with the softer textures of their surroundings. His later glass tends to be paler, but this simply makes the drawing more prominent. On the other hand, he was not incapable of variation in his manner, as the attractive blue and purple glass in the lancets at Godmersham indicates, or the later gothic style of the great west Jesse window at All Saints', with lively small figures on clear blue and red grounds, standing among the trails of pale pinkish mauve and yellowish green foliage. There are also some admirable windows in his characteristic manner. At Heytesbury, for example, there is a whole series of Gibbs windows which, although on closer examination rather pale in tone, give an attractive impression of warm colour to the church without making it undesirably dark. There are also excellent, rather brighter windows in the south aisle at Brigham, glittering gold, red and green, with lively drawing and bold patternwork. Perhaps the most interesting Gibbs window, also of the 1860s, is at Dropmore, with very powerfully drawn figures, strong rough-bearded faces, and a daringly simplified ram and apple tree, all in very bright shades of red, pink, mauve, deep blue and copper yellow.[17]

Notes

1   Of Butterfield's clear glass it should be mentioned that early specifications prescribe Newcastle crown glass. Crown glass was blown and spun flat. In the 1850s this gives way in secular work to sheer glass, the polished blown cylinder glass invented in 1838 and popularized by its use in the Crystal Palace, 'Cathedral rolled glass' was used for later church work.

A valuable general discussion of Victorian stained glass is the series by T. F. Bumpus, 'Stained Glass in England since the Gothic Revival', *A*, (62) 1899, p. 202, to (66) 1901, p. 361, referred to below as TFB.

The following makers executed glass for Butterfield:

THOMAS WILLEMENT

Highbury Chapel, S, 1843 (chest)

Coalpit Heath, E (*Bristol Mirror*, 9 October 1845)

St Augustine's Canterbury, 1845–9, not extant ('Works Executed in Stained Glass by Thomas Willement', British Museum Add MSS. 52143)

MICHAEL AND ARTHUR O'CONNOR

Dorchester Abbey, 1847–8 (correspondence, Oxford Architectural and Historical Society)

Kinwarton, E (*B*, (5) 1847, p. 605)

Horfield, not extant (*E*, (7) 1847, p. 37)

London, Christ Church Hoxton, not extant (*E*, (9) 1849, pp. 378 and 399).

Ashwell, E, 1851 (*BE*)

Ottery St Mary, two Lady Chapel S (*E*, (13) 1852, pp. 84–5)

London, All Saints' Margaret Street, clerestory 1853, SE 1857 (TFB)

Baldersby, E (*B*, (15) 1857, p. 613)

London, Christ Church Endell Street, not extant (*B*, (17) 1859, p. 396)

Great Bookham, SE (*E*, (20) 1859, p. 53)

Caistor, E. and (not extant) W, 1860–3 (AAS, (VII) 1863–4, pp. ix, lxxxv)

London, St Matthias Stoke Newington, aisles (*E*, (22) 1861, pp. 215–6 and 312–3)

Pinchbeck, E, 1855 (signed) and W, 1861 (*BE*)

Winchester College chapel SW, 1862, not extant (tower restoration accounts)

JOHN HARDMAN

Ottery St Mary, N transept E, clerestory, E, etc 1849–57 (correspondence, Hardman Collection)

Grazeley, E, 1850 (*ibid.*)

Clehonger, E, 1850 (*ibid.*)

West Lavington, E and side, 1850–2 (*ibid.*)

Alfington, E, 1851–2 (*ibid.*)

Cumbrae College, E and S, 1851–4 (*ibid.*)

London, St Andrew Wells Street, 1852, not extant (*ibid.*)

Osnaburgh Street convent, 1852–3, not extant (*ibid.*)

Dorchester Abbey, SE, 1853–4 (*ibid.*)

Australia, Sydney, Alexandria North, 1853 (*ibid.*)

Marlston, E, 1853–4 (*ibid.*)

Langley, set, only west extant, 1854–5 (*ibid.*)

Great Yeldham, E, 1854–61 (*ibid.*)

Sudbury St Peter, E and W, 1854–60 (*ibid.*)

Limber Magna, 1854–5, not extant (*ibid.*)

Blickling, E, 1854–5 (*ibid.*)

London, St Mary Magdalen Munster Square, 1857 (*ibid.*)

Yealmpton, E, 1857–9 (*ibid.*)

Rugby School Chapel, SW, 1859–64 (*ibid.*)

Barley, *E* (*B*, (30) 1872, p. 551)

Hitchin Holy Saviour, N aisle, 1880 (chest)

WILLIAM WAILES

Chirton, E, 1850 (*BE*)

Cumbrae College, oratory (*B*, (9) 1851, p. 533)

Fredericton Cathedral, E. 1852 (Clarke, *Anglican Cathedrals Outside the British Isles* p. 57)

London, St Matthias Stoke Newington, E, not extant (*E*, (14) 1853, p. 269)

Hathersage, not extant (*E*, (15) 1854, p. 359)

Lincoln, St Anne's Bedehouse chapel, only W tracery extant (*B*, (12) 1854, p. 549)

London, St John Drury Lane, not extant (*E*, (17) 1856, p. 428)

Ampfield, E and W, 1857 (Notebook 13) and Keble Memorial, 1866 (J. T. Coleridge, *Memoir of John Keble*, London 1869, p. 274)

Baldersby, W (*B*, (15) 1857, p. 613)

Balliol College Chapel, 1858, not extant (correspondence, college archives)

Hursley, E and some others, c 1858 (Notebook 18; Coleridge, *Keble*, pp. 333–5)

United States, Baltimore St Luke, E, 1859–65 (accnts)

Limber Magna, E, 1859 (accnts)

Winchester St Cross, W, chancel (not extant) and S transept (*B*, (23) 1865, p. 764)

Tamworth, E (*ILN*, (58) 1871, p. 179; TFB gives Gibbs)

Weston upon Trent, SE (*B*, (30) 1872, p. 472)

HENRI GERENTE

London, All Saints' Margaret Street, aisles and W, 1849–53, not extant (*Architectural History*, (8) 1965, pp. 75, 79–80)

WARD AND NIXON

London, St Paul Shadwell, not extant (*E*, (8) 1848, p. 322)

CLAYTON AND BELL

London, Battersea College chapel, not extant (*E*, (19) 1858, p. 341)

FREDERICK PREEDY

Bamford, E, 1860 (chest, 'superintended' by Butterfield)
Alvechurch, south aisle (*BN*, (7) 1861, p. 842)
Baldersby, aisles and clerestory (*BE*)
London, St Michael Paternoster Royal, not extant (*E*, (28) 1867, p. 315)

JAMES POWELL

London, St Michael Paternoster Royal, not extant (*E*, (28) 1867, p. 315)
Great Berkhamsted, aisle, 1869–70 (chest)

WILLIAM MORRIS

London, Christ Church Albany Street, aisle, 1864 (Mr A. C. Sewter kindly informed me
of the correct date)
Dalton, W 1868–9, others probably contemporary (*ibid.*)
Tamworth, NE (*ILN*, (66) 1875, p. 191; stonework designed by Butterfield)

LAVERS AND BARRAUD

London, St John Hammersmith, E, 1859, not extant (accnts, TFB)
Bromham, chancel, 1868–9 (*B*, (27) 1869, pp. 431–2)
Blunsdon St Andrew, E and SE, 1868 (*B*, (26) 1868, p. 120)

HEATON, BUTLER AND BAYNE

Great Berkhamsted, W, 1867–70 (chest)
Clevedon St John, E, S transept E, aisles and W, 1877–9 (Elton diaries)
Enfield St Mary Magdalene, E, 1883 (accnts)
Caterham Guards chapel, 1885–7 (accnts)
Harrow Weald, N aisle, 1889–92 (accnts)

ALEXANDER GIBBS

Newbury St John, c 1860, not extant (TFB)
Latton, chancel, 1860–1 (*B*, (19) 1861, p. 688; accnts)
London, St John Hammersmith, aisles, 1863–73 (TFB)
Brigham, S aisle (*B*, (23) 1865, p. 753; accnts)
Winchester St Cross, N transept (*B*, (23 1865, p. 764)
Wokingham St Sebastian, W, c 1864 (*BE*)
Godmersham chancel (*CB*, October 1865)
Milton Ernest (*B*, (23) 1865, p. 929)
Dropmore, E, c 1866 (*BE*)
Fulham Palace chapel, c 1867 (TFB)
Beech Hill, c 1867 (*BE*)
Heytesbury, E, chancel side, transepts and W, 1867 (Heytesbury Collection)
Great Waldingfield, E 1869, W 1877 (*BE*)

London, All Saints' Margaret Street, S aisle c 1869, W 1877 (TFB)

London, St Alban Holborn, W, 1870, not extant (TFB)

London, St Matthias Stoke Newington, W, c 1870, not extant (TFB)

United States, Baltimore St Luke, N transept and aisles, c 1870 (Phoebe Stanton, *The Gothic Revival and American Architecture*, p. 301)

Weston upon Trent, E (*B*, (30) 1872, p. 472)

Alvechurch, E, 1873 (*BE*)

Cheddar (*B*, (31) 1873, p. 413)

Rugby School chapel, S transept (*Meteor*, 30 October 1873)

United States, Emmorton St Mary, Maryland, series of 15, c 1873 (accnts: Stanton, *op. cit.*, pp. 289, 292)

Babbacombe, chancel, 1874 (TFB)

Keble College chapel (*B*, (34) 1876, p. 495)

Knook ('I am very glad to hear that you all so much like the stained glass. I liked it very much myself. I have no doubt that Knook will make a remarkably pretty interior': Butterfield to Lord Heytesbury, 7 March 1876, Heytesbury Collection)

Winchester College chapel, 1877, not extant (Walford Memorial accounts, college archives)

Tottenham, 1876 (TFB)

London, St Augustine's Queen's Gate, chancel 1876, clerestory and W 1880–6, mostly destroyed (TFB)

Winterborne Monkton, E (*BN*, (35) 1878, p. 253)

Christleton, W (*ILN*, (71) 1877, p. 539)

West Deeping, chancel, c 1878 (*BE*)

Ottery St Mary, S transept (*B*, (36) 1878, p. 1051)

London, St Clement City Road, 1879, not extant (accnts)

Dublin, St Columba's College chapel, W, 1880 (accnts; TFB)

Chipping Barnet, E, 1880–2 (accnts, TFB)

Ascot Priory, side, c 1885 (*BE*)

Perth Cathedral, c 1890 (TFB)

Tadlow, 1861–6 (chest), Sellindge, SE, 1863 (accnts), Lyminge, E, 1864 (accnts) and Leslie Kirk on the Green, 1890 (accnts) are very likely by Gibbs, and deserve mention. Tamworth, E (TFB) and Enfield (TFB) are misattributions.

2   Butterfield to John Hardman, 1 September 1843, Hardman Collection.

3   Butterfield to J. L. Patterson, 29 April 1847, Oxford Architectural and Historical Society.

4   A. J. B. Hope to Henry Tritton, 19 April 1852, Tritton Collection.

5   Bumpus, *London Churches*, 2, p. 253.

6   Law, *op. cit.*, p. 164; *BN*, (5) 1859, p. 487.

7   Notebook 18; Coleridge, *Keble*, pp. 333–5.

8   Butterfield to the Master, 19 March and 20 December 1858, Balliol College archives.

9   Butterfield to Hardman, 19 January and 25 September 1852, (Grazeley) n.d. 1850, 25 February 1850, 8 March 1856 and 7 October 1857, Hardman Collection.

10 *Ibid.*, (Ottery) 19 January 1852, 1 February 1855, 27 March 1856 and 28 April 1854.

11   *Ibid.*, 25 September 1852, 25 March 1854 and September 1849.

12   *Ibid.*, 19 January 1852, 15 November 1854, 28 February, 27 and 30 July 1855, (Sudbury) 6 July 1855, 31 August and 5 December 1856.

13   *Ibid.*, 30 September 1859, 22 February 1860, 17 December 1859, 7 January and 1 February 1860.

14   *Ibid.*, 26 January and 25 February 1861, and Hardman to anon., December 1860, and to Butterfield, 19 February 1861.

15   *Ibid.*, February and April 1861, and Butterfield to Hardman, 2 and 30 April 1861.

16   Diaries, 25 May, 19 and 27 July and 12 November 1878.

17   There are various detailed glass designs in the Starey Collection, some in colour and all probably late in date, but it is not clear whether they represent Butterfield's proposals to a glass maker or *vice versa*.

Stone furniture

Stone furniture requires no more than a brief mention here. Butterfield designed some eighty fonts, which have been discussed earlier. The most important of his dozen stone pulpits have also been mentioned. The earliest, such as Coalpit Heath (204), Canterbury Cathedral[1] and Huddersfield, are of plain stone with traceried panels. Huddersfield has thick colonnettes and a ribbed trumpet stem. The remaining pulpits are polychromatic: solid and glittering at All Saints' (X), a pierced play of planes at Babbacombe (XVI) and more simply at St Augustine's Queen's Gate, paler and trumpet-stemmed at Tottenham. Christ Church Albany Street (355) is the last, a surprisingly fine classical design in pale alabaster, an octagon raised on marble columns, with its upper arcading filled by Byzantinesque tracery.[2] It provides an interesting suggestion of how Butterfield might have handled the pulpit for St Paul's Cathedral, a commission which he did not execute.[3]

A number of churches, chiefly of the 1840s and 1850s, have low stone walls at the entrance to the chancel, simply buttressed and arcaded (206). The design in *Instrumenta Ecclesiastica* is uncharacteristically elaborate. At Great Mongeham the wall, like its wrought iron gates, forms a square grid pattern. Yealmpton has a superb screen wall in grey and red marble. The most richly marbled example is at All Saints', with segment-headed arcading, pierced traceried panels and a fine fossil grey coping inlaid with streaks of white.

The original plan for All Saints' had included a high stone screen, but this was 'waived to please the Bishop' in a compact between him and Beresford-Hope. 'He, I suppose, then would have preferred none. I from aesthetic considerations would have preferred the high one; so the low screen and gates which gave the principle, were actually agreed to.'[4] The existing stone screen at Cumbrae (155) gives some indication of the type of screen which Butterfield had intended. It is derived from the

474

355 Christ Church Albany Street, pulpit

356 Dalton church, reredos; and glass by
William Morris (Gordon Barnes)

medieval stone screen at Great Bardfield in Essex, but has marble columns, a cross instead of a rood, and less decorative tracery. The tracery and cross are kept high up, so that the view of the altar from the nave is in no way interrupted. As the *Ecclesiologist* said of the screen originally filling the chancel arch at Perth Cathedral, 'It was the architect's desire to combine a complete separation of choir and nave, with a degree of lightness and *pervisibleness* (if we may coin a word), and in this he has most completely succeeded'.[5]

Later screens were more often of wood (278) or metal (201), and low stone walls became less common as Butterfield began to draw nave and chancel into a single architectural space. High screen walls, as at Rugby and Dundela (52, 165), are treated as pierced architectural members rather than inserted fittings.

Reredoses are (356) also normally part of the architecture: simply an inlaid or arcaded wall surface. The detailing varies in different periods of Butterfield's work. The earlier decoration normally consists of flat tile patterns, in self-contained rectangles and circles. Gradually more relief is introduced. The central panel usually contained a cross, and this is raised; circles of coloured marble are slightly sunk. Sometimes in the 1860s the cross is given emphasis by a delicately hooded outline, which rises above the sill of the east window. The patterning becomes centrifugal, twisting tendrils inlaid in mastic. Later reredoses tend to be thicker in detail, with a raised gabled central portion, sometimes with lumpish pyramid-topped buttresses, as at Enfield. But a prominent piece such as this, or the sculptured reredos at St Mary's Warwick, very rarely occurs before the last churches, and even then is exceptional.[6] The one case is which Butterfield treated a reredos as an independent piece of rich stone furniture rather than an elaboration of the east wall itself was at Perth Cathedral, where a grand grey and grey-blue reredos buttressed in grey-pink and inlaid with tiles was placed against the white east wall in 1882. It was removed in 1910, and now stands in a vestry.[7]

Notes

1   *E*, (8) 1847, p. 57.
2   Made by Earp, 1882–5 (accnts).
3   *E*, (19) 1858, p. 320.
4   A. J. B. Hope to William Dyce, 22 November 1851, Aberdeen Art Gallery.
5   (12) 1851, p. 26. Other screens which have disappeared were in Merton and Balliol College Chapels.
6   The reredos at West Lavington dates from 1882 (accnts).
7   Drawings, Victoria & Albert Museum.

Wooden furniture

The first quality to emphasize in Butterfield's wooden furniture is its diversity –
diversity of type, style, and even material. We can perhaps best begin by indicating
something of the diversity of type. Imagine, for example, that we are approaching a
church designed by Butterfield. At the entrance to the churchyard we might be confronted by a gate, sturdily braced like that illustrated in *Instrumenta Ecclesiastica*, its
boarding punched with quatrefoils, surmounted by a row of spikes. Other designs
survive for gates for Waresley church, with a criss-cross 'English oak fence', and also
for a private house in Whiteknights Park, Reading.[1] Most such gates have of course
perished in the weather, but there is an attractive double gate at Bromham (357)
which is probably Butterfield's Alternatively, there might be a wooden lych gate,
although these are almost as rare as gates. There is a very early example of 1845 at
Jedburgh,[2] with thin curved braces, but with a straight roof and corner posts which
distinguish it from the design in *Instrumenta Ecclesiastica*. The hipped gate at Ashwell
must be a little later.

Within the churchyard there may have once been wooden grave crosses, but these
have rarely survived the years. The porch is then approached, and although this is
part of the architectural structure rather than furniture, a wooden porch will be
designed in very much the same constructional architectural spirit as the lych gate.
Very likely it will protect a good oak door by Butterfield, perhaps traceried and
panelled like that at Chirton. Inside, especially in churches of the 1860s and afterwards, there may be a box-like panelled internal porch to preserve the warmth.
Close to the door is an almsbox, possibly following the *Instrumenta Ecclesiastica* design,
square on a slender column, strapped with iron. Wood and iron are again combined
in Butterfield's church chest designs; there is an admirable chest at Waresley. Another
combination can be seen in panelled and traceried organ cases (358) with rows of
painted pipes, like that at Kinwarton. There are equally striking contrasts in treatment between the spare structuralism of, for example, the bier design in *Instrumenta
Ecclesiastica*, a spare skeleton of wooden ribs, and the unnecessary solidity of some
other furniture, which seems to aspire to the qualities of masonry rather than woodwork. The pews, for example, may be buttressed and battlemented. Or there may be
a tall, crocketed font cover like that at Wavendon, wonderfully solid, with ample
lucarnes and a burst of foliage at its apex, suspended on marvellously elaborate ironwork balances (231). At Baldersby the architectural parallel seems deliberate, for
the font cover is steep and sheer like the church spire (234).[3] Still more perplexing is
the wooden clock on the wall above it, gabled, and picked out with dials, decorative
circles and pseudo-structural lines on a dark ground which at first sight suggest
inlaid work in two coloured woods.[4]

357 Bromham, churchyard gate

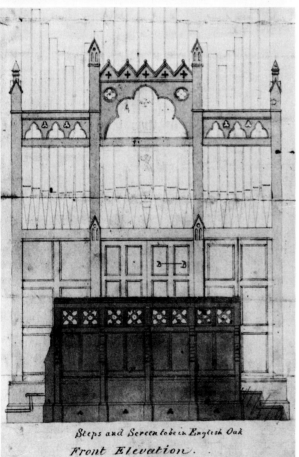

358 Winchester St Cross, design for organ case (R.I.B.A.)

Steps and Screen to be in English Oak

Front Elevation.

359 Baverstock church, interior and screen   **360** Avington church, altar rails

It is probably this architectural treatment of woodwork which an unsympathetic obituarist had in mind when he claimed that Butterfield 'seems never to have grasped the intrinsic differences between wood and stone'.[5] Yet not only is such a generalization impossible when the varied treatment of different furniture types is considered, but equally when a single type is traced through Butterfield's whole career. The development is various. With wooden moveable lecterns, for example, which are designed as bookrests on a single stem, the style parallels his architecture, beginning with the solid early carpentry of Hellidon or the *Instrumenta Ecclesiastica* designs, square and boldly tenoned, becoming attenuated and highly chamfered in the 1860s, and returning to a renewed simplicity in late examples such as that, matching the screen, at Baverstock (359, 365). Yet with screens the development is very different, for the earliest phase is not at all solid. There is a delightfully elegant chancel screen of 1847 at Kinwarton, with a row of pierced panels under a horizontal crenellated beam, and a foliated cross rising above on a crocketed ogee arch (173). There are also successful side screens at Dorchester and Ashwell, with thin traceried arches between buttressing upright posts. The Godmersham screen (109) of 1865 is by comparison very bare, but still slender, while the Dropmore screen (110) is richly cusped, but with more massive uprights. The last chancels screens of the 1880s, however, at Foxham (278), Baverstock (359), and Kingsbury, are all thoroughly solid both in construction and detail. While the Kinwarton screen had been inspired by late gothic examples, the model was now early gothic structural carpentry; and this change in style reflected a change in attitude, for while Butterfield had regarded the early screens simply as furniture, he had now incorporated them into his architecture.

Most furniture types are much less consistent in their stylistic development. Some indeed, are apparently quite arbitrary in their diversity within a single phase: altar rails, for example (360). Contrast the elegant traceried web of the Scottaw altar rails of 1858 with the astonishing Amesbury design of 1853 – post, braces and rail reduced to a single circle-punched piece (180, 187).[6] There are, however, two types which deserve special attention, because their stylistic development is relatively clear, and helps to reveal some of Butterfield's principles in designing woodwork. These are firstly pulpits, and secondly seating.

Butterfield designed some ninety pulpits. Of these seventy have stone bases rather than wooden stems. Nearly all the wholly wooden pulpits date from before the mid-1850s, and they are in fact the dominant type in the first period. Some have trumpet stems, but splayed octagonal feet are more common, and they are all excellent pieces of straightforward carpentry. Their chief variation is in the type of tracery in the pulpit panels, which grows bolder and more forceful. The tense tracery of the *Instrumenta Ecclesiastica* design is characteristic of the early 1850s, and there is an even simpler version at Langley, where the same converging lines are punched through the panel layers. The Langley pulpit also illustrates Butterfield's practical attitude to construction. It has the same thick corbels supporting its bookboards which at Dorchester (362) were criticized by the *Ecclesiologist* as 'not well designed constructionally', because they were glued rather than tenoned into place. Butterfield's reply was very revealing of his attitude to construction: corbels are ' "blocks" as a carpenter would call them . . . Anyone accustomed to general joiners' work is aware that these sort of things are used in it abundantly, and "glued" . . . You can put your hand under any piece of furniture, and find them . . . I have simply used, visibly, that sort of work which is concealed, more or less, in most joiners' work.'[7] He is not concerned with reviving methods which he regards as outdated; it is rather a case of downright common honesty. The ladder steps of the same pulpit are designed in just this spirit.

For their date the sound simplicity of Butterfield's pulpits of 1847 at Avington and Thanington (361) are an astonishing forecast of the much better known solid structural early gothic furniture designed for the Morris firm by Philip Webb. Some examples, such as the Milton furniture, had been seen by Webb, although there were other architects designing equally good work by the mid-1850s, so that Butterfield's influence on Webb's design need not have been direct. In 1847, however, before Street or William White had built their first churches, Butterfield was probably alone in designing furniture of this type, and he thus provides a link between the rather lighter simple furniture of Pugin and the earliest work of Webb and Morris. Butterfield's other woodwork of the late 1840s, such as altar rails and stalls, can share these qualities, but his pulpits are their best demonstration.

The later stone based pulpits are by comparison disappointing, although some of the first are strikingly simple. Amesbury (214), for example, with its thick columns, and Latton (363), where the pulpit is open, with no boarding between the columns, are remarkably solid and architectural, as if the woodwork was influenced by the masonry base. The panel tracery continues to be interesting. At Milton Ernest (391) and Neen Sollars the tracery is set under straight triangular gables; at Chaddesley Corbett (191) and Great Waldingfield there is strong cinquefoiled arcading punched with small traceried circles. Relatively simple examples occur as late as 1874–6 at Knook and West Deeping which are variations of the Latton and Waldingfield types.

More often, however, the designs were much richer. Open pulpits of the Latton type now have rich cusping in the openings. A large group of pulpits are in a neo-perpendicular style, with thin buttresses, square traceried openings and doubled-up bookboard corbels. The simpler examples of this type are unattractive, their detail thin and mechanical, normally in a light wood. They are more interesting when a darker wood gives a more substantial quality, and the woodwork is linked to the stone base by applied corbels, as at Harrow Weald. At St Mary Castlegate, York, the base is enlivened by miniature stone flying buttresses, and other pulpits have two colours of stone used in the base.

361 Thanington church, pulpit

362   Dorchester Abbey, pulpit

363   Latton church, pulpit

364   Christleton church, lectern
        design (R.I.B.A.)

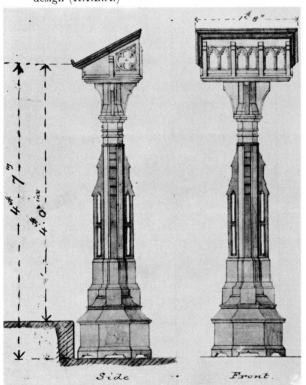

365 Hellidon church, stalls

The richest later type of pulpit has complex tracery of a late geometric style, with narrow circular moulding profiles, braced bookboard corbels at the angles, and radiating wooden corbels from the stone base. Very often walnut and oak are both used, so that dark and light woods are contrasted, and there is also sometimes foliage carving. Most such pulpits now seem somewhat indigestible, but they undoubtedly show Butterfield's willingness to handle woodwork with elaborate refinement, and the best, such as that at St Bees, have a real splendour.[8]

With seating – the commonest of all types of wooden furniture in Butterfield's church work – there was less room for such elaboration, except in the few cases where canopied stalls were required. At St Augustine's Canterbury there are attractive canopies in an early gothic style, while those in Fulham Palace chapel are thinner in detail; but more often the stalls merely have tall panelled backs, as at Keble. Consequently, although chancel stalls and nave seats follow the same development as pulpits, they always retain a certain simplicity, and the later examples are often as rewarding as the earliest.

The first phase is again remarkable for its simple structural carpentry. Hellidon is perhaps the most remarkable example of rustic cheapness, for its poppyhead stalls look as if they could have been rudely sawn into shape (365). Poppyheads are very common in the 1840s and 1850s, more often in stalls than seats, although the nave at Coalpit Heath is filled by a charmingly simple set of poppyhead bench ends. They are not often so rudimentary, for most are either carved with foliage or shaped to a sharp edge. Similarly, the bold cross-strutted stall fronts at Avington (172) are exceptional; traceried fronts are more common, although the knobbly elaboration

366 Milton church, stalls   **367** Langley church, seats

of the Yealmpton stalls is an extreme. A few of these stall fronts, such as Milton and Trumpington, are brilliantly simplified (366). The Milton design in particular is of the highest quality. There are also some first-rate nave seats of the 1850s, with clean chamfered square ends, such as those at Langley (367). Butterfield's rather surprising and undoubtedly charming low box pews at Trumpington (368) and Scottaw, with traceried sides and crenellated tops, also date from the 1850s.

Shortly before 1860 there is again a change in style, and new types of design are developed. The bolder form of stall front has punched foliate openings, normally set in square panelling. In the priest's stall this is sometimes effectively combined with a raised trellis pattern. A more delicate but equally simple treatment is plain rectilinear panelling, pierced to form an open grid in front. One of the earliest examples is at Stibbard, although here the backs are trefoil-punched. Many other stalls combine grid fronts with traceried backs, or traceried fronts with square panelled backs.

Nave seats sometimes employ similar grid fronts, and their backs may again be square, punched, or traceried. There is a fine set of traceried seats at Keble, but this is the least common type. Thus the bench end is commonly of more visual importance than the back. Although square bench ends do not disappear, the ends are more often cut away to curved, hunchback forms, sometimes pierced at the elbow and foot, nervously notched and chamfered (369). Another form, less common, consists of spare concave curves, reducing the end to its structural minimum. Both types can form fascinating, tense silhouettes.

In spite of their gothic chamfers and quatrefoils there is an expressive structural economy in seats like those at Flitwick (185). Nor is this 'functionalism' merely super-

368 Trumpington church, pews

369 Barley church, seats

ficial. Butterfield's pamphlet on the design of *Church Seats and Kneeling Boards* (370), first published as an article in the *Church Builder* of July 1885, shows a section across a seat, with the figure of a man kneeling on a kneeling board, with his hat on the floor in front of him ('in full view of the person to whom it belongs, and entirely free of the possibility of its being kicked by the person to whom it does not belong'). He had argued for more than thirty years for kneeling boards of the type used in Germany and Italy, rather than the traditional English hassock. 'The hassock and carpet are the rich man's tradition, and they usually mean appropriation. A hassock is a stumbling-block, even to the youngest and most agile, in entering any seat, and it permanently occupies a large piece of floor, to the great hindrance of standing with ease and comfort. It is always in different stages of decay, raggedness, and nastiness, and in town Churches at least, it harbours vermin. It can never be cleaned. The poor man, as may be seen in any Church where some unusual effort has not been made, is not provided with this article.' The ideal seat should therefore be equipped with a fixed kneeling board to raise the knee five inches from the ground. The arms should rest on the back of the seat in front which should rise no more than 14 inches above the seat, or the arms of the kneeler would be forced upwards. A low back also supported the spine when sitting, while allowing the shoulders 'liberty to move freely above it. . . . There is no need for a sloping back when the shoulders are thus free. Overmuch effort, as it seems to me, has been often made to produce a too easy and lounging seat for Church use.'

370   Church seats (*Church Builder*, 1885)

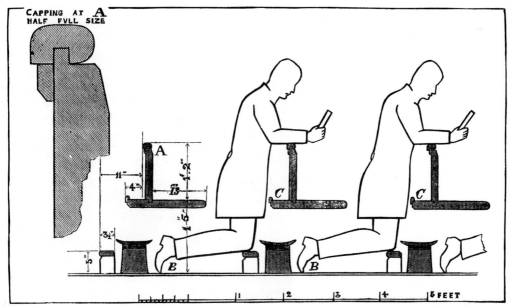

There were varying opinions on the comfort of Butterfield's pews. The pamphlet included testimonies from clergy to the effect that '*You* have made my people kneel'. Others were more doubtful. Butterfield had to write to an anxious Lord Heytesbury, 'I assure you they are comfortable.'[9] The architect H. Roumieu Gough described them frankly as 'instruments of torture'.[10] He can hardly have represented 'the vast majority' which he claimed, for Butterfield's pamphlet was popular enough to be reprinted, and there seems to have been little desire anywhere to replace his pews, although it is true that hassocks are used in most of them. But like any standard anthropomorphic shape, his design was intolerant of variations in height. There was justice on both sides when a lady guest of Lord Coleridge took Butterfield to task for the extreme discomfort of his seats – 'But are you not a little undersized?' was the caustic answer.[11]

Apart from fixed benches Butterfield also designed moveable seats, including a covered settle for use as a sedilia, very similar to the type of which William Morris was so fond. This design appears in *Instrumenta Ecclesiastica*, together with various benches, desks and stalls, and also an impressively simple pair of wooden chairs with upright backs. One version is plain, and the other traceried. A variant of the traceried form occurs in a delightful set of chairs in Wavendon church (371). Very likely Butterfield also designed the excellent rush-seated chairs, with tall, slightly curved ladder backs, which he provided for St Peter's Sudbury in 1857 (372). The seats chosen for All Saints' were again of a similar type, but with shorter backs.

In secular work there was also a demand for simple wooden furniture, to which

371   Wavendon church, chair

372 Sudbury St Peter, restored interior with chairs (*Illustrated London News*, 1857)

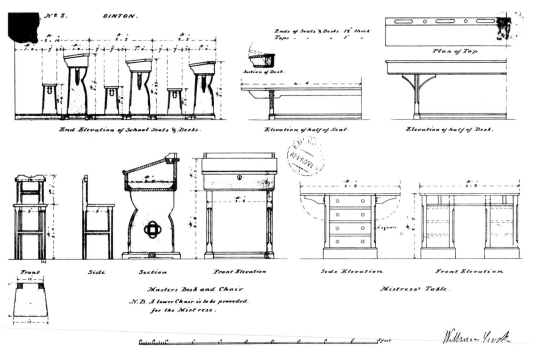

373 Dinton school, furniture designs (Wiltshire Record Office)

374 Keble College, library table design (R.I.B.A.)

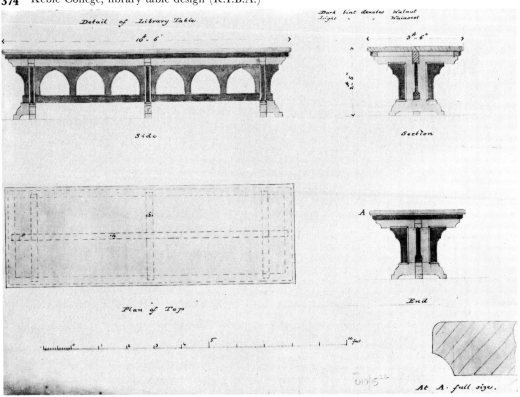

Butterfield readily responded. His school plans (373) often include robust desks and work tables like those he illustrated in *Instrumenta Ecclesiastica*. Built-in furniture was also required – cupboards, dressers and sometimes bookcases. Fittings of this type were often similar to his church furniture of the same period: the great cross-strutted servery at St Augustine's Canterbury, for example, with its quatrefoil perforations and neat iron hinges; or the rich gothic library fittings, including a grandly braced long table at Keble (374).

But the most important secular furniture was that designed for Milton Ernest Hall. There was a whole range of fittings here, including battlemented doorcases, tall bookcases with neat set-backs, and even some wooden garden furniture and a hipped, weatherboarded boathouse, although this, like the bowling green shelter which Butterfield designed for Lord Nelson at Trafalgar House in a similar style, has unfortunately disappeared.[12] Fortunately an early photograph survives (375), showing the start of a somewhat sombre rowing party.[13]

The furniture has survived, although it is now scattered among Benjamin Starey's descendants. It is thought to have been made by a local craftsman in Bedford. The severest designs are the dining room chairs, stiff and formal, with a slight curve to the

375 Milton Ernest Hall, boathouse (Colonel Hogg)

back and back legs. The sitting room furniture does not seem to have been designed by Butterfield, although it is interesting to notice that photographs show a round-seated Sussex chair of the type produced by William Morris.[14] There is, however, an astonishing triple settee which Butterfield apparently later left to the Stareys, with thin curving arms, turned legs and elegant stretchers, painted with small panels of flowers and delightful zebraesque patterns of dark brown and pale creamy yellow.[15] The date of this settee is unknown, and it could be simply a decoration by Butterfield of a bought piece. Whatever the exact story, the result is an exceptionally striking and attractive example of Victorian painted furniture.

Much of the bedroom furniture at Milton Ernest was also painted, particularly in the children's rooms, white with stripes and cinquefoliate stars picked out in red. There are mirrors, beds and cane-seated chairs in this style, with knobbly turned legs. The effect is undoubtedly very gay. There was rather more serious furniture for the adult bedrooms (376), but still very attractive, the cane seated chairs especially slender in construction, and like the tables and mirrors made of soft coloured walnut, inlaid prettily with stars and other patterns in sycamore and ebony.

The Milton Ernest furniture probably dates from 1858, when the house was first

376 Bedroom furniture from Milton Ernest Hall (*Country Life*)

occupied. [16] Together with the Sudbury chairs, it is sufficient to establish Butterfield's reputation in this field. When three of his pieces were exhibited in 1953, Peter Floud wrote of Butterfield's work: 'The small amount of domestic furniture which he designed appears to have been far in advance of its time and to have anticipated some of the ideas later developed not only by Morris and Webb but also by Godwin.'[17]

Notes

1   R.I.B.A.

2   W. H. Teale, *Six Sermons Preached at the Consecration of St John the Evangelist Jedburgh*, Edinburgh 1845.

3   Other good tall covers are at Ashwell and Merton College. The most elaborate of all was at All Saints'.

4   R.I.B.A., similar clock design for St Augustine's Queen's Gate; accnts.

5   *R.I.B.A. Journal*, (VII) 1900, p. 246.

6   Other interesting plain designs are at Avington (1847), Feckenham (1853), Landford (1858), Lyneham (1863) and Winchester Hospital chapel (1868). Good examples with richer tracery are at Aston Cantlow (1850), Mapledurham (1863), Blunsdon St Andrew (1868), Milsted (1872) and Ault Hucknall (1887).

7   (15) 1854, pp. 146, 180-1.

8   Probably of the 1860s.

9   12 September 1865, Heytesbury Collection.

10   *BN*, (50) 1886, p. 87.

11   Stephen Coleridge, *Memories*, London 1913, p. 82.

12   Notebook 19; accnts, 1859.

13   Kindly shown me by Colonel and Mrs Willoughby L. Hogg.

14   *Ibid.*

15   *Ibid.*

16   There is no subsequent entry in Butterfield's accounts, which begin in 1859; but on the other hand Benjamin Starey's journal does not mention the furniture designs. The mirror design is sketched at the back of Butterfield's continental notebook.

17   Peter Floud et al., *Exhibition of Victorian and Edwardian Decorative Arts, Catalogue*, Victoria & Albert Museum, London 1952, p. 31.

Embroidery, wallpaper, books

Butterfield's interest in EMBROIDERY is evidenced by the fact that he saw through the press Mary Barber's *Some Drawings of Ancient Embroidery*, which he states in his preface was 'written at my suggestion'. It is a beautifully produced collection of lithograph drawings, chiefly of figures and floral details, published by Henry Sotheran in 1880. Butterfield had earlier illustrated three attractive embroidery designs in *Instrumenta*

377 Milton Ernest Hall, drawing room (Colonel Hogg)

378 Milton Ernest church, book covers

Ecclesiastica: a funeral pall, with crocketed gold circles on blue or purple; an altar frontal loosely powdered with flowers; and another with fleur-de-lys and dots set in a formal diagonal pattern. Unfortunately nothing executed in this fresh early style has come to light, and even where later designs are recorded, few examples remain.[1] The best is undoubtedly a green silk frontal given by the Duke of Newcastle to All Saints' in 1889 (XXV): an Agnus Dei in the centre on a pale maroon ground diapered white, and censing angels, stars and seraphim on either side in wonderfully subtle shades of gold, orange, chestnut, grey and pink. This must be one of the finest surviving frontals of its date, and once more demonstrates Butterfield's mastery of colour. The crimson frontal at Christ Church Albany Street is a simpler Agnus Dei design. Closer to Mary Barber's medieval examples are a splendid white frontal with seraphim, stars and thistles also at All Saints', a crimson frontal with fleur-de-lys and seraphim at Keble, and another white frontal at Sedgeberrow, where Mary Barber's husband was rector (161). It is more difficult to place the banner at Sedgeberrow, a distinctly more original design, with an eagle and formalized flowers on a red ground. However, a photograph of a room at Milton Ernest taken in about 1870 shows a firescreen embroidered with quite striking simplicity in a comparable style, so that they may indicate Butterfield's influence.

The same is true of the delightfully fresh climbing tendrils and flowers of the WALLPAPER (377) at Milton Ernest.[2] Although Butterfield probably did not design his own wallpapers, Warington Taylor, manager of the Morris firm, was impressed enough by his tastes to advise E. R. Robson that 'those beautiful papers of Butterfield's may be had of Arthur, Sackville Street. Wall papers for rooms I mean.'[3] Coleridge, on the other hand, was less happy with 'the worms' chosen for his London dining room by Butterfield in 1868.[4] Unfortunately the Senior Common Room at Keble, where one of his choices survives, was papered as late as 1884.[5]

It is scarcely easier to get a fair impression of the many designs for BOOK COVERS which occur in Butterfield's accounts. They include 'designs for various book covers' for Spottiswoode in 1861, among them possibly the bold formalized diamond-edged designs which have survived.[6] Certainly the handsome, if less remarkable, bound books which can be found in Butterfield's churches must be by the same hand (378).

Notes

1 Recorded designs are frontals for Keble College Chapel, 1870 (Notebook 11) and 1876 (made by Miss Brett; *Church Times*, 28 April 1876); Christ Church Albany Street, 1882 (made by Wantage sisters; *Parochial Report for 1882–3*, p. 5; discovered by Anthony Symondson and illustrated in *Country Life*, 1 June 1967, p. 1403), Caterham, c 1887 (large drawing, Starey Collection), Enfield, 1889 (accnts; drawing, Starey Collection;

not extant), All Saints, 1889 (accnts; drawing, Starey Collection; made by the East Grinstead sisters, *Church Congress Report*, 1890, pp. 91 and 364) and probably also St Mary Woolnoth, 1879 (payment to Miss Brett, Restoration Fund Accounts, Guildhall; not extant).

2 Kindly shown me by Colonel and Mrs Willoughby L. Hogg.

3 c 1865, Fitzwilliam Museum.

4 E. H. Coleridge, *op. cit.*, 2, p. 158.

5 Accnts.

6 Starey Collection.

Metalwork

It will be appropriate to conclude this brief survey of Butterfield's contribution of the applied arts with his metalwork, for this was the field in which he first made his reputation. He had, as we have seen earlier, introduced himself to the Cambridge Camden Society through his suggestion that they should take an interest in CHURCH PLATE, and in March 1843 he took the responsibility for selecting artists and superintending their work for the Society. Until 1850 he was personally responsible for almost all the plate produced under the scheme, and although other architects produced approved designs in the 1850s he remained in control until 1857, when he was succeeded by G. E. Street. Butterfield, however, kept his high reputation as a designer. His plate, which had been shown at the Great Exhibition of 1851, was again exhibited at the International Exhibition of 1862. John Keith and Son, official manufacturers to the Ecclesiological Society until 1867, were still producing plate in the 1860s 'under the inspiration which he originally received . . . from our friend Mr Butterfield.'[1] Throughout his life he continued to receive commissions for plate from patrons who did not support him as an architect.

The consequence is that the short list below of documented examples is a mere fraction of the 'prodigious output of plate in the mediaeval manner' by Keith and Butterfield which, in the opinion of Mrs Shirley Bury, took place from 1843 onwards.[2] Sufficient, however, has already been discovered to give a clear impression of Butterfield's standards. Like Pugin, who had begun a little earlier to accomplish the same transformation in Roman Catholic plate design which Butterfield achieved for the Anglicans, he modelled his style on the few medieval examples of English church plate which were known in the 1840s. Common sources are one reason for the striking similarities between some of their chalices, although Butterfield designed nothing like Pugin's late gothic filigree tabernacles. They also both suffered 'many trials and great difficulties, arising from the want of tools, the inexpertness of workmen, and the entire novelty of the kind of work', in securing adequate standards of execution.[3] Neither was entirely successful in overcoming these problems. Keith's plate normally seems undeservedly mechanical, thin, even very slightly cheap. He was eventually replaced by another maker, Barkentin, in 1867, because William Burges and other younger designers were demanding higher standards; and in the early 1870s Butterfield again transferred, to Hart, Son, Peard and Company, who executed all his later plate. Pugin had been similarly dissatisfied with his manufacturer, John Hardman of Birmingham. Butterfield, who commissioned a large number of windows from Hardman, must have seen Pugin's metalwork at his factory, and in 1851 he asked the firm to cut a seal in brass 'for the use of some religious ladies.' This was probably the only case in which Pugin designed metalwork for Butterfield. It is interesting that Butterfield wrote: 'It is very nice in design but struck me as deficient in finish and workmanship.'[4]

Nevertheless Butterfield's plate is consistently sound, and some of his earliest work (379), such as the set of 1844 at Jedburgh, is of impressively high quality. His designs always remained close to the standards which he set in *Instrumenta Ecclesiastica*. The plate is of wrought silver or silver-gilt, engraved, and often decorated with enamels and jewels. The chalices have a circular bowl, a foliated hexagonal foot, and a rather tall stem with an involved knop; perhaps a little too slender for convenience, but very attractively proportioned. Later examples, such as the jewelled chalice at Southwark or the plain chalices at Enfield, are still only slight variants of the designs published in the 1840s. The designs differ only in details: some chalices are encrusted

379 Kemerton church, chalice and flagon and Highnam church, chalice

380 All Saints' Margaret St, chalice of 1861 (Goldsmiths)

with jewels; others have elaborate embossed figure designs on the foot; sometimes the bowl and often the knop is pierced; or the bowl may flicker with wavy rays, a motif taken from early 17th century Roman Catholic Recusant chalices. One of the most interesting chalices (380), at All Saints', Margaret Street, has raised ribbing on its knop which is probably intentionally related to the font in the same church. Similarly, the rectilinear tracery of the Keble chalices can also be found in the chapel stalls.

Patens are much simpler, engraved with symbols and an inscription. Some alms dishes are similar but a little bolder, with the design perhaps picked out with blue enamelling. More commonly a figure design hammered in relief filled the bowl, taken from Fra Angelico or some similar source. Alms dishes could be of pewter or brass instead of precious metal. The flagons (379) are particularly attractive, full swelling shapes with wonderfully curvaceous handles and spouts. Sometimes the body is of glass, although mounted in the same silver or silver-gilt frame. Although they are less original than later flagons designed, for example, by Street, Butterfield's flagons exemplify the High Victorian sense of form.

The altar cross in *Instrumenta Ecclesiastica* with its diapered arms and symbols of the Evangelists might be thought more characteristic of Butterfield himself, but the altar candlesticks are also thick and swollen. The comment is typically functional, and yet aesthetic. 'In these, as in chalices, a knop is not to be dispensed with. They must also have a spreading bowl, and a pricket, or spike.' They could be ordered from Potter of South Molton Street.[5] Butterfield also designed classical jewelled candle-

381   *right* Kinwarton church, corona

382   *opposite left* Rugby parish church, candlestick

383   *opposite right* Dropmore church, candlestick

sticks for Christ Church Albany Street, and perhaps elsewhere. A number of churches where he worked have hanging coronae (381) of lights, although simpler than the designs published. More impressive are the tall standard lights, which vary from the massive embossed lion-based stem at Rugby to the delicate skeletal frame and crown at Dropmore (382, 383).

These are closely related to Butterfield's lecterns. The Brigham lectern (390) is comparable to the Dropmore standard.[6] The earliest lecterns, such as Kilndown, are much sturdier, with splendidly conventionalized eagle bookrests, thick ringed stems, conical bases and lion feet. Others have double bookrests instead of the eagle, while the especially fine lectern at Christ Church Albany Street (384) has flamboyant buttressing rather than lions at its base. For these early lecterns the maker was generally Potter. In general the later lecterns, made by Hart, were less massive. Perhaps the most attractive are those which combine thick stems with twisted tendrils, as at St Augustine Queen's Gate; and certainly the most astonishing is at St Patrick Hove, with a figure of the saint niched in the central stem between two slender Celtic round towers (385, 386).

There is much other brasswork in Butterfield's churches: ample flagons for fonts, oil lamps (387), and occasionally verger's or pastoral staffs. He also designed a few desks in brass in his last years, and he frequently incorporated brasswork in screens and rails. These, however, are rarely entirely of brass, and it will be best to consider them with Butterfield's ironwork.

At the time of his death 'an old crafts' architect' wrote to the *Building News* that

385 St Augustine Queen's Gate, lectern

386 St Patrick Hove, lectern

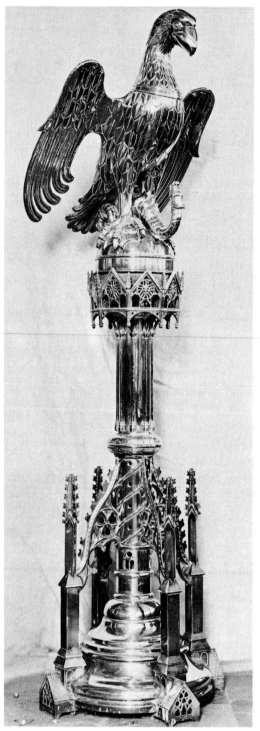

384 Christ Church Albany St, lectern
(Mary Farnell)

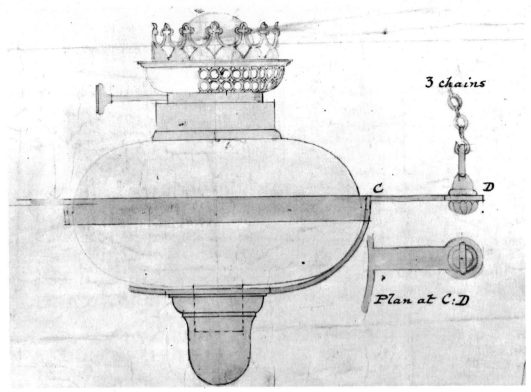

387 Copythorne Church, oil lamp (Starey Collection)

388 Chanter's House, Ottery St Mary, lantern
(Starey Collection)

389 Cubbington church, altar rails

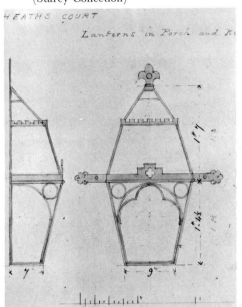

390 Brigham church, screen and lectern

391 Milton Ernest, chancel screen

Butterfield 'at one time engaged in practical smithery himself, and had the run of the workshops of a leading firm' in London.[7] Certainly the wrought ironwork of his earlier churches show a strong feeling for the material. Hinges are worth a special look at Chirton, for example, or St Augustine's Canterbury (167); later examples can also be excellent, but they tend to be more stiffly twisted, with hierarchic bands. The fresh charm of the first examples is perhaps best expressed by the delightful door handle and lock at Coalpit Heath (199). Other examples, like the iron corona at Kinwarton or the church brazier design in *Instrumenta Ecclesiastica*, were of robust, bold simplicity (15, 381, 388). Although no such church braziers are recorded, until recently there was an astonishing gothic grate in the refectory at Osnaburgh Street. At Dorchester the terse ladder-like pulpit steps have an appropriately spare daring rail, decorated only by a twist of foliage and a curled form like a bedspring (362). And if later designs are less inventive, the consistent quality remains: weathercocks, unmistakable bootscrapers, elegant curving gas light brackets (18), and so on.[8]

'Mr Butterfield's forte', however, as the *Ecclesiologist* observed of Perth Cathedral, was for screenwork.[9] Here his imagination never flagged. The earliest examples are relatively simple and open, ogee headed at Aston Cantlow (206) and Cumbrae (103), severely rectilinear at Great Mongeham, and thorn spiked in the Wavendon tower screen. Then at Cubbington in 1852 he filled the iron frame of the altar rails with feathery brass foliage (389) picking out the ironwork with red and black paint. The use of two metals also helps to distinguish supports from ornament. These rails, which were made by Skidmore of Coventry, led on to the much more successful combination of gilding, iron and brass in the splendid chancel gates at All Saints', this time carried out by Potter.[10] Butterfield had now formalized the foliage, and in the equally impressive side screens he first used a 'strap-like treatment of foliation', a feature of Butterfield's metalwork which was especially admired by Eastlake.[11] Similarly when Gerard Manley Hopkins, 'fagged with looking at pictures' at the Academy, looked into All Saints' 'to see if my old enthusiasm was a mistake', he felt 'more than before Butterfield's want of rhetoric and telling, almost to dullness, and even of enthusiasm and zest in his work – thought the wall mosaic rather tiresome for instance.' But even so the chancel side arches and 'the touching and passionate curves of the lilyings in the ironwork under the baptistery arch marked his genius to me as before'[12] (157, 235).

Several attractive screens of the 1860s are low and open, running right across the chancel arch and not merely gates in low walls as at All Saints'. St Alban's Holborn was the first, and very much in the manner of All Saints' (14). The best surviving brass screen of this type is at Brigham, much thinner, a straight run of bare hoops (390). The wrought iron screens are richer but looser; the modest example at Milton Ernest has low sides and higher gates, hinged on still higher posts which twist over

392 Wellington Barracks, design for fountain (R.I.B.A.)

backwards at the top (391). This variety of style continues into the 1870s, in both rails and screens. The Milsted altar rails, for example, use metal tracery in a wooden frame. And at the same time Butterfield began to use the twice-twisted leaf motif, the hallmark of his last metalwork designs, with increasing frequency.

The leaf, usually coloured and edged in gold, appears in most altar rails from the late 1870s, ranging from the simplest as at Ardleigh (198) to the splendid iron and brass rails in Rugby parish church (200). The astonishing high painted metalwork screens which Butterfield designed for St Bees (201) in 1886 and subsequently for St Augustine's Queen's Gate and elsewhere are as sinuously writhing as the rails. Still more fantastic was his proposal for a fountain at Wellington Barracks (392), with suspended gunmetal urns, tilted pitchers like cannons, and a grotesque wrought iron canopy with cannon balls at the top.[13] Altogether Butterfield designed more metal furniture in his last years than at any other time, showing an inventiveness that is often lacking in other work from the same years. It has an old man's hand, rather stiff and contrived despite the chosen forms. Bumpus called the last screens 'puerile';[14] and so they are in a sense, for Butterfield's imagination had started with metalwork, and here it was ending.

Notes

1   *E*, (25) 1864, p. 221.

2   Shirley Bury, *Copy or Creation*, catalogue of an exhibition at Goldsmiths' Hall, London 1967; referred to below as CC:

Kemerton, chalice and flagon, 1843 (CC)

Jedburgh, plate, 1844 (Teale, *Six Sermons*)

Kilndown, lectern (*E*, (3) 1844, p. 127)

London, Christ Church Albany Street, flagon, 1844 (CC), lectern (*E*, (9) 1849, p. 378) and candlesticks, 1884 (accnts; drawing, Starey Collection)

Bussage, chalice, 1845 (*BE*, *Gloucestershire*, 1, p. 141)

Oxford, Lincoln College, lectern, now at Waddington (*E*, (6) 1846, p. 38)

Kingsbury St Andrew, formerly Wells Street, lectern (*E*, (7) 1847, p. 79)

United States, Philadelphia St James the Less, altar plate, 1847 (Stanton, *The Gothic Revival and American Church Architecture*, ch. III)

Calcutta Cathedral, lectern (*E*, (8) 1848, p. 266)

Danby, altar plate (*E*, (8) 1848, p. 261)

Wick, altar plate, 1848 (*BE*, *Gloucestershire*, 2, p. 405)

Ogbourn St Andrew, plate, 1849; destroyed 1861 (Register of Baptisms, Wiltshire Record Office)

Highnam, chalice and almsdish, 1850 (CC)

Fredericton Cathedral, altar plate, almsdish and lectern, 1851 (Stanton, *op. cit.*, pp. 139–41)

Barnsley, chalice and flagon, 1854, and candlesticks (*BE*, *Gloucestershire*, 1, p. 97)

London, All Saints' Margaret Street, chalices, 1854 (CC) and 1861 (accnts, CC); lectern, c 1859 (drawing, Starey Collection)

London, St John Drury Lane, lectern, c 1856 (drawing, Starey Collection)

London, St Matthias Stoke Newington, flagon, 1857 (CC) and candelabra (Starey Collection)

Fellingham, pastoral staff, 1858 (accnts; not extant)

Oxford, Balliol College, candlesticks and altar plate, 1858–61 (*E*, (19) 1858, p. 260; accnts)

London, St John Hammersmith, standing candelabra, c 1859 (drawing, Starey Collection)

Newbury St John, standing candelabra, c 1860 (drawing, Starey Collection)

Alvechurch, lectern, 1861 (accnts)

London, St Alban Holborn, plate and candlesticks 1862 (accnts; like the All Saints' chalices, illustrated in J. B. Waring, *Masterpieces of Industrial Art and Sculpture at the International Exhibition*, London 1862, 1, p. 20 and 3, pl. 233.)

Portsea, Holy Trinity (demolished), candlesticks, 1862 (accnts)

Rangemore, plate, 1864–8 (accnts)

Tadlow, cross and standard lights, c 1865 (accnts; restoration accounts, chest)

Godmersham, candlesticks (*CB*, October 1865)

Winchester St Cross, lectern (*B*, (23) 1865, p. 764) and standing candelabra (Starey Collection)

Babbacombe, chalice 1866 (accnts), lectern, candlesticks and altar cross 1871 (drawings, Starey Collection)

Hove St Patrick, lectern, 1867 (drawing, Starey Collection)

Bishop of St Albans, pastoral staff, 1867 (drawing, Starey Collection)

Oxford, Keble College, two chalices and cruets, 1870; lectern and candlesticks, 1876 (*B*, (34) 1876, p. 402; lectern drawing, Starey Collection)

London, St Leonard Shoreditch, flagon, c 1870 (drawing, Starey Collection)

Rugby School chapel, candlesticks, c 1870 (drawing, Starey Collection)

Bishop of Cape Town, processional cross, c 1870 (drawing, Starey Collection)

Cowley St John, chalice, six candlesticks and six vases, 1871 (drawings, Starey Collection)

London, All Saints' Margaret Street, processional cross, 1872, and chalice, 1876 (drawings, Starey Collection)

London, St Barnabas Rotherhithe, chalice and flagon, c 1872 (drawing, Starey Collection)

London, St Augustine Queen's Gate, lectern, 1873 (drawing, Starey Collection)

Tottenham, candlesticks, 1875, and lectern, 1877 (drawings, Starey Collection)

Cork Cathedral, chalice (*BN*, (30) 1876, p. 185)

Portsmouth St Michael, chalice, 1876 (drawing, Starey Collection)

Bishop of Exeter, processional cross, 1877 (drawing, Starey Collection)

Clevedon St John, chalice and cruet, 1878 (Elton diaries)

Lancing College, chalice, 1878 (accnts; drawing, Starey Collection)

Rugby church, altar vase, 1878, and candlesticks, 1885 (accnts; drawings, Starey Collection)

Axbridge, St Michael's Home, lectern, 1879, and flagon, and candlesticks, 1889 (drawings, Starey Collection)

Qu'Appelle, chalice, c 1880 (drawing, Starey Collection)

Wantage St Mary, altar cross and standing candelabra, c 1880 (drawings, Starey Collection)

Enfield St Mary Magdalene, two chalices, cruets, candlesticks and vases, 1883–9 (accnts)

Waltham on the Wolds, altar cross, 1883 (accnts)

Edmonton St Mary Fore Street (demolished), plate, 1884 (accnts)

Ault Hucknall, two chalices, 1887 (accnts)

Biggleswade, altar cross, 1887 (accnts)

Lincoln Cathedral, two chalices, 1887 and 1889 (drawings, Starey Collection)

Stowlangtoft, chalice and flagon, 1888 (drawings, Starey Collection)

Zanzibar, St Andrew Kumgani, chalice, 1888 (drawing, Starey Collection)

Dover Castle church, candlesticks, vases and lectern, 1889–90 (accnts; drawings, Starey Collection)

London, Southwark Cathedral, chalice and flagon 'with help of Lady Ofrington's jewels', 1890 (accnts)

Bournemouth St Augustine, chalice, flagon, almsdish, candlesticks and altar vases, 1892 (drawings, Starey Collection)

Sudbury St Gregory, chalice, 1892 (drawing, Starey Collection)

Rev. H. T. Wood, chalice and flagon, 1892 (drawings, Starey Collection)

London, St Paul Rotherhithe, chalice, c 1893 (drawing, Starey Collection)

3 *Instrumenta Ecclesiastica*, pl. LV.
4 Butterfield to John Hardman, August and 29 November 1851, and A. W. N. Pugin to John Powell, August 1851, Hardman Collection.
5 Pl. LVII.
6 Neither is documented, but the Brigham screen is in the same style, and all probably date from 1865–6; also, compare the moveable metal desk design in *Instrumenta Ecclesiastica*.
7 (78) 1900, p. 332.
8 Perhaps one should add bells, in which Butterfield took a characteristic interest. At Anstey he rehung the peal with a chiming hammer invented by the Rev. H. B. Ellacombe, by which 'a whole peal of bells may be easily chimed by one person' (*B*, (30) 1872, p. 352). At Ardleigh he urged strongly 'against recasting the five old bells. I do not see the need. Incorporating the old work with the new work, is in my opinion the truer way. The modern mind has an excessive liking, I think, for making everything brand new. It may, perhaps, give a little more trouble to preserve the old, but not trouble of a costly character, and I doubt whether the new bells would not gain in quiet mellow tone, by being harmonised with the old ones' (Butterfield to Rev. G. Hales, 30 January 1892, Ardleigh chest).
9 (12) 1851, p. 24.
10 *B*, (10) 1852, p. 308; *BN*, (5) 1859, p. 488.
11 *History of the Gothic Revival*, p. 259.
12 Notebooks, p. 248.
13 Accnts, 1886; drawings, R.I.B.A. There were other designs for Chelsea and Windsor barracks.
14 *London Churches*, 2, p. 308.

Chronology

NOTE: numbers in brackets are completion dates.

1814   Born 7 September.

1831   Apprenticed 3 March to Thomas Arber, builder of Pimlico, for five years. The indenture implies that Butterfield had begun working for Arber six months earlier.

1833   25 April Arber adjudged bankrupt; 7 June indenture cancelled.

1833–7 Architectural student; pupil of E. L. Blackburne for most of this period; student member of Architectural Society.

1837   Enters competition for Gillingham church, Dorset.

1838–9 Architectural assistant at Worcester, probably to Harvey Eginton.

1840   Sets up office at 38 Lincoln's Inn Fields.

1842   Moves to 4 Adam Street, Adelphi.
        Highbury Chapel (43).
        Letters published in *Ecclesiologist*, February and October.

1843   Enters Swindon St Mark competition.
        Presents Shottesbrooke drawings to Oxford Architectural and Historical Society.
        Accepts responsibility for Cambridge Camden Society scheme for plate and other church furniture.

1844   11 May elected a member of Cambridge Camden Society.
        St Augustine's College, Canterbury (48).
        Coalpit Heath church and parsonage (45).
        Publishes *Instrumenta Ecclesiastica* I and *Elevations, Sections and Details, of St John Baptist Church, at Shottesbroke, Berkshire.*

1845   Enters Eton College chapel restoration competition.
        Publishes *Instrumenta Ecclesiastica* II–VII.

1846   Dorchester Abbey restoration (53).
        Publishes *Instrumenta Ecclesiastica* VIII–XI.

1847   Perth Cathedral (90).
        Adelaide Cathedral (78).
        Publishes *Instrumenta Ecclesiastica* XII.

1848	Frederichton Cathedral completion (53).
	Yealmpton restoration and school (63).
1849	Alfington school, house and church (50).
	Cumbrae College (51).
	London, All Saints' Margaret Street, and clergy house and school (59).
	London, St Matthias Stoke Newington, and parsonage and school (58).
	Ottery St Mary restoration (50).
	Oxford, Merton College restoration and extension (63).
	West Lavington church and parsonage (50).
1850	Ashwell, restoration and cottages (60).
	London, Osnaburgh Street convent (52).
	Plymouth, St Dunstan's Abbey (63).
	Publishes *Instrumenta Ecclesiastica*, 2, cemetery designs.
1851	Huddersfield St John (53).
	Exhibits plate at Great Exhibition.
	Visits Austrian Empire.
1852	Amesbury restoration (53).
	Publishes *Instrumenta Ecclesiastica*, 2, school designs.
	Visits France.
1853	Cowick, Hensall, Pollington and Wykeham, churches, schools and parsonages (54).
1854	Langley church and school (55).
	Milton church (57).
	Milton Ernest Hall, cottages, farms, watermill and church restoration (64).
	Oxford, Balliol College chapel (57).
	Visits France and northern Italy with Benjamin Starey.
1855	Alvechurch, restoration, school and parsonage (61).
	Baldersby church, school, parsonage, agent's house and cottages (61).
	Waresley church (63).
	Visits Paris Exhibition and Rhineland.
1856	Bamford church and parsonage (62).
	Great Bookham school and cottages (66).
	St Mawgan restoration, school and parsonage (63).
1857	Winchester College restoration (82).
	Visits France.
1858	St Bees restoration (87).
	Winchester St Cross restoration (93).
	Elected to Athenaeum Club.
1859	Braunston cottages (61).
	London, St Alban Holborn and clergy house (63).
	Newbury St John and parsonage (62).
	Visits France.
1860	Rugby School (86).

1861	Hunstanton town plan (62).
1862	Manchester, St Cross Clayton (66).
	Exhibits plate in International Exhibition.
	Visits Austrian Empire.
1863	Winchester Hospital (68).
1864	Dropmore church and parsonage (67).
	Penarth St Augustine (66).
1865	Babbacombe church (74).
	R.I.B.A. proposal of Gold Medal rejected by general meeting.
1866	Oxford, Keble College (86).
	Death of William Butterfield senior.
	R.I.B.A. Council again proposes Gold Medal, but Butterfield withdraws when opposition apparent.
1868	Visits Paris and Rome.
1870	London, St Mary Brookfield (75).
	Visits Germany.
1872	Visits Germany.
1875	Rugby St Andrew (96).
	Elected member of Architectural Association.
1876	Belfast, St Mark Dundela (91).
1877	Melbourne Cathedral (86).
1880	Chanter's House, Ottery St Mary (83).
1881	Elected Fellow of the Society of Antiquaries.
1884	Awarded R.I.B.A. Gold Medal.
1885	Ascot Priory Chapel (86).
	Publishes *Church Seats and Kneeling Boards*.
1886	Moves to 42 Bedford Square.
1891	Death of sister, Anne Starey.
1892	Withdraws from most practice.
1895	Last recorded architectural work, at All Saints' Margaret Street.
1900	Dies 23 February at 42 Bedford Square.

Select Gazetteer

NOTE: Major works in italics, minor works in roman type.

England

BEDFORDSHIRE

Biggleswade, Bromham, Marston Mortayne and Millbrook restorations; *Milton Ernest Hall*, farm buildings, cottages, church restoration and *Milton Mill*.

BERKSHIRE

Ascot Priory Chapel, Avington restoration and parsonage, Beech Hill church and parsonage, *Letcombe Bassett school* and restoration, *Newbury St John's parsonage*, Marlston restoration, Shaw school and chancel, Wantage Convent novitiate wing, King Alfred's School wing, St Mary's School wing, and church west end, and Wokingham St Sebastian.

BUCKINGHAMSHIRE

Dropmore church and *parsonage, Great Woolstone parsonage*, Lavendon restoration, *Wavendon restoration*, and Wooburn restoration.

CAMBRIDGESHIRE

Balsham restoration, *Trumpington restoration* and *schoolhouse*, and *Tadlow restoration*.

CHESHIRE

Christleton Church, Great Budworth, High Legh and Marton restorations.

CORNWALL

St Mawgan parsonage, school and restoration.

CUMBERLAND

Brigham restoration, Lamphlugh church and *St Bees restoration*.

DERBYSHIRE

Ault Hucknall restoration, Bamford church and *parsonage*, Hathersage and Monyash restorations.

DEVON

Abbots Kerswell restoration, *Alfington school, house* and church, *Babbacombe All Saints, Castle Hill school, Exeter Grammar School.* Morebath restoration, *Ottery St Mary restoration, Chanter's House,* and Patteson Cross, *Plymouth St Dunstan's Abbey school,* and *Yealmpton church* and *school.*

DURHAM

Belmont church.

ESSEX

Ardleigh church, and Colchester St Helen's chapel and Hadstock restorations.

GLOUCESTERSHIRE AND BRISTOL

Bristol, Highbury Chapel and Horfield restoration: *Coalpit Heath church* and *parsonage,* Hewelsfield restoration, *Poulton church* and *school,* and completion of *Wick church.*

HAMPSHIRE

Braishfield church, Bournemouth St Augustine's church, Burley and Copythorne chancels, *Emery Down church,* Heckfield almshouses and restoration, Hursley lodges, Mattingley restoration, *Northington school,* Sparsholt restoration; and Winchester, College restoration, St Michael's chancel, St Cross restoration, and *Royal Hampshire County Hospital.*

HERTFORDSHIRE

Aldenham House Home Farm and cottages, Anstey restoration, *Baldock rectory, Barley church,* Berkhamsted restoration, *Chipping Barnet church* and *Hitchin Holy Saviour.*

HUNTINGDONSHIRE

Abbotsley restoration and *Waresley church.*

KENT

Ash restoration, Buckland restoration; *Canterbury,* Cathedral pulpit, *St Augustine's College,* St Mildred's restoration and *Broad Street school; Dover St Mary sub Castro restoration, Godmersham restoration,* Great Mongeham restoration, Kilndown lectern, *Langley church* and *school,* and Milsted and Thanington restorations.

LANCASHIRE

Manchester St Cross Clayton.

LEICESTERSHIRE

Braunstone Cottages and *Kirby Maxloe Cottages* and former school.

LINCOLNSHIRE

Caistor, Friskney and Hagnaby restorations, *St Anne's Bedehouse Chapel, Lincoln,* Limber Magna and Pinchbeck restorations, *Pinchbeck Bars church* and *vicarage,* Stickney restoration, *Tattershall school* and West Deeping restoration.

GREATER LONDON

Ashford church; Battersea Sir Walter St John's School; *Enfield St Mary Magdalene* and *parsonage;* Fulham Palace chapel; *Hammersmith St John* and parsonage; Harrow Weald All Saints; *Holborn St Alban* and *clergy house; Kensington St Augustine Queen's Gate* and *clergy house;* Kingsbury Holy Innocents; *Marylebone All Saints' Margaret Street, clergy house* and *schools; St Pancras, St Mary Brookfield,* and Christ Church Albany Street restoration; *Stoke Newington St Matthias* and school; *Tottenham All Hallows; Westminster, 14 Burleigh Street, Strand; Woolwich St Michael Borgard Road.*

NORFOLK

Colkirk and Holt restorations, *Hunstanton town plan* and *terrace,* Scottaw and Stibbard restorations.

NORTHAMPTONSHIRE

Braunston and Dodford restorations, *Hellidon restoration* and *school,* and Wootton restoration.

NORTHUMBERLAND

Etal church

OXFORDSHIRE

Dorchester restoration, Little Faringdon parsonage, Horton church, Mapledurham restoration, Milton church; and *Oxford, Balliol College chapel, Keble College* and *Merton College chapel restoration.*

RUTLAND

Ashwell cottages and restoration.

SHROPSHIRE

Neen Sollars and Hopesay restorations.

SOMERSET

Axbridge St Michael's Home, Cheddar restoration, Clevedon St John, *Gaer Hill church,* and *Wraxall inn* and school.

STAFFORDSHIRE

Rangemore church, *Sheen parsonage* and church completion, and Tamworth and Weston upon Trent restorations.

SUFFOLK

Bacton, Ellough, Great Waldingfield and Lawshall restorations, Ipswich St Mary Stoke, and Ringsfield and Sudbury St Gregory and St Peter restorations.

SURREY

Bisley Gordon Boys' Home, *Caterham Guards Chapel*, *Great Bookham* restoration, *school* and *cottages*, and *Weybridge St Michael*.

SUSSEX

Ardingly College Farm, Battle, Bexhill, East Grinstead Sackville College, Hastings All Saints' and St Clement's restorations, *West Lavington church* and *parsonage*, and West Tarring restoration.

WARWICKSHIRE

Aston Cantlow school and restoration, Cubbington and *Kinwarton restorations*; *Rugby St Andrew's church*, Bath Street school, and *Rugby School*; *Thurlaston school chapel* and *Wilmcote school* and *parsonage*.

WILTSHIRE

Aldbourne restoration, *Amesbury restoration* and cemetery chapel, Ashton Keynes, *Baverstock*, *Blunsdon St Andrew*, Broad Blunsdon and Castle Eaton restorations, *Charlton by Downton parsonage* and *school*, Chirton, Cliffe Pypard and Dinton restorations, *Foxham church*, *Heytesbury restoration*, *Highway church*, Knook restoration, Landford church, Latton and Lyneham restorations, *Netherhampton church*, *Ogbourne St Andrew parsonage* and restoration, *Salisbury Theological College* and St Nicholas Hospital restoration, and West Harnham, *Whiteparish* and Winterborne Monkton restorations.

WORCESTERSHIRE

Alvechurch School, *parsonage* and *church*, and Chaddesley Corbett restoration.

YORKSHIRE

Baldersby church, *parsonage*, *school*, *cottages* and *agent's house*, Bursea chapel, *Butterwick cottages*, Cautley church, *Cowick church*, *parsonage* and *school*, Dalton church, *Hensall church*, *parsonage* and *school*, Huddersfield St John, *Hutton Buscel school* and restoration, *Pollington church*, *parsonage* and *school*, *Sessay church*, *school*, *cottages* and *bridge*, Ruston cottages, *Wykeham church*, *parsonage* and *school*, Yedingham chancel and *York St Mary Castlegate restoration*.

Wales

CARDIGANSHIRE

Aberystwyth St Mary, *Elerch church* and Llangorwen church porch and bellcote.

GLAMORGAN

Penarth St Augustine.

Scotland

Cumbrae College, Jedburgh school and *Perth Cathedral.*

Ireland

Belfast St Mark Dundela and Dublin St Columba's College chapel.

Africa

Seminaire de Saint Paul Ambatoharanana, Cape Town St Saviour Claremont completion and Victoria West church.

Australia

Adelaide and *Melbourne Cathedrals*

Canada

Fredericton Cathedral.

India

Calcutta Cathedral lectern; Colabah St John restoration.

Index